Teaching Music in Today's Secondary Schools
A Creative Approach to Contemporary Music Education

Second Edition

Malcolm E. Bessom
Editor, *Music Educators Journal,* and Director of Publications, Music Educators National Conference, Reston, Virginia

Alphonse M. Tatarunis
Director of Music and Media Services, Danvers (Massachusetts) Public Schools

Samuel L. Forcucci
Professor of Music, State University of New York College at Cortland

Holt, Rinehart and Winston
New York   Chicago   San Francisco   Atlanta   Dallas   Montreal   Toronto   London   Sydney

Photographs by Lee Stevens, Gainsboro Studio
Drawings by Paula Ann Tatarunis, M.D.

Library of Congress Cataloging in Publication Data

Bessom, Malcolm E
  Teaching music in today's secondary schools.

  Includes bibliographies and index.
  1. School music—Instruction and study.
I. Tatarunis, Alphonse M., joint author. II. Forcucci,
Samuel L., joint author. III. Title.
MT1.B555 1980   780'.72973   79–23828
ISBN 0–03–021556–0

Copyright © 1980, 1974 by Holt, Rinehart and Winston
All rights reserved
Printed in the United States of America
    1   2   3   039   9 8 7 6 5 4 3

MTI
.B55

In memory of
four outstanding music educators

Robert A. Choate
Dean, School of Fine and Applied Arts, Boston University

James Fitzpatrick
Associate Professor of Music, School of Music, University of Miami

Harry Kobialka
Associate Professor of Music, Crane School of Music,
State University of New York College at Potsdam

Henry Lasker
Music Teacher, Newton High School, Newtonville, Massachusetts

JUL 2 6 '89

LIBRARY
SAINT MARY'S COLLEGE
NOTRE DAME, INDIANA

LIBRARY
SAINT MARY'S COLLEGE
NOTRE DAME, INDIANA

Preface

Teaching Music in Today's Secondary Schools: A Creative Approach to Contemporary Music Education was first written after a period of widespread research and far-reaching innovation in the field of music education, at the beginning of an exciting new era in teaching. In just the few years since, there have been so many changes in education and so much new thinking in the field that the authors have produced this revised and enlarged edition to make the text current, germane to contemporary issues, and of increased practicality and flexibility.

It has been written primarily for prospective teachers of music in the secondary schools, whether they will be active in junior or senior high schools or in the formats of middle schools, nongraded schools, and open classrooms. In addition, this text should prove valuable to graduate students, in-service teachers, and department heads who are in search of practical techniques for revitalizing their programs.

Several volumes on teaching music in secondary schools are available. This revised edition differs from them in several important respects, and it expands on topics that have been ignored or treated only superficially elsewhere:

1. First, the authors have perceived the importance of much recent thinking and current practice in teaching. We have incorporated such diverse topics as behavioral objectives, concept teaching, mastery learning, programmed learning (including learning activity packages), criterion-referenced testing, and management systems for learning. Throughout, the text is concerned with the development of a curriculum having both substance and flexibility. To this end, a philosophy based on aesthetics and the fostering of aesthetic sensitivity still undergirds the methods, practices, and techniques that we present.

2. Because music education is an aesthetic component of general education, the thinking of both general educators and music educators about learning processes has been carefully digested and integrated in the presentation of instructional techniques.

3. Three opening chapters orient the reader to the role and qualities of the music educator in the secondary school; the teacher's understanding of the subject; the foundations for developing teaching strategies; the way to maintain teaching strategies; the purpose and value of music in secondary education today; and the structure of a balanced music curriculum.

4. Considerable space has been devoted to the organization of a music curriculum for general students, not just for performers or special music students. It is our feeling that fostering a lasting love of music for all students is at the core of music education, and to this end several chapters have been given over to general music classes; music listening, history, and literature classes; humanities and related arts courses; and courses in music theory and composition for the general student. We offer new insights and specific practices, for example, in renovating general music classes for both middle and junior high schools and in writing lesson plans for them. At the same time, we offer a significant amount of material about the vocal program, the instrumental program, rehearsal techniques, and performance practices.

5. Supplementing information in other chapters, we have devoted one full chapter to individualized learning. We explain establishing an environment for individualization through independent study, music labs, programs utilizing technology, open and informal classrooms, and nongraded schools. Another full chapter is devoted to students with special needs. This chapter includes programs for exceptional children (the speech impaired, emotionally disturbed, mentally retarded, learning disabled, deaf and hard of hearing, visually handicapped, and physically handicapped) and programs for gifted and talented children.

6. Realizing that there is no one way to teach music effectively in any given situation in any school, we have provided a variety of approaches and practical, proven techniques on which the teacher can draw, experiment, and enlarge. Still, we make definite, specific recommendations when we believe we must take a clear stand.

7. Finally, we offer practical guidance in dealing with various administrative factors that concern the successful music teacher—problems of scheduling, practices in measurement and evaluation, relations with school administrators, room and building facilities, public relations, guidance and career education, adherence to the copyright law, and other topics.

Although we have used the generic "he" throughout, in order to avoid complexities of wording, we do not mean to imply by any means that music is the province of men. On the contrary, we hope that this book will widen the number of women and men who teach music successfully, thereby the number of their students, girls and boys, who go to successful experiences or careers in music.

The contents of this book derive from our many years of experience in teaching music classes of many kinds at each level of instruction; in developing music curriculums and experimenting with new techniques and formats; in supervising and administering programs of music education; and in working with prospective music teachers in the schools and at the college level. We also have communicated with music educators in a variety of teaching situations across the country, have done our own recent research in music education, and have called upon a certain degree of common sense to guide us in writing. We hope that this revised text will serve the profession well in moving educators to imaginative teaching in today's schools, with the goal of developing creative, musically educated students for today's society.

We wish to thank the following reviewers for their suggestions in helping us to prepare this edition: Barbara Bair, University of North Carolina at Greensboro; Irma H. Collins, Murray State University; Richard Hishman, Illinois Wesleyan University; Charles M. McDermid, Michigan State University; Dwight E. Nofziger, University of Northern Colorado; Rosalie R. Pratt, Montclair State College; Robert J. Tuley, University of Southern Mississippi; Larry F. Tynes, James Madison University; Thelma O. Williams, Glassboro State College.

M.E.B.
A.M.T.
S.L.F.

Contents

part 4   Supportive Elements in a Music Education Program   299

The Teacher,
the Student,
the Curriculum

Part 1

The Successful Music Teacher

1

The skill a teacher requires is not far different from that required of a skilled
symphony conductor: the sensitivity to the human instruments he deals with,
the need to draw them out, whip them up, hold them back, bring out
this voice and hush another, the rare ability to hear all the parts and yet
retain a grasp of the larger whole toward which all are striving.

KENNETH E. EBLE
A Perfect Education[1]

A SCHOOL does not operate in a vacuum. Today's school is, in fact, a
microcosm of the world at large; it is filled with the loves, fears, and
violence, the understanding and misunderstanding, the concern and dis-
interest, the trust and distrust, the blind confusion and knowledge, the
encouragement and discouragement, the confrontation and escape that
characterize all of today's society. More than ever before, today's students question their environment, look objectively at established institutions, seek their own sets of values, search for their own means of expression, and frequently discover expressive outlets in artistic endeavors.

It is only natural, then, that the arts should have the potential for being
among the most vital elements in a student's education, especially as educators move toward the humanization and personalization of the curriculum. There is no question that music, of all the arts, has become the
strongest voice in the socioaesthetic outcry of youth. Irwin Sonenfield has
appropriately observed that "for the young, the gap between a desire for
the reassurance of absolute values and the observation that there are no
such values has been bridged by music."[2] He sees music as youth's replacement for religion "as the source of the most absolute convictions."

[1] Kenneth E. Eble, *A Perfect Education* (New York: Macmillan, 1966), p. 108.
Copyright © 1966 by Kenneth E. Eble; reprinted by permission of Macmillan Publishing Co., Inc.

[2] Irwin Sonenfield, "The Mystical Rite of Youth Culture," *Music Educators
Journal,* 59:6 (February 1973), p. 30.

This celebration of philosophical, psychological, spiritual, sexual, and technological truth through music is most obvious, of course, outside the school in the pop–rock expressions of youth culture. The fact that such expressions are constantly changing creates no paradox in the embodiment of absolutes, for among the majority of youth only the present has real meaning: Truth lives from day to day, and eternity is relived weekly. Through the work of capable teachers, music can take on a similarly expanded significance as a means of self-actualization within the school, and it can do so within a much broader context than the pop–rock idiom alone. Faced with the need for a more humanistic approach to all aspects of societal living and with the prospect of ever-increasing leisure time, attention to education in the affective domain and the development of aesthetic sensitivity are now seen as basic facets of the school's commitment. Consequently, the shaping of music education and the development of this sensitivity are major tasks for teachers who are in constant contact with young people. Although professional organizations, commissions, and study groups can do much in defining the place of music in American society and in our schools, still it is the diversified body of individual music teachers who will advance the cause of music education.

THE MUSIC TEACHER IN PROFILE

Who is the secondary school music teacher? There is no one answer, for he functions in a unique instructional situation where he is identified by a variety of names—band director, general music teacher, orchestra conductor, instrumental specialist, theory teacher, choral director, and many more. In some schools the music teacher assumes only one of these titles and all the duties connected with it, while in other schools he may be multititled—perhaps band director, general music teacher, and choral director all rolled up into one very busy person. The secondary school music teacher in general is no more identified by a single pattern of school structure than he is by a single title. Indeed, he finds himself in a wide assortment of grade-level organizations, and sometimes even in a completely nongraded school. He may be assigned to either a three- or four-year high school or to a consolidated regional school, which could include grades six to twelve. He may be on the staff of a junior high school where the grade organization ranges from one to four years; or he may be a faculty member in a middle school, where he would be involved with either grades five to eight or six to eight.

The structure of the school in the secondary phase of education is certainly too varied to fit a compact description, and within it the music teacher's own special quarters are hardly more uniform. Music facilities at the secondary level range from the well-constructed and carefully planned music suite to improvised rehearsal facilities in auditoriums (one of the better places), gymnasiums, and cafeterias. They may also be classroom facilities shared with other departments, necessitating the continual movement of pianos, phonographs, recordings, and other equipment and materials.

The variety in music facilities is probably surpassed only by the diversity in scheduling, which in recent years has been placed in the trust of a computer. In one community, the choral director who worked with a 150-voice glee club found it necessary to sign up over 250 students in order for the computer to schedule the number he desired. In the process of scheduling, the computer would invariably be confronted with over 100 conflicts. In the same community one year, the band director was shocked to discover that all his first-chair players, who were seniors, had been scheduled for advanced placement courses that were programmed for the same period. Once students have been scheduled, the number of times each class or performance group will actually meet can vary from every day to once a week, either after school, before school, or during the school day.

Thus, in terms of his title, the conceptual and physical structure of the school he works in, and the schedule he follows, a general image of the music teacher is difficult to draw. We can be sure, though, of one thing that will distinguish him—his teaching. Within the complexity of the secondary school, music teachers have managed to be successful under adverse as well as ideal conditions. For while adequate facilities and reasonable scheduling are contributing factors in determining the level of a teacher's success, in the final analysis success or failure depends upon the individual teacher. The concern of this chapter, therefore, is to give an overview of those qualities and understandings that contribute to the development of the successful music teacher—qualities and understandings that will be seen in more detail in subsequent chapters as they relate to more specific teaching experiences.

Qualities of the Successful Music Teacher

The music educator spends approximately one third of his life influencing the musical growth and development of others. In discussing the importance of the teacher's role, Lindly Stiles said, "Teachers are curators of all our yesterdays and the architects of our tomorrows. Always they accomplish their mission through the minds and talent of others. To do is noteworthy; but to be able to do and to devote one's energies to helping others learn is man's noblest work."[3] Therefore, it is necessary for anyone contemplating a career in teaching to realize there are certain essential qualities that contribute to teaching success. The person who chooses teaching for a career, and is well suited, takes the first step toward a rewarding and productive life. On the other hand, the individual who makes the wrong choice will find personal unhappiness, and of even greater consequence, he will contribute little to the growth and development of his students.

The teacher's *personality* is probably the most important quality contributing to his success or failure. Personality can be described as the sum of an individual's personal traits, which blend together to make him a stimulating teacher, a tolerable teacher, a dull teacher, or a teacher who is sometimes stimulating, sometimes tolerable, and sometimes dull. Successful teachers have variable traits, but often their personalities are marked by human understanding; tolerance; cooperativeness; democratic judgment; warmth and friendliness; a love of children; a deep interest in their work; a sense of involvement, dedication, and willingness; an informed outlook; intelligence, knowledge, and a capacity for growth; talent and skill; a receptivity to new ideas and situations; organizational ability; clarity of thought and expression; emotional stability; good health; a neat, distinctive appearance; individuality; and creativity.

The importance of the teacher's personality should not be minimized since the student who likes the teacher, and believes the teacher likes him, will learn more effectively than the student who does not like his teacher and senses a reciprocity of feeling. The pupil-teacher relationship is proving more influential in the learning process than the selection,

[3] Lindly J. Stiles, "The Best Should Teach," *Wisconsin Journal of Education*, 90:8 (March 1958), p. 7.

organization, and presentation of the subject matter to be taught. It should be emphasized, however, that at no time should a teacher sacrifice his educational objectives because he believes a particular action will influence his students and make them like him more. On the contrary, student–teacher respect must be attained within the framework of a learning situation, whether in the classroom or in performance, where teacher and pupils are working toward a mutually understood and educationally desirable outcome.

While liking young people and enjoying their association is an attribute of the successful educator, in every teacher's career there are inevitably some students whom it is difficult or impossible to like. This is a necessary fact to recognize, but it is not by itself a sign of conflict or maladjustment. The real problem arises when a teacher finds *few* students that he likes. Such a statement as "I like teaching, but I can't stand the kids" is an indication that he must either strive to improve his attitude or find a new means of earning a living. For while students may be able to learn without teachers or even in spite of teachers, it is impossible to be a teacher unless there are pupils.

Good *humor and cheerfulness* are two more qualities that characterize the successful music teacher. These must never be confused, though, with the deadly sarcasm and ridicule used by some teachers under the guise of good fun. Such sarcasm can reach the uncontrollable point where teacher and pupils are locked in constant wits-matching combat. The teacher who really has a good sense of humor can laugh with the class at spontaneous jokes and then return to complete the lesson at hand; he can introduce a flavor of humor into the rehearsal as a change of pace, a form of relaxation, or a means of making a specific instructional point; and he can laugh at himself when necessary. As Gilbert Highet indicated, "The real purpose of humor in

teaching . . . is *to link the pupil and the teacher*, and to link them through enjoyment."[4] When people laugh together they are no longer separated by such barriers as age differences, pupil–teacher differences, or intellectual differences. Instead, they become a group that is totally committed to the shared feeling of enjoyment brought about by a particular incident or set of circumstances.

The music teacher must also have *maturity and emotional stability*. The band director, for example, who is subject to fits of temper as a result of a personal problem at home, or because he had a late playing job the night before, will only contribute to the anxiety of his band members rather than create an atmosphere that is conducive to a productive rehearsal. A good example of the dangers of emotional instability is exhibited by the chairman of the music department whose senior choir receives a II rating at a music festival while the freshman choir, directed by another staff member, receives a I rating. From that moment on he asserts his authority, as a defense mechanism, and makes life miserable for his family, his students, and especially his associates. The person who has a serious emotional problem will not be able to function as a teacher because that problem and he himself—not his students—are the center of all that is important to him. This teacher needs professional help. If it is not sought, his presence in school will continue to be a disturbing factor, not only to himself but also to other staff members, the administration, parents, and especially the students. This is not to say that the teacher should disguise his true feelings in class. On the contrary, he should avoid playing a role and should feel free to share his personal experiences, opinions, attitudes, and emotional responses along with his intellectual understandings. But when his re-

[4] Gilbert Highet, *The Art of Teaching* (New York: Vintage Books, 1950), p. 55.

sponses indicate an emotional problem, they have no place in the classroom.

Another important quality of the successful music teacher, and possibly the most misunderstood, is *knowledge of what is to be taught*. Very often knowledge in a particular area is superficial. For example, the teacher of Harmony I may know little more than the material covered in the course outline. Yet, the knowledge that is really required in this instance involves fluency with *all* traditional harmonic techniques, familiarity with the principles of contrapuntal writing, knowledge of orchestration and instrumentation, understanding of contemporary techniques, and acquaintance with a wide variety of music literature to be used to illustrate harmonic and compositional principles. The belief that "basic knowledge" is enough to teach a particular subject is erroneous, since it is necessary to have an in-depth knowledge and understanding to determine what is really basic. This means that learning, through both formal and informal study, must be a continuous process in the development of the successful teacher. His mind must remain openly receptive to improvement, innovation, and change.

The successful teacher, regardless of his subject or position, also has a kind of *personal magnetism* that attracts, interests, and holds young people. He has a personal feeling of duty toward his students and his subject. His classes are approached with imagination and enthusiasm, and decisions regarding what, when, and how to teach are a fusion of knowledge and common sense. His attractiveness is further related to his broad interests, which reach beyond his subject area but are reflected in his stimulating approach to his own field. Part of this magnetism, too, derives from the fact that as a music teacher he continues to be a practicing musician; he is not only capable of getting others to make music, but also can make music himself, as an emo-

tional outlet or a form of self-expression. He is unique in a world of conformists and constantly observes his environment and the people in it with sensitivity and compassion. All these factors, then—a pleasing personality, a sense of humor, maturity and stability, extensive knowledge, and a certain magnetism (a vibrant style or charisma)—are distinctive qualities that characterize the successful teacher.

The Role of the Teacher

We have seen from his various titles that the music teacher in the secondary school wears many different hats. But whether he is a choral director, theory teacher, or band director, he also functions in various nonteaching roles. The music teacher, for example, will be influential as a *counselor*, advising the student whose career objective is involved with music, or even the student who seeks help with a personal problem. Although most secondary schools have extensive and well-organized guidance departments, many student musicians will turn naturally to the music teacher for assistance. The amount of time given to this area is difficult to estimate, and its importance should not be underestimated or taken casually. In his counseling capacity, the teacher must remember that his function is to *advise*, and his advice should not be presented in such a fashion that the student and parent will view it as infallible information or judgment.

Another important function of the music teacher is as a *community-relations agent*: keeping the administration, faculty, students, parents, and community informed about the objectives, activities, and scope of the music program. This could take many forms, such as preparing newsletters, submitting pictures and articles to the newspaper, or making appearances as a guest speaker at PTA or service club meetings. In the public-relations process, one must be aware that it is the music

LIBRARY
SAINT MARY'S COLLEGE
NOTRE DAME, INDIANA

program and its effect upon the students, and *not* the music teacher himself, that is the subject being presented to the public. The students must not be exploited to enhance the music teacher's reputation. However, the teacher whose prime interest is the musical growth and development of his students will soon discover that their success will reflect naturally on him. In establishing community relations, the teacher may find himself involved in some of the following activities: organizing and maintaining music–parent groups; serving on committees to organize community music activities; organizing and directing community bands, orchestras, and choruses; assisting local libraries in selecting music books and recordings; working as a professional musician, such as a church choir director, church soloist, organist, member of a professional orchestra, or supper–club entertainer; organizing a summer recreational program for band, orchestra, chorus, or music drama; and providing guidance and teaching for adult music-education courses.

Still another role of the music teacher is that of being a musician among musicians and an educator among educators—in short, an *educator–musician*. As such, he must be cognizant of the research, trends, and changes in his own field and in general education. He must serve on curriculum committees involved in music reorganization and as a member of study groups concerned with the over-all scope of secondary education.

Although the importance of these and other related responsibilities cannot be denied, the most important function of any teacher is obviously . . . to teach. As a teacher he is concerned with:
   –Developing goals and objectives
   –Motivation
   –Selection and organization of material
   –Presentation of material
   –Evaluation
   –Maintaining effective classroom control

These areas of concern are not limited to music in conventional classroom situations; they also must be considered by the teacher who is involved with performance groups.

Developing Goals and Objectives

The music teacher must decide which of the school's goals are best attained through music and then set up subsequent music objectives that will facilitate the attainment of these goals. This is not to say that music should attempt to fit into a pattern of goals that are reached only, or more appropriately, through other areas of the curriculum; rather, it assumes that the goals of aesthetic education are a part of the *school's* philosophy, not just the philosophy of the music department. While it is possible for some goals to be fulfilled by more than one subject area, the music teacher is faced with the task of choosing and realizing those goals that are best achieved through *music's unique contribution*. A specific example of the relationship between goals and objectives is presented in Table 2-2, beginning with the immediate instructional objective and leading to the school goal. (A more detailed discussion of goals and objectives appears in Chapter 2, as well as in other chapters that relate to specific areas of the curriculum.)

Motivation

The music teacher cannot assume that his acceptance of the role and duties related to teaching will evoke automatic and reciprocal acceptance by the student of his role as the learner. On the contrary, as he approaches the teaching situation the teacher will discover that it is necessary to inspire (motivate) students so that they will want to learn and develop their musical potential. In this process of motivation, the role of the teacher is quite complex and cannot be described as a particular procedure to be followed, a set of rules and regulations that will ensure success, or a hierarchy of characteristics to be used as a guide. However, George J. Mouly does give us some insight into this complexity when he describes the teacher's role:

> . . . if special mention had to be made of relevant qualifications, sensitivity to children's needs and ingenuity in harnessing their motives in the direction of desirable goals would be among the most important. It means the teacher will have to provide moral support to the child who is frustrated by the demands of the school, a change of work for the child who is bored, special projects for the child whose interests have not yet been tapped by the school's routine. He will have to keep a nice balance between difficulty and ease of material so that the child is neither frustrated nor bored, and this he will have to do not only for one child but for some 30 children, each of different ability, interests and background. He will have to get children to learn material in which they have no great interest and to develop those interests, relying in the meantime on his personality and his prestige as a person concerned only with their welfare.[5]

Currently there are a number of theories of motivation, but the one that seems to have attained the greatest general acceptance is that of the late psychologist Abraham H. Maslow. His theory revolves around the idea that man is motivated by a hierarchy of needs as illustrated in Figure 1-1. However, Maslow's hierarchy is not absolute, but rather an idealization of the way motives emanate. As the individual receives gratification on a particular level, the other levels become more important to him. Maslow was also quite careful to point out that complete fulfillment on one level is not necessary before interest in the other levels can develop.

The lowest level and the basic foundation

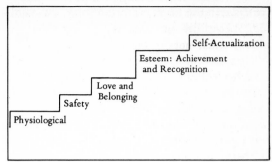

FIGURE 1-1. Maslow's Hierarchy of Needs[6]

Self-Actualization
Esteem: Achievement and Recognition
Love and Belonging
Safety
Physiological

of Maslow's hierarchy is man's *physiological* needs. These provide man with the drive to attain food in order to avoid starvation, search for water to avoid thirst, and so on. If the needs on this level are not adequately met, they will dominate man's drive and hamper his movement to other motivational levels. However, Maslow argued that these conditions are quite rare in our society today, and his concern was more with what motivates man after his physiological needs are met.

The next step is the desire to achieve a feeling of security—*safety*. This quest for a stable environment is found in children as well as adults. Moreover, while some adults are able to hide their feelings of insecurity, children are not. When the child discovers that his world has been disrupted, he becomes discouraged and apprehensive. Such insecurity has a definite influence upon the child in terms of his ability to function to the peak of his capacity in a learning situation. Understanding this, the teacher must try to establish a rapport with his students that will provide them with the stability and security they need.

Love and belonging is the next plateau in Maslow's hierarchy. Here, the individual is moving away from himself, seeking to form relationships with other human beings and to

[5] George J. Mouly, *Psychology for Effective Teaching*, 2d ed. (New York: Holt, Rinehart and Winston, 1968), pp. 340–341.

[6] See Abraham H. Maslow, *Motivation and Personality* (New York: Harper & Row, Publishers, 1954).

become a member of a group or of many groups. At this level, the child who has difficulty establishing satisfactory relationships with his classmates and teachers will find it difficult to function as a learner.

The need for *self-esteem* through achievement and recognition is a very important consideration, for it is at this level that instruction is operational. Each student must be given the *opportunity* for success and satisfaction. If he is constantly frustrated by failure, he may seek recognition by other means that could be detrimental (such as vandalism and disruptive forms of behavior).

At the peak of Maslow's hierarchy is the need for *self-actualization*. The person who reaches this level is one who has satisfied all his basic needs but still has a feeling of discontent. Now he must have the freedom to do what he wants to do, to become what he wants to become in order to achieve peace of mind and joy. An example of the search for self-actualization is the successful businessman who seeks political office or appointment to some form of governmental service in order to realize complete fulfillment.

Most of man's motivations are learned—those related to his survival being the exception. Beyond the first level of the hierarchy, motives are acquired as a result of life experiences. Therefore, the music teacher, in order to create interest and enthusiasm among his students, must consider several factors. First, he should recognize those motives that the student develops himself. A student's interest in music may be either intrinsically or extrinsically related to the subject. For example, one student may sing in the choir because he derives satisfaction from participating in fine music performances, whereas another may join the choir in order to be with his friends or to go on an exchange concert. In either case, the teacher should capitalize on the motive and help each student develop more complex and sophisticated motives which will

create a continued need that must be gratified. Although both types of incentives are valid and effective in the learning situation, Mouly has pointed out that extrinsic ones can be of little value and even harmful in certain circumstances: (1) when they do not derive from the student's own goals in relation to the experience, but are imposed by the authority of the teacher; (2) when the incentive is emphasized to the degree that it becomes an end in itself and replaces the real goal (grades being a good example because they often become more important to a student than whether he is learning something worthwhile); (3) when a group incentive is appropriate for only certain members of the group (such as one that is effective with the gifted student but not with the average or dull student); and (4) when the incentive creates emotional conflicts (such as the reward that can be obtained by only one member of a class and thus leads to disappointment for many).[7]

Another factor the teacher must consider is whether or not the student's aspiration level (the level of achievement that he sets for himself) is realistic. If it is too high, it will lead to unnecessary failure and frustration. On the other hand, if the level of aspiration is too low and easily reached, the student will be denied the opportunity for greater achievement and will become bored for lack of a challenge.

Both reward and punishment can be used to motivate the student, and both have positive and negative elements. The positive aspect of a reward is that the student associates something pleasant with a particular experience and there is a strong inducement to repeat the activity. Interest and enthusiasm are generated by a pleasant experience. On the negative side, however, the student who least needs the motivation often receives the

[7] See Mouly, *op. cit.*, pp. 279–280.

reward, and there is also the danger that a student will develop an expectation that everything he does must be rewarded. Punishment is a positive incentive when it serves as a deterrent and when the student understands that it is a particular act or behavior that is being censured and not himself. But punishment can also have detrimental effects, as when a student is punished but is not shown how to improve his performance to avoid further punishment. It can also be self-defeating when it is used over a long period of time, making the student discouraged and anxious. In addition, the constant use of punishment can destroy teacher–pupil rapport, leading to antagonism and resentment that make learning difficult.

Many teachers believe that praise is superior to reproof as a motivational device. However, after reviewing available data, H. O. Schmitt concluded that there is no basis for this belief.[8] What is evident is that both praise and reproof lose their effectiveness if they are not used judiciously. Continuous praise, for example, becomes meaningless if it is given when it is not deserved. Students are quick to recognize its insincere use. On the other hand, the teacher who constantly criticizes his students does nothing but injure and belittle if his comments are never interspersed with praise.

Another factor in motivation is competition. This can be a successful device, particularly when it exists between groups rather than between individuals. The danger of competition between individuals is that the loser may develop a negative self-concept. It can also lead to poorer performance on the part of the student who constantly faces failure. If competition is fair and offers all class members the opportunity to be winners, then it

can serve to increase interest in class and individual performance.

As the music teacher works with students to establish a series of motives, he must always be mindful of individual ability. Tasks must be challenging but not discouraging; there must be more prospects of success than of failure. The student must have the opportunity to increase his self-esteem through music experiences, to have the satisfaction of achievement, and whenever possible to receive some recognition for his achievement.

Selection and Organization of Material

The complete structure and organization of a music course or a performance class, with its long-range and day-to-day objectives, will influence the teacher's selection of what is considered important to teach. In turn, what is important will be influenced by the teacher's knowledge of the specific subject; contact with current trends, innovations, improvements, and changes; available facilities and materials; and some knowledge of the ability level of the students to be taught.

The teacher must be certain that his organization and planning are in line with reality —with what can be realistically accomplished within a particular situation, with a particular group, and within a particular time period. For example, the choral director who plans an ambitious program, even though he knows that his students have had little or no previous choral experience, that scheduling conflicts have kept the more experienced singers out of his group, and that he meets his chorus only once a week, has lost touch with reality. The final outcome of such organization will lead to the anxiety of his students and contribute to his own utter frustration.

The mark of the professional teacher is *detailed preparation for teaching*. Time must be devoted to thinking about *what* is going to be taught (selection), *how* it is going to be taught (method), *why* it is going to be taught

[8] H. O. Schmitt, "The Effect of Blame on Incentives in Learning," *Psychological Monographs*, 53:3 (1941).

(priority), and *when* it is going to be taught (sequential organization). The teacher who accepts the responsibility of detailed preparation understands the importance of his role in contributing to the growth and development of his students. This acceptance is further indication of the teacher's complete commitment to provide his students with only the best he has to offer, whether it is in a general music class or in a high school orchestra.

In addition to organizing the selected material to meet his students' needs, the teacher must also furnish them with a sense of security by establishing a classroom atmosphere that is warm, creative, businesslike, and democratic. If these conditions exist in the teaching–learning situation, the problem of classroom discipline will take care of itself. However, the teacher who is well organized but dominates the class, who does not provide opportunities for student involvement, and who establishes arbitrary goals that the students do not understand, will find that discipline can be a problem and that control is possible only by autocratic methods.

Presentation of Material

The next phase of teaching is concerned with the active contact of teacher and students in the learning situation. Highet has appropriately suggested that we adopt, in classroom presentation, the techniques used by the advertising industry: "Make it vivid . . . ," "Make it memorable . . . ," and "Make it relevant. . . ."[9] Within this frame of reference, teaching must be *vivid* in order to attract, to interest, and to hold the student's attention; material must be *relevant* or it should not be presented; and both must be *memorable* or learning will fade in the students' minds and be forgotten.

Classroom presentation is further enhanced

[9] Highet, *op. cit.*, p. 240.

and communication is improved when the teacher is *clearly understood* by his students. Difficulty in such communication is often attributed to a student's inability to comprehend (1) the teacher's verbalization of what is to be learned, and (2) abstract concepts that are presented without adequate explanation and concrete illustration. The band director, for example, who demands a "fine clarinet tone" talks in abstraction until he reinforces his demand with illustrative recordings, explanation, or self-demonstration of that ever-ambiguous "fine tone."

Patience and understanding in regard to the rate of pupil progress, comprehension, and achievement are also significant considerations related to presentation. The teaching process and the learning process both take time, and the development of understanding on the part of the student is not immediate. Thus, while the teacher may make plans to present certain material quickly, he will soon discover that his actual rate of presentation is directly influenced by the rate at which his students learn. The teacher whose presentation is balanced with patience and understanding will give students opportunities for personal success and gratification; a purpose and sense of direction toward desired goals; opportunities to express individual ideas; clarification when there is confusion; alternatives that will account for individual differences; encouragement, when there is discouragement, through guided discovery; and opportunities to acquire those habits that help to develop good practice and study skills.

Evaluation

After the teacher has decided what is worth teaching and has presented his material to the learner, he needs to carry through by determining exactly what the student has learned, and by evaluating the effectiveness of materials, organization, and methods of presentation as they relate to the achievement of desired behavioral changes. The teacher should operate under the premise that if it is worth spending time to teach, then it is worth spending additional time to determine whether the teaching has been successful.

In organizing a program to evaluate pupil progress, Magnuson, Larson, and Shellhammer, writing for the California State Department of Education, recommended that the process of evaluation include any and all available methods of acquiring information related to pupil behavior and personality; be concerned primarily with the growth of the student as an individual rather than growth as it relates to some group or some national standard; be a continuous, built-in part of every step in teaching; furnish information of a quantitative and a descriptive nature; and finally, provide for cooperative involvement of the teacher, the pupil, and the parent.[10] It is important that evaluation be viewed in terms of its dual function: It is not only a means to determine what students have accomplished, but also, in the broader sense, to provide the teacher with information on the effectiveness of his role in the teaching-learning process.

Maintaining Effective Classroom Control

Adolescents go through a turbulent period of rapid physical, mental, and emotional growth as they make the transition from childhood to adulthood. They also must make many social and personal adjustments while they are involved simultaneously in the task of learning. Some of these adjustments, as Kenneth Hoover has pointed out, include:

(1) achieving new and more mature relations with his peer group, (2) achieving emotional independence of adults, especially his parents,

(3) desiring and achieving socially responsible behavior, and (4) acquiring an adequate value system to guide behavior.[11]

Although some students are problems, the music teacher should know that adolescents also have many positive personality characteristics that make them exciting and sensitive people to teach. For example, they have:

—courage enough to take a chance
—ability to adjust to change
—great energy, vitality, and drive
—a good sense of humor
—capability of deep serious thought
—a strong sense of fair play, disliking the person who is "unfair"
—loyalty to organizations and causes
—ability to question contemporary societal values, institutions, and philosophies
—a sense of honesty, which can be brutally frank.[12]

The music teacher who is striving to develop techniques for effective classroom control must be aware of these adolescent characteristics and adjustments. Classroom control should not be associated with blind, uniform conformity by all members of the class. Instead, the teacher must help each student to develop inner discipline, within the framework of the personal and social adjustments facing the student. The concept of uniform discipline for all students has changed, and in today's secondary schools there is, as Hoover has said, an "acceptance of variations in behavior by individuals and even the toleration of variations for a single individual as he is faced with changing conditions."[13]

[11] Kenneth H. Hoover, *The Professional Teacher's Handbook* (Boston: Allyn and Bacon, Inc., 1976), p. II–23.

[12] Herbert A. Otto, "The Personal and Family Strength Research Projects: Some Implications for the Therapist," *Mental Hygiene*, 48:3 (July 1964), pp. 439–450.

[13] Hoover, *op. cit.*

[10] See Henry W. Magnuson, Carl A. Larson, and Thomas A. Shellhammer, *Evaluating Pupil Progress* (Sacramento: California State Department of Education, 1952), pp. 4–5.

Maintaining effective classroom control is one of the major concerns of the new and prospective music teacher—and it should be! No matter how well the teacher knows the subject or how well the material is organized for class presentation, if the teacher does not have the skill to control students in the class, it will be impossible to create an atmosphere conducive to learning. Developing such a skill is a very personal and individual task. A technique that proves effective for one teacher in a particular disciplinary situation will not necessarily work for another teacher in a similar situation, nor even for the same teacher in a different situation. Therefore, music teachers each must work out, within the framework of their personality, their philosophy, and the school policy, disciplinary techniques that work. Although there are many variables in the development of effective classroom control, Wilburn Elrod has suggested the following guidelines:

(1) Attempt to be firm and fair in your treatment of students. . . .
(2) Be consistent in your behavior in the classroom. . . .
(3) Attempt to be thoroughly planned and well organized each day that you teach. . . .
(4) Make few rules in the beginning. . . .
(5) Try to maintain a sense of humor. . . .
(6) Make your class interesting. . . .
(7) Provide students with feedback about their work and attempt to make it quick and positive. . . .
(8) Know your students. . . .
(9) Be yourself. Know yourself. . . .
(10) Be flexible. . . .
(11) Know your subject. . . .
(12) Practice what you preach. . . .[14]

A new approach to school discipline has been advocated by William Glasser, director of the Educator Training Center of Los Angeles. The Glasser approach involves parents and assigns to each student the responsibility for his or her own behavior. Glasser emphasizes the following:

—A personal approach: I care enough about you to be involved, to be your friend. Spend a few seconds throughout the day reinforcing involvement.
—Value judgment. Ask students to evaluate their own behavior.
—Planning. Work with students to formulate alternatives. Build success into the plan.
—Commitment. Build a way to check back, follow up. Give positive reinforcement.
—No excuses. Eliminate discussion of excuses to show you know the students can succeed.
—No punishment. It removes the responsibility from the student. They have to understand that they are responsible for themselves.
—Never give up. Hang in longer than the student thinks you will.[15]

The major criticism of Glasser's approach is that it is too time-consuming and indulgent. It was introduced in the Boston school system in 1975 under a program that was federally funded by the Emergency School Aid Act, devised to assist with problems related to segregation. In 1978, one of the coordinators of the Boston program, Claudia Davis, reported that even though it was time-consuming and indulgent, the approach nevertheless had given teachers a new sense that they could be in control of their schools again.[16] Success of the Glasser plan was reported also in Detroit, where it was used in thirty-six schools; in Greensboro, North Carolina; and in the Harlingen (Texas) High School, which has an enrollment of 2500. William Borgers, the prin-

[14] Wilburn Elrod, "Don't Get Tangled in Discipline Problems," Music Educators Journal, 63:4 (December 1976), pp. 48–50.

[15] Gloria Negri, "A New Approach to Discipline," Boston Sunday Globe, January 22, 1978, p. 7. Reprinted by courtesy of the Boston Globe.

[16] Ibid.

cipal at Harlingen, reported that the Glasser approach "has changed the discipline structure from punitive to nonpunitive. It is a quieter type of discipline. The whole idea is that the teacher and student can solve the problem together."[17]

Finally, is classroom control important to teacher success? According to Elrod, "Research indicates that more teachers fail because of inability to cope with interpersonal relationships with people than fail due to a lack of subject matter knowledge."[18]

THE MUSIC TEACHER IN CONTACT WITH THE SUBJECT

Notwithstanding the importance of classroom control, the successful music teacher also must be in control of the subject. He must have an in-depth knowledge of the broad spectrum of music, not simply of the European classical heritage. "Reverence for the classics in our time," wrote Aaron Copland, "has been turned into a form of discrimination against all other music."[19] The perpetuation of this discrimination in our schools has been the result of music teachers assuming the position of connoisseurs and allowing to be used in their classes only the music that has been considered "good" by a single group of experts, or music that has withstood the leveling of time. It is difficult, however, to accept such a position. Certainly such composers as Palestrina, Monteverdi, and Beethoven were not motivated to compose their music for some future audience; rather, they wrote for their respective contemporary audiences. This is also true of today's composer, who seeks rec-

ognition in the concert hall within his lifetime, not at some future, undetermined moment in history. Furthermore, the teacher must recognize that music does not have a narrow, singular meaning in contemporary society—that there are many different *musics*, which contribute to the fulfillment of the varied needs of people at any one time. He must recognize the full scope of music and prepare himself for a broad involvement in it.

Recognizing the Scope of Music

Participants in the Tanglewood Symposium on music in our society (organized in 1967 by the Music Educators National Conference) recognized the necessity of freeing music education from its traditionally narrow approach, wherein young people have been presented with only those aesthetic values that were related to nineteenth-century tastes. The Tanglewood Declaration recommended that the program of music education include:

Music of all periods, styles, forms, and cultures. . . . The musical repertory should be expanded to involve music of our time in its rich variety, including currently popular teenage music and avant-garde music, American folk music, and the music of other cultures.[20]

In recent years, music educators have expanded the scope of their programs and redefined the meaning of "serious music." Within the framework of the teen-age subculture, for example, students accept their own form of popular music as a "serious" idiom. They have close identity to teen music since it is composed, performed, and patronized by members of their own subculture, and it

---

[17] *Ibid.*

[18] Elrod, *op. cit.*, p. 50.

[19] Aaron Copland, *Music and Imagination* (New York: Mentor Books, 1959), p. 28.

[20] Allen Britton, Arnold Broido, and Charles Gary, "The Tanglewood Declaration," in *Documentary Report of the Tanglewood Symposium*, Robert A. Choate, ed. (Washington, D.C.: Music Educators National Conference, 1968), p. 139.

sings of love, acceptance, independence, and the constant struggle with adult standards and values. The music educator must be aware that the average teen-ager comes to class with some well-defined and well-established music preferences, and the general feeling toward music is positive: *they think music is great!* By building on the positive values they already have, the teacher has the opportunity of providing young people with further experiences to develop their understanding of music. We must not repeat mistakes of the past and continue to take an isolationist's point of view by setting up pure and absolute values of musical excellence. Such values are false because they are incomplete, and they serve only to degrade, in the eyes of students, the music from which they have received pleasure and enjoyment.

The music teacher must accept the reality and values of popular music; it must be recognized as a strong influence upon the development of the music tastes of young people. He must also accept the existence and values of other types of music—values that do not exist for just individually exclusive groups of music consumers. For with proper understanding, a person can enjoy the best of jazz along with Bach, the best of popular theatre music along with string quartets, the best of electronic music along with opera, and the best of folk, ethnic, and popular music along with Mozart, Brahms, and Stravinsky. Such cosmopolitan taste is a desirable goal of music education if students (and music teachers) are to participate in the totality of musical expression for the fullness of aesthetic enjoyment.

Recognizing the full range of today's music *does not* mean the abandonment of tradition. It merely means putting our music heritage—both past and present—into proper perspective as it relates to man. If man is to participate fully in the music of his time, then the music teacher is faced with the problem of providing the following experiences: (1)

familiarity with contemporary music techniques involved in atonal music, electronic music, and aleatoric music; (2) experiences with music of other cultures and civilizations, such as the musics of Africa, Asia, the Orient, and the American Indian; (3) awareness of the full stream of popular music from rock to Broadway; (4) understanding of the wide range of styles in the fields of blues and jazz; and (5) acquaintance with the vast repertoire of American folk music.

Expanding the scope of music education to include these areas has required not only a change in the attitude of music teachers but other changes as well. First, the area of teacher education has been expanding to include a background in ethnomusicology; contemporary music trends; American folk music, blues, and jazz; pop-rock and disco music; and the instruments associated with these musics. Secondly, the performance-centered curriculum in the high school has been augmented to include more opportunities in music for those students not interested in performance, and performance classes are expanding their objectives beyond the teaching of performance skills, allowing some time to concentrate on the development of music understanding that will have functional value in adult life.

The Teacher's Background

If the music curriculum is to encompass a comprehensive range of types and styles of music, and if it is to include a wide variety of offerings to meet the needs of all students, then the teacher must assure himself that he has the proper training. Traditional teacher-education programs are criteria based, with all prospective teachers being required to accumulate a given number of credits and have reasonable success in the following areas:

Musical Background
–Theory, harmony, and counterpoint
–Composition and arranging

—Music history and literature (including pop, jazz, and so on)
—Applied music: major instrument or voice
—Functional piano (for nonpiano majors) and knowledge and functional use of social instruments such as the guitar
—Conducting
—Methods and materials in the secondary school
—Student teaching in the secondary school

Professional Background
—Educational psychology
—Child and adolescent growth and development
—Educational measurement
—Technological hardware and software
—History and philosophy of education

General Educational Background
—English literature, composition, or drama
—Art survey
—Humanities
—Related arts
—Social sciences
—Speech
—Liberal arts electives

In recent years there has been a trend in teacher education to develop a curriculum based upon competency or performance. Competency-based programs organize the curriculum in smaller units called instructional modules, rather than in courses, and each module has specific objectives and criteria for achievement. Thus, to qualify for certification, the prospective teacher would be responsible for demonstrating certain competencies rather than passing particular courses. The Commission on Teacher Education of the Music Educators National Conference set forth the following as desirable musical competencies to be exhibited by music teachers:

Producing Sounds (Performance)

All music educators must be able to:
Perform with musical understanding and technical proficiency. . . .
Play accompaniments. . . .
Sing. . . .
Conduct. . . .
Supervise and evaluate the performance of others. . . .

Organizing Sounds (Composition)

All music teachers must be able to:
Organize sounds for personal expression. . . .
Demonstrate an understanding of the elements of music through original composition and improvisation in a variety of styles. . . .
Demonstrate the ability to identify and explain compositional choices of satisfactory and less satisfactory nature. . . .
Notate and arrange sounds for performance in school situations. . . .

Describing Sounds (Analysis)

All music educators must be able to:
Identify and explain compositional devices as they are employed in all musics. . . .
Discuss the affective results of compositional devices. . . .
Describe the means by which the sounds used in music are created. . . .[21]

Alfred North Whitehead once warned that all teachers must observe two educational commandments: "Do not teach too many subjects," and again, "What you teach, teach thoroughly."[22] The first part of Whitehead's

[21] "Qualities and Competencies for Music Educators," *Teacher Education in Music: Final Report* (Washington, D.C.: Music Educators National Conference, 1972), pp. 5–7; see also the recommended standards on pp. 26–33.

[22] Alfred North Whitehead, *The Aims of Education and Other Essays* (New York: The Free Press, 1967), p. 2.

statement is a warning that should be heeded by the music teacher who finds himself involved in a diversity of assignments, even though they are all involved with music. In one community, for example, the music teacher directed five choruses and the marching band, and taught a daily theory class in the high school. In addition, his duties involved four other choirs and a class of retarded students in the junior high school. Under these unbelievable conditions, the teacher commented, "I have enough time to do everything—except get ready to do it!" The teacher who must work under such pressure conditions will find that thorough teaching is an impossibility. For although it is desirable to have a certain amount of competence in a number of areas of music, few teachers are outstandingly successful without concentrating on one special area. The music teacher who wishes to be thorough in a particular sphere should increase his competencies in that area as specified in the following list:

Choral Music

- Knowledge of choral literature and of the history of choral styles and forms; acquaintance with past and current performance practices
- Understanding of the human voice and the techniques used to teach singing to a group and to individuals
- Knowledge of and skill in using choral techniques related to the development of good tone, balance, blend, good pronunciation and enunciation, and so on
- Skill in choral arranging and original composition
- Knowledge of how to organize a choral group; that is, recruiting members, auditioning singers, assigning parts, selecting suitable music, and so on
- Ability to play the piano

Instrumental Music—Orchestra

- Knowledge of orchestral literature, and of the history of orchestral styles and forms; acquaintance with past and current performance practices
- Ability to play stringed instruments, and knowledge of the playing requirements of all other orchestral instruments
- Familiarity with the latest materials and techniques used to develop string players, such as those of Suzuki and Bornoff
- Ability to read a condensed score and a full score
- Knowledge of how to organize an orchestra; that is, recruiting members, assigning chairs, selecting music, and so on
- Skill in and knowledge related to arranging, orchestration, and composition for orchestra
- Skill in making minor string repairs

Instrumental Music—Band

- Knowledge of band literature and acquaintance with past and current performance practices
- Knowledge of the transposition of all instruments and the skill to read a full or condensed band score
- Knowledge of the playing requirements of all band instruments
- Skill in composing and arranging for the band
- Knowledge of how to organize a concert band, marching band, wind and percussion ensemble, and stage band
- Skill in making minor instrumental repairs
- Knowledge of the techniques used in the development of a band program; that is, instrumental demonstrations, choosing instruments, selecting instructional materials, and so on

Theory, Harmony, and Composition

—In-depth understanding of, and the skill to apply in practice, both traditional and contemporary harmonic techniques

—Above-average ability in playing the piano

—Understanding of and skill in using techniques of composing, arranging, and orchestrating

—Understanding of forms of music, form in music, and various techniques of analysis including those of Heinrich Schenker and Rudolph Reti

—Extensive knowledge of music literature (traditional, contemporary, folk, rock, jazz, and so on), in order to illustrate where and how composers have used a particular technique being studied in class

General Music and Related Classes

—A thorough knowledge and understanding of the music of various periods and styles

—Knowledge of the characteristics and instruments of American folk music, jazz, music theatre, popular music, teen music, and music of other cultures

—Knowledge of the relationship of music to the other arts, and an understanding of the fundamental styles and developments in those arts

—Knowledge of new instructional practices, such as the compositional approach, lab classes, individualized learning, and so on

—Knowledge of and skill with audiovisual media and technological equipment

—Ability to play the piano

—Facility with the Autoharp, guitar, and recorder

—Knowledge of suitable materials that are available for singing, listening, and general historical and stylistic understanding

—Special ability to relate to all the students, regardless of their levels of interest and capabilities in music

The additional background needed by the effective general music teacher is, more or less, applicable to teachers of courses in music appreciation, music history, music literature, and the related arts. Their more specific competencies are suggested in those chapters devoted to each course. Similarly, the background needed by teachers who work with stage bands, pop–rock bands, folk-singing groups, and music theatre is presented in Chapter 14.

The acquisition and expansion of knowledge and skills needed to teach a particular course can be realized by two methods, or more effectively by a combination of both. The first, which we might call the formal method, includes (1) graduate study on the college or university level; (2) attendance at workshops, conferences, and lectures sponsored by the Music Educators National Conference and other professional organizations; (3) participation on curriculum organization committees at the state and local levels; and (4) continued study in applied music. The second and equally important method, the informal, includes (1) involvement with certain segments of music literature as a professional musician; (2) individually directed research into material related to the course being taught; (3) attendance at concerts, recitals, and other performances; and (4) keeping in touch with current trends in music through such publications as *Music Educators Journal, American Choral Review, American Musicological Society Journal, Journal of Music Theory, Stereo Review, Down Beat,* and *Ethnomusicology.* Many teachers recognize the value of the formal method; too many, however, overlook the value of the informal method, which is essential. In many cases, the latter is also the most practical method, since the teacher can direct his study to very precise, personal needs. Especially important is an understanding of what MENC's Commission on Teacher Education has called "the developmental process involved in becoming a successful teacher. [Music educators] are aware that certain competencies and qualities are essential for the first-year teacher and that other competencies and qualities are acquired only through a commitment to continuous study and self-evaluation."[23]

Who, then, is the secondary school teacher who guides learning experiences in music? He is a man or woman with one or more titles, teaching in one or more areas of music education, and assigned to one or more of the structural concepts of the "secondary school." If he is a successful teacher, he is undoubtedly distinguished by certain qualities of personality

[23] *Teacher Education in Music, op. cit.,* p. 33.

that give him a distinctive "style," and he effectively fills several roles related to the teaching situation. Although he has competencies in several areas of music education, he has probably specialized in one area and has continued his own education, formally or informally, to be exceptionally knowledgeable in that area. He recognizes the full range of music in today's society and, by maintaining an open mind, keeps up to date so that he may bring the full range of music to his students in developing their understanding and ability to make independent and knowledgeable judgments as consumers or performers. He understands the unique contribution of music to education, and pursues a course of teaching that recognizes essential principles of child growth and development, the teaching of aesthetic sensitivity, and the process of learning. Such is the image of the successful music teacher in today's schools.

Discussion Questions and Projects

1. From your reading and from your personal experience, compile a list of those qualities that you feel are most important in a teacher (in various areas of music education) and explain why they are important.
2. Explain, with specific illustrations, how the need for esteem in Maslow's hierarchy of needs can influence instruction in a general music class and in a performance class.
3. How can the music teacher use such incentives as reward, punishment, praise, and reproof with positive results in a general music class, a beginning instrumental class, a music theory class, and a marching band?
4. Before he can provide realistic guidance, what kinds of information must a teacher have concerning a student who is interested in a career in music?
5. Develop, for presentation to a secondary school principal, a strong justification for the inclusion of rock, jazz, and ethnic musics in all phases of music instruction.
6. Visit a general music class or performance class in a secondary school and report on the techniques the teacher uses to maintain classroom control.

Selected References

BERNARD, HAROLD W., and WESLEY C. HUCKINS, eds. *Readings in Human Development.* Boston: Allyn and Bacon, Inc., 1967.

BRUNER, JEROME S. *The Process of Education.* New York: Vintage Books, 1963.

GORDON, EDWIN. *Psychology of Music Teaching.* Englewood Cliffs, New Jersey: Prentice-Hall, Inc., 1971.

GORDON, SOL. "Education and The Impulse Life of the Child," *Phi Delta Kappan*, 47:6 (February 1966), pp. 310–314.

HARLOW, HARRY F. "Motivation as a Factor in the Acquisition of New Responses," in J. S. Brown, et al., *Current Theory and Research in Motivation*. Lincoln, Nebraska: University of Nebraska Press, 1953.

HIGHET, GILBERT. *The Art of Teaching*. New York: Vintage Books, 1950.

HYMES, JAMES L., JR. *Behavior and Misbehavior*. Englewood Cliffs, New Jersey: Prentice-Hall, Inc., 1955.

MASLOW, ABRAHAM H. *Motivation and Personality*. New York: Harper & Row, Publishers, 1954.

PULLEAS, EARL V., and JAMES D. YOUNG. *A Teacher Is Many Things*. Bloomington: Indiana University Press, 1968.

REIMER, BENNETT. *A Philosophy of Music Education*. Englewood Cliffs, New Jersey: Prentice-Hall, Inc., 1970.

Foundations
for Developing
Teaching
Strategies

2

An effective . . . classroom exists for the accomplishment of
certain end results: otherwise, decisions are made and activities
implemented without reason or purpose.

A SCHEME FOR MANAGEMENT BY OBJECTIVES[1]

TIME IN THE SECONDARY SCHOOL is limited, and with ever-increasing demands in a competitive curriculum for a return to basics, music study
easily could be neglected. Music also must be considered basic. If music
is to be a vital offering for all students in the secondary school, then
teachers must continue to center it around the unique contribution it
makes toward the growth of the individual—*the development of the sensitivity of each person to the aesthetic content of music*. It is true that
there is a wide range of musical capacity and sensitivity, but every person
is capable of finding some satisfaction and enjoyment as a consumer or
producer of music on some level and in some medium. With this fact in
mind, the successful music teacher recognizes various aesthetic theories
and develops a continually unfolding philosophy of music education as
a foundation for practical work in the classroom. Such a foundation derives from an understanding of aesthetic sensitivity, the learning process,
and the development of goals and objectives.

[1] *A Scheme for Management by Objectives* (Tucson: Educational Innovations
Press, Inc., 1973).

AESTHETIC SENSITIVITY

An aesthetic product—whether it is a work of music, a painting, a poem, or some other type of art—is considered a form of communication between the creator and the beholder. However, the everyday process of communication and the process related to an aesthetic product are quite different. In ordinary communication, the transmitter of a particular message selects *what* he wants to communicate and *how* he wants to communicate it; the connection is completed when the receiver gets the message and it evokes the desired action. The success of this process depends upon a minimum of interference between the sender and receiver. Thus, how the message-signal is organized and the quality of the medium selected for transmission are quite important: If the choice is poor, the message might be misunderstood.[2]

The communication process related to an aesthetic product does not necessarily begin with a complete message, especially if the art form is music. A composer, for example, may have just a fragment of an idea—a melodic phrase, a harmonic progression, a rhythmic pattern—that he explores and expands upon through manipulation of the aesthetic components that make up the music medium (rhythm, melody, harmony, form, texture, dynamics, tempo, and so on). During the period of creation, there is great interaction between the composer and his medium of expression; he shapes and structures the aesthetic components, and during the process they, in turn, influence his subsequent decisions and choices. As he works, the composer is quite subjective, and the creation embodies the sum of the knowledge, understanding, and skill he had before he began

his composition, as well as what he has newly learned in the process of creating.[3]

Once the composition has been completed and has been heard by the listener, the transmittal cannot be categorized as communication per se, because the work does not have a set message that is supposed to evoke a set response. What happens between the composer and listener is, in Bennett Reimer's terms, a *sharing* of the whole and parts of the composition. The listener cannot have the same insights and feelings about the composition as the composer because he brings to bear on it a different set of music capabilities, processes, and attitudes. To the new work he brings a set of past experiences with music, and through listening he has the opportunity to discover and gain some new insights related to the aesthetic components of music. Increasing the listener's ability to perceive these components in any work, familiar or unfamiliar, is the music teacher's task in developing aesthetic sensitivity.

"Aesthetic sensitivity" is one of those often-nebulous terms that are bandied about by educators. It need not be, however; it can be defined in a relatively simple way. *Aesthetic sensitivity is the ability to perceive and understand the components of an artwork, the handling of those components by the artist (composer), and the interrelationships among them.* It does not matter whether the person's response to these components is positive or negative, whether he finds them enjoyable or displeasing, appreciates them highly or little, values them or not; nor does it matter whether the response is primarily emotional, intellectual, or physical. Possessing aesthetic sensitivity is being fully aware of the expression inherent in an aesthetic product (through processes of recognizing, identifying, distinguishing, and relating); and while it is the basis for personal reaction, judgment,

---

[2] See Bennett Reimer, *A Philosophy of Music Education*, (Englewood Cliffs, New Jersey: Prentice-Hall, Inc., 1970), pp. 45–48.

[3] See Reimer, *op. cit.*, p. 50.

and value, it is clearly distinct from these factors.

Robert W. Buggert and Charles B. Fowler have written that appreciation is a "by-product of understanding. Conceivably, disliking a piece of music might be as natural a result of understanding as learning to enjoy it. Once the student understands the music he listens to, he will acquire his own set of appreciations. The musical art should be accessible in all its forms, although the choices people make within that selection are personal choices."[4]

Thus, there are two interdependent parts to the aesthetic experience (see Table 2-1)—one of them being measurable and teachable, and the other being nonmeasurable and nonteachable (except in the dictatorial sense that one can try to indoctrinate, brainwash, and impose a personal set of values on another, and perhaps try to manipulate feeling and emotion through some device such as biological feedback). The nonteachable part has been described by Reimer as "the feelingful reaction" to what has been perceived.[5] Any attempt to directly teach or affect the way a person reacts or feels when he hears a piece of music deteriorates the aesthetic experience to the level of a hunt for some ingredient or "message" that has been placed in the music by a clever composer to be uncovered by the equally clever listener. For years music teachers spent much of their time trying to teach the "beauty," "excitement," "delight," "meaning," or "depth" of various "classics" in thousands of "music appreciation" classes.

The other part of the aesthetic experience, which *can* be directly taught, is concerned

Table 2-1.

AESTHETIC EXPERIENCE	
SENSITIVITY TO AN AESTHETIC PRODUCT	RESPONSE TO AN AESTHETIC PRODUCT
(Teachable and Measurable)	(Nonteachable and Nonmeasurable)
Perception of	Reaction to
Rhythm, Melody, Harmony, Form, Texture, Medium, Dynamics, Tempo, Style, and so on.	Rhythm, Melody, Harmony, Form, Texture, Medium, Dynamics, Tempo, Style, and so on.
▽	▽
Involves	Involves
Awareness Observation Recognition Identification Reference Distinction Discernment Characterization Association Relation Comparison Classification Analysis Synthesis Integration Discovery Conceptualization Comprehension Insight Understanding	Feeling Emotion Affection Subjectiveness Personality Imagination Attitude Taste Interpretation Quality Meaning Significance Criticism Decision Choice Evaluation Acceptance Rejection Judgment Appreciation

with the perception of the aesthetic components that make up a piece of music. These include (1) percepts related to the basic elements of music—rhythm, melody, harmony, and form—and to the expressive elements of music—dynamics, tempo, and tone color; and (2) percepts related to how these elements are organized within a particular music style or period. Music teaching, whether performance or nonperformance, that provides experiences built around fundamental music concepts also

[4] Robert W. Buggert and Charles B. Fowler, *The Search for Musical Understanding* (Belmont, California: Wadsworth Publishing Company, Inc., 1973), p. viii.

[5] See Bennett Reimer, "The Development of Aesthetic Sensitivity," *Music Educators Journal*, 51:3 (January 1965), pp. 33–36.

furnishes the teacher with the type of curricular content that can be evaluated to measure the result of his teaching. (In developing an understanding of simple song form, for example, the teacher evaluates his results through the student's ability to recognize, aurally and visually, this structural organization in familiar and unfamiliar music.)

The teacher who provides for the development of aesthetic sensitivity through an understanding of basic concepts (concepts of sound and structure that apply to all types of music) will discover that he is not limited to ". . . any fixed set of objects as proper objects of veneration . . ."[6]; he can build his program from the broad expanse of all available *musics*. He is not bound to one approach of organization and presentation, but has a variety of alternatives (e.g., listening, performing, composing). He is not restricted to the use of a particular composition or style for the development of a specific concept, but can reintroduce and reinforce the same concept through many compositions of various styles, over and over again. He is not confined to a learning experience that demands only an immediate acquisition of knowledge or mastery of a skill, but can employ a process in which concepts are presented and clarified through progression from the simple to the complex, from the general to the specific, and from the concrete to the abstract. And he is not enslaved to being a source of mere factual information, but rather is a guide to the exploration, through student involvement, of those music concepts that can be used to make sense out of sounds, discover personal meaning in music, and increase personal enjoyment.

Good teachers have always taught concepts, but until the 1970s they did not teach them as the nucleus of music understanding in any substantial, widespread way. Now the aesthetics-centered, concept-oriented music program has provided the teacher with the long-needed, broad, musically-intrinsic objective, and the fundamentals of understanding, around which a strong, meaningful curriculum can be built—whether in the nongraded school, the open school, the middle school, or the traditionally scheduled junior or senior high school.

LEARNING PROCESS

Since the beginning of the century, a number of theories of learning have been developed by psychologists. These can generally be considered in terms of the two broad categories suggested by Ernest R. Hilgard: the association or stimulus–response theories, and the field or cognitive theories.[7]

The association theories include those of Thorndike, Guthrie, Hull, Skinner, and Gagné. Edward L. Thorndike developed a theory known as *connectionism*,[8] stating that a set of habits is acquired through trial and error, with the result that an appropriate response becomes associated with a particular stimulus. Thorndike applied three principles to the learning process. First was his principle of readiness, meaning that a sensory impression is associated with an impulse to act, and when the tendency toward an action exists, fulfilling the action is satisfying, but not fulfilling it is annoying. (He did not mean readiness, then, in terms of maturation level.) Secondly, his principle of exercise stated that associations are strengthened through prac-

---

[6] Harry S. Broudy, "The Case for Aesthetic Education," in *Documentary Report of the Tanglewood Symposium*, Robert A. Choate, ed. (Washington, D.C.: Music Educators National Conference, 1968), p. 10.

[7] See Ernest R. Hilgard and Gordon H. Bower, *Theories of Learning*, 3d ed. (New York: Appleton-Century-Crofts, Inc., 1966).

[8] See Edward L. Thorndike, *The Psychology of Learning* (New York: Teachers College, Columbia University, 1913).

tice. He later emphasized that the importance lay in the repetition of the associations, not of the original situation that gave rise to the association.[9] The third principle was that of effect: an association is strengthened or weakened by its consequences (reward and punishment). Thorndike deemed motivation to be an important factor: ". . . practice without zeal—with equal comfort at success and failure —does *not* make perfect, and the nervous system grows *away* from the modes in which it is *exercised with resulting discomfort.*"[10] He explained that habit alone does not explain much of human behavior, and that "practice without zeal" leads to unproductive drill. Motivational elements that Thorndike considered important were interest in the work, interest in improvement, significance, problem-attitude, attentiveness, absence of irrelevant emotion, and absence of worry.

E. R. Guthrie was an early behaviorist, believing in observable responses. His theory of *contigious conditioning* is summarized in a statement in his book *The Psychology of Learning*: "A combination of stimuli which has accompanied a movement will on its recurrence tend to be followed by that movement."[11] Guthrie's theory suggested that to encourage a behavior, it is necessary to know the cues leading to it and then arrange for the desired behavior to occur when those cues are present; conversely, it is important to see that undesired behavior does not occur in the presence of these same cues. Or, as defined by Hilgard, "what is being noticed becomes the signal for what is being done."[12] It was also Guthrie's belief that the more stimuli there are to be associated with the desired behavior, the less likely it is that other stimuli will be distracting and cause an undesired behavior. Applying this to music, it could be said that it is best to practice in the exact manner that is to be required later in performance.

Clark L. Hull believed strongly in a reinforcement theory requiring a reduction in drive (satisfying a need) or a reduction in a drive stimulus.[13] Habit was a key element in his concept of *systematic behavior*. Hull's theory stated that the strength of habit depends on how much remains to be learned and on the number, rather than amount, of reinforcements to a particular response. Habit is strongest when need reduction is great, and learning is maximized at this point when there is also little delay between response and reinforcement. Thus, drive activates habit, and the strength of the habit determines the potential of the response.

Another behaviorist is B. F. Skinner, who is known for his theory of *operant conditioning*.[14] Skinner distinguishes between respondent behavior, wherein responses are elicited by identifiable stimuli, and operant behavior, wherein responses are emitted without identifiable stimuli. He believes that most human behavior is operant and he does not attach much importance to respondent behavior. The principal factor in Skinner's operant conditioning is his belief that the association between a stimulus and the desired response is strengthened by immediate reinforcement

[9] See Edward L. Thorndike, *The Fundamentals of Learning* (New York: Teachers College, Columbia University, 1932); and *The Psychology of Wants, Interests, and Attitudes* (New York: Appleton-Century-Crofts, Inc., 1935).

[10] Thorndike, *The Psychology of Learning, op. cit.*, p. 22.

[11] E. R. Guthrie, *The Psychology of Learning* (New York: Harper and Brothers, 1935), p. 26.

[12] Hilgard and Bowers, *op. cit.*, p. 92.

[13] See Clark L. Hull, *Principles of Behavior* (New York: Appleton-Century-Crofts, 1943).

[14] See B. F. Skinner, *Science and Human Behavior* (New York: The Macmillan Company, 1953); and *The Behavior of Organisms* (New York: Appleton-Century-Crofts, 1938).

(food, a prize, praise, recognition, and so forth, rather than traditional long-range reinforcers such as grades, a diploma, or the promise of a lucrative position). In addition, a stimulus that accompanies a reinforcement can itself have reinforcing value. Skinner's research led to the use of teaching machines and other forms of programmed instruction (including textbooks) that indicate to a student immediately whether his response is correct or incorrect. The application of this theory forces a teacher to define desired behaviors.

Robert Gagné, a contemporary behaviorist, has had a considerable influence on the behavioral objective movement in education. Gagné's position is that behaviors to be taught are derived from an observation of human performance.[15] Based on such observation, a series of behavioral objectives is written, with rudimentary behaviors being prerequisite to more complex ones. Then, the teacher is able to arrange an appropriate sequence of learning experiences to realize those objectives.

All the behavioral learning theories, as well as Thorndike's prebehavioral connectionism, take on both their values and their limitations from the fact that they are concerned only with observable phenomena or overt stimulus-response situations; they ignore internal mediating events as being unknowable. Whereas they are basically concerned with muscular response, trial-and-error procedures, and acquired habits based on learned responses, the second basic category of learning theory—cognitive theory—is concerned with the process of the central nervous system, problem-solving insight, and cognitive understandings of relationships based on learned facts. It is to the second category that Edward C. Tolman, Gestalt psychologists such as Kurt Koffka and Wolfgang Kohler, and the Swiss developmental psychologist Jean Piaget have contributed.

Cognitive processes are central to Tolman's theory of *sign learning*, which states that behavior is directed toward a goal and the student follows signs to that goal.[16] He learns meanings rather than movements. Instead of habit leading to response, as in association theory, an expectancy of something at the end leads to action. The learner sees various means of approaching his goal, based on prior experience, and his activity is then guided by his expectancy. Knowledge is acquired through the relationship of means to end rather than in terms of behavior and reward. In this relationship there is a togetherness of elements—of signs, actions, and confirmations of the goal.

Closely related to Tolman's theory is the *Gestalt theory*, which was introduced to the United States in the late 1920s and early 1930s.[17] The Gestalt approach emphasizes perceiving relationships of the parts to the whole and of the means to the end. Problems are solved in terms of reasoning, their organization, and their intrinsic qualities. According to this theory, organization in the learning experience comes both from processes inherent in the learner and from the structure of the environment being dealt with. It is important that all necessary factors be available for observation, for this affects the ease or difficulty with which understanding is achieved. Hilgard has offered an illustration of this point:

In the favored arrangement the problem is so structured that significant features are per-

---

[15] See Robert M. Gagné, *The Conditions of Learning* (New York: Holt, Rinehart and Winston, 1965).

[16] Edward C. Tolman, *Purposive Behavior in Animals and Men* (New York: Appleton-Century-Crofts, 1932).

[17] See Kurt Koffka, *Principles of Gestalt Psychology* (New York: Harcourt, Brace, 1935); and *The Growth of the Mind* (London: Kegan Paul, Trench, Trubner and Co. Ltd., 1924).

ceived in proper relationship, and distracting or confusing features are subordinated. Some mathematics teachers make problem solution difficult to grasp because they go through derivations step by step without an overview of where the steps are leading or what the articulating principles are. They teach the necessary operations, but the final insight eludes the students because of the manner in which the proof is arranged.[18]

Educators have long recognized the difficulties involved in applying the results of pure psychological research to a teaching situation. However, there have been a few recent researchers who have produced theories that lend themselves more readily to practical application in the classroom. In the field of behaviorism, Gagné's work is an example. And in the field of cognitive theory, Jean Piaget's contributions are well known.

Through observations of children in both clinical and experimental situations, Piaget developed a theory of the development of thought processes from infancy to adolescence.[19] He has indicated the existence of four major stages of development: (1) sensorimotor, during the first eighteen months of life; (2) preoperational, extending from eighteen months to about the age of seven; (3) concrete operations, extending from seven to about eleven or twelve years of age usually; and (4) formal operations, beginning in pre- or early adolescence. The preoperational stage is characterized by the child's rudimentary use of symbols, but he manipulates reality intuitively. He has an egocentric orientation to symbols at this point and must reason in terms of each perception individually. When he reaches the stage of concrete operations, the child is able to manipulate mentally symbols related to his immediate experience. Trial and error is internalized, taking place in his mind without observable action. His thinking is no longer dependent on perceptions, and he is able to draw relationships among more than two things simultaneously. The stage of formal operations is both a qualitative and quantitative extension of the last. The student's handling of symbols here extends to envisioning hypothetical situations and relations, and to means of verifying them. Two concepts connected with Piaget's theory are those of conservation and reversibility. Conservation is the student's ability to see that one element does not change though others related to it may, or that an element may remain constant in one dimension but not in others. Reversibility refers to the student's ability to reverse a procedure, so that, having conserved the original concept, when something changes he can think back to its original state. Piaget's theory can have considerable application to music education; it shows how a concept can be introduced to students at certain levels.

Another psychologist whose work has had an effect on educators in recent years is David P. Ausubel. In *The Psychology of Meaningful Verbal Learning*, Ausubel distinguishes between reception learning (when material is presented to the student in finished form) and discovery learning (when the content to be learned is actually discovered). He points out that reception learning is not necessarily rote, and that verbal learning has been abused because of such practices as

. . . premature use of verbal technics with cognitively immature pupils; arbitrary presentation of unrelated facts without any organizing or explanatory principles; failure to integrate new learning tasks with previously presented materials; and the use of evaluation procedures that merely measure ability to recognize discrete facts or to reproduce ideas in the same words

[18] Hilgard and Bowers, *op. cit.*, pp. 241–242.

[19] See Jean Piaget, *The Language and Thought of the Child* (Cleveland: The World Publishing Company, 1965).

or in the identical context as originally encountered.[20]

Ausubel is known for his theory of subsumption, which states that learning occurs within a cognitive structure of hierarchically organized units of classification, having decreasing inclusiveness from the broadest of concepts through subconcepts to units of specific data. In relation to this, he has pointed out that discovery learning—a commonly used technique since the 1960s—may be unproductive if the student does not have a cognitive structure to which he can relate what he discovers. Ausubel has written:

> Discovery learning is a psychologically more involved process than reception learning because it presupposes a problem-solving stage that precedes the emergence of meaning and the interiorization of information. But reception learning, on the whole, appears later developmentally and, in most instances, implies a greater degree of cognitive maturity. The young child learns most new concepts and propositions inductively through autonomous discovery, although self-discovery is not essential if concrete-empirical props are available. Reception learning, however, although occurring earlier, is not really prominent until the child is both capable of internal mental operations and can comprehend verbally presented propositions in the absence of concrete-empirical experience. . . .[21]

Ausubel's theory, then, would recommend renewed attention to verbal learning (or a different balancing of verbal and discovery approaches) at the secondary school level, especially in such courses as general music, harmony, and music theory. An emphasis on discovery and the development of broad inclusive concepts would be maintained in the lower grades and would provide the cognitive structure to which later reception learning could be related.

Out of the reality of the classroom, rather than adopt any one learning theory, educators generally have developed an eclectic approach to the learning process. If there is anything unified about current thinking, it is that educators today tend to view learning in terms of behavioral changes involving the student's entire personality. These changes occur in (1) *the cognitive domain*, referring to the acquisition of concepts and principles related to knowledge, comprehension, application, analysis, synthesis, and evaluation; (2) *the affective domain*, which refers to learning related to the development of interests, values, attitudes, feelings, and appreciations; and (3) *the psychomotor domain*, concerned with learning related to developing muscular coordination in association with sensory perception.

The following list of learning principles is an eclectic one that draws on a number of learning theories. Like all principles and all theories, the ones listed here are generalizations. None is intended as an absolute condition for learning. However, they have proved to have practical application in many learning situations, and the music teacher should find them a valuable guide in organizing learning experiences.

1. The total environment has an influence upon the success or failure of the learner.

2. The learner must experience a greater degree of success than failure in the process of learning. Consistently learning from mistakes alone has a negative effect on the learner's subsequent efforts.

3. What the student is learning must be of significant value to *him* and should contribute in some way to his self-awareness and competence.

---

[20] David P. Ausubel, *The Psychology of Meaningful Verbal Learning* (New York: Grune & Stratton, 1963), p. 18. Used by permission.

[21] Ausubel, *op. cit.*, p. 17.

4. Learning takes place when the learner is actively involved in a personal manner.

5. Learning experiences must be related to the developmental characteristics of the learner.

6. Aspiration level is directly related to the learner's motivational level.

7. Learning is more efficient when the student understands its purpose and need, and can see where various steps in the learning sequence are leading.

8. Learning is more effective when the student is stimulated by not only the substance but the process of learning.

9. Learning is a problem-centered solving process.

10. Successful learning is more apt to take place when the learner is concerned with one thing at a time.

11. Many short learning experiences over a long period of time are often more efficient than long learning experiences over a short period of time, particularly in the development of skills.

12. The development of conceptual understanding involves the process of perception, conception, and application.

13. Learning is reinforced when smaller details are related to basic concepts and when basic concepts are related to larger frames of reference.

14. Learning is more effective when a variety of techniques, methods, and media is employed to examine a single concept.

15. Immediate application of learning is the basis of relevancy and recall.

16. Learning is reinforced by a constant process of synthesis, regardless of the amount of analysis.

17. Learning is most effective when knowledge and understanding are balanced with imagination and intuition.

18. Learning is a continuous process that is evolutionary and cyclical, not additive.

19. The learner must be constantly cognizant, through feedback, of the result of his efforts.

20. Learning is a process of individual inquiry that leads to discovery.

In applying these eclectic principles of learning, the teacher should be cognizant of recent research regarding the functioning of the brain. The cerebral cortex has two hemispheres —the left one, known as the "major hemisphere," and the right one, known as the "minor." Although these labels have been applied only in modern times, the dominance of the left hemisphere probably dates far back. In his book *The Origin of Consciousness in the Breakdown of the Bicameral World*, Julian Jaynes presented the fascinating theory that humans had no "inner life"—no introspection, will, or ability to imagine—until about 10,000 B.C. Prior to that, according to Jaynes, they had language but lacked consciousness and were guided by habit. Problems were solved by inner, godlike voices coming from the right hemisphere of the brain, whereas speech was generated by the left side. Eventually, society became too complex to be directed by these voices; humans developed awareness and, Jaynes wrote, the fading voices—their utterances now written down—gave rise to religions. In time, the left hemisphere became dominant, although right-hemisphere voices still might break through occasionally, as in the hallucinations of schizophrenics.

Although this theory may explain the source of the left hemisphere's dominance, we need to go beyond such a mystique to consider the function of both hemispheres in learning and to see the right hemisphere as more than a source of "voices" and hallucinations. Both parts work together in a complementary manner. In *most* persons, but not all, the left hemisphere is dominant. This side of the brain handles analytic, logical thinking, including language. It works by fragmentation, processing information sequentially, one item at a time. The left side provides musical response by breaking down the whole—identifying a chord change, noticing a modulation from E-flat major to C minor, recognizing the augmentation of a particular rhythm pattern, and so on. The right hemisphere, in contrast, is intuitive and holistic in processing information. It provides orientation and overall recognition by integrating many aspects simultaneously. The right side also deals with spatial patterns, and it may be that the recognition of pitch occurs there. By handling the complexities of sound simultaneously rather than sequentially, the right side processes the artistic aspects of music, leading a person to identify a piece of music by, say, its title or style as a result of an overall impression, and leading to an aesthetic response.

Music perception is clearly a function not of either hemisphere alone, but of both working together. An emphasis on music as an "academic" subject to be dissected would focus on left-hemisphere functions, just as an emphasis on the emotional qualities of music would focus on right-hemisphere functions. However, full musical recognition and response involves *both* sides of the brain. It can be understood, then, that a student who experiences strong left-hemisphere activity may not respond to music as a whole, even by trying to shift analytical gears rapidly. A student who experiences strong right-hemisphere activity, conversely, may respond well intuitively but may be weaker in fragmentary, verbal analysis. Focusing on one hemisphere can weaken activity in the opposite hemisphere. Therefore a student focusing on an analysis of parts should not be expected to respond aesthetically to the whole at the same time. Progressive focusing, however, can lead to a different result: If, after left-hemisphere analysis, we turn to right-hemisphere integration, then we achieve sudden insight.

What is learned is recalled or not recalled by the brain depending on the degree to which the original learning situation is relived and on the degree to which the subjective state of the learner (at the time of learning) is recaptured. Thus, Gilbert Highet's previously cited premise about following the lead of the advertising world and making a lesson vivid has its foundation in the workings of the brain. If the learning experience is not vivid, then the information or skill being taught must be repeated many times. In addition, as Thomas A. Regelski has pointed out:

> learning must be encountered or applied to *situations* similar or related to the kind the learner can be expected to encounter in life. Thus it should be generalizable, rather than too highly specific, and should be highly varied and increasingly refined at subsequent levels (that is, a "spiral" curriculum).
>
> Returning to a learning over and over again to strengthen it should be done in a context where sheer repetition (rote or imitative learning) gives way to *increasing independence* and to occasions for students to use independently what they have learned.[22]

The dominance of the left hemisphere seems to occur around ten years of age; therefore, middle-school students—those in the early stages of secondary education (as defined in this book)—are at a crucial point in their development. Regelski noted that

> around this time—typically the fifth and sixth grades—reactions negative to music class can become set, as for example when some boys become disaffected with singing or when instrumental students rebel against practicing page after page of whole notes that are not as rewarding as playing "by ear" or playing melodies with an accompaniment (taped on cassette if necessary). Music classes should dwell more upon right-hemisphere kinds of musical learning, while using the other mode

[22] Thomas A. Regelski, "Who Knows Where Music Lurks in the Mind of Man?—New Brain Research Has the Answer," *Music Educators Journal*, 63:9 (May 1977), p. 36.

of consciousness when and as it is useful in enhancing musical, metaphoric thinking.[23]

Although split-brain research has provided some useful information for music educators, much research must be done before we can be reasonably sure of how the brain functions in a learning situation. In fact, various studies report contradictory results. It should be noted, for example, that more than one-third of the population is either left-handed or ambidextrous to some extent (a significant fact when you consider that in most activities the *left* side of the brain controls the *right* side of the body). Of these people, more than one-third are *not* left-hemisphere dominated (better than one out of nine people); their speech functions, for example, are either right-hemispheric or ambilateral. The preceding descriptions of hemisphere functions, then, might be either reversed or combined for a large number of students. There is also some evidence of differences in lateral dominance between males and females. And it may also (and quite likely) be that hemisphere functions differ with the extent of music training. Consequently teachers should not draw, at this point in the research, any definite conclusions about how brain dominance affects learning. *Some* conclusions for *some* students are suggested by existing research, but teachers should watch for the results of further research.

DEVELOPING GOALS AND OBJECTIVES

Every teacher soon discovers that all subject matter areas in the secondary school receive instructional direction from statements of goals and objectives. In order to avoid organizational confusion, it is important to know and understand the difference between goals

and objectives. A *goal* is best described as a statement that is (1) broad in intent and purpose, (2) general and timeless, (3) open to many interpretations, and (4) not measurable as stated.[24] For example, here are two goal statements; the first is related to education in general, and the second one to music. Notice how they meet our criteria:

—The development of responsible citizens.
—The development of each individual's musical talent.

To have goals is important, but it is not enough. Goals do provide a general direction and a point of departure for instructional organization, but teachers need more definitive statements that will provide signals to indicate that goals have been achieved. These more definitive statements are the *objectives*. As teachers organize their objectives, it is important that they recognize the various levels, and understand how these levels interrelate with each other and with the goals. The various levels of goals and objectives are as follows:

School goals will provide information as to where the music program can make its unique contribution to the total development of each student.

Broad music goals will state, in general terms, how the music program intends to contribute to the achievement of school goals.

Program objectives will present, in more specific terms, those musical behaviors in the *total* music program that will result in attainment of the broad music goals.

Course objectives will state in more specific terms the musical behaviors students will

[23] *Ibid.,* p. 38.

[24] *A Scheme for Management by Objectives, op. cit.,* p. 1.

exhibit as the result of a particular music course.

Instructional objectives are the specific *behavioral objectives* the teacher uses in preparing his lessons for a day, week, or some other segment of instruction.

Table 2-2 shows how these five levels are related through the selection of objectives in one particular area. The program objective given in this table is just one of a large number of possibilities. For a more complete presentation of program objectives, refer to Table 2-3.

Notice that the goals and objectives on the first four levels in Table 2-2 and those in Table 2-3 are not written in specific behavioral terms, although they indicate observable behaviors. At the instructional level, however, the teacher should write behaviorally stated objectives that adhere as much as possible to the criteria suggested by Robert F. Mager—which have been generally accepted in educational circles:

> First, identify the terminal behavior by name. . . . Second, . . . [describe] the important conditions under which the behavior will be expected to occur. Third, specify the criteria of acceptable performance. . . .[25]

Following Mager's criteria for the development of behavioral objectives on the instructional level will provide the teacher and the student with the specificity that is lacking in statements of goals and objectives on the program and course levels. A behavioral objective will specify the *task* (observable behavior) that the student must perform, the *condition* under which the particular task will be performed, and finally the *criterion* that determines whether the task has been performed

[25] Robert F. Mager, *Preparing Instructional Objectives* (Palo Alto, California: Fearon Publishers, 1962), p. 12.

Table 2-2.

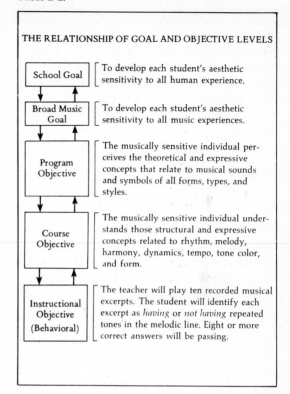

THE RELATIONSHIP OF GOAL AND OBJECTIVE LEVELS

School Goal — To develop each student's aesthetic sensitivity to all human experience.

Broad Music Goal — To develop each student's aesthetic sensitivity to all music experiences.

Program Objective — The musically sensitive individual perceives the theoretical and expressive concepts that relate to musical sounds and symbols of all forms, types, and styles.

Course Objective — The musically sensitive individual understands those structural and expressive concepts related to rhythm, melody, harmony, dynamics, tempo, tone color, and form.

Instructional Objective (Behavioral) — The teacher will play ten recorded musical excerpts. The student will identify each excerpt as *having* or *not having* repeated tones in the melodic line. Eight or more correct answers will be passing.

successfully. Remember, a behavioral objective must have *a task, a condition, and a criterion*. The omission of the criterion would imply that the task must be completed without any errors. The following statements are examples of the three parts of a behavioral objective:

> *Task:* the student will identify meter signatures by ear
> *Condition:* when the teacher plays fifteen recorded musical examples
> *Criterion:* ten or more correct answers will be considered passing

Here are the same three segments put together into a behavioral objective:

> When the teacher plays fifteen recorded musical examples, the student will identify

Table 2-3. PROGRAM OBJECTIVES

Behavior	The musically sensitive individual:
Knowledge	1. is familiar with a wide range of music compositions, representative of all kinds of music;
	2. knows important facts about the historical and artistic development of music, including social implications, stylistic eras, and so on;
	3. has knowledge of composers and compositions as they relate to the development of music;
	4. has knowledge of the place and types of music in contemporary society; and
	5. has knowledge of the relationship of basic music concepts, both theoretical and expressive, to various types and styles of music.
Understanding	1. perceives the theoretical and expressive concepts that relate to musical sounds and symbols of all forms, types, and styles;
	2. recognizes the different criteria employed in realizing and evaluating various types of music, and understands the performance problems involved in the interpretation of music of a particular style, instrument, instrumental combination, voice, or vocal combination;
	3. understands the close relationship between music and the other arts; and
	4. can discriminate among performances of artists and among compositions of a like nature.
Skill	1. has the ability to recognize, aurally and visually, the structural elements of music, form generalizations about them, and apply these generalizations in listening to other compositions and performances, both familiar and unfamiilar;
	2. has the facility and independence to express himself musically—i.e., individually or in a group, vocally or instrumentaily, or through music composition; and
	3. experiments with his own interpretation of a particular composition and seeks the opinions of his teacher and other musically interested persons.
Attitude	1. is aware of the diversity of music tastes and is considerate of the differing music preferences of others;
	2. respects and encourages the musical expression of others;
	3. works to improve his musicality through formal and informal study;
	4. seeks personal enjoyment through music experiences of all kinds;
	5. reads books related to music, collects recordings, and attends music performances; and
	6. is aware of school and community music offerings.

Behavior	The musically sensitive individual:
Appreciation	1. is aware of the feelingful aspect of music;
	2. recognizes the place of music in the school and in society;
	3. recognizes the need of all individuals for aesthetic expression and aesthetic reaction; and
	4. respects the artistic performance of all *musics* and their artists.
Habit	1. seeks to play and sing in school and community groups;
	2. develops good study and practice habits;
	3. is selective in the quality of music performed, records collected, performances attended, and music listened to; and
	4. listens to all music with discrimination regarding interpretation, tone quality, precision, and so on.

the meter signatures by ear. Ten or more correct answers will be considered passing.

In writing behavioral objectives, the choice of words, especially the verbs that describe the behaviors, is very important. Such verbs as "know," "appreciate," "understand," "enjoy," "interpret," and "like" are acceptable for the higher objective levels, but they are too vague, too imprecise, to be of functional value on the instructional level. They do not convey to either the instructor or the student the exact behavior expected as a result of student-teacher interaction, or at least how that behavior is to be exhibited and recognized. Examples of verbs that have greater accuracy and are less ambiguous include "arrange," "list," "classify," "tap," "clap," "sing," "play," "move to," "harmonize," "match," "name," "choose," and "divide." Such verbs would be acceptable in a behavioral objective.

Although behavioral objectives are now widely accepted, it must be realized that they cannot be applied equally well to all phases of education. They are best suited to cogni-

tive learning. Benjamin Bloom identified six categories of learning in the cognitive domain: (1) *knowledge* (remembering facts, terminology, classifications, principles, theories, and so on); (2) *comprehension* (being able to translate, interpret, or infer); (3) *application* (putting knowledge to use in solving a problem); (4) *analysis* (being able to distinguish elements, find relationships, and discern the principles of organization); (5) *synthesis* (being able to piece together elements through independent thought to produce something communicative, a plan for doing something, or, at a higher level, a set of abstract relations); and (6) *evaluation* (being able to judge appropriately in terms of the inherent qualities of an item or in terms of external criteria such as usefulness or effectiveness).[26] Table 2-4 illustrates that behavioral objectives can be written for each of these categories. However, it should be noted that criteria for acceptable performance are not indicated in the objectives given in the cate-

[26] See Benjamin S. Bloom, ed., *Taxonomy of Educational Objectives; Handbook I: Cognitive Domain* (New York: Longman, Inc., 1956).

gories of synthesis and evaluation. There are some instances in which the evaluation of performance must be open-ended; individual actions can vary considerably, and it would often be inappropriate to impose definite criteria on someone's creative work or personal judgment.

In the affective domain, David R. Krathwohl has identified five learning categories: (1) *receiving* (that is, being receptive, as evidenced by awareness, willingness, or attention); (2) *responding* (as manifested in a lack of resistance, voluntary action, or an active desire to seek a satisfactory experience); (3)

valuing (including recognition of traditionally accepted values as well as the formation of personal preferences and the development of firm convictions); (4) *organization* (establishing a personal hierarchy of values); and (5) *characterization by a value complex* (formulating a strong philosophy that effects a set and a broadly encompassing outlook).[27] Although behavioral objectives in the affective domain can state particular behaviors and

[27] See David R. Krathwohl, Benjamin S. Bloom, and B. B. Masia, eds., *Taxonomy of Educational Objectives; Handbook II: Affective Domain* (New York: David McKay Company, Inc., 1965).

Table 2-4. COGNITIVE BEHAVIORAL OBJECTIVES

Category of Learning	Behavioral Objective
Knowledge	Presented with fifteen pictures of instruments of the band and orchestra, all of them previously studied in class, the student will correctly name at least thirteen.
Comprehension	Given the scores for both familiar and unfamiliar compositions, the student will interpret each meter signature by demonstrating the appropriate conducting pattern to be used.
Application	Given an eight-measure figured bass line, the student will harmonize the upper three parts, following practices previously covered in class. Five mistakes or fewer will be considered satisfactory.
Analysis	Given the score for the first movement of Beethoven's *Sonata No. 16 for Piano*, Op. 31, No. 1, the student will identify in writing, with reference to specific measure numbers, the thematic material in the exposition, how this material is manipulated in the development, and how it is used in the recapitulation. Two or more references to the exposition, three or more to the development, and two or more to the recapitulation will be deemed satisfactory.
Synthesis	Given the basic chord progression for a twelve-measure blues, as well as a set of words, the student will compose an original composition for voice, bass guitar, guitar, electric piano, and drums.
Evaluation	Given a score and a tape of his own singing, the student will judge his performance in terms of precise intonation, distinct pronunciation and enunciation, suitability of tone quality to enhance interpretation, and rhythmic and melodic accuracy.

the conditions under which they will be observed, there will be no clear-cut criteria to measure performance. This is because of the fact that affective objectives, by their very nature, are value-laden. A rigid level of conformity is impossible (and undesirable as well) because there are many ways for students to show their interests, values, appreciations, habits, and attitudes, all of which can vary greatly with each person as they are influenced by the area of study, the school, home conditions, social conditions, and other factors. Thus, the evaluative portion of affective behavioral objectives must remain open-ended, and the inapplicability to the affective domain of the three criteria for writing behavioral objectives must be recognized as an inherent weakness. Within this framework,

the music teacher's major concern should be the development of objectives that allow individual expression and variation to occur naturally. Table 2-5 provides examples of such objectives in the affective domain.

In the psychomotor domain, music skills range from such acts as playing the trombone, involving both physical and mental processes, to listening, which is almost purely mental. It is difficult for music educators to agree with Benjamin Bloom's belief that the psychomotor domain has little functional value in the classroom, for psychomotor learning plays an integral part in the development of music skills. To help the teacher discuss skills as they relate to each other, how they are used, and their various levels of difficulty, Elizabeth Simpson organized a tentative hierarchical

Table 2-5. AFFECTIVE BEHAVIORAL OBJECTIVES

Category of Learning	Behavioral Objective
Receiving	After a series of listening lessons on the music of the classical guitar, the student, at the teacher's suggestion, goes to the music listening center and listens to several recordings of classical guitar music on his own time.
Responding	Provided with the opportunity to participate in a variety of extraclass activities, the student chooses to participate in the activities of the jazz club.
Valuing	After reading material for and against federal support of the arts, the student voluntarily writes to his senator and congressman urging increased appropriations for federal support of the arts.
Organization	Provided with the time and materials, the student, on his own initiative, chooses to research a music topic that interests him.
Characterization by a Value Complex	Note: This level is beyond the goals of music education. However, as Richard Colwell has stated, ". . . the music profession offers numerous examples of individuals whose value systems center around the musical experience. The two aspects of this level are . . . generalized set, and . . . the integration of these beliefs and values into a total philosophy or *world view*."[28]

[28] Richard Colwell, *The Evaluation of Music Teaching and Learning* (Englewood Cliffs, New Jersey: Prentice-Hall, Inc., 1970), p. 177. Reprinted by permission of Prentice-Hall, Inc., © 1970.

system that parallels the affective taxonomy devised by Krathwohl. It must be noted that Simpson's is not a genuine hierarchy and cannot be adhered to rigidly. Its principal weakness lies in the fact that so little research has been done regarding the nature and development of aural skills.

Simpson organized her taxonomy of psychomotor skills into seven major categories: (1) *perception* (sensory awareness of objects, qualities, and relations, involving stimulation of one or more sense organs, then distinguishing among the stimuli and selecting a cue for response, and finally translating the meaning of the cue into action); (2) *set* (mental, physical, or emotional readiness to act); (3) *guided response* (observable action, under a teacher's guidance, that may be either imitative or trial and error); (4) *mechanism* (a learned response developed to the point of its being habit); (5) *complex overt response* (a complex motor act that is performed smoothly and efficiently, either with confidence or with the ease and control of an automatic action); (6) *adaptation* (the ability to adjust an action to increase its appropriateness or suitability); and (7) *origination* (the ability to develop new skills).[29]

In the preceding pages, we have seen some of the difficulties involved in writing behavioral objectives in accordance with Mager's guidelines. Although behavioral objectives are widely accepted, there are many educators who question whether *all* objectives should or really can be stated in behavioral terms. W. James Popham, professor of education at U.C.L.A., was a long-time proponent of the use of *only* behavioral objectives; in recent years, however, he has written that while most objectives should be behavioral, there are exceptions. When a teaching goal has

enough merit, it should be pursued even though there is no immediate way to measure whether the goal has been achieved. Popham has offered an example:

Suppose our aim is to have children acquire a certain attitudinal predisposition which will be manifest, by definition, only after they become adults. Our best hope for assessment is to isolate predictor behaviors which are currently measurable and use these as proxies for the long-term goals. This is a defensible plan, *if* we can isolate proxy behaviors in which we can be confident. But since we have really just begun to get very sophisticated and circumventious in our measurement approaches, there are long range goals for which we presently can't find suitable proxies. . . . What troubles one about ever voicing this "permit" . . . is that too many teachers may employ it as an excuse for business as usual, and today's business as usual in American education is unacceptable. . . . Too few teachers employ a sufficiently large proportion of measurable objectives to be able to discern whether the bulk of the instructional efforts are satisfactory.[30]

George F. Kneller, professor of education at U.C.L.A.'s Graduate School of Education, recommends that behavioral objectives be replaced by what he calls "specified objectives." Kneller wrote that these

. . . are chosen, or specified, by the school according to its own philosophy of education, and they are specified only for certain subject matter which the school considers basic. Certain specific content (or skills) could be required of all students at certain levels, and the students could be tested on how well they have acquired it. . . . At another level, a level at which standardization is difficult, impossible,

[29] Elizabeth Simpson, *The Classification of Educational Objectives, Psychomotor Domain* (Urbana: University of Illinois, 1966); see Colwell, *op. cit.*, pp. 102–104, 169–172.

[30] W. James Popham, "Must ALL Objectives Be Behavioral?" *Educational Leadership*, 29:7 (April 1972), p. 608. Reprinted with permission of the Association for Supervision and Curriculum Development and W. James Popham. Copyright © 1972 by the Association for Supervision and Curriculum Development. All rights reserved.

or undesirable, the individual teacher should specify objectives, to be achieved by either the individual student or groups of students, in accordance with (a) a theory of knowledge and value adopted by the teacher himself, and (b) the talents and choices of the student. . . . Two subjects where rigorous evaluation is quite impossible [are] art and music."[31]

Kneller further questions the behaviorists' claim that a teacher using behavioral objectives can provide for individual needs either by developing objectives for each student or by adjusting predetermined class objectives. He points out that the number of possible objectives for one course could run as high as two thousand (a behaviorist claim) and that the teacher who develops individual objectives for a class of thirty could be working with sixty thousand objectives!

Elliot W. Eisner, professor of education and art at Stanford University, is another critic of behavioral objectives. He notes that despite all the work that has been done in developing taxonomies of objectives and their application to various subject areas, ". . . teachers seem not to take educational objectives seriously. . . ."[32] Eisner has questioned the actual usefulness of objectives:

> . . . When teachers plan curriculum guides, their efforts first to identify over-all educational aims, then specify school objectives, then identify educational objectives for specific subject matters, appear to be more like exercises to be gone through than serious efforts to build

tools for curriculum planning. If educational objectives were really useful tools, teachers, I submit, would use them. If they do not, perhaps it is not because there is something wrong with the teachers but because there might be something wrong with the theory.[33]

According to Eisner, one of the first limitations to the function of educational objectives "is that the dynamic and complex process of instruction yields outcomes far too numerous to be specified in behavioral . . . terms in advance."[34] For example, there are times in a teaching situation when an opportunity arises unexpectedly to illustrate an important idea, to make a significant point, or to introduce a new concept. The teacher cannot predict in his objectives when such dynamic opportunities will arise, but they do arise, and they sometimes turn a lesson or a series of lessons about so that the student learns something worthwhile that had not been specifically planned.

Another limitation is the failure to take into account "the particular relationship that holds between the subject matter being taught and the degree to which educational objectives can be predicted and specified."[35] In the areas of science and mathematics, it should be possible to state quite exactly the desired behavioral outcomes of a particular sequence of instruction. But in the arts, such specificity is not always possible nor in some instances even desirable. In the area of creativity, for example, the desired behaviors cannot be easily described, and the creative work should really be, as Eisner has said, "something of a surprise to both teacher and pupil."[36]

Still another point of confusion relates to the use of objectives as standards to evaluate

[31] George F. Kneller, "Behavioral Objectives? No!" *Educational Leadership*, 29:5 (February 1972), pp. 399–400. Reprinted with permission of the Association for Supervision and Curriculum Development and George F. Kneller. Copyright © 1972 by the Association for Supervision and Curriculum Development. All rights reserved.

[32] Elliot W. Eisner, "Educational Objectives: Help or Hindrance?" *The School Review*, 75:3 (Autumn 1967), p. 253. Published by the University of Chicago. Copyright © 1967 by The School Review.

[33] *Ibid.*

[34] *Ibid.*, p. 254.

[35] *Ibid.*, p. 255.

[36] *Ibid.*

student achievement when the learning outcomes do not lend themselves to precise measurement. There are some areas where a fixed standard can be applied, but when the teacher evaluates an aesthetic work his student has produced, the teacher cannot apply a particular standard of measurement. Instead, he must use his own judgment as a musician or artist, viewing the work much as a professional critic does and offering suggestions for either improvement or, better, alternative procedures.

Finally, Eisner has questioned the need for developing objectives prior to the selection of curriculum content and activities, referring to a statement that had been made by James B. MacDonald:

> Objectives are viewed as directives in the rational approach. They are identified prior to the instruction or action and used to provide a basis for or a screen for appropriate activities.
>
> There is another view, however, . . . [which states] that our objectives are only known to us in any complete sense after the completion of our act of instruction. No matter what we thought we were attempting to do, we can only know what we wanted to accomplish after the fact. Objectives by this rationale are heuristic devices which provide initiating sequences which become altered in the flow of instruction.[37]

MacDonald's point might be likened to the use of an outline by a writer. A preliminary outline is fine for sketching ideas and sequence. But very often, in the course of writing, some ideas become less important than originally thought, others become more important, and logic, in actual practice, dictates a different sequence or even a different emphasis in the writer's conclusions. An accurate outline may often be written only after the fact.

There is no need for the music teacher to deal with objectives by taking an unwavering position. Opposing viewpoints have been presented here because there are both advantages and disadvantages to the use of behavioral objectives. It is advisable, then, to use them in any area of music instruction where they can provide guidance in directing instruction and in evaluating both learning and the instructional pattern, but to avoid behavioral objectives where they seem inappropriate, would tend to restrict creativity, or would impose a strict measurement on something that cannot be precisely measured. The teacher should feel free to switch direction, strategy, or objectives in the middle of a lesson if appropriate, to seize the moment and make the most of the unexpected. But whether a course is altered during the process or not, the teacher should not begin instruction without having certain objectives in mind. Some of the objectives may be open-ended, but without them, instruction will wander aimlessly.

[37] James B. MacDonald, "Myths About Instruction," *Educational Leadership*, 22:7 (May 1965), pp. 613–614. Reprinted with permission of the Association for Supervision and Curriculum Development and James B. MacDonald. Copyright © 1965 by the Association for Supervision and Curriculum Development. All rights reserved.

Discussion Questions and Projects

1. Define the following terms: (a) aesthetic sensitivity; (b) goals; and (c) instructional objectives.
2. Select several features of both association and cognitive learning theories and explain how they might be applicable to music education.

3. What is the value of the specificity of a behavioral objective?
4. What is the value of the nonspecificity of a school goal or of a broad music goal?
5. Select five learning principles from those listed on pages 29–30 and clarify the significance of each for the teaching-learning process in band, chorus, theory class, and individual instrumental or vocal lessons.
6. Write three instructional objectives. Be sure you can identify the task, the condition, and the criterion.

Selected References

ALLPORT, GORDON W. *Pattern and Growth in Personality*. New York: Holt, Rinehart and Winston, 1964.

AUSUBEL, DAVID F. *The Psychology of Meaningful Verbal Learning*. New York: Grune & Stratton, Inc., 1963.

BOYLE, J. DAVID. "Behavioral Objectives: Is What People Are Saying About Them Really True?" *Music Educators Journal*, 63:6 (February 1977), pp. 60–63.

————, ed. *Instructional Objectives in Music*. Vienna, Virginia: Music Educators National Conference, 1974.

BRAND, MANNY. "Student Teaching: The Emotional Cycle," *Music Educators Journal*, 65:2 (October 1978), pp. 54–55.

CAMPBELL, DAVID N. "Behavioral Objectives—The Grand Charade," *Today's Education*, 65:2 (March–April 1976), pp. 43–44.

DE CECCO, JOHN P. *The Psychology of Learning and Instruction: Educational Psychology*. Englewood Cliffs, New Jersey: Prentice-Hall, Inc., 1968.

DIMOND, STUART J., and J. GRAHAM BEAUMONT. *Hemisphere Function in the Human Brain*. New York: Halsted Press, 1974.

EISNER, ELLIOT W. "Educational Objectives: Help or Hindrance?" *The School Review*, 75:3 (Autumn 1976), pp. 250–260.

FINCHER, JACK. *Human Intelligence*. New York: G. P. Putnam's Sons, 1976.

FRANKLIN, ELDA, and A. DAVID FRANKLIN. "The Brain Research Bandwagon: Proceed with Caution," *Music Educators Journal*, 65:3 (November 1978), pp. 38–43.

GAGNÉ, ROBERT M. *The Conditions of Learning*. New York: Holt, Rinehart and Winston, 1965.

GATES, ANNE, and JOHN L. BRADSHAW. "The Role of the Cerebral Hemispheres in Music," *Brain and Language*, 4 (1977), pp. 264–293.

HART, LESLIE A. *How the Brain Works*. New York: Basic Books Publishers, Inc., 1975.

HILGARD, ERNEST R., and GORDON H. BOWER. *Theories of Learning*. 3d ed. New York: Appleton-Century-Crofts, Inc., 1966.

KIBLER, ROBERT J., LARRY L. BAKER, and DAVID T. MILES. *Behavioral Objectives and Instruction*. Boston: Allyn and Bacon, Inc., 1970.

LATHROP, ROBERT L. "The Psychology of Music and Music Education," *Music Educators Journal*, 56:6 (February 1970), pp. 47–48, 141–145.

MORGAN, DOUGLAS N. "Concepts and Music Education," *The Journal of Aesthetic Education*, 2:4 (October 1968), pp. 117–123.

O'KEEFE, VINCENT. "What Are Behavioral Objectives All About?" *Music Educators Journal*, 59:1 (September 1972), pp. 50–55.

ORNSTEIN, ROBERT E. *The Psychology of Consciousness.* New York: The Viking Press, 1972.

PIAGET, JEAN. *The Language and Thought of the Child.* Cleveland: The World Publishing Company, 1965.

REGELSKI, THOMAS A. *Arts Education and Brain Research.* Reston, Virginia: Music Educators National Conference/Alliance for Arts Education, 1978.

————. *Principles and Problems of Music Education.* Englewood Cliffs, New Jersey: Prentice-Hall, Inc., 1975.

————. "Who Knows Where Music Lurks in the Mind of Man?—New Brain Research Has the Answer," *Music Educators Journal,* 63:9 (May 1977), pp. 30–38.

REIMER, BENNETT. *A Philosophy of Music Education.* Englewood Cliffs, New Jersey: Prentice-Hall, Inc., 1970.

SAMPLES, BOB. *The Metaphoric Mind.* Reading, Massachusetts: Addison-Wesley Publishing Co., Inc., 1976.

SKINNER, B. F. *Science and Human Behavior.* New York: The Macmillan Company, 1953.

THORPE, LOUIS P. "Learning Theory and Music Training," in Nelson B. Henry, ed. *Basic Concepts in Music Education.* The Fifty-Seventh Yearbook of the National Society for the Study of Education. Chicago: NSSE, 1958.

ZIMMERMAN, MARILYN PFLEDERER. "Percept and Concept: Implications of Piaget," *Music Educators Journal,* 56:6 (February 1970), pp. 49–50, 147–148.

The Balanced
Music
Curriculum

3

Curriculum must assume a place at the center of music.

DAVID McALLESTER
at Tanglewood[1]

IN RECENT DECADES, since the United States moved to the threshold of the space age, music education has faced a series of tremendous challenges. On October 7, 1957, when the launching of the Soviet Union's Sputnik I was announced, the reality of cold-war competition jarred the United States. A type of scientific hysteria followed, and few escaped criticism for the outrage of not being the first nation in outer space. It was not long before the American educational system became the scapegoat. Teachers were blamed for poor-quality teaching, schools for not teaching the right subjects, and, as in other periods of crisis, quick and simple solutions were sought for complex problems. Provoked by urgent cries from both educational and noneducational quarters, many school administrators and school boards decided that increased requirements in science and mathematics—regardless of a particular student's needs, capabilities, or interests—would be the best, most expedient solution.

There was no question that these subjects needed appropriate emphasis at all levels, but a proper balance had to be maintained. "We will not be panicked," said James E. Allen, Jr., then New York State Commissioner of Education, "into special emphasis upon science and math-

---

[1] David McAllester, "Curriculum Must Assume a Place at the Center of Music," in *Documentary Report of the Tanglewood Symposium*, Robert A. Choate, ed. (Washington, D.C.: Music Educators National Conference, 1968), p. 138.

ematics to the exclusion of all other subjects."[2] Responding to the concern over an impending educational imbalance, the American Association of School Administrators chose as the theme of its 1959 convention "The Creative Arts in Education." During this meeting a resolution was passed that stated, in part, that all school systems should strive to maintain

> . . . a well-balanced school curriculum in which music, drama, painting, poetry, sculpture, architecture, and the like are included side by side with other important subjects such as mathematics, history, and science. It is important that pupils, as a part of general education, learn to appreciate, to understand, to create, and to criticize with discrimination those products of the mind, the voice, the hand, and the body which give dignity to the person and exalt the spirit of man.[3]

Additional support for music education came from the National Association of Secondary School Principals in a position paper published in 1962. Stressing the need for a balanced curriculum and the importance of the arts as part of the comprehensive high school, the paper stated:

> The arts are subject disciplines which emphasize the use of the intellect as well as the development of sensitivity, creativity, and the capacity to make reasoned, aesthetic decisions in extending the range of human experience. The arts give direction to man's patterns of living from the setting of his table to the expression of his most cherished aspirations. The arts constitute a vast communication system which complements man's cognitive word system. . . .[4]

[2] Quoted in Lyman V. Giner, "Let's Keep Our Balance in Education," *NEA Journal* (February 1958), p. 80.

[3] American Association of School Administrators, *Official Report, 1958–1959* (Washington, D.C.: AASA, 1959), pp. 248–249.

[4] *The Arts in the Comprehensive High School* (Washington, D.C.: National Association of Secondary School Principals, 1962), p. 5.

PRELUDE TO CONTEMPORARY MUSIC EDUCATION

While support for the arts in the immediate post-Sputnik period, such as that offered by the AASA and NASSP, was comforting and gratifying, in reality it was empty rhetoric. Music was, in fact, being considered a postscript to the total program of education, a frill in a society that was busy trying to "catch up." One of the activities that came under specific attack was the marching band. For example, one critic, Donald Ivey, wrote:

> Who hears the music when fifteen shapely coeds are twirling their batons and wiggling everything else? I have no quarrel with the marching band; frankly I am sincerely amazed that the members can play anything at all while engaged in the formations demanded of them and in the temperatures at which they must perform. The point here is that the entire enterprise . . . cannot be defended as musical.[5]

Some of the factors contributing to the precarious position of music education at that time were reported by Eugene Youngert, a senior associate who assisted James B. Conant in the latter's 1957 study of the comprehensive high school.[6] Youngert reported that the major obstacle standing in the way of student enrollment in music was the secondary school principal's belief that the school day had to consist of six periods. The student who took five academic subjects and physical education obviously had difficulty in scheduling music, even if he wished to elect it. Some of the lesser causes Youngert cited for the downgrading of music were:

[5] Donald Ivey, "An Eclectic Concept of Music Humanities," *Music Educators Journal*, 51:6 (June–July, 1965), p. 35.

[6] James B. Conant, *The American High School Today: A First Report to Interested Citizens* (New York: McGraw-Hill Book Co., 1959).

- Pressures of the academics—especially in a six-period day;
- Lack of sympathetic understanding on the part of pressured counselors;
- Timidity of music teachers who fail to realize that the "front office" is yielding to others who are *not* timid;
- Thinness of some music programs that don't deserve support. . . .
- Principals' ignorance of what a good music program is;
- Willingness of music to be a suppliant for charity—band, orchestra, choir parents' clubs, candy sales, and that sort of stuff. The academics are never suppliants for charity.[7]

In his initial report, Conant suggested that the high school be organized around a seven- or eight-period day, with each period as short as forty-five minutes if necessary. With such a flexible schedule, students would not have difficulty in electing the arts. In a follow-up report, published in 1967, Conant showed that 74.2 percent of the schools studied had devised schedules that permitted students to take music or art in any one year along with English, science, mathematics, foreign language, social studies, and physical education.[8]

As music educators attempted to maintain balance within the complete spectrum of general education, they also tried to attain a balanced perspective within the music program itself. A now standard reference work, *Basic Concepts in Music Education,*[9] which appeared in 1958, provided direction for placing music in the mainstream of education and for promoting a curriculum centered upon its unique values. But the insecure position that music held in the schools caused curriculum designers to move in diverse directions during the following years. Some music educators, for example, interpreted statements such as that of the AASA to mean that the music program should be geared to the masses only; they defined "masses" in the weakest manner possible and reduced their programs to pablum offerings. Others drew from the same statements the idea that if music is equal to other courses in the curriculum it should be taught academically. The MENC-NEA publication *Music for the Academically Talented Student* (1960) was one manifestation of this broad drive to make music "respectable" and secure in its position. Although the intellectual aspect of music education did need reinforcement, this movement generally disregarded the most important factor in teaching music—that of providing for aesthetic experience.

Actually, music curriculums were not in danger of being reduced in most school districts during the 1960s, but the broadened emphasis on science and mathematics in education did cause many music educators to evaluate their programs, and a good number found much in need of improvement. They questioned the validity of concentrating on music for what amounted to little more than sheer enjoyment, while the equally important phase, music for a deeper aesthetic experience, received little or no attention. A study by the National Education Association also pointed out that the secondary school music program stressed music performance for those students who had the ability and interest, rather than stressing the importance of having every student learn something of value about music before he graduated from high school.[10] At

[7] Eugene Youngert, "Music: Necessity, Not Frill," *Music Educators Journal*, 50:1 (September-October 1963), p. 82.

[8] James B. Conant, *The Comprehensive High School: A Second Report to Interested Citizens* (New York: McGraw-Hill Book Co., 1967), p. 45.

[9] Nelson B. Henry, ed. *Basic Concepts in Music Education.* Fifty-Seventh Yearbook of the National Society for the Study of Education, Part I (Chicago: NSSE, 1958).

[10] See *Music and Art in the Public Schools*, Research Bulletin 1963–M3 (Washington, D.C.: National Education Association, 1963), p. 54.

this point, a conflict between education and recreation goals had to be resolved before music education could assume its proper place in the total program of the secondary school.

Music educators accepted the challenge that was hurled at the entire education profession and no longer justified the place of music in the curriculum by extrinsic values that were not unique to music. They abandoned the "seven cardinal principles" (formulated in 1918 by the Commission on the Reorganization of Secondary Education and concerned with health, social development, and various lofty ideals) and instead began to justify their efforts on the basis of the development of aesthetic sensitivity. While the performance of vocal and instrumental music remained an integral part of the secondary school music program, teachers began to broaden their objectives beyond the attainment of performance skills to include the equally important acquisition of music understanding. Courses were organized or further developed for students who were not interested in performance. These courses met a variety of interest and ability levels, and they fell into such categories as music appreciation, history, and literature classes; theory, harmony, and composition for both the future musician and the future consumer of music; related arts courses and music as part of the humanities; and courses in learning to play instruments that were especially suitable for private enjoyment, such as the guitar and piano.

Regardless of the type of music course, there was general agreement by the late 1960s that the teacher must provide experiences to further music understanding. Such understanding was expected to take the student beyond present awareness of music; apply to the solution of immediate tasks or problems; provide fundamental music *concepts*, not just facts, which would contribute to future musical growth; and provide some insight regarding the purpose and function of music as an aesthetic expression, relating to the past, the present, and its possible directions in the future.

CMP, The Yale Seminar, and MMCP

The search for a more substantial curriculum was greatly aided by the availability of federal and foundation funds. In 1963, for example, MENC received a grant of $1,380,-000 from the Ford Foundation to set up and administer the Contemporary Music Project for Creativity in Music Education (CMP). The Project had actually begun in 1959 as the Young Composers Project—a Ford-funded program administered by the National Music Council to place young composers in public school systems; the composers wrote for specific school performing groups and shared the experience of the creative process with students. Under the 1963 grant to MENC, the original program continued for another five years (under the title "Composers in Public Schools"), but the Project as a whole was expanded. It now established seminars and workshops at colleges and universities around the country "to help teachers build a better understanding of the analysis, performance, and teaching of contemporary music."[11] Pilot projects were also established in public schools "to determine methods for presenting contemporary music to children and for emphasizing creativity through music improvisation and composition."[12]

In 1965, CMP sponsored a seminar that led to a definition of comprehensive musicianship. Reporting on that seminar at a later time, William Thomson spoke of it as "a quiet but certain revolution that now is pledged to strip the accumulation of words and procedures in our music teaching down to the true essentials, matters that are rele-

[11] "Contemporary Music Project," *Music Educators Journal*, 59:9 (May 1973), p. 36.

[12] *Ibid.*

vant to all music, and with that as a beginning, to build up a new body of information and sets of techniques which may enable the novice musician to develop as an intelligent and concerned listener, producer, and teacher of music—music of the past, present, and future."[13] Following the seminar, regional Institutes for Music in Contemporary Education were held to find ways of applying the principles of comprehensive musicianship. Thirty-six institutions participated in these six regional Institutes by conducting two-year experimental programs between 1966 and 1968.

Meanwhile, in 1964, the U.S. Office of Education had sponsored the Yale Seminar on Music Education, the objective of which was to examine ways of improving elementary and secondary music education and to indicate directions for research.[14] The Yale Seminar drew upon the talents of musicologists, theorists, and performing musicians, but unfortunately left music-education specialists out. Its recommendations reinforced the academic approach and spurred the Juilliard research study on music-curriculum materials for the elementary school (made available in 1970), but the Seminar advanced the aesthetic basis of music education hardly at all.

Among federally-funded projects, the one that was most influential was the Manhattanville Music Curriculum Program (MMCP), launched in 1965 under the direction of Ronald B. Thomas.[15] MMCP encouraged students to learn by what has been called the "compositional approach." Students at all levels were given the opportunity to compose, perform, and analyze music in order to gain an understanding of music structure and process. Working in a laboratory atmosphere, they were able to discover music concepts as they searched for solutions to compositional problems.

Although the compositional approach gained considerable support through the influence of MMCP, and later of CMP, its potential had actually been recognized by music educators of the past. Over forty years ago, for example, Will Earhart wrote:

The appreciative and the creative (or re-creative) attitudes are therefore one. . . . This is the reason why we have found . . . that the students in our harmony classes, where the work is based almost exclusively on original composition, often develop a rich and true appreciation more rapidly than do the students in our appreciation classes. . . . It is the reason too, for our having an almost incredible amount of improvising and notating of original melodies and songs . . . from the kindergarten throughout the grades.[16]

James Mursell also understood the value of teaching an understanding of music through creative work. In 1948, he wrote:

. . . Musical composition from its humblest to its highest level is an act in which feeling is transmuted into a pattern of tone and rhythm. Thus it is an act in which all phases of musical responsiveness are evoked. . . . Musical composition may very properly be fostered not only in the lower grades, not only in the elementary school, but on all levels and in a great many situations. . . . I am inclined to think that one of the basic troubles with many

---

[13] William Thomson, "New Math, New Science, New Music," *Music Educators Journal*, 53:7 (March 1967), p. 30.

[14] See Claude V. Palisca, ed., *Music in Our Schools: A Search for Improvement* (Washington, D.C.: U.S. Office of Education, 1964).

[15] See Ronald B. Thomas, *MMCP Synthesis* (Elnora, New York: Media, Inc., 1971).

[16] Will Earhart, *Will Earhart: Teacher, Philosopher, Humanitarian*, Clifford V. Buttelman, ed. (Washington, D.C.: Music Educators National Conference, 1962), p. 126; a paper originally read at the 1930 convention of the Music Supervisors National Conference in Chicago.

of our standard plans of music education is that they hold people in stereotypes for many years and crush out of them that musical originality, individuality, and confidence for which even the best of skills are no substitute at all.[17]

MMCP workshops at colleges and universities during the ensuing years interested many music educators in the compositional approach. Teachers attending the first workshop, for example, were given the following assignments: a two-minute composition using "nonmusical" objects; a piano composition using only the perfect fifth and the major second; a twelve-tone composition in three moods for instruments available in class, which of necessity led to the investigation of serial literature; a twelve-tone composition for such unorthodox instrumental combinations as flute, saxophone, cello, and piano, which drew participants to an investigation of the potential of each instrument and of principles of orchestration; a semi-improvisational work for voices, clarinets, and percussion; and a composition created by committee. Stimulated by such experiences, the teachers instituted compositional activities in their own music programs, and soon the movement was widespread.

Tanglewood, CMP, and Local Projects

During the later 1960s, three factors evoked other changes in music education: the Tanglewood Symposium, CMP, and localized projects. Concern for the role of music in today's society and education resulted in the convening of a symposium sponsored by the Music Educators National Conference in the summer of 1967. Under the direction of Robert A. Choate, leaders from all phases of American life—academic, religious, artistic, governmen-tal, industrial, labor, and others—who were closely related to or interested in various aspects of music met at Tanglewood, Massachusetts. After a week of plenary meetings and panel discussions, a three-day "post-session," limited to members of the field of music education and some consultants, was held to determine the implications and conclusions that could be drawn from the week's presentation. The result was the *Tanglewood Declaration,* which stated in part:

> We believe that education must have as major goals the art of living, the building of personal identity, and nurturing creativity. Since the study of music can contribute much to these ends, *we now call for music to be placed in the core of the school curriculum.*
>
> The arts afford a continuity with the aesthetic tradition in man's history. Music and other fine arts, largely nonverbal in nature, reach close to the social, psychological, and physiological roots of man in his search for identity and self-realization.
>
> Educators must accept the responsibility for developing opportunities which meet man's individual needs and the needs of a society plagued by the consequences of changing values, alienation, hostility between generations, racial and international tensions, and the challenges of a new leisure.[18]

Among the major changes advocated by the Tanglewood Symposium were the teaching of music of all types, forms, styles, periods, and cultures (see quotation, page 15), programs to meet the needs of the general student who has been largely omitted from music education at the secondary level because of the emphasis on performing groups, consideration of the uses of educational technology, and attention to the needs of special education students. Those concerns led to MENC's publication of special issues of

---

[17] From *Education for Musical Growth,* by James L. Mursell, pp. 169–170. Copyright, 1948 by Ginn and Company. Published by Ginn and Company.

[18] Robert A. Choate, ed., *Documentary Report of the Tanglewood Symposium* (Washington, D.C.: Music Educators National Conference, 1968), p. 139.

Music Educators Journal devoted to an in-depth treatment of specific topics: youth music (November 1968), urban education (January 1970), technology in music teaching (January 1971), music in special education (April 1972), music in world cultures (November 1972), music in open education (April 1974), careers and music (March 1977), and the arts in general education (January 1978).

A second factor in the reshaping of music education at this time was the Contemporary Music Project, which received a new grant from the Ford Foundation in 1968, as well as financial support from MENC. During the following five years, until its conclusion in 1973, CMP was involved in three major programs: Professionals in Residence to Communities, which placed both composers and performing musicians in communities "to serve the cultural interests of these communities and to encourage cooperation and innovation among the various artistic, civic, and educational institutions in the communities"[19]; the provision of grants to selected teachers to develop ways of implementing the concept of comprehensive musicianship; and a program of workshops, publications, and consultative services to promote the principles and practice of comprehensive musicianship. Comprehensive musicianship promulgated a common-elements approach to the study of all musics (the idea that certain elements are present in the music of any culture, tradition, or style); the philosophy that students should function as musicians, becoming involved in activities that encompass all aspects of musicianly behavior; and the application of the principles of comprehensive musicianship through an integration of compositional, analytic, and performance activities, through breadth and depth of course materials, through involvement in immedi-

[19] "Contemporary Music Project," *loc. cit.*

ately useful experiences, and through independent projects.

The third major influence during the later 1960s was the expansion of local projects to develop creative, innovative programs. This was encouraged by federal funding that had been made available by the Elementary and Secondary Education Act of 1965. Central to the development of new materials, techniques, and courses through these projects were several factors in balancing the curriculum. For example, educators recognized the need to balance courses in music performance with nonperformance classes. If music was to remain an integral part of general education in the secondary school, then provision had to be made to furnish music experiences for the large number of students who were not interested in performance. Since these students would make up the bulk of the music-consuming public, their needs could not be ignored.

Another factor was a balance in courses within both the performance and nonperformance areas—that is, offering opportunities for specialized performance groups in addition to the traditional band, chorus, and occasional orchestra; and offering music theory, literature, and related arts courses to supplement general music. Experiments also involved attempts to extend the range of modes of learning. Compositional practices, the discovery technique, independent projects, and new technological devices were all employed by teachers trying to strengthen their programs.

Still another factor was the concern over the imbalance created by stressing eighteenth- and nineteenth-century music of the European tradition—a concern raised by the Tanglewood Symposium. To justify this emphasis, some music educators insisted that it was their *duty* to familiarize students only with music of the "highest artistic and cultural merit." Charles Fowler, writing in the *Music*

Educators Journal, showed the indefensibility of this rationale:

> We exalt our art, but in doing so, we sever it from the common level of experience. Our blunder is that we have treated music as a highly specialized type of consciousness and thus, without realizing it, fenced it off for the elite.[20]

By 1970, the profession at large was admitting that the pluralistic nature of American society has extensive implications for music education; it realized that there never did exist, and does not exist today, a single, elite, preferred American culture toward which all people must be herded. Rather, American society is a composite of many cultures and subcultures—those of the black-, Mexican-, Indian-, and Puerto Rican-Americans, other ethnic groups, and the vibrant teen social structure. This diversity of cultural groups has nurtured and produced a variety of musics, all having their own set of traditions, techniques, and aesthetic values. In supporting a balance of all these styles in the music curriculum, Wiley L. Housewright wrote:

> The diversity of music is an immutable fact. Different types and styles of music represent different points of view that exist simultaneously. Juxtaposition need not mean conflict. One can enjoy rock 'n' roll in one situation, and Bach and Babbitt in another. Cosmopolitanism is a more important goal of music education than elitism because it encompasses taste not only for Beethoven but for all kinds of musical art.[21]

Ignoring current modes of musical expression and the music styles indigenous to minority cultures amounts to a disregard of both modern society and an individual's heritage and self-awareness. It constitutes the imposition of a single value system upon the entire community. Although students should definitely become acquainted with the music of past eras and the social and cultural forces that led to their creation, they must also have the opportunity to understand the musics to which they relate as members of both special cultural groups and contemporary society as a whole.

Foreign Influences

During this period of space exploration, music teachers also discovered that there had been unique developments in music education in other countries that could be adopted in the United States. For example, the German composer Carl Orff believed that children should be allowed to discover music for themselves, and that the learning processes of children should follow the same pattern as the learning processes of the race. Just as primitive man had developed bodily movement and dance to simple rhythmic drum beats, Orff recommended that children use drums suitable to their physical size and skill, adding bodily movement to the rhythms. Within this frame of reference, Orff's approach to teaching rhythm was based on patterns of speech, further reinforced by bodily movement.

Primitive man's melodic experimentation was also adopted by Orff, for he advocated that children should first learn songs with one or two pitches, or at the most, the five tones of a pentatonic scale. Eventually, the child's tonal experiences are expanded to include other scale steps.

To help children understand the concept of intervals, Orff advocated that every child should have the opportunity to play a simple melody instrument. He specified the design

[20] Charles B. Fowler, "The Case Against Rock: A Reply," *Music Educators Journal,* 57:1 (September 1970), p. 39.

[21] Wiley L. Housewright, "Confrontation with Tomorrow," *Music Educators Journal,* 55:9 (May 1969), p. 29.

of these instruments in an exact manner to ensure accuracy of pitch. Most of them resemble marimbas and xylophones, except that they are low in height and the bars are removable; only those tones that the student knows are used. As new tones are learned, the appropriate bars are brought into use.[22]

In the public schools of Palo Alto, California, another European approach was successfully adapted. Pupils there learned to read and sing by using techniques adapted from the method of the Hungarian composer Zoltán Kodály. The foundation of this system, as adapted by Helen Richards, was singing. This program, begun in nursery school and developed logically and gradually throughout the grades, used charts to introduce rhythm syllables, tone syllables, and hand signals representing relative pitches. Awareness of the beat was considered of prime importance. After suitable experience in hearing music and experiencing the beat, the pupils progressed to written notation. Initial melodic experience was limited to a pentatonic tonal system.[23]

The work of Shinichi Suzuki of Japan also became prominent in the United States during this period. Suzuki's approach to string instruction startled American music educators who were having difficulty in developing students' interest in stringed instruments. He had not only devised a system that was successful in developing technique and musicality, but also attracted thousands of students, including many preschool children, to the

violin. (Suzuki's method is outlined in Chapter 11).[24]

Among the new developments that music teachers were caught up in by the early 1970s was the issue of open education. The trend toward open education in the United States derived from changes during the post-World War II period in the British primary schools. These innovations did not receive much attention here until England took a long look at its educational system in the mid-1960s and subsequently published its 1967 Plowden Report, which stated that "the child is the agent in his own learning." "There is little place," it stated, "for the type of scheme which sets down exactly what ground should be covered and what skill should be acquired by each class in the school."[25]

Actually, informal education (as this philosophy came to be known) had been promoted earlier by England's Hadow Committee Report in 1934, and giving free rein to the child to teach himself had been a central thesis of John Dewey's progressivism, which was popular in the 1920s and 1930s. However, what developed in postwar Britain was significantly different from progressivism because the teacher still maintained control—still planned, coordinated, evaluated, and guided. As the Plowden Report stated, "From the start, there must be teaching as well as learning."[26]

Along with this report, considerable inter-

[22] See Stanley Chapple, "Some Fundamental Values in Music," *Music Educators Journal*, 48:4 (February–March 1962), p. 76; and Beth Landis and Polly Carder, *The Eclectic Curriculum in American Music Education: Contributions of Dalcroze, Kodaly, and Orff* (Washington, D.C.: Music Educators National Conference, 1972).

[23] See Helen Richards, "The Legacy from Kodaly," *Music Educators Journal*, 49:6 (June–July 1963), p. 28; and Landis and Carder, *op. cit.*

[24] See also, John Kendall, *The Suzuki Violin Method* in *American Music Education* (Washington, D.C.: Music Educators National Conference, 1973); and Malcolm E. Bessom, "Faces of Suzuki," *Music Educators Journal*, 58:7 (March 1972), pp. 54–57.

[25] Plowden, Lady Bridget, et al. *Children and Their Primary Schools: A Report of the Central Advisory Council for Education*, vol. 1 (London: Her Majesty's Stationary Office, 1967), Part 5, items 529 and 539.

[26] Quoted in Charles E. Silberman, *Crisis in the Classroom: The Remaking of American Education* (New York: Vintage Books, 1971), p. 209.

est was generated in the United States by the dissemination of information from American teachers who had visited the British primary schools, by a series of articles by Joseph Featherstone in *The New Republic* in 1967,[27] and later by material in Charles Silberman's widely read *Crisis in the Classroom*. During the second half of the 1960s, several open education projects in the United States became particularly well known. For example, in 1964, Lore Rasmussen set up a mathematics learning center in Philadelphia that expanded each year afterward and received considerable attention.[28] In 1965 Marie Hughes began an open classroom project in the Tucson schools for disadvantaged Mexican-American children.[29] Several advances came in 1968: In that year, Lillian Weber began her open corridor at P.S. 123 in Harlem;[30] the New School of Behavioral Studies in Education at the University of North Dakota (later the Center for Teaching and Learning) began to provide a new type of teacher education and to assist the state in its plans to convert North Dakota elementary schools to open education;[31] and Vermont produced its *Vermont Design for Education*, listing seventeen objectives for schools in that state,

many of them fundamental to the concept of open education. (Objective one: "The emphasis must be on learning, rather than teaching."[32]) Within four years, over thirty public and twenty-five private Vermont schools were working toward open education. In 1969 the Education Development Center in Newton, Massachusetts, began an advisory program to help schools create open classrooms, and by the beginning of the seventies music educators found themselves in a position where they had to develop new techniques and new attitudes in order to keep up with this widespread movement in general education.

Although the movement spread rapidly at the elementary and middle-school levels, the open concept was just beginning to touch secondary schools by the early 1970s. The notable exceptions were Philadelphia's Parkway School, known as the "school without walls," and Newton's Murray Road High School.[33] There were also several open high schools in Vermont, and by this time a few colleges were also offering full teacher-education curriculums in open education. (In addition to North Dakota's New School, early degree programs were offered at the City College of New York and at Newton College of the Sacred Heart.)

Music educators found that the arts continue to hold an important position in Britain's informal classroom, on which America's open classroom is largely based. John Blackie, a former chief inspector of primary schools in England, in his book *Inside the Primary School*, wrote that the arts are "essential just as much as the 3Rs." "Everything that we know about human beings generally, and children in particular, points to the importance of the arts in education. They are the

[27] Featherstone's articles have since been reprinted in Joseph Featherstone, *Schools Where Children Learn* (New York: Liveright, 1971).

[28] See Ewald B. Nyquist and Gene R. Hawes, eds., *Open Education: A Sourcebook for Parents and Teachers* (New York: Bantam Books, 1972), pp. 146–153.

[29] See Silberman, *op. cit.*, pp. 311–318.

[30] See Walter and Miriam Schneir, "The Joy of Learning—In the Open Corridor," *The New York Times Magazine*, April 4, 1971, pp. 30+; also, "Open Door, New York City: A Report by the Program Reference Service" (New York: Center for Urban Education, 1971).

[31] See Henry S. Resnik, "Promise of Change in North Dakota," *Saturday Review*, 54:16 (April 17, 1971), pp. 67–69, 79–80.

[32] See Chapter 8, p. 181.

[33] Both high schools are described in two chapters in Ronald Gross and Paul Osterman, eds., *High School* (New York: Simon & Schuster, Inc., 1971).

language of a whole range of human experiences and to neglect them is to neglect ourselves."[34] Similarly, the Plowden Report stated that "art is both a form of communication and a means of expression of feeling which ought to permeate the whole curriculum and life of the school."[35] (For a discussion of the philosophy of open education and its application to music education, see pages 179–187 of Chapter 8.)

The 1970s and the Challenge of the 1980s

By the middle 1970s the education system was once again a focal point of public criticism. This time, the criticism did not stem from a single source, such as being late reaching outer space, but from many factors. For example, declining school enrollments brought about the closing of many schools and a significant reduction in the nation's teaching force, but school costs were not reduced proportionately. Such economic factors as an increase in energy costs coupled with the devaluation of the U.S. dollar precipitated a constant increase in operational costs, which offset any savings that might have been realized from school closings and staff reductions. One of the most frustrating factors to taxpayers was that while education costs were going up, SAT scores were on the decline, and many high school graduates could not pass basic-skill competency tests. The public was asking the familiar questions, "Why can't Johnny read? Why can't Johnny write? Why can't Johnny add?" No longer was the blame put on the student who failed; it was placed on the school board, the superintendent, the principal, and the teacher. All were being held accountable.

[34] John Blackie, *Inside the Primary School* (New York: Schocken Books, Inc., 1971), p. 113.

[35] Plowden, *op. cit.*, p. 247.

The overall solution to the problem of quality education at this point had a familiar ring to music educators. In order to save money and improve instruction, there was a demand for a *return to the basics* and for the elimination of all educational frills. At a time when music education was experiencing some practical trends, including an interest in music career education and a growing awareness of special education needs, still, in the mid-1970s, music was being looked on as one of these "frills." As Fred Hechinger wrote deploringly in *The New York Times:* ". . . frills in schools around the country have come to be such subjects as music, art, foreign languages, and a variety of cultural and humanistic topics."[36]

In November 1976, the National Committee on Instruction of the Music Educators National Conference adopted a position paper that stated, in part, that

> . . . music is basic in education, that music, along with the other arts, deserves a prominent position in the curriculum of the elementary and secondary schools, and that the important contributions of music to the aesthetic and cultural objectives of education are more than sufficient to justify that position. At the same time, the Conference recognizes that music can make other contributions to the educational and personal growth of the student and that these ancillary contributions may be highly valued in some communities. The diverse benefits of music instruction will accrue to the student regardless of the motivation that initially led to the inclusion of music in the curriculum and regardless of the relative values placed on the various outcomes.[37]

Unfortunately, MENC's statement that music is basic to the education of all children had

[36] Fred M. Hechinger, "The Basic No-Frills Box," *The New York Times*, November 9, 1976; reprinted in *Music Educators Journal*, 63:8 (April 1977), p. 39.

[37] "The Role of Music in the Total Development of the Child," *Music Educators Journal*, 63:8 (April 1977), p. 59.

little impact. The general attitude was well described by Charles Fowler:

> In comparison to the obvious usefulness of the basics—reading, writing, and arithmetic—the arts appear to be impractical, even superfluous. American schools are fundamentally pragmatic and education is essentially instructional, serving a particular and practical purpose. Viewed from this perspective, the arts are not the stuff that livings are made of; they do not ensure that people will get ahead; and they do not guarantee success.[38]

This was indeed a time of contradictory trends. While arts education was struggling for survival and music/arts educators were losing their jobs, the National Endowment for the Arts reported that between 1965 and 1975 the arts were flourishing and growing in our society. Professional orchestras, for example, doubled in number during that period; resident professional theatres quadrupled; councils for the arts quintupled; and the increase in professional resident dance companies was sevenfold.[39] Why this dichotomy? It seemed, as the Arts, Education, and Americans Panel put it, to be the result of the lack of "connection between our desire for art and our need for art."[40] Moreover, the schools and the teachers responsible for arts education had neglected to tap the available resources of artists, musicians, arts institutions, orchestras, theatre companies, and so on. In support of the arts as an integral part of education, John

Edward Ryor, then president of the National Education Association, told the Arts, Education, and Americans Panel, chaired by David Rockefeller, Jr.:

> Quality education in its most fundamental sense cannot be separated from the culture of a society. The quality of the culture is expressed in its arts and its humanities. Those who say they can be removed from the curriculum are calling for the rape of education, for a return to "training" at the expense of "learning."[41]

The Rockefeller Panel itself wrote in 1977 that it

> supports the concept of "basic education," but maintains that the arts, properly taught, are basic to individual development since they more than any other subject awaken all the senses—the learning pores. We endorse a curriculum which puts "basics" first, because the arts are basic, right at the heart of the matter. And we suggest not that reading be replaced by art but that the concept of literacy be expanded beyond word skills.[42]

Such beliefs were the basis of a growing movement in the mid- and late-1970s toward arts-in-general-education programs—the use of the arts in teaching other subjects in the curriculum.

The overall challenge to arts educators in general and music educators specifically has not changed. It was the same in the 1950s, 1960s, and 1970s, and remains the same in the 1980s: to overcome the indifference toward and ignorance of the arts in our society. If music is to enter the mainstream of life in the United States, if it is to become a real part of "basic education," and if it is to receive financial support during periods of economic stress, then the music programs in the schools must consider the social relevance of music, the role

[38] Charles B. Fowler, "Integral and Undiminished: The Arts in General Education," *Music Educators Journal*, 64:5 (January 1978), p. 30.

[39] National Endowment for the Arts, "Supplementary Fact Sheets, Challenge Grant Program for the Arts," *Preliminary Notification and Application Information: Challenge Grants*, pamphlet, October 14, 1976.

[40] The Arts, Education and Americans Panel, *Coming to Our Senses: The Significance of the Arts for American Education* (New York: McGraw-Hill Book Company, 1977), p. 11.

[41] *Ibid.*

[42] *Ibid.*, p. 6.

that it plays in people's lives. Music educators must adhere to the philosophy that our foremost purpose is to foster an understanding of music that leads to lasting appreciation of and participation in music activities, that through aesthetic experiences life is enriched and its beauty is intensified.

In the late 1950s, Sputnik forced us to recognize the importance of science education. In the 1960s, with the help of President Kennedy, there was a recognition of the importance of physical education. Now, as music educators cope with the 1980s, the time has come to acknowledge the power and urgency of the arts in everyone's education.

THE ROLE OF MUSIC IN SECONDARY SCHOOLS

The task of organizing a balanced music program in today's secondary school is quite complex. It is influenced by such factors as the availability of time within the school day and classroom space within the school plant; the number of teachers on the music staff and their particular areas of specialty; the attitudes of students, administrators, and parents toward the importance of music; and the amount of funds appropriated to support the music program. An additional factor is the balance between performance and nonperformance classes, general and special music courses, and the development of music understanding and performance skills in all performance classes. Stated in the most simple terms, the role of music education in secondary schools is *to develop music understanding and appreciation through the ability to perceive and react—to experience music aesthetically*. This role is realized through a basically two-pronged approach, which (1) provides opportunities for the musical growth of *all* students as a part of the *common experience* of

general education, and (2) discovers the musically talented and furnishes them with experiences that extend *beyond* those in the core of general education.

The key words here are "musical growth."[43] The inclusion of any performance or nonperformance class, or of general or special music courses, can be justified only when it furnishes those developmental experiences[44] that contribute to the student's continuous musical growth. In defining musical growth, James Mursell noted that it is a process by which the individual student reorganizes and reshapes his personality (behavioral change), as musical meanings become more readily understandable (through concepts and percepts) and are broadened and expanded through music experiences (selected music literature and developmental experiences) that have continuity of organization and serve a useful purpose to the student.[45] For example, a student beginning violin study has little or no skill in playing the violin; he will be unable to decode a page of music notation and relate it to his instrument, and he will not be able to play in an ensemble. At the end of a year of study, however, he will probably have developed some facility on the instrument (behavioral change). This will be because of (1) developmental experiences (private lessons and playing in the beginning orchestra); (2) selected music literature (instructional material used in the lessons and the repertory of the orchestra); and (3) understanding music concepts and percepts (developing the skill to read notation related to a particular fingering).

[43] See James L. Mursell, *Education for Musical Growth* (Boston: Ginn and Company, 1948), Chapter 3.

[44] James Mursell wrote that the developmental experience is the prime mover in musical growth and that it is characterized by five processes: arresting, compelling, revealing, fulfilling, and making conscious. See Mursell, *ibid.*, pp. 99–100.

[45] *Ibid.*, Chapter 3.

The Aesthetic Basis of Music Education

There is little disagreement that music education should be aesthetic education, and that musical growth cannot be achieved without aesthetic growth. In an address before the Southwestern Division of the Music Educators National Conference, E. Thayer Gaston spoke of the aesthetic basis of music in this way:

> It must be clear . . . that the reason for having music is not only the joy of its beauty, but because of its contribution toward profundity of feeling which is a result of aesthetic experience. Music is first and foremost for aesthetic growth and development, not to teach citizenship, not to teach poise, not for community ego gratification. All of these latter achievements may derive from music, but they are not why music should be taught.[46]

It is unfortunate that the unique values of music have been overlooked for years by teachers and administrators in their struggle to promote music in education. Instead, music in the schools has been sanctioned for a variety of purposes that could be met equally well by other subjects in the curriculum. As we have come to learn more about the nature of man, however, educators, psychologists, and social scientists have learned that aesthetic experience is a basic need in life. It is a principal element in man's meaningful relationships with other men. For the sole purpose of strengthening aesthetic experience, music belongs in the school.

In the broadest sense of the word, *aesthetics* (derived from the Greek word meaning "perceptive") has been defined as the theory of the beautiful, with concern for discovering (1) those components that contribute to the effectiveness and enjoyment of art; (2) how these components originated, were developed,

and are organized to produce a work of art; and (3) what the place of art is in the life of man and in his society. More specifically, *music aesthetics* is concerned with man's intellectual and emotional relationship and reaction to music. The music educator who organizes his program to develop the aesthetic sensitivity of his students must consider and understand the dual nature of the aesthetic experience—the *cognitive* aspect, both perceivable and teachable, which deals with concepts related to the dimensions of tone (pitch, duration, intensity, and timbre) and their combined manipulation (rhythm, melody, harmony, and form), and the *affective* reaction to the organization of these elements, which is *not* teachable. While the cognitive is related to man's intellectual capacity and his ability to increase his knowledge, understanding, and skill, the affective deals with man's feelingful reaction to a piece of music and is within the realm of his emotions. The level of one's feelingful reaction to music is determined by the level of his knowledge, understanding, and skill; therefore, both aspects are interrelated and inseparable. (See Chapter 2, pages 23–25.)

Within the framework of the secondary school, the teacher is faced with the problem of how to organize the music program to increase the level of each individual's aesthetic sensitivity. The "music appreciation" class seemed to be the principal answer at one time. Although the basic premise was quite valid, its narrow curriculum and limited focus seemed to be concerned more with the development of "appreciation" for selected composers and their "great" works than with providing each student with the necessary discriminatory tools to enable him to make his own independent appreciative or aesthetic judgments. Today, we realize that if the music program is organized to develop aesthetic growth, then the same broad music goal will be applicable for both performance and nonperformance classes: *to develop each student's*

[46] Quoted in Harry S. Broudy, "Art Education Substantiated," *Music Educators Journal*, 54:4 (December 1967), p. 46.

aesthetic sensitivity to and through all music experiences. The chorus, the band, the orchestra, the stage band, and the rock combo must all become laboratories in which students have the opportunity to analyze how composers have manipulated the materials of music to produce a particular composition. The general music class, no longer limited to the presentation of only traditionally "great music," must move from ritual to relevancy by becoming an open forum for experiencing all types of music. For example, students can be helped to find answers to why they like a certain rock or folk tune. Is it because of the performer's rendition, the intervallic arrangement of the melodic line, a rhythmic pattern that is repeated on the bass guitar and cymbals, a distortion created by a reverb unit that produces a unique sound, the repetitive nature of the words, or perhaps the effect of the chord changes (which the student could either play on his guitar or pick out on the piano)? In each instance—whether in a performance or nonperformance class—students can be introduced to the materials and processes of music so that their sensitivity to the sounds of music will deepen cognitively and affectively.

Music Education for Today's Society

The role of music education in America seems to have run a full cycle of development. In the early part of the twentieth century, a young MENC worked diligently to put music into the classroom. Today, however, music educators face the equally difficult task of opening that classroom to the world, of releasing music education from the confines of the school and making it a relevant part of man's experience as it relates to the society in which he must live. The strength of music education lies in the total art and social functions of music. This becomes increasingly so as a new, expanded leisure unfolds, affecting both social institutions and individual habits,

values, and personalities. The real potential and success of music education is quite limited when it is viewed only in terms of "public school music," as the field was once called. But it will blossom fully as the profession accepts its societal responsibility and assists the musical growth of *all* people—preschool, school age, and adults. It is significant that three-and-a-half years after the Tanglewood Symposium, when the MENC published the first comprehensive set of goals in its sixty-four-year history, it stated its goals in this way: "MENC shall conduct programs and activities to build a vital musical culture, an enlightened musical public."[47] The essence and focus of this goal was actually set forth at Tanglewood by sociologist–music educator Max Kaplan:

> Not only is music education a crystallization in microcosm of its parent art, it leads directly and powerfully into the entire destiny and state of music—both amateur and professional, on the concert stage and in the home. How music will in the future become a creative element of creativity, performance, and listening will in good measure emerge from what is being thought now in the minds and training institutions of its sages and technicians.[48]

Clearly, today's music educator must realize that his classroom is the community, his subject all musics, and his students all persons. He must be cognizant of the plurality of his students' backgrounds and cultures, and of the plurality of music tastes, values, and needs that exist in our society. To dogmatically establish one set of absolute goals and objectives, to fence them off by one concept of quality, learning, and fulfillment, and then to

[47] "Goals and Objectives for Music Education," *Music Educators Journal*, 57:4 (December 1970), p. 24.

[48] Max Kaplan, "Values, Leisure, and the Aesthetic," a paper prepared for the Tanglewood Symposium, "Music in American Society," July 1967.

expect each man to consummate his particular need is absurd. As man searches for his own identity and self-realization, his music needs and values will be influenced by a unique set of social, cultural, economic, and educational pressures. With such a multiplicity of unique determinants, it is understandable why there exists in the United States today such a diversity of musics. Many music educators must abandon the missionary role they have assumed regarding man and his music. They must place themselves in the center of society, and instead of hoping to show a few souls the glories of a limited veil of "great music," turn instead to helping all men find their responsive places in the totality of musical expression.

THE SECONDARY MUSIC CURRICULUM

A systematic and sequential development of the secondary school music curriculum, throughout the middle school and senior high school, is imperative if (1) music is to be accepted by students and administrators as a serious discipline important enough to be studied, and (2) music education is to have any effect on the vitality of out-of-school cultural activities. Music teachers must plan their work so that they will know what behavioral changes should occur, both immediately and over a long term, as the result of a particular course or particular lesson. They must also know what music materials and experiences (collected in the form of courses) can be used to elicit these changes, and what methods of evaluation are best to measure the degree of change in terms of newly acquired music learning. A sequence of both performance and nonperformance classes is necessary to the development of a comprehensive program. Although each of these categories, and each course within either

category, will have a different outward appearance, all must be based on the same fundamental goals and objectives and must function collectively in achieving those goals.

General and Special Music Classes

Music classes of a general nature should be offered on all levels of the secondary school as part of the core of general education. These general music classes are usually offered only through the middle school, and whatever their organization may be, their objectives should be the same—the development of aesthetic sensitivity through conceptual understanding. It is essential that the content of the general music class be geared so that all experiences are oriented toward *personal involvement* with music in order to expand the individual student's knowledge, skill, and understanding of music.

Developing conceptual understanding through related *percepts* (the perceivable elements of the basic concept) is not restricted to any particular type of music instruction, to any grade level, or to any ability level. A single concept can be presented repeatedly throughout the grades by progressing sequentially from the general to the specific, the simple to the complex, following Mursell's *cyclical*[49] and Bruner's *spiral*[50] approach. This type of organization is illustrated by Table 3-1, which shows how one aspect of the concept of melody can be presented at various levels.

Through the general music class, the student can become involved in music in a variety of contexts (as a creator, performer, and listener) and can learn the basic concepts underlying the general structure of all musics. After the middle school, general music is

[49] See Mursell, *op. cit.*, p. 364.

[50] See Jerome S. Bruner, *The Process of Education* (New York: Vintage Books, 1963).

usually followed by special courses that pursue an understanding of the same concepts, but through more specialized investigation. Too often, music in the later phase of secondary education emphasizes the acquisition of performance skills to the exclusion of all else. As important as these skills are, a diversity of experiences should continue in the high school and specific concentration should be available through nonperformance classes as well. Among the possible courses that might be offered are the following:

–Music listening, music literature, music history
–Music theory
–Related arts and humanities
–Directed individual study in composition, arranging, and musicology

Such courses as these are not intended only for students who plan to follow music as a profession. They should be designed for all interested students as special ways of becoming involved in music outside of performance. (Detailed information on organizing and teaching general and special courses of this sort is provided in Chapters 4 through 7.)

Performance Classes

The secondary school music teacher, who for years concentrated his efforts on building bigger and better performance groups and feeder systems to sustain them, has discovered in recent years that he is being held accountable on *educative* terms. Consequently, music educators have had to reassess the

Table 3-1.

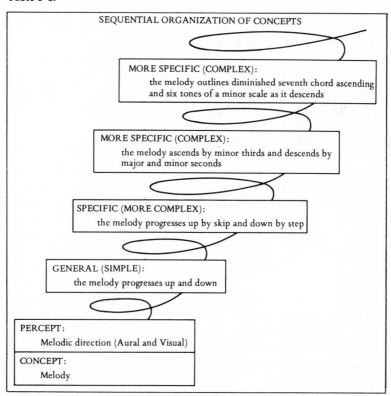

role of bands, orchestras, and choruses. Without abandoning their quest for quality performance, they are now pursuing the equally important dimension of nurturing aesthetic growth through the development of music knowledge and understanding, in addition to skill, as a regular part of the performance class. The teacher whose objectives have been similar to those of a professional conductor must now devise objectives that are more educative in nature and then assume the dual responsibility of teacher–conductor, with the emphasis being placed on his role as a teacher. This reassessment has not reduced the importance of performance in the curriculum: rather, it has broadened the purposes of performance classes, emphasized that they are an integral part of the total music curriculum, and underscored the necessity of structuring a sequential performance program throughout the secondary schools. (Techniques of making the performance class educative are discussed in Chapter 12, as well as in portions of Chapters 10 and 11.)

Vocal Music

Since many students have their first real experience as members of a performance group in the early middle school, the teacher will find it essential to establish at this early stage the understanding that the middle school chorus is an extension of the general music class and is another opportunity for students to further their musical growth. In this way, students on all levels of the secondary school will accept and expect the vocal class to provide more than the development of techniques for public performance.

Opportunities for vocal music at the high school level must be organized so that the needs of all students who wish to perform, regardless of ability level, will be served. Sometimes, one or several choruses open to all students are organized more for ease in scheduling than for serving the students' individual needs. This can prove quite frustrating both to students with limited vocal ability and to those who are above average. A more suitable plan is to offer vocal courses on a nongraded basis, with membership in each group related to the student's competency (determined by audition, not by grade placement). With ability as the prime criterion for membership, a variety of vocal offerings needs to be provided:

—Mixed chorus (a nonselective group for students with limited ability)
—Girls choir and boys choir (selective or nonselective groups for students of average ability)
—Concert mixed choir and advanced girls choir (selective groups for students of above-average ability)
—Small ensembles (provided for students of all ability levels)
—Voice class (for interested students who exhibit some vocal potential)

(A more detailed discussion of techniques for organizing and teaching the vocal music program is presented in Chapter 10.)

Instrumental Music

As with the vocal music program, opportunities for instrumental performance need to be organized so that the needs of all students who wish to perform, regardless of ability level and area of interest, will be served. A wide variety of instrumental groups, including orchestras, bands, and small ensembles, should be provided, with membership determined on a nongraded basis directly related to the student's competency. Unlike those directing the vocal program, instrumental teachers often have the opportunity to become more closely involved with individual instrumentalists, through private or group lessons. Because of this relationship, individual student needs and playing abilities are known, and teachers can make a more educated determination about particular music organizations in which students should seek membership. Therefore, both selective and nonselective performance organizations on various ability levels should be a part of the secondary school program. In the middle school and junior high school, these offerings could include:

—Instrumental lessons for beginning, intermediate, and advanced students in either class or individual instruction
—Beginners band and orchestra (nonselective groups that provide initial ensemble experience)
—Advanced nonselective band and orchestra (groups designed for players who are more advanced and experienced)
—Small ensembles (a wide variety of groups organized for different ability levels)

The senior high school program must also offer instrumental opportunities for students at various ability levels in small and large ensembles. Students who wish to begin instrumental study at this level should not be neglected and ought to be provided with group instruction classes. As student proficiency grows and interests vary, offerings in the pop-rock-jazz area can be included, and student-organized, student-directed groups should be encouraged. Wherever possible, offerings in the high school should include the following:

—Wind ensemble and string ensemble (ensemble and class instruction for students with limited competency)
—Intermediate band and orchestra (selective groups for students with advancing performance ability who do not yet qualify for the more selective organizations)

—Advanced band and orchestra (selective groups for students with a high level of performance ability)
—Marching band (a selective group open to students of intermediate and advanced bands)
—Small ensembles (selective groups for traditional and innovative combinations of instruments in various idioms)
—Jazz band (a selective group organized to accommodate students on various ability levels)
—Miscellaneous offerings (piano classes, guitar classes, and so on)

(Chapter 11 presents a detailed discussion of organizational and instructional techniques for a comprehensive instrumental music program.)

The multiplicity of offerings presented in this overview of a balanced curriculum is designed to meet the specific needs of individual students whose backgrounds, abilities, and potentials are wide in range. The basic curriculum that has been outlined here works toward this end, but it is incomplete unless provisions are also made within these and other classes and activities for the physically and mentally handicapped, the intellectually and musically gifted, and the culturally deprived. Music education must pursue a comprehensive curricular structure. It is clear, too, that if music educators are to establish the aesthetic basis of music as the foundation of their programs, if they are to promote not only a quality school program but also a vital musical culture, and if they are to release the creative and responsive potential of the individual, then music must not only be placed in the core of the curriculum—curriculum must assume a place at the center of music.

Discussion Questions and Projects

1. Make a survey of several high schools in your area to determine whether the basic objectives of the performance classes have been expanded beyond the development of performance skills to include the development of conceptual understanding. If so, how?
2. Carry on a class discussion using the following statements as points of departure: (a) A student can be a member of a performance group for years and never grow musically. (b) Only the *best* music literature must be used in all music classes if the integrity of music education is to be upheld. (c) Many music educators give lip service to the use of all kinds of music in their classes but are still practicing the "connoisseur approach." Why? (d) Music educators must view music in American society as it is, not as what they think it is or what they wish it were.
3. Using Table 3-1 as a guide, organize a spiral growth pattern for the following percepts: three-part form, tempo, dynamics, consonance–dissonance.
4. Establish criteria for evaluating the curriculum of a lower middle school, an upper middle school, and a senior high school as it relates to adequacy in number and variety of course offerings, flexibility in scheduling, competency of the teaching staff, the availability of materials, and adherence to current trends and philosophies in music education.
5. Make a survey of nonmusic teachers and administrators to discover their attitudes toward music as part of the "return-to-the-basics" movement. Determine the reasons behind their attitudes.

Selected References

ANDREWS, FRANCES M., and NED C. DEIHL. "Development of a Technique for Identifying Elementary School Children's Musical Concepts," *Journal of Research in Music Education*, 18:5 (Fall 1970), pp. 214–222.

ARTS, EDUCATION AND AMERICANS PANEL. *Coming to Our Senses: The Significance of the Arts for American Education*. New York: McGraw-Hill Book Company, 1977.

BESSOM, MALCOLM E. "Arts, Education, and Americans: The Rockefeller Panel Releases Its Report," *Music Educators Journal*, 64:1 (September 1977), pp. 78–81, 91–93.

BRINKLEY, ROBERT. "The New Rock and Music Education," *Music Educators Journal*, 55:6 (May 1969), pp 31–33.

BROIDO, ARNOLD, and CHARLES L. GARY. "Is Your Music Program for Real?" *Music Educators Journal*, 55:7 (March 1969), pp. 31–33.

BRUNER, JEROME S. *The Process of Education*. New York: Vintage Books, 1963.

BURKE, FRED G. "The Human Imperative," *Music Educators Journal*, 59:9 (May 1973), pp. 18–22.

CHOATE, ROBERT A., ed. *Documentary Report of the Tanglewood Symposium*. Washington, D.C.: Music Educators National Conference, 1968.

"Contemporary Music Project," *Music Educators Journal*, 59:9 (May 1973), pp. 32–48.

EDDINGS, JOHN M. "Two Trends in Teaching Music: The Comprehensive and the Cross Cultural," *Music Educators Journal*, 56:1 (September 1969), pp. 69–71.

GARY, CHARLES L., and BETH LANDIS. *The Comprehensive Music Program*. Washington, D.C.: Music Educators National Conference, 1972.

GEORGE, LUVENIA. *Teaching the Music of Six Different Cultures in the Modern Secondary School.* West Nyack, New York: Parker Publishing Company, 1976.

GOECKE, NORMA. "What Do They Mean by 'Back to Basics'?" *Music Educators Journal,* 63:3 (November 1976), pp. 30–33.

HAACK, PAUL A. "Music Education: Aesthetic or Anesthetic," *Music Educators Journal,* 55:2 (October 1968), pp. 52–53.

HECHINGER, FRED M. "Back-to-the-Basics Impact," *Today's Education,* 67:1 (February-March 1978), pp. 31–32.

HENKE, HERBERT H. "The Renaissance Is Up to You," *Music Educators Journal,* 55:6 (February 1969), p. 33.

HOFFMAN, BURTON R. "The Arts in Society and Education," *Music Educators Journal,* 59:7 (March 1973), pp. 28–32.

KAREL, LEON C. "Music Education: Strategies for Survival," *Music Educators Journal,* 65:3 (November 1978), pp. 30–35.

KLOTMAN, ROBERT H. "When You Go Back to the Basics, Take Music Along," *Music Educators Journal,* 64:1 (September 1977), p. 77.

LANDIS, BETH, and POLLY CARDER. *The Eclectic Curriculum in American Music Education: Contributions of Dalcroze, Kodaly, and Orff.* Washington, D.C.: Music Educators National Conference, 1972.

MOTYCKA, ARTHUR, ed. *Music Education for Tomorrow's Society: Selected Topics.* Jamestown, Rhode Island: GAMT Music Press, 1976.

NEWMAN, GRANT. "Doublethink and Music Education," *Music Educators Journal,* 56:8 (April 1970), pp. 59–60.

PALISCA, CLAUDE V., ed. *Music in Our Schools: A Search for Improvement.* Washington, D.C.: U.S. Office of Education, 1964.

REIMER, BENNETT. "Education for Aesthetic Awareness: The Cleveland Area Project," *Music Educators Journal,* 64:6 (February 1978), pp. 66–69.

———. "Patterns for the Future," *Music Educators Journal,* 63:4 (December 1976), pp. 22–29.

RENFIELD, RICHARD L. "Arts Education: What Value?" *Music Educators Journal,* 54:4 (December 1967), pp. 36–38.

ROCKEFELLER, DAVID, JR. "The Arts in American Education," *Today's Education,* 67:2 (April-May 1978), pp. 33–34.

TAYLOR, HAROLD. "Music: An Educational Force," *Music Educators Journal,* 54:4 (December 1967), p. 39.

THOMAS, RONALD B. *MMCP Synthesis.* Elnora, New York: Media, Inc., 1971.

WEHNER, WALTER L. "The Endless Stream That Never Arrives," *Music Educators Journal,* 59:1 (September 1972), pp. 24–27.

———. *Humanism and the Aesthetic Experience in Music: Education of the Sensibilities.* Washington, D.C.: University Press of America, 1977.

WESLEY, DONALD C. "What the Rockefeller Report Should Mean to the Teacher," *Today's Education,* 67:2 (April-May 1978), p. 4.

WILLIS, THOMAS. "Youth Music on Their Terms," *Music Educators Journal,* 56:9 (May 1970), pp. 56–59.

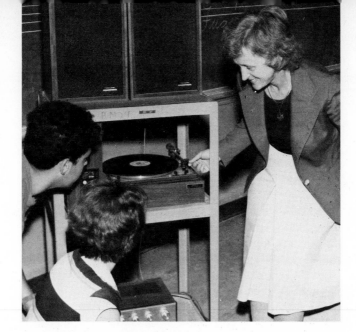

Music Education Through Nonperformance Classes

Part

General Music Classes

4

Experiences are passed on from one man to another. Abel knew that.
And now we know it. But where is the bridge placed—at the end of the
road, or only at the end of our vision? Is it all a bridge, or is there no bridge
because there is no gulf?

CHARLES IVES[1]

THE COURSE in general music, long associated with the junior high school,
has now been broadened in scope, content, and philosophy to become
the central part of a continuous, developmental music program that
begins in the elementary school, continues in the middle school, and
extends through the junior high school or, for some students, even
beyond.

Such a course at the secondary level had its inception in the junior
high school as a part of the exploratory program in general education
for which that school had been organized. The need for this type of
program was recognized by administrators and teachers alike around
1910 because high school students were discovering too late, if at all,
exactly what their interests and abilities were. The sharp, abrupt change
in method of instruction between the traditional eight-year elementary
school and four-year high school was also a contributing factor in the
evolution of a new school organization. In response to these concerns,
the junior high school provided a bridge between the elementary level,
with its self-contained classes, and the high school, with its strict
departmentalization.

After more than half a century, the junior high school today holds

[1] Charles Ives, *Essays Before a Sonata* (New York: W. W. Norton & Co., 1961), p. 5.

an established place in our educational system, even if it has never fully achieved a level of maturity commensurate with its potential. In recent years, it has lost part of its unique position through the continued downward extension of the secondary phase of education into the middle school. With the introduction of the middle school, secondary education begins in either the fifth or sixth grade on the assumption that elementary, basic skills of learning can be adequately acquired in the first four years of school. By this point, the middle school student, like the junior high student, is ready for a more departmentalized program that will introduce him to the structural components of the various disciplines. Many educators also support the middle school concept because the students of a (5)-6-7-8 grade-level organization are more closely aligned in their physical, emotional, and psychological needs than those of the traditional 7-8-9 grade organization of the junior high school.[2]

The general education program of both the middle and junior-high grades reveals to pupils the major fields of learning, and by the eighth or ninth grade starts each student thinking about a career or occupation that he feels may likely be of interest and benefit to him. As a result, generalized courses, such as General Science and General Music, are included in the curriculum. A sequence of study areas under this plan covers a wide range of information about a particular subject. The instructional materials in these courses are not isolated into separate areas; rather, they are fused together into a larger body of information. A course in General Mathematics, for example, would include algebraic, geometric, and trigonometric concepts. This approach not only introduces the student to higher mathematics at an early age, but also serves the exploratory function of acquainting the student with the content of the more specialized courses he will encounter at senior high school and college levels.

Two basic educational approaches are currently employed in our middle and junior high schools. The first of these, an older concept and one that is still commonly found, assumes simply that an effective and productive program of instruction results when emphasis is placed upon the development of general understanding. This approach permits the combining of traditionally segmented courses in subject-matter fields of the senior high school into broader courses that are more germane to the needs of younger secondary students, even though the specialized subtopics are not covered to any degree of depth. The exploratory nature of courses in this phase of education hopefully fosters further interest for in-depth study in a particular subject area to be provided at the high school level.

More recently a new learning procedure of exceptional merit has been advanced—one that is in accord with currently accepted educational practices and promises to strengthen the program. This procedure stems from the curriculum reform movement that began in the mid-1950s, and it gained impetus as a result of the Woods Hole Conference of 1959, convened by the Education Committee of the National Academy of Sciences. Again, the main objective is the promotion of general understanding, but in this approach learning is designed to promote understanding through comprehension of the very structure of the subject matter. It is a concept-centered approach that deals with the constituent elements of a subject and their basic relatedness. The teaching and learning of *structure*, rather than simply the mastery

[2] See Pearl Broad, "The Middle School: Trends Toward Its Adoption," *The Clearing House; A Journal for Modern Junior and Senior High Schools*, 40:6 (February 1966), p. 331.

of facts and techniques, is at the base of understanding. To be sure, the task of education has always been one of presenting subject matter effectively so that maximum learning takes place, and this approach does continue the concentration on broad areas of subject matter. However, in this new process knowledge is not handled superficially or haphazardly, for by organizing and presenting the subject in structural terms, then specialized studies, observations, and experiences can always be related to the student's basic understanding.

In application, this approach provides that students initially undertake to learn a general idea rather than a skill—a central concept of the discipline that can then be used as a basis for solving subsequent problems as special cases of the idea originally mastered. The general idea, whatever its nature, always derives from comprehension of the underlying structure. As psychologist Jerome Bruner has stated in his report on the Woods Hole Conference, "Grasping the structure of a subject is understanding it in a way that permits many other things to be related to it meaningfully."[3] This foundation for relationship provides a direct path to accomplishing the classic problem of transfer or application of learning. A second important factor reported by Bruner is that "unless detail is placed into a structured pattern, it is rapidly forgotten. Detailed material is conserved in memory by the use of simplified ways of representing it."[4] In short, the new philosophy provides that functional and purposeful learning can be acquired and applied if it is obtained through a program that places emphasis upon the fundamental structure of a subject. This basic approach is highly recommended for today's programs in

General Music; it is one that has far-reaching possibilities.

TRADITIONAL PRACTICE IN GENERAL MUSIC

Younger secondary school students need broad experience in understanding, feeling, and expressing themselves through the arts. At this particular age level—from the fifth through the ninth grades—students have a natural interest in and capacity for music; they need every opportunity to learn more about the art and to enjoy it fully. The general music concept is very much in keeping with the exploratory function of this stage of education. It provides an opportunity for all pupils to become familiar with the components of music expression, allows for a fuller awareness of the total dimensions of contemporary living, of which the arts are a vital part, and encompasses a variety of activities out of which a continuing interest and participation in one or more areas of music can emerge.

Virtually all students take the general music courses, and for many of them in the seventh and eighth grades it is the *final* opportunity for organized music instruction. More important, it has unfortunately become for many the final or near-final stage of musical *growth*—a negative outcome that has been the result partly of the dull, unstructured organization of many available teaching materials, but principally because of the lack of creative thought given to the design of the program beyond the sixth-grade level.

The Lack of Focus

General music is a term that has come to mean almost as many things as there are school systems offering the course. Only recently have there been signs of a thoughtful

---

[3] Jerome S. Bruner, *The Process of Education* (New York: Vintage Books, 1963), p. 7.

[4] *Ibid.*, p. 24.

assemblage and evaluation of the considerably divergent opinions among educators as to what constitutes a good general music program. The implication of all-inclusiveness in the course title has perhaps contributed to the traditional lack of specificity. Today, after years of planning, examination, experimentation, and re-evaluation, the course has been strengthened considerably, at least through the beginning level of the middle school; and very fine instructional materials are now available for these early grades. Widely fluctuating practices still prevail, however, in the area of the junior high school, with the result that some educators have suggested dismissing general music once and for all at that level. Such a step would be as regrettable as the practices that produced it.

The state of these practices must be recognized before a really strong curriculum can be developed. Paradoxically, the general music program has been both overly fixed and overly flexible. It has been fixed in its description of the youths who make up the classes and in its basic provisions for dealing with students whose backgrounds, interests, talents, and understandings have only recently come to be recognized as too divergent to be fixed. On the other hand, the program has been flexible in the areas of subject content, presentation of materials, and depth endeavor —areas where basic structure and content have long been needed but neglected. The absence of clearly defined goals for the course has reduced flexibility to haphazardness, resulting in a lack of focus.

A careful study of over fifty representative curriculum guides on general music from across the nation reveals that there is considerable agreement from program to program about desirable outcomes. There is agreement, for example, on the educative purpose of the course and on the obvious needs for using quality music and for developing understanding and enjoyment of music. A large number

of programs also emphasize performance and the acquisition of performance skills. Primary goals of the course, however, reveal a marked difference of opinion. In some situations, emphasis is placed upon human values with the primary purpose directed toward personal growth and enhancement of life through the study of music. No one surely can find fault with such a goal, but in itself it amounts to mere vacuous rhetoric and offers little guidance for designing an effective curriculum. In other situations, the primary emphasis is on music as an end in itself, with the objective being the development of an "appreciation of good music" (whatever that phrase may mean), or of individual vocal or instrumental musical abilities or both. Often, this type of goal, as worthy as it sounds, is supported by a program of activities without far-reaching or long-lasting application.

The Lack of Structure

A typical procedure in the general music course has been to include any particular facet of music that is considered interesting and appropriate (and what aspect of music is not interesting or appropriate in some way to some group?), but with little if any attention being given to understanding basic concepts embodied in the chosen music. The extent to which a class has developed a certain study area has sometimes been left solely to the discretion of the participating members. Although pupil–teacher planning is a valid teaching technique, it must relate closely to the conceptual knowledge, skill, and understanding to be developed. On occasion, "pupil–teacher planning" has resulted from pupil rejection of what the teacher had originally planned, leading to the complete abandonment of conceptual study and to a concentration instead on almost anything that would keep the class *entertained*—and quiet! More often, though, each teacher has decided what *areas* (not concepts) of music would be studied, the extent of concentration, and the order of presentation—a procedure that relies too much on personal taste and ability, rather than on the basic structure of the discipline, and results in widely differing programs from school to school within even a single school system. At the other extreme, some state departments of education and individual school systems have guides that spell out prescribed programs in detail, to the degree that one known guide cites specific days in each month of the school year when certain songs are to be sung! Such precision, if followed closely, is as restrictive as the other practices are aimless.

Certainly no course in the school curriculum can have been as indefinite and changeable as general music has been in some communities. Even within individual schools, one may find students taking a general music course one year that bears little resemblance to the same course the previous year. Although change in materials and activities from year to year is necessary for improvement of the curriculum and to meet class and individual needs, still the lack of a central, basic structure, around which classes can orbit in different but related paths, cannot be accepted as compatible with any thoughtful program of educative experience.

The Lack of Integration

The organizational device that has been traditionally employed in the general music class has been the unit study plan, with the focal point of the unit ranging from music to nonmusic topics. The particular *theme*, the materials considered, and the depth of endeavor all depend on the amount and availability of source material, on the resourcefulness of both teacher and students, and too often on what else is being taught in the school to which music can be artificially related. Like all other areas of the curriculum, general music programs are a direct reflection of the organizational ability, personality, musical ability, and leadership ability of the persons involved in their conduct and development. Obviously, this results in a wide variety of programs. The important fact, however, is that this variety is in many instances not supporting a common understanding of the role of general music nor the most direct, effective, and creative means of accomplishing its goal. It is the type of variety that tends to work against the integration of understanding and skills related to the structure of the discipline.

This lack of integration has also been caused in the past by a one-sided view of the modes of experience that are available. The scope of personal involvement was limited because singing was the principal class activity (following the custom in the elementary school). Students sang and learned many songs—some of which were of excellent quality, although others were trite, contrived, and too juvenile in subject matter. The justification for the singing-centered general music program—still reflected in some of the basic music book series—was the old cliche, "everyone has an instrument for singing!" Eventually, experiences in listening, playing instruments, responding rhythmically, and creating original music were added because music educators became conscious of an important fact: In order to fulfill the diverse music needs of all students, a broad range of music activities are necessary. It is true that everyone has a voice for singing, but it is equally true that few fulfill their music needs through singing alone. The case against a singing-dominated classroom has been clearly set down by Bennett Reimer:

> The songs children can sing are inevitably of limited complexity compared with their powers of musical perception and reaction. The gap between the ability to sing and the ability to

experience music musically grows wider as children grow older, until in upper elementary and junior high grades the disparity has usually become painful for both students and teachers. No amount of searching for songs which "appeal," which are "psychologically acceptable," which are "masculine" for the boys or "touching" for the girls, will make up for the fact that a diet of songs is inadequate for the increasingly sophisticated needs of children. This is especially true if the general music program, from the very start, has helped children come to grips with many kinds of music of a wide diversity of musical complexity. With an ever-broadening acquaintance with the riches available in the realm of music the likelihood that song-singing alone will satisfy aesthetic needs is, and should be, small.[5]

DEVELOPING A STRONG PROGRAM

The expanded general music class, with its stress on multimusic experiences for maximum class participation, has been an improvement over traditional practices, although three basic ingredients have still been lacking in many programs: (1) defined objectives (both long-range program objectives and short-range operational objectives), which will provide the focus for the course; (2) a sequential approach to understanding basic music concepts, which will provide the needed structure for the course; and (3) a flexible but directional and comprehensive organization of the course that will provide for varied experiences and the integration of learning.

Teachers and students have sometimes become so involved with class activities that they have lost sight of the particular goal toward which these activities can lead. While singing, listening, playing, and creating are all enjoyable, and enjoyment is a desirable musical outcome, the general music program has had to abandon the game-and-entertainment syndrome and become concerned with the more important area of what students are *learning about music*; otherwise, it cannot justify its rightful place as an integral part of general education in the secondary school. It follows, then, that the general music curriculum needs to be organized so that it can develop in each student an understanding of the basic concepts related to the theoretical and expressive elements of music. For "conceptual development," Woodruff has written, "is not simply one of several interests for an educator; it is rather the essence of his concerns."[6]

Course Outline

The practice of dissecting a body of music knowledge into a series of unrelated lessons for the general music program is no longer acceptable. Today's general music teacher must have a plan that outlines the material to be covered during the course in order to achieve the stated course objectives. Some school systems have detailed curriculum guides that provide the teacher with the course objectives, course sequence, suggested activities, materials to be used, and so on. A more popular approach is the course outline, which provides the teacher with the course objectives (Table 4-1 is an example) and a course sequence (Table 4-2 is an example), and leaves the teacher free to determine what teaching strategy and materials are best suited to the particular class.

[5] Bennett Reimer, *A Philosophy of Music Education* (Englewood Cliffs, New Jersey: Prentice-Hall, Inc., 1970), pp. 117–118. Reprinted by permission of Prentice-Hall, Inc., © 1970.

[6] Asahel D. Woodruff, "How Music Concepts Are Developed," *Music Educators Journal*, 56:6 (February 1970), p. 52.

Table 4-1. COURSE OBJECTIVES FOR THE GENERAL MUSIC CLASS IN A UNIT ON
MUSIC OF THE TWENTIETH CENTURY

Behavior	The musically sensitive person:
Knowledge	1. knows the similarities and differences in the melodic, rhythmic, and harmonic structure of the different styles of twentieth-century music; 2. knows the names of composers, performers, and compositions in the various categories of twentieth-century music; 3. knows the social, political, and economic forces that contributed to the development of the various styles of twentieth-century music; 4. knows what new and traditional sound sources are used to produce twentieth-century music; and 5. knows that there are subcategories of popular music, jazz, and contemporary classical music.
Understanding	1. understands the techniques used by serial composers; 2. understands how electronic-music composers create musique-concrète compositions; 3. understands the basic technique of improvisation in playing jazz; 4. understands how the guitar and other amplified instruments changed popular music; and 5. understands how music is produced on a synthesizer and by a computer.
Skill	1. aurally distinguishes the various styles of jazz; 2. aurally distinguishes the various styles of popular music; 3. aurally distinguishes the various styles of contemporary classical music; 4. can compose a simple twelve-tone composition; and 5. can create a simple musique-concrète composition.
Attitude	1. tolerates the preferences of others in twentieth-century music; 2. listens to many types of twentieth-century music on recordings and on the radio with discrimination regarding the selection of works; 3. encourages friends to become familiar with many kinds of twentieth-century music; and 4. encourages school and community music directors to include contemporary music in their repertoires.
Appreciation	1. receives intellectual and emotional gratification through listening to all varieties of twentieth-century music; 2. has respect for the artistic performance of all kinds of twentieth-century music; 3. believes in the artistic value of the musics of the twentieth century; and 4. has become more selective in choosing twentieth-century music to listen to.
Habits	1. listens to many types of twentieth-century music on recordings and on the radio with discrimination regarding the melodic, rhythmic, and harmonic structure; and 2. attends concerts of jazz, rock, and contemporary classical music.

Table 4-2. GENERAL MUSIC COURSE OUTLINE FOR UNIT ON MUSIC OF THE TWENTIETH CENTURY

I. Analysis of melodic, rhythmic, harmonic, and formal structure in twentieth-century music
   A. Popular music
      1. Historical background
      2. Rock
      3. Country-western music
      4. Disco music
   B. Jazz
      1. Historical background
      2. Traditional styles
      3. Big-band styles
      4. Bebop and cool jazz
      5. Free-form jazz
      6. Third-stream music
   C. Contemporary classical music
      1. Historical background
      2. Atonal music, including twelve-tone
      3. Neo-Classical and neo-Romantic music
      4. Electronic music
      5. Aleatoric music

II. Analysis of new and traditional sound sources in twentieth-century music
   A. Popular music
      1. Guitar
      2. Amplified instruments
      3. Traditional instruments
   B. Jazz
      1. Instrumentation in traditional jazz
      2. Instrumentation in big-band jazz
      3. Instrumentation in modern jazz
   C. Contemporary classical music
      1. Traditional instruments
      2. Pure electronic sound (synthesizer, computer)
      3. Musique concrète

The Development of Sequence

The lack of attention to the structure of music has been a basic flaw in traditional general music practices. It seems only logical that music teachers should teach *music*—the materials of music. Yet, effort has often been dissipated in teaching geography or history through music, irrelevant facts about composers' lives, an identification of terms rather than sounds, or such pat definitions as "program music is music that tells a story." To facilitate understanding of all kinds of music and increase the potential for personal enjoyment, an understanding of the basic concepts of music structure is essential.

"Children should be introduced to the structure of music," wrote John Goodlad, "through a carefully planned, sequential curriculum as rigorous and well-organized as the best math curriculum."[7] This statement, of course, should not be interpreted, or *mis*-interpreted, to mean that the sequence must be so rigorously organized that unrealistic objectives are arbitrarily established regarding the presentation of specific music concepts, activities, and music literature for each level, each month, each week, or each day. On the contrary, while structural organization, the introduction of concepts, and the cyclical development of their related percepts from the simple to the complex (as illustrated in Table 3-1) must follow a logical and evolutionary sequence, there is no preset time at which a particular percept must be presented, a particular activity undertaken, or a specific piece of music literature examined. "Rigorous" in this sense does not mean strict or inflexible.

Once the sequence has been established, the ability of the class will guide the teacher in determining the rate and level of conceptual presentation that is commensurate with the students' ability and level of musical growth. Furthermore, once class ability has been established and percepts on specific levels have been chosen, then the teacher must organize to present and reinforce these percepts through a variety of activities and materials—*not just one*. The teacher will need to determine what music literature can best serve as the center of a particular activity; again, there should be no restriction on the type of literature to be used. As Bennett Reimer has said, "The general music teacher is a specialist in teaching about melody, rhythm, harmony, tone color, texture, form, style, through particular pieces of music *but in ways which show how these elements operate in all music. The skills required for doing this successfully are as complex as any in education.*"[8]

[7] John I. Goodlad, "Music's Place in Education," in *Creative Approaches to School Music*, Marion S. Egbert, ed. (Chicago: American Music Conference, 1967), p. 2.

[8] Reimer, *op. cit.*, p. 117.

A general music program organized sequentially to foster musical growth through conceptual understanding provides the teacher with the needed concrete nucleus for curriculum planning. As the hub of the program, music structure is not restrictive, since it is possible to perceive almost any basic structural concept through a variety of experiences and through a wide selection of music literature.

Organizing for Conceptual Understanding

The general music specialist whose class is organized to develop aesthetic sensitivity through conceptual understanding works with a five-point organizational plan. He must:

1. Understand and be able to verbalize about each broad concept.

2. Analyze and understand those percepts, related to a particular concept, that the student must perceive in order to acquire conceptual understanding.

3. State in his long-range and daily instructional planning the desired behavioral changes in the student that should result from class experience.

4. Select a teaching strategy and music literature that will be suitable for the development of a particular concept.

5. Develop techniques of evaluation to measure the effectiveness of his lesson organization and presentation as well as the degree of behavioral change that has occurred. This provides the teacher with feedback for revision.

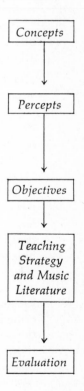

Concepts

Percepts

Objectives

Teaching Strategy and Music Literature

Evaluation

In order to illustrate how this plan can be applied, let us consider in some detail the organization of just one conceptual area—*rhythm*. It should be stressed, however, that the concepts related to rhythmic structure will be only superficially understood unless they are related to other conceptual areas as well.

1. *Concept:* The first step in the plan is to state the basic concept to be developed. For example:

Rhythm, in its broadest sense, is concerned with the temporal motion of musical sound. It is an organization of sounds and silences of varying durations that creates a series of time patterns related to an underlying pulsation.

2. *Percepts:* The second step is to outline those percepts that will support and contribute to the student's understanding of the broad concept. The following are examples of percepts related to rhythmic structure.

a. BEAT—Rhythm is generally governed by a felt unit of time, known as a *beat,* which marks off durational values and organizes the flow or motion of the music. The beat is continuous, even during moments of silence.

b. ACCENT—Certain beats are more prominent than others—sometimes because of an audible emphasis of sound, but more naturally because of their primary placement in a sequence of time values. Such beats are said to be *accented.* The combination of stressed and unstressed, strong and weak beats gives the music a feeling of *pulsation.* (Thus, pulsation is more than beat; it is a pattern of accented and unaccented beats.)

c. METER—*Meter* is the measurement of rhythmic motion through the organization of time values in relation to a given unit of time. It provides a mathematical basis for measuring both regular pulsa-

tion and variable groupings of sounds and silences in rhythmic patterns. Meter is represented symbolically by a *meter signature,* which specifies the unit of measurement and determines the normal sequential order of heavy and light beats.

d. POLYMETER—Music may be organized in two or more meters simultaneously. This superimposition of meters is referred to as *polymeter.*

e. CHANGING METERS—Some music is organized so that two or more meters are used in succession rather than simultaneously. *Multimetric changes* may occur at widely spaced intervals or as often as every measure.

f. RHYTHMIC PATTERNS—Sounds and silences of varying durations can be grouped in relation to the beat to create a variety of *rhythmic patterns.* Such patterns may be classified as even or uneven, and the relationship of sounds and silences within a pattern are perceived as longer, shorter, or the same.

g. SYNCOPATION—A rhythmic pattern within a given meter may be characterized by an irregular, unexpected, shifted accent that is known as *syncopation.*

h. POLYRHYTHM—Music involving two or more series of sounds simultaneously may present contrasting rhythmic groupings at the same time. Coexistent, contrasting rhythmic patterns constitute *polyrhythm.*

i. TEMPO—The interpretive aspect of rhythm can be perceived in terms of varying degrees of over-all fast or slow motion. The pace of the music is referred to as *tempo.*

j. NOTATION—The relative duration and metric organization of rhythmic sounds and silences can be represented by graphic symbols. This system of representation is called *notation.*

3. *Objectives:* Based on the percepts outlined, the teacher can now develop long-range operational objectives identifying behaviors to be observed. For example, the student who has grasped an over-all concept of rhythm should be more discriminative in:

a. determining the basic beat and pulsation of selections he hears;

b. recognizing the basic metric structure of a piece of music, the organization of rhythmic patterns as they relate to metric units, and rhythmic deviations from the established meter;

c. identifying even and uneven rhythms aurally and visually, as well as the use of accents in regular and irregular patterns;

d. following the development of rhythmic motifs, patterns, and phrases throughout the music;

e. recognizing different and characteristic rhythms when comparing music for the waltz, polka, and other dance forms, including more recent and contemporary dances;

f. recognizing rhythmic devices used in contemporary music, such as irregular meters, multimetric changes, syncopation, and polyrhythmic and polymetric combinations;

g. understanding and using the symbols of rhythmic notation, such as meter signatures, note and rest values, and other durational signs;

h. interpreting rhythmic notation as it relates to a melodic line.

On the instructional level, the teacher will develop specific behavioral objectives (with task, condition, and criterion) for a particular lesson. The following behavioral objectives, for example, might be suitable for lessons in which the teacher wishes to develop some knowledge and understanding of percepts related to the concept of rhythm:

a. Given twenty notated music examples without meter signatures, the student will analyze each example and write in the correct signature. Five mistakes or fewer will be considered passing.

b. The teacher will play ten music examples on the piano, and the student will identify these examples by ear as "even," uneven," or a "combination" of both. Three mistakes or fewer will be considered passing.

c. Given a notated sixteen-measure melodic excerpt, the student will analyze and then label each measure as "even," "uneven," or a "combination" of both. Two mistakes or fewer will be considered passing.

d. Given a notated sixteen-measure melodic excerpt, the student will write "S" over each measure containing syncopation. Four mistakes or fewer will be considered passing.

e. The teacher will play ten music examples at the piano, and the student will identify whether these examples are in triple or quadruple meter. Three mistakes or fewer will be considered passing.

4. *Teaching Strategy and Music Literature:* The fourth organizational step is the selection of music literature and the mode of presentation. Here, the following considerations should receive serious attention.

a. The existing level of the students' music understanding, knowledge, and skill should determine the selected level at which a concept and its related percepts are organized.

b. The grade-age level at which the lesson is to be presented will help to determine the materials and experiences selected for examining the concept.

c. The relevancy of the music literature to be used and the suitability of the experience, as these relate to the students' personal music backgrounds and to their community-home-school environment (suburban, innercity, or rural), should influence the teacher's choice.

d. Each lesson not only must contribute to the development of aesthetic sensitivity through conceptual understanding but also must reinforce a positive rapport among the class, the teacher, and *music*.

For example, the general music specialist who has chosen multimetric change as the percept for lesson organization has reached a level of complexity and abstraction that will be difficult for the students to comprehend if, in their music backgrounds, they have had little experience with the beat, accent, meter, meter signatures, rhythmic patterns, and rhythmic notation, or with how these percepts relate to music they have performed, listened to, and composed. Whether in the middle school or the junior high school, the class with limited conceptual understanding must first become acquainted with the simpler rhythmic percepts before the students can perceive, with understanding, the effect of multimetric change in such songs as "Who Has Seen the Wind?" by Carlisle Floyd,[9] or "Evening" by Charles Ives (as shown in Figure 4–1). However, the general music class with a more advanced understanding of meter and its related percept will easily perceive the metric changes in, for example, the sea chantey "Shenandoah," which shifts readily from $\frac{4}{4}$ to $\frac{3}{4}$, or the short piano piece *Lament*, by Zoltán Kodály, which changes from $\frac{5}{4}$ to $\frac{3}{4}$ to $\frac{7}{8}$ to $\frac{4}{4}$ within four measures (as shown in Figure 4-2).

To reinforce further the understanding of multimetric change, the following experiences could be used:

a. Students can be encouraged to find, analyze, and perform songs with changing meters. In their music textbooks will be found such examples as "Tom Cat" by Igor Stravinsky,[10] and the Spanish folk song "La Madrugada."[11]

b. Students can be encouraged to find, outside of school, music with metric changes, and to bring it to class for analysis, discussion, and performance. Such music may be encountered in their private music studies, informal music activities, and in their own record collections.

c. Opportunities can be provided for class and individual composition incorporating metric changes. These compositions may be purely rhythmic in nature (as illustrated in Figure 4-3), or they may be melodic and harmonic as well.

d. Through listening and following the score (analysis), students can be led to discover where metric changes occur in compositions such as the following:

   —Bartók, "Syncopation" (in *Mikrokosmos*, Volume V, No. 133), a good example of $\frac{5}{4}-\frac{4}{4}$ interchange, with measures 15–17 in $\frac{3}{4}$.

   —Debussy, *Prélude à l'après-midi d'un faune*, containing measures of $\frac{9}{8}, \frac{6}{8}, \frac{12}{8}$, and $\frac{3}{4}$.

   —Ravel, "Chanson romanesque" (the first in a set of three songs entitled *Don Quichotte à Dulcinée*), involving a continuous shift from $\frac{6}{8}$ to $\frac{3}{4}$.

   —Stravinsky, *Petrushka*, the first tableau, measures 30–42.

[9] Found in Robert A. Choate, et al., *New Dimensions in Music; Mastering Music* (New York: American Book Co., 1970), pp. 250–251.

[10] Found in Robert A. Choate, et al., *New Dimensions in Music; Experiencing Music* (New York: American Book Co., 1970), p. 201.

[11] Found in Beth Landis, *Exploring Music 7* (New York: Holt, Rinehart and Winston, 1971), p. 151.

FIGURE 4-1. Charles Ives: "Evening"

Now   came still Eve - ning on,   and   Twi - light gray

had   in her so - ber liv - ery   all   things_ clad;   Si - lence ac - com - pan - ied;_

From *114 Songs* by Charles E. Ives. Privately printed by the composer, Redding, Conn., 1922.

FIGURE 4-2. Zoltán Kodály: *Lament*

From *Classics to Moderns*, Copyright © 1962, Consolidated Music Publishers, Inc., New York. Used by permission.

5. *Evaluation:* The fifth step in this plan concerns two processes—student evaluation and self-evaluation.

Student evaluation involves measuring the degree to which student behavior has changed as a result of a particular lesson or group of lessons, and determining what generalizations have been formed that are applicable to the same or similar problem-solving situations. For example, the evaluation of a student who has been introduced to multimetric change may be carried out through (a) class discussion; (b) a formal written exam in which he has to identify unfamiliar notated music excerpts that contain metric alterations, either with or without given meter signatures being provided; (c) performing, with understanding and relative ease, music that includes two or more meters; (d) composing and performing, with skill and understanding, music with shifting meter signatures; and—the most diffi-

cult—(e) identifying aurally the occurrence of metric changes.

It should be emphasized that the cognitive behavioral area, which deals with the development of music understanding through the accumulation and recall of knowledge and the development of intellectual skills and abilities, lends itself more readily to immediate evaluation than does the affective behavioral domain, which is concerned with the feelingful reaction to music as it influences the development of music values, taste, interest, and appreciation (none of which should be considered measurable according to any absolute standard).

In the area of self-evaluation, the teacher is concerned with the influence of his lesson organization and presentation upon his students. Therefore, he must consider the pace of the lesson and the various materials and techniques of presentation that have been used, such as (a) the *quality, clarity,* and

FIGURE 4-3. Multimetric Composition for Percussion*

*Composed by sixth-grade students, Public Schools, Danvers, Massachusetts.

relevancy of both materials and experiences, (b) the *effectiveness* of that portion of lesson time that was teacher dominated, (c) the amount of *pupil response and participation* in class activity and discussion, and (d) the opportunity provided for *student inquiry and discovery.* He must further analyze his motivative techniques as they relate to the development of student interest, and whether the level of questions and activities he has used has stimulated or hindered class motivation.

ORGANIZING CENTERS

The organization of a curriculum around structural and expressive concepts involves over-all planning of two types—the selection, first, of a set of *organizing elements,* and second, of a set of *organizing centers.*

Organizing elements include concepts, ideas, problems, skills, and even values. They may be as specific as "the perception of polymeter" or as wide open as "the understanding of

Music Education Through Nonperformance Classes

good tone quality." In a visualized diagram of the curriculum, these elements would appear as vertical factors, extending upward from one stage of learning to another, and providing continuity and sequence. The basic element would remain constant throughout, but its setting, the experiences related to it, and its relationship to other organizing elements would become more complex and varied as the students move from one level of understanding to another level.

Organizing centers include units, types of experiences, materials (books, recordings, films), activities, and modes of inquiry. These, too, may be specific or general—as narrowly focused as a film on an orchestra rehearsal or as broad as the topic of Romanticism in music. In a visualized diagram, organizing centers would appear as horizontal factors, delineating what is to be taught, what materials may be used to teach it, and what forms of presentation may be employed. Thus, a single organizing element will extend through numerous organizing centers, and a single organizing center can involve numerous organizing elements.

Units are an important and widely employed form of organizing center, and considerable thought must be given to their selection. Frequently, units appear to be chosen because the unit "theme" is a convenient catch-all, and too frequently there appears to be little connection between one unit and the next. However, while it is true that basic concepts can be presented through an almost unlimited number of unit topics, it must be realized that the use of certain units will often limit the selection of appropriate materials and activities. When units are chosen wisely, on the other hand, they not only allow a good deal of freedom in matters of presentation, but also provide, within themselves, a sequence that reinforces the students' grasp of basic concepts. John Goodlad has provided a good set of criteria to apply in the selection

of a unit or any other form of organizing center:

The good organizing center for learning:
. . . encourages student practice of the behavior sought.
. . . is economical in that it contributes to the simultaneous attainment of several educational objectives.
. . . encompasses ability floors and ceilings of the group.
. . . builds on what has gone before and prepares for what is to come.
. . . buttresses and supports learning in other fields.
. . . has educational significance in its own right.
. . . is comprehensive in that it permits inclusion of several ideas and several catchhold points for differing student interests.
. . . ties together students, ideas, and materials in some meaningful fashion.
. . . has capacity for movement—intellectual, social, geographic, or chronological.[12]

In the early middle-school grades, traditional approaches have included units constructed around music of the Americas (usually in the fifth grade) and music of other nations (usually in the sixth grade). These organizing centers arose in the general music program because traditional social studies curriculums were often based on these subjects. Surprisingly, they have been retained as primary units in many music programs in spite of the fact that the curriculum reform movement in social studies has developed other, more relevant approaches. Although correlation with other fields can be interesting and valuable, the music specialist, in selecting units, must be concerned with much more than an attempt to update his program to match the new social studies. Instead, he should always work from the standpoint of

[12] John I. Goodlad, "The Teacher Selects, Plans, Organizes," in *Learning and the Teacher*, 1959 Yearbook (Washington, D.C.: Association for Supervision and Curriculum Development, 1959), pp. 55–58.

organizing units around the discipline of music itself. This does not exclude the possibility of a wide variety of traditional unit themes; it simply implies the need to make the unit musically relevant.

Well-defined behavioral objectives will provide the teacher with guidelines for selecting learner interests and, if desired, community situations that lend themselves well as broad organizing centers. Thus, such topics as "Music in Our City," "Music and the Dance," and "The Science of Music" can still be the basis of useful units *if* they are supported internally by attention to the structure of music. But units that imply nonmusic or semi-music centers of activity—such as "Music and Transportation," "Westward Ho!" or "Music at Harvest Time"—would be inappropriate. Within them, good conceptual teaching may occur, but the unit topics themselves do not offer *musical* reinforcement or continuity. To relate this to Goodlad's criteria, such a unit would not have musically "educational significance in its own right." If the teaching is good, lessons do not have to be hung on a nonmusic frame to create interest.

By the seventh grade, students are generally receptive to a more formal approach to unit organization; this is a good level for developing units that will bring together and unify the varied, exploratory experiences of the lower grades in a manner that will increase the individual's response to music. For this reason, it is suggested that *broad conceptual areas may themselves become organizing centers.* Individual units built around tone, rhythm, melody, harmony, form, style, interpretation, and function can provide logical sequence and continuity, as well as extensive freedom in the selection of materials and activities. Such units, of course, should not be confined only to the development of structural concepts suggested by the title. For example, a unit on form would perhaps be organized around basic design principles of unity and variety and around basic forms such as binary, ternary, rondo, variations, and so on; but the unit should not neglect concepts related to other broad areas such as rhythm, melody, or interpretation.

Finally, if this type of plan is successfully realized at the seventh-grade level, an appropriate set of organizing centers for eighth-grade general music classes might be derived from basic styles and types of music. Thus, while a seventh-grade unit on "style" might develop concepts related to those factors that create a music style (the treatment of basic elements, for example), or broad concepts of historical, nationalistic, or individual styles, the approach could be widened at the eighth-grade level to develop an understanding of specific styles. Organizing centers in this plan, designed to synthesize conceptual understanding, might include units on early music, baroque music, music of the classical and romantic eras, contemporary classical idioms, electronic music, folk music, ethnic musics, music theatre, popular music in America, rock, and jazz.

Hopefully, the general music specialist will be aware that organizing centers should be formulated to accommodate sequence through the total span of the general music program—not simply grade by grade as self-contained levels. If the total sequence is considered, then conceptual understanding can be developed in an over-all plan that leads from *exploration* to *analysis* to *synthesis*. Each of these three stages is basic to each level of learning, but throughout the total program the broad emphasis should shift from one stage to the next as the student develops.

Within selected units, there will also be suborganizing centers, consisting of various activities, modes of inquiry, and specific materials. It is not necessary, however, for all students to be involved at the same time with the same organizing center, activity, or material, nor even with the same element. In fact, an individualized package of experiences, suited to each student's particular interests, needs, style of learning, and rate of learning, is highly desirable.

One means of working toward individualization is to have a flexible organization in which the whole class is developing an understanding of the same precepts but through different activities. For example, lessons designed to reinforce an understanding of ternary form might allow students to choose one of the following: (1) singing familiar and new songs for the purpose of analysis to identify those in ABA form; (2) composing a melody, a percussion piece, or an electronic work in an ABA pattern; or (3) listening to familiar and new compositions on records and tapes, with or without scores, to discover which are written in ternary form.

Another organizational possibility, which moves further toward individualization is the "music lab." In the lab, the students are *not* all working with the same concepts or percepts at the same time. Rather, activities are unrelated to one another, and all the experiences are not required of every student. For instance, at any one time, a student may choose (1) to learn the style characteristics of early jazz through listening, reading, and discussion; (2) to develop skill in aurally identifying instruments of the band or orchestra through listening to tapes and recordings; or (3) to learn to play guitar accompaniments to a variety of songs employing only the primary chords, using a capo for transpositions.

Because of the many considerations involved in individualizing a program, the subject will not be developed further at this point. However, Chapter 7 is completely devoted to individualization and offers numerous suggestions in terms of music labs, the use of technology, open classrooms, nongrading, and other topics—many ideas being applicable to the general music class.

Whether the teacher prepares units to in-

volve all class members simultaneously, initiates an entirely individualized approach, or creates an organizational plan combining the two, there are several centers of activity that deserve special attention: singing, instrumental performance, listening experiences, and music theory and reading (including composition).

Singing

The singing renaissance that we are experiencing in the United States is centered on youth, and it has evolved largely because of the interest of young people in the folk, rock, and other popular idioms of music that penetrate our lives daily through one medium or another. This interest is especially noticeable among junior-high-age boys, who in the past have expressed a negative attitude toward singing, designating it as an activity strictly for girls. The new "singing America" offers the teacher a direct path to working effectively with young voices.

In general, the voices of the early middle-school boys and girls (grades 5 and 6) are alike in range since the vocal bands or cords do not lengthen and thicken appreciably until the time of puberty. However, in quality there is a discernible difference. The girl's voice, for example, has been likened to the light sound of the flute, whereas the boy's voice has a noticeable brilliance and body that increases until his adolescent change occurs. The possible vocal range at this time extends from C^1 to Eb^2:

FIGURE 4-4

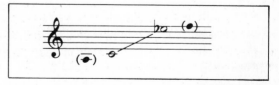

At this stage of vocal development, it is quite evident that two problems are encountered in the production of tones below C^1. First, if the voice is pushed to attain volume, the sound becomes quite harsh; and second, if the voice is not supported with sufficient breath, it develops a lifeless, breathy quality. In the extreme upper range, above Eb^2, there are also two common problems: flat singing, which results from insufficient breath support; and a shouty, strident tone quality that is attributed to forcing the tone.

The middle-school singer must not be sold short; he is capable of an aesthetic experience through artistic singing. The teacher must not settle for the insipid, low-keyed, one-dynamic-level, breathless, unphrased, sing-song type of vocal performance so commonly heard and accepted. Fifth and sixth graders who are dealing successfully with involved mathematical concepts, a second language, and other intellectual and physical challenges must receive a similar challenge through singing. The following focal points indicate areas of achievement that are not only possible but must be demanded:

1. Attention to *good phrasing*, with an explanation from the teacher why it is necessary and what factors govern good phrasing.

2. Attention to various *dynamic levels* and changes in *tempo*, and to their relationship to song interpretation.

3. Instruction in *breath control* and why good singing is impossible without it.

4. Experience in following a conductor, with an explanation of how hand or baton motions are related to dynamics and tempo changes.

5. A continued development of conceptual understanding through singing—by attention to structural elements of songs performed and expressive elements involved in the style of performance.

The voices of junior-high-school or later-middle-school singers (grades 7 and 8) offer the general music teacher his greatest challenge. Students at this age are beginning to experience the psychological and physiological changes that occur during puberty, as well as the startling effect these have on the vocal mechanism. If the general music specialist is to continue to nurture an interest in singing and to guide each student through these changes, he must be cognizant of what is happening and what he must do to cope with the problem.

For many years music educators devoted their attention only to the changes that occur in boys' voices. However, girls also experience a slight but important vocal adjustment. Although the female larynx grows proportionately less than that of the male, the new sound produced by adolescent girls, which at first is quite weak and breathy (grade 7), eventually gains in richness and body in the lower register and greater resonance and a wider range in the upper register (by grades 11 and 12). During the junior-high years, girls are usually classified as sopranos and altos, although in reality most are mezzo-sopranos.

The change in the teen-age boy's voice is considerably more involved and demands closer and more constant attention on the part of the teacher. Prior to the time when puberty begins to manifest itself, a boy finds his voice behaving reasonably well and quite manageably. It is a rather confusing experience for a young boy, during the initial stages of puberty, to discover that the seemingly normal process involved in singing suddenly begins to play tricks on him. He finds it difficult to sing songs that prior to this time he could handle with reasonable accuracy and personal satisfaction. What is actually happening to him is that his larynx is in the process of practically doubling in size, with the adjoining muscles and fibrous tissues thickening and becoming stronger. As a result, the vocal cords produce tones that are

FIGURE 4-5

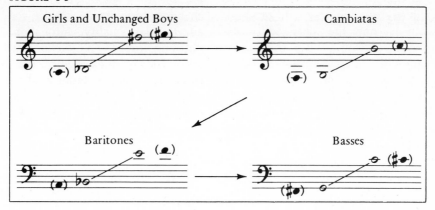

lower in pitch and heavier in quality. During the early stages of vocal change, the process of singing no longer seems to be natural, and the boy finds that he must concentrate in order to effect the coordination needed to produce tones accurately with his more mature vocal cords. Although the process of voice changing is, for the most part, a gradual but relatively quick one, with the complete change usually accomplished over a period of a few weeks, there are cases in which the change has been considerably more prolonged. The music teacher must be constantly alert to beginning signs (such as a lowering of the speaking voice, the cracking of the singing voice, and noticeable physical changes)[13] in order to help guide boys through this sensitive period in personal vocal development.

Varying opinions prevail among authorities regarding *how* boys with changing voices

[13] See Warren Joseph, *The Relationship Between Vocal Growth in the Human Adolescent and the Total Growth Process* (Unpublished doctoral dissertation, Ph.D., Boston University, 1959); and the same writer's articles, "A Summation of the Research Pertaining to Vocal Growth," *Journal of Research in Music Education*, 13:2 (Summer 1965), pp. 93–100; "Vocal Growth Measurements in Male Adolescents," *Journal of Research in Music Education*, 17:4 (Winter 1969), pp. 423–426.

should sing, and even about *what* they should sing. Some music educators prefer to identify these boys as "alto-tenors," the implication being that boys with changing voices would sing the same part as those girls who have been assigned to a lower part. This provides for two-part singing, or three-part singing where the class includes boys who have experienced a more complete change and have become baritones. Other music educators prefer to identify the boys as "cambiatas." The implication here is that there is more than one stage involved in vocal change, and thus, more than two- or three-part singing can be achieved. Figure 4-5 shows the ranges and voice classifications commonly found in grades 7 to 9.

Perhaps the most important factor to keep in mind while working with boys who are experiencing vocal mutation is that their voices are in a seemingly abrupt, yet constant process of change. This is a period of their development that can be an extremely interesting and educative experience for them. Certain boys, in their quest for producing low tones, will force their "unchanged" voices downward, thus producing tones that are breathy and throaty, have little volume, and lack resonance. This, they feel, is their way of hurrying the developmental process and proving their coming manhood. Other boys, who are definitely on their way, will produce low tones but use only the "changed" parts of their voices, refusing to use the upper tones that are still available. The best vocal sounds are produced when boys are not limited to using one of their so-called two voices, but sing normally, allowing their vocal cords to respond freely and naturally throughout their total range as needed.

Working individually with students is one way of accurately pinpointing the voice change. However, there are less time-consuming ways of classifying voices. One suggestion is to sing songs that have an octave leap near the beginning, progressively raising, then lowering, the key. Songs used for this purpose should not be limited to material in the standard junior-high-school song books, but should include music from the current repertoire of the teen culture. A less songlike procedure is to begin at middle C and sing upward diatonically, having each student determine the pitch of his highest comfortable tone; the process can be reversed to determine the lowest comfortable pitch.

Once the music teacher has determined the various voice classifications among his students (being aware that periodic reclassification may be necessary), he will realize that unison singing will *not* serve the vocal range requirements of all voices. Part singing thus becomes a necessity, and it is helpful to have boys with changing voices participate in part work where the music is specifically written so that they are singing the main melody. This gives them an opportunity to sing a part that is readily identifiable. This type of song arrangement, then, would provide opportunities for the girls, who generally are not experiencing any real difficulty in adjusting, to sing parts that are more challenging for them.

The best results are obtained from a program that (1) continuously gives attention to the basic principles of vocal production ap-plicable to all voices, unchanged, changing, or changed (principally breath control, which affects tone quality, intonation, resonance, phrasing, range, and diction); and (2) provides students in each voice classification with suitable singing material to develop the full range and quality of the individual voices with comfort and musical satisfaction.

Instrumental Performance

There are innumerable ways in which instruments of almost every conceivable type can be used in the general music classroom. The use of instruments to accompany singing activities offers the students further opportunities to become involved with matters of timbre, rhythmic precision, phrasing, interpretation, taste, and general, all-around sensitivity to music—to say nothing of the pure enjoyment that may be derived from making music instrumentally.

Opportunities to utilize the talents of students who have attained proficiency on band and orchestral instruments should not be overlooked. These can be rewarding experiences, not only for the performers themselves but also for the other students who generally respond enthusiastically to "live" instrumental supplements to the program. Many students who have been studying an instrument privately or with a class are delighted to be able to apply what they have learned, either in a solo performance, an accompaniment or descant to class singing, or a demonstration of their instruments. The use of such instruments develops the basic concepts being examined in other phases of the music program, and can also be a means for initiating an investigation of the acoustical basis of musical sound. Those students who are studying the piano can be involved in many ways—not only to provide accompaniments, but also to play important themes prior to a listening activity, to illustrate various harmonic concepts, or to play student compositions. The piano, of course, should not be limited to the use of the teacher and piano students alone. Every student should have the chance to explore and experiment at the keyboard, in both directed and free activities.

Informal instruments can also be used effectively for accompaniment purposes. Melodic instruments such as resonator bells, harmonic instruments including the Autoharp, and the wide variety of percussion and friction instruments available all have their place in the classroom. An important consideration here is the selection of instruments that will be stylistically suitable for accompanying a particular song. This selection should be put to the students since it provides a natural opportunity to increase discrimination. The teacher's preferences should not be imposed on the class; rather, when a difference of opinion arises, the selection should be examined in a musical manner—both intellectually and through trial performance—to determine which instruments would be most appropriate and effective.

The Autoharp is especially popular because it offers a simple means of introducing harmonic background to singing. It operates in several commonly used keys, is easily learned, and provides a sufficient number of chords. Although the Autoharp is now used as a "professional instrument" by some folk singers, the teacher may find that older students in general music classes prefer a more "complete," more sophisticated instrument for harmonic performance. Aside from the piano, the answer to this problem lies with the guitar, which can hardly be classified any longer as only an informal instrument because of its wide and artistic use by professionals and amateurs alike. Every teacher of general music today needs a working knowledge of the guitar, just as he does of the piano. Although it requires a great deal of skill for truly accomplished playing, the guitar

can be effectively employed through the use of just a few basic chords and a capo for transposition. It is not difficult to involve students with the guitar, either. Even those with no previous experience can learn simple fingerings for basic chords rather quickly, and simple strumming can be substituted for the more complicated picking achieved by advanced players.

Because of the popularity of the guitar as a youth instrument, its use in the class can be helpful in involving even those few students who otherwise seem indifferent. There is no need to fear that students will feel they are being patronized as long as the guitar is introduced as a legitimate instrument and is used in a musically sensitive manner. Aside from accompaniment possibilities, the guitar is particularly suited to instruction in theoretical concepts, for its fretted fingerboard provides a visual as well as aural approach to intervals, chords, and scalar structures. The strumming motion of the right hand also assists students in feeling metric organization.

A number of schools have begun separate classes in guitar, outside of the general music course, because student interest has been so high. Whether it is taught separately or employed within the general music framework, a basic principle is to teach just a few chords and then develop a large repertoire before attempting the trickier fingerings and strums. With this approach, and with the aid of self-instructional materials, all the students should be able to use the guitar with moderate success by some point in the semester.

Listening Experiences

A quality program in general music provides abundant opportunities for students to come in contact with the widest possible range of music. To extend this range beyond their own performance capabilities, opportunities can include not only the use of recorded tapes and discs, but also provisions for live performances in the classroom or auditorium by student and professional groups; class trips to local or regional concerts, festivals, and musical productions; and the use of films, selected radio or television broadcasts, and videotapes (for use on closed-circuit television or in cassette form for the individual classroom).

An important factor in exploring the resources for listening experiences is an openness to the scope of musical expression. Educators today do not classify music as our predecessors did—namely, classical or "serious" music on the one hand and popular music or "everything else" on the other. Classrooms, which at one time reverberated exclusively with the mystique of sophisticated, tried-and-tested brands of music, have fortunately opened up to include a variety of unsophisticated, informal types, many forms of contemporary music, and innovative, avant-grade expressions of both professional and nonprofessional creators. This is all for the good, for each type of music is a valid, acceptable form within a given set of values, and each is suitable in the general music course if it is properly presented.

Contemporary classical music is one area of music literature that especially needs more attention in the schools. This music cannot be dismissed as too complex, too experimental, or too recent to be proven worthy, and therefore bequeathed to students of the twenty-first century for serious consideration. There is no avoiding the importance of contemporary music; it is the musical expression of *our* people in *our* time, and what can be more relevant? Students are naturally close to this music and are amazingly responsive to the works of twentieth-century composers. This applies not only to music written for traditional media, but also to works created in the broad field of electronic music, for many sound sources and compositional techniques are now shared by the fields of classical music, rock, and jazz. Resource materials, which were scarce in this area not too many years ago, are now plentiful. Several record companies have large catalogs of contemporary works, and there are several good texts available for the teacher's own reference.

Another area deserving increased attention in listening activities is folk music, which has traditionally been little more than the staple of vocal performance in the classroom. The study of folk and ethnic music—and especially American idioms—can be a topic for unit concentration or can be introduced intermittently in conjunction with other forms and styles to teach various concepts. If the organization of the lessons is stylistic, the study of folk and ethnic music can be presented (1) from the standpoint of music representative of particular groups (for example, lumbermen, pioneers, American Indians, seamen, blacks, the Jewish people, industrial workers, and so on); (2) in a functional social setting (for example, music to accompany work, worship, ceremony, and play); (3) in a quasi-chronological format (for example, music of colonial days, the early Republic, the Civil War, and on through the urban folk music developed by Dylan, Baez, Saint-Marie, Paxton, and others); or (4) according to regional traits (for example, folk music of the Southern mountains, the deep South, the West, New England, Western Europe, Africa, or the Orient and Middle East). Resources for presenting this material are abundant.[14] Ethnic music of almost every conceivable area of the world is now available on recordings, including the great wealth of America's folk literature. Many of these recordings are of excellent quality and are supplemented with liner notes or enclosed booklets containing useful information for the teacher.

[14] See, for example, Barbara B. Smith, ed., *Music in World Cultures* (Washington, D.C.: Music Educators National Conference, 1972).

The broad area of popular music—which makes up most of the students' out-of-school listening—also should be part of the general music class. The class should hear representative selections from rock, disco, country-western music, rhythm-and-blues/soul music, and even what is known as "middle-of-the-road" music. America's best-known indigenous music—jazz (from traditional styles to free-form jazz and the jazz-rock fusion)—certainly should play an important role in the course. All too long, music educators turned their backs on this music, leaving it up to students to seek their own way through the wide assortment of styles. For the most part, the results of that practice tended to be purely emotional responses; yet beneath the immediate surface appeal these idioms are as endowed as any other music with subsurface ingredients that only the sensitive, discriminating listener will discover. Realizing this truth, knowledgeable teachers in recent years have introduced popular music and jazz styles in the classroom on an equal basis with other types of music to teach students to be more intelligent, discriminating consumers.

Many leading music educators long have supported the inclusion of popular music and jazz in the curriculum. For example, William Cornog, in an address before the Tanglewood Symposium in 1967, said: "Man the Player is playing like mad outside the schools, outside the whole respectable scholastic world—in literature, in art, in music—and this has always been so. The schools have not always known where the action is."[15] Supporting this point of view, Charles Leonhard recommended that music teachers "move out of the comfortable rut of traditional music and a status quo music program into the challenge and ex-

citement of the new music. . . ."[16] He also encouraged the profession to "face the fact that we are subjecting students in schools to music that receives scant, if any, attention from them outside the school."[17] Two years after Tanglewood, the Music Educators National Conference lent its "official" support when its president, Wiley L. Housewright, stated:

> Church choirs, marching bands, choruses, and orchestras do not fully satisfy the musical appetites of the young. Hundreds of thousands of American youth want more. Their drive, their enthusiasm, their creativity, and their enormous fund of talent have produced new music—vibrant, original, and honest. . . .
>
> Many youths feel that art music is antiquarian, interesting only to young conformist candidates of the snob establishment; many adults view youth music as too sensual, boisterous, simplistic, and unmusical. Somewhere between the two extremes lies the truth. Art is nonexclusive. Sophisticated styles never obliterate the simpler forms. Both can coexist as necessary and significant communicative expressions. One musical art cannot repress another.
>
> There is much to be gained from the study of any musical creation. Rock, soul, blues, folk, and jazz cannot be ignored. . . . Music education must encompass all music. If student musical attitudes are to be affected by music education, the music teacher's openness to new music serves as a necessary model. The Music Educators National Conference . . . not only accepts rock and other present-day music as legitimate, but sanctions its use in education.[18]

It is important to emphasize that the teacher who uses popular music should avoid adopt-

[15] William H. Cornog, "These Essences," in Robert A. Choate, ed., *Documentary Report of the Tanglewood Symposium* (Washington, D.C.: Music Educators National Conference, 1968), p. 28.

[16] Charles Leonhard, "The Next Ten Years," *Music Educators Journal*, 55:1 (September 1968), p. 50.

[17] Charles Leonhard, "Human Potential and the Aesthetic Experience," *Music Educators Journal*, 54:8 (April 1968), p. 110.

[18] Wiley L. Housewright, "Youth Music in Education," *Music Educators Journal*, 56:3 (November 1969), p. 45.

ing the "disc jockey approach," playing popular tunes one after another with little or no concern about how they relate to the lesson at hand. Such an approach uses popular music merely as entertainment, as a time filler, or as a reward when students have behaved well during the "teacher's portion" of the class. The purpose of the general music class is to educate. Therefore popular music idioms should be introduced to help students learn music concepts and their related percepts; to develop their music knowledge, understanding, skills, appreciation, attitudes, and habits; in short, to help young people increase their aesthetic responsiveness to music. For example, Carole King's "A Natural Woman" can be used to demonstrate triple meter; the Beatles' "Lucy in the Sky with Diamonds" can illustrate changing meter ($\frac{3}{4}$ to $\frac{4}{4}$); the Mahavishnu Orchestra's "Celestial Terrestial Commuters" might be used in a lesson on free meter; Paul McCartney's "My Love" illustrates off-beat accents; the Main Ingredient's "Summer Breeze" is representative of binary form, and Skylark's "Wildflower" of binary form with immediate repetitions; and so on. Although certain popular recordings have become standards and can be used effectively years after their initial release, it is important for the teacher to keep in touch with *current* hits, among which is a great deal of excellent teaching material. Up-to-date reading and listening in popular music are musts for the fully aware specialist in general music.

Music literature, both of past eras and of the twentieth century, needs to be considered in some sort of a historical framework. Since a composer or performer-composer is a product of his own time, an understanding of the social and historical setting in which a composition was created can help lead the listener to a deeper understanding of the music. Yet, while certain historical facts should be considered in the presentation of a listening experience, and while chronology may be a useful organizing device, history itself should not be the governing objective. Only those facts that contribute to an understanding of the *music* should enter the presentation.

The broad objective should be the development of listening skills through *the understanding and perception of structural, stylistic, and interpretive concepts.* No one approach is necessarily best for accomplishing this goal, and a number of different approaches are employed successfully by teachers. Some instructors like to develop listening skills through a format based on various forms, textures, and types of composition. Others prefer to use a stylistic approach, building upon the elements of composers' styles, period styles, idiomatic styles, or national styles. The reason no one approach is best is simply that no one approach suffices; in practice, almost every possible approach can and should be used during the course of the year to develop listening skills. The particular concept to be examined and the particular music selected will be principal determinants in the methods of presentation.

Earlier it was stated that a functional and flexible sequential organization of the general music program is one that employs variable topic units in grades 5 and 6, element-and-form-oriented units in grade 7 to bring together and reinforce basic concepts, and stylistic units in grade 8 to broaden the students' understanding. Whether this format or another is used, it is important that listening activities be integrated with the activities undertaken in singing, playing, and composing. *This integration should be founded on a musical rather than a topical basis.* Programmatic, social-interest, or social studies correlations—at one time the principal organizing factors in general music programs—have little to do with the development of music understanding and often serve only to delay the integration of music experiences. Jerome Bruner, whose creative thinking is applicable to all subjects, has aptly spoken of one of these points in stating that "the unity of knowledge is to be found within knowledge itself, if the knowledge is worth mastering. To attempt a justification of subject matter . . . in terms of its relation to the child's social activities is to misunderstand what knowledge is and how it may be mastered."[19]

False interest and activity topic centers are readily available for illustration. For example, singing a song about a locomotive in grade 5 and then listening to Honegger's *Pacific 231* or Villa-Lobos' *The Little Train of the Caipira* is basically a contrived topical relationship that does not in itself serve any real music education purpose. Nor does singing a sea chantey and listening to Debussy's *La Mer* necessarily promote conceptual understanding through integrated activities. The program *would* have an integrated structure, however, if the singing activity involved a sea chantey with a call-and-response pattern and a work song incorporating the same principle, and if the related listening experiences drew upon music featuring the same or related structural concepts (such as recordings of authentic African music, the chase choruses in Chicago jazz, "trading fours" in modern jazz performances, the interplay between soloist and orchestra in a concerto, or the antiphony heard in, say, a Gabrieli canzona).

To illustrate this approach further, let us select one of the concepts related to rhythm, as presented on page 76. Perhaps the class has been working on a song in which one rhythmic pattern is predominant. It might be an arrangement of "America, the Beautiful," in which the first four-measure rhythmic phrase

[19] Jerome S. Bruner, *On Knowing: Essays for the Left Hand* (New York: Atheneum, 1967), p. 121.

is repeated and repeated, a current rock melody based on a recurring syncopated figure, or perhaps an aria such as Verdi's "Di Provenza il mar," with its seven-note rhythmic motif, or Mozart's "Non più andrai," which is characterized by a three-note dotted figure. If perception of repeated rhythmic patterns is the objective, then related listening activities might involve such a wide variety of styles as Beethoven's *Symphony No. 7*, an example of music from India featuring a tala, a big-band jazz number based on a rhythmic riff, or Chopin's *Prelude No. 7*, with its six-note rhythmic motif.

Any lesson or unit, then, that is organized around structural or interpretive elements can draw upon a number of music styles for integrated listening lessons. Units organized to develop stylistic understanding, such as those suggested for grade 8, would, in a sense, be planned in the opposite direction. That is, listening materials and performance selections would be drawn from the one style being examined, but in this case the activities would lend themselves to the perception of a number of concepts previously presented individually. The focus and supporting materials of each of these approaches can be seen in Figure 4-6.

It becomes obvious that each approach feeds the other, and one might logically ask the age-old question of which comes first. In the lower grades, listening experiences based on both procedures will be valuable in build-

FIGURE 4-6

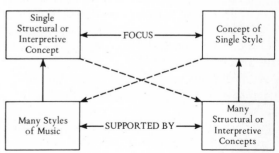

ing an over-all sound structure in which the child can operate. But as the same basic ideas are spiraled upward through more complex forms and are experienced in more detail from different angles and in different contexts, there comes a stage where concentration needs to be on the analysis of individual concepts in order that the subsequent synthesis will yield generalizations of greater depth. It is for this reason that a sequence of structural concepts leading to stylistic concepts has been recommended for the traditional junior-high-school years. For a student can perceive the individual structural concept through its presentation in a variety of styles without really understanding those styles per se; but he cannot come to understand the special characteristics that yield a concept of a particular style unless he can first perceive those characteristics as individual structural elements. At this point in the spiral, then, the focus of listening activities would best begin at the left of the diagram (Figure 4-6).

Since many techniques for presenting listening lessons in the general music class are closely related to those employed in the more specialized music-listening or literature class at the high-school level, the reader is referred to Chapter 5, where specific techniques are discussed in some detail.

Music Theory and Reading

Some music educators compare music-reading ability to reading a language. This view maintains that just as a person in the United States is considered illiterate if he does not have a functional ability to read and write the English language, so may a person be considered musically illiterate if he does not have a functional understanding of the graphic language of music. Because of the dual connotations of the words "literate" and "illiterate," however, this view cannot be justifiably accepted without qualifications. "Literate" in a specific sense means "the ability to read and write," but in a wider sense it is often interpreted as "well educated" or "cultured." Thus, any reference to literacy or illiteracy in music should have only *one*, restrictive connotation: the ability or inability to read and write music notation. The lack of such ability in no way means that an individual is musically uneducated. He may be highly sensitive to music and may possess and utilize a broad understanding of music, even though he may have no understanding of notation. At the same time, it is only by combining the visual with the aural effect that a student can develop to his utmost potential his ability to deal with the totality of music experience.

Throughout his schooling, for example, a student may be exposed year after year to an explanation of the meaning of the top and bottom numbers in a meter signature. Yet, when he listens to a new work, it matters very little whether he knows what the exact notation is. What *is* important is that he can *feel* and *follow* the basic beat, the metric organization, and deviations from them. This distinction also applies to other aspects of notation and the sounds they represent. We must distinguish, then, between the development of a student's aesthetic sensitivity and the development of means available to him for widening his involvement in music experiences.

Certainly a functional understanding of notation is *one* of the keys to *complete* contact with music, but it is not the key to music sensitivity. Therefore, while the importance of continuing the reading phase of the general music program through each level of classes should not be dismissed, it must nevertheless be recognized that an understanding of and sensitivity to the content of music are the first concern. The aural effect should always precede the visual. If this is accomplished, then there need be no great concern over teaching music reading. For the appropriate time for acquiring a functional knowledge of notation is only when the need arises. The student who has grown in his responsiveness to music and who continues to grow will eventually reach a stage where the bits and pieces of notation he has learned will no longer be serviceable. *Then* he will be ready for a more complete understanding of the graphic representation of music; and *then,* if he so desires, he will also learn notation—with or without a teacher!

While the need for functional reading ability must precede its acquisition, this does not mean that a structured reading program is not important throughout the middle school. The structured program lays the foundation for mastery when the need arises, and in the meantime it assists the development of music understanding in the broader sense of that phrase.

By the sixth grade, the development of understanding the basics of notation should reach the end of its first cycle. It may be expected that by this level, the musically growing student should understand the function of key signatures and how to find the tonic note, know the meaning of meter signatures and grasp the relativity of rhythmic notation, understand pitch designations by notes and accidentals, and be able to read simple melodies *at his own pace* by means of syllables, letters, or numbers. In the seventh and eighth grades, elements of theory and reading should be pulled together and reinforced to provide the opportunity for students to develop their skills further. Although some teachers like to present theory at this level in a concentrated unit, it is more practical to review the subject and introduce new concepts throughout the program as the elements of theory relate to other music experiences. In fact, if a class has had such a weak background in music reading in the lower grades that there is little or nothing to build

on, it is highly questionable whether the teacher should try to *begin* a reading program at this level through a concentrated unit. When this situation exists, it would seem justifiable to say that time is more effectively spent in concentrating on the broader goal of musical responsiveness.

The continuous interpolation of theory instruction in all areas of classroom activity must be made interesting. Unfortunately, theory has been, and still is in many instances, taught as a series of dull, monotonous, and personally unrewarding exercises. Some of our newer texts present attractive and highly successful approaches (without the use of nonmusic gimmicks). Always remember, however, that the real key to creating interest is relevance. When the teacher communicates the *need* for understanding a theoretical concept, then it can be interesting. Among the legitimate and profitable techniques for continuing theory instruction are the use of thematic charts or transparencies in conjunction with listening activities; playing rhythmic and other instrumental accompaniments from scores; class evaluation of expressiveness in interpreting songs as it relates to the score (in terms of dynamics, tempo markings, phrasing, and so on); visually comparing similar and different sections of a song before learning it; playing melodies and chords on the keyboard from notation; following scores while listening; transferring traditionally notated chords to tablatures for use in playing the guitar, and vice versa for adapting guitar tablatures to keyboard performance; creating chordal accompaniments by synthesizing pitches in melodic lines; playing the key tone and having students find their beginning pitches in part music; and recording, by means of notation, original student compositions. There are many other possibilities, of course, each of which can further reading ability without isolating theory into a dull, mechanical learning process. Such techniques as these also suggest an approach to the evaluation of reading ability: Since memorization of notational symbols does not in itself indicate an ability to respond to their meanings, written tests of the identification sort are often meaningless. Evaluation should be based largely on observable behaviors in class and individual performances.

An excellent means of developing notational understanding while promoting musical growth in other areas is the compositional approach. Given a minimal amount of information regarding notation, students can learn a great deal about theory and reading by having the opportunity to compose their own music. We know now that composition, once the province of a few chosen people, is an area of music activity in which many can engage with reasonable success. Henry Lasker, the late composer and educator who devoted many years to teaching creative music to secondary school students, reported that young students with no previous experience in composition can produce some exciting works—even fully orchestrated compositions—without being subjected to rules and traditions.[20] He proved this point year after year in his classes by establishing a creative climate, giving the students a free rein, and letting them *discover* the techniques required to compose the music they hear within themselves. As their works unfolded, in various forms and styles, for various performance media, and of various lengths, the students came to grasp in a very personal way basic concepts of rhythm and meter, pitch, harmony, motif, phrase, period, contour, sequence, inversion, unity and variety, form, instrumentation, and interpretation.

Students may begin composition in many ways: by creating a melody for an original or

[20] See Henry Lasker, *Teaching Creative Music in Secondary Schools* (Boston: Allyn and Bacon, Inc., 1971).

previously written text, by developing a rhythmic idea, by expanding on a melodic motif, or perhaps by exploring the possibilities of a harmonic progression. Experimentation at the keyboard, even by nonpiano students, may offer a start; or a vocal improvisation could become the basis of an idea to be worked out in composition. The possibility of writing for nontraditional instruments should not be overlooked either. For example, many experiments with musique concrète and electronic music can develop from working with just simple equipment; two tape recorders alone are quite flexible resources in the hands of imaginative students. (See some of the suggestions offered in Chapter 6 on theory classes.) In composing electronic music, a student will obviously need to develop his own system of notation. (This may also be true for some students in writing for traditional sound media if their understanding of notation is still limited. Nevertheless, the compositional act and concepts that derive from it are the important matters here; therefore, creative activity should not be denied to students who must devise their own form of notation as a first step.) Aleatoric composition may also be an interesting departure for the class. Recent activities have involved such unorthodox procedures as assigning certain sounds to objects and different surface areas around the classroom; the composition takes shape as the students move around the room in different directions (from left to right, from floor to ceiling, from wall to wall, and so on).

Whatever approach the students may take as a start, the process of developing their musical thoughts leads them, with the teacher's guidance, to a discovery of the materials, methods, and shapes of music. Because it is their own creation at the center of activity, learning certain concepts about sounds, structures, and styles—linked with related listening experiences—has relevance. Thus, students in general music classes can, should, and will come to grips with music theory, and will grow through the experience (more than theoretically), if theory is made an integrated rather than isolated part of the program, if it is made interesting, and if it is structured to meet their needs *as those needs evolve.*

DEVELOPING THE LESSON

Every lesson must be considered as part of a larger sequence of learning experiences; it must relate to what has gone before and to what is ahead. At the same time, the importance of the individual lesson as a *major* learning experience needs to be recognized. As such, it requires preparation in as thorough a manner as if it were the *only* lesson. Each of the factors discussed in terms of the overall program—instructional objectives, sequential organization, and concept teaching—will give direction to the preparation of a lesson. In addition, organizing elements and organizing centers will have to be selected. In the following sections on planning, presenting, and evaluating a lesson, the discussion is organized around a specific example to show how these basic ideas can be put into practice.

Writing the Lesson Plan

Preparing a *written* lesson plan is an important step toward successful teaching. In this plan, the teacher delineates a teaching strategy to realize the behavioral changes described in the instructional objectives. The beginning teacher will discover that the success of a lesson is frequently in proportion to the detail of a step-by-step plan. Nothing is as terrifying to the inexperienced teacher as not knowing what to do next in the middle of a teaching situation. Referring to a carefully written plan can get the novice teacher back on course when the lesson goes off on a tangent.

The amount of detail in a good lesson plan depends on several factors: (1) how much experience the teacher has had—the more experienced the teacher, the less detailed plans tend to become; (2) how often the teacher has taught the particular lesson—new material usually requires more detailed planning; and (3) how complex the lesson is—even in working with familiar material, if the lesson is somewhat complicated or draws on numerous examples, the teacher may need more extensive "reminders" written down to be sure that nothing important is passed over. The lesson plan should contain the following components:

1. *Instructional objectives:* Behavioral objectives will indicate the expected outcomes of the lessons for the learner.

2. *Teaching procedure:* The teaching strategy will be broken into a step-by-step procedure that shows how instructional materials will be used, the intended sequence, and alternative steps if a lesson happens to run short, move off on a tangent, or otherwise run into difficulties.

3. *Equipment and materials:* There is less chance that the teacher will forget needed equipment and materials if they are listed in the lesson plan.

4. *Review and evaluation:* In this part of the plan, the teacher records his or her immediate reaction to the success of the lesson and makes notes to answer such questions as "Have the instructional objectives been achieved?" "Were the objectives realistic for this particular class?" "How successful was the teaching strategy?" "Were the instructional materials satisfactory?" "What can be done to improve the lesson?" "Is a reiteration with different materials called for?" and so on.

Developing Instructional Objectives

A misconception that defeats many lesson plans in their relationship to the total general music program is the notion that the goal of the lesson is for students to memorize what is presented as factual information. Although a certain amount of memorization is involved, the teacher should plan for the goal of *learning to learn* through an understanding of concepts that may be perceived in a variety of situations. Thus, definite concepts must be kept in mind, specific instructional objectives must be established, and materials must be selected that are likely to lead to the desired behaviors.

Let us assume that a lesson is to be planned for a middle-school or junior-high class that has had limited music experience. The length of the class meeting is forty-five minutes. The concept of rhythm and the percepts of beat and tempo have been selected as the main organizing elements in the lesson, and within a sequence of varied activities that will be used to develop these percepts, listening has been selected as the organizing center for this particular class meeting. With appropriate behavioral objectives in mind, two brief compositions have been chosen that seem suitable: the "Hornpipe" from Handel's *Water Music* and the "Pizzicato Polka" from Shostakovich's ballet *The Age of Gold*. The selection of these two works now permits us to enlarge upon our behavioral objectives for this lesson. They might be outlined in the following manner:

1. Given a written "quick quiz" (see Table 4-3) containing the terms "rhythm," "tempo," "hornpipe," "arco," "Handel," "polka," "Shostakovich," and "pizzicato," the student will match these terms with given descriptive phrases. Two mistakes or fewer will be considered passing.

2. During the playing of familiar and unfamiliar recorded music, the students will raise their hands when they hear the tempo change. If three-quarters of the class makes

Table 4-3. GENERAL MUSIC CLASS—QUICK QUIZ

Name_____Date_____Section_____

Match each term in the left column with the appropriate description in the right column by placing the number of the term in the space provided beside the description.

1. Rhythm
2. Tempo
3. Hornpipe
4. Arco
5. Handel
6. Polka
7. Shostakovich
8. Pizzicato

Brass instrument_____

Violin bow_____

Composer of "Pizzicato Polka"_____

Gives music a feeling of movement_____

Sailors' dance_____

Speed of the music_____

Composer of "Hornpipe"_____

Bohemian dance with quick steps and a hop_____

Plucking strings with the fingers (detached tones)_____

Playing strings with a bow (smooth)_____

the correct response, the initial presentation will be considered successful.

3. When the teacher plays two recorded examples of string music, the student will perceive and identify by a show of hand which of the examples is pizzicato and which is arco. If three-quarters of the class makes the correct response, the initial presentation will be considered successful.

Organizing the Teaching Procedure

The presentation of a lesson needs to involve several types of classroom interaction—for example, instruction by the teacher, experience with the music, discussion by the students, and if possible within the time limits of a single class period, more than one mode of inquiry (listening, performing, composing). Depending on the students' attention span, age level, and level of understanding, the balanced variety of modes of inquiry may be accomplished through a series of related lessons rather than within each single lesson. (In the illustration provided here, only listening is involved, although the presentation is varied through aural, oral, and visual factors.)

To begin, the teacher must motivate his students to get involved in the experience at hand, and should share with them the objectives to be realized. But motivation does not stop there; it has to be maintained throughout the lesson by establishing a series of problems to be solved, and these must be problems within their ability for solution. (As the sample lesson continues below, it will be seen that the problems presented before each listening segment are appropriate for a class with limited background. A class with a more advanced level of understanding would be given problems of a more complex nature in regard to the same basic concepts.)

The framework of the entire lesson should provide sufficient time for the class to experience the whole before the parts, to concentrate on specific points through analysis, and finally to pull the whole together again through synthesis. Furthermore, every attempt must be made to reach and involve each student actively in the presentation. This requires that the teacher devise suitable questions and activities that take into account the students' varying abilities, attitudes, and interests, and that a suitable procedure for class response be established. In the case of a listening lesson, for example, the teacher must establish the need for quiet during the actual listening portions of the period in order to ensure that everyone will have the opportunity for uninterrupted listening. He must also present listening objectives for each segment that direct the students toward *active listening*. And he should indicate that unless questions are addressed to the class for group response, students with answers to offer should raise their hands for recognition. This offers as many students as possible the opportunity to participate. In many instances where members of the class merely call out the answers, there is undue confusion and one or two students can dominate discussion to the point where other students who also know the answers are not motivated to respond.

In continuing the sample lesson related to beat and tempo, the following material has been organized under three headings: *Discussion* (for class analysis and synthesis), *Instructions for Listening* (for motivation and the presentation of problems to be solved), and *Music Sequence* (for active listening).

Discussion No. 1: Using familiar songs, current rock numbers, or music heard in previous lessons, the students should be encouraged, through class discussion, to express what they already know about rhythm. For example: (1) rhythm gives music movement; (2) tempo indicates the speed with which a piece of music is performed; and (3) the beat is continuous and marks off intervals of time.

Instructions for Listening No. 1: The class is asked to determine whether, in the composition to be played, the tempo and beat remain the same or change. During all listening, students are told to tap the beat lightly.

Music Sequence No. 1: "Hornpipe" from *Water Music* by George Frideric Handel.

Discussion No. 2: Most of the students should have recognized that there was a tempo change; the teacher asks for a show of hands by those who perceived the change. Although some students will simply follow the class leaders and raise their hands, the technique is acceptable at this early point in the lesson. It will provide *some* feedback, but more importantly will indicate to those who perceived no change that they will need to pay closer attention, individually, to the music and to their tapping of the beat.

Instructions for Listening No. 2: The same music is to be played again in its entirety, and this time the students are asked to write down on paper (a) where the tempo change occurs—at the beginning, in the middle, or at the end; (b) whether the tempo changes by becoming faster or slower; and (c) what the mood of the music is (happy, sad, majestic, mysterious, and so on), how the mood is affected by the tempo and tempo change, and whether any accompanying activity is suggested (that is, what could one do to the music?).

Music Sequence No. 2: "Hornpipe."

Discussion No. 3: The students are told to check their own written answers against the conclusions reached in class discussion. As a result of the discussion, the class should indicate that the tempo changed at the very end of the composition, where it slowed down. At this point the diagram in Figure 4-7 is pre-

FIGURE 4-7

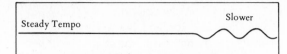

sented to visualize the tempo change as it occurs in the "Hornpipe." (Diagrams such as this may be drawn on the board, prepared on a chart, or shown through the use of an overhead projector transparency.) Through a discussion of the tempo and the spirit of the music, the students will recognize its gaiety and probably its suitability for dancing. At this point the title of the work and the name of the composer are given, and if "hornpipe" is a new term, the teacher explains that it is a sailors' dance.

The discussion thus far has been open and the students have not been asked to indicate their decisions in an individual, private manner. Rather, they have been given the opportunity to evaluate themselves, checking their own thoughts against the consensus of the class. Self-evaluation of this sort can be valuable in prodding students toward more independent listening.

Instructions for Listening No. 3: Another composition is to be played, and the students are asked to determine (a) where the tempo change occurs—at the beginning, in the middle, or at the end; (b) whether the tempo changes by becoming faster or slower, and whether the change is sudden or gradual; and (c) whether the tempo, after the change, remains the same to the end of the composition, or whether it changes again.

Music Sequence No. 3: "Pizzicato Polka" from *The Age of Gold* by Dmitri Shostakovich (entire selection).

Discussion No. 4: The students are instructed to close their eyes and raise their hands to respond to the questions: "Who be-

FIGURE 4-8

| Steady Tempo | Faster – Faster | Steady Tempo |

lieves the tempo changed near the beginning?" "In the middle?" "Toward the end?" (The "middles" have it.) "Who thinks it became slower?" "Faster?" (There is continuous acceleration.) With the show of hands having given the teacher some feedback on a more individual basis (understanding that this is the first hearing of the polka), the class is instructed to open their eyes, and a general discussion follows to determine that the tempo changes again at a later point (some students *were* correct in saying it changed toward the end), returning to the same tempo as at the beginning. The diagram in Figure 4-8 is now presented for discussion and explanation.

Instructions for Listening No. 4: To evaluate whether the students, individually, can perceive tempo changes, the teacher instructs them to close their eyes, listen to the same composition once again, and raise their hands during the playing when the beat gets faster, keeping their hands raised until the music reverts to the original tempo. During this second listening, the students are also asked to determine the mood of the music.

Music Sequence No. 4: "Pizzicato Polka."

Discussion No. 5: To begin, the teacher comments on the success or failure of the class to perceive the tempo changes. Then, through discussion, the class should recognize the gaiety of the music and agree that it, too, is quite suitable for dancing, although the middle section, with its increased tempo, might become hectic. The class is now given the title of the composition and the name of the composer. In the discussion that follows,

"polka" should be recognized as another dance, and the new term "pizzicato" is explained through demonstration with a violin or other stringed instrument.

During the demonstration, the students become familiar with (a) pizzicato, the technique of playing a stringed instrument by plucking the strings; (b) arco, the technique of playing a stringed instrument with a bow; (c) how the fingers are used to change the pitches of the strings, and the fact that when a string is shortened its pitch becomes higher, whereas when a string is lengthened its pitch becomes lower. Several opportunities for such recognition are provided during the demonstration.

Instructions for Listening No. 5: To provide the students with the opportunity to distinguish between pizzicato and arco, the first segment of the polka is played, followed by a segment of the hornpipe. The students are asked to determine whether the first or second segment is an example of pizzicato, and to describe in their own words the difference between the arco and pizzicato sounds heard on the recordings.

Music Sequence No. 5: Segments of the "Pizzicato Polka" and the "Hornpipe."

Discussion No. 6: The first sequence should be recognized as the one featuring pizzicato. During the discussion, the students might describe the arco passage as smooth and the pizzicato passage as short and detached.

Instructions for Listening No. 6: To complete the lesson, both compositions are played again in their entirety, if time permits. (This should be possible since both are quite brief.) The students are asked now to compare the two selections and to determine how the different moods and styles of the dances are affected by the rhythm and manner of performance.

Music Sequence No. 6: "Hornpipe" and "Pizzicato Polka" (entire selections in an uninterrupted sequence).

Discussion No. 7: The students should discover that the over-all tempos of the two compositions do not differ very much, but that the internal changes *are* different. They will probably decide that the style of each dance is affected more by something else about the rhythm, and may determine that this "something else" is the type of rhythms involved rather than the tempo of the rhythms. (This discovery may provide the teacher with the basis for subsequent lessons on different rhythmic patterns, accents, and metric concepts.) To close the lesson, a quick quiz is given (see Table 4-3).

Selecting Equipment and Materials

The necessary tools for presenting this sample lesson include recordings of the compositions, a record player (or if the material has been pretaped, a tape recorder), an overhead projector and transparencies (or large charts and cards), a violin or other stringed instrument, and finally—most important—an imaginative teacher who can take a lesson plan that has been organized on paper and make it come alive in the classroom.

Some words of caution are in order in using audiovisual equipment (which media specialists refer to as hardware): (1) do not wait until the last minute before the lesson to check whether the equipment is in working order; (2) if the hardware needed is not part of the general music classroom equipment and must be borrowed from the school's media center, reserve it several days in advance of the lesson; and (3) ask your media specialist (the person responsible for the AV hardware) whether backup equipment is available should the hardware break down in use or just prior to the lesson (in which case, it is also wise to have a substitute plan for the class).

Evaluating and Reviewing the Lesson

Immediate evaluation can be made during the presentation of a lesson. In the sample given here, evaluation has been carried out partially through class discussion, partially through individual "blindfold" response, and partially through a written quiz. In addition, other techniques should be applied after the lesson has been completed—techniques that will undoubtedly carry over into other class periods. For example, overhead transparencies or cards, showing the music terms used during the lesson, can become focal points for an evaluation-discussion. In relation to the sample lesson, the following items would receive attention: (1) the degree to which students understand the meanings of the terms "rhythm," "tempo," "beat," "arco," and "pizzicato"; (2) an evaluation of what has been learned about beat and tempo from the two compositions heard in class; (3) the knowledge that Handel composed the "Hornpipe" and that Shostakovich wrote the "Pizzicato Polka"; (4) an opportunity for aural identification of each composition and an opportunity to relate the music to the tempo diagrams shown earlier; and (5) an opportunity to perceive pizzicato and arco passages in other compositions that are unfamiliar, including nonclassical music.

In subsequent class meetings, other methods of evaluation, review, and expansion should be undertaken. For example, the students can be allowed to experiment with the violin in order to understand better the principle involved in changing the pitch of a string. They can also be encouraged to bring to class, for analysis and discussion, recordings with tempo changes, recordings with arco and pizzicato passages, and music being studied privately or in school groups in which they can discover how tempo changes are indicated. Composing original melodies or rhythmic scores will provide still another opportunity for them to experiment and discover how different tempos influence the character of music. A few might want to create music for a violin solo, using arco and pizzicato techniques. In class performance, attention can also be focused on the same rhythmic factors as a means of review, and the manner of performance will provide another means of evaluation. Finally, the students should have the opportunity for optional, individual listening to other music by Handel or Shostakovich, to other polkas or hornpipes, or to other types of music based on dance rhythms.

PROVISIONS FOR GENERAL MUSIC

Much has been said about planning objectives, structuring a concept-oriented curriculum, and developing relevant experiences through various organizing centers, but these factors alone will not provide for a successful general music program. The finest curriculum on paper must still be brought to life by a creative teacher, working within sufficient class time in proper facilities and employing quality teaching materials and equipment.

Whether the curriculum is thought of as "student-centered" or "learning-centered," the key to successful experiences is a well-prepared, finely tuned teacher. Classes cannot be left to the whims of a "piano-plunking singing teacher" whose objectives are indeterminable. For years we have heard it said that music specialists are needed in the elementary grades. By now it should be apparent that specialists are also needed for secondary general music classes—not just musicians, but *general music specialists*. Too often, we find teachers who have been trained primarily as instrumental or vocal directors assigned to general music classes instead of, or in conjunction with, classes more directly related to their backgrounds and knowledge. More discouraging is the fact that many teachers who work and prefer to work with only general music classes have no more special training in this area than the instrumental and vocal specialists.

Any teacher specializing in general music today requires a solid and up-to-date understanding of young people in grades 5 through 9—an understanding of not only their educational needs, but also their social and emotional needs, feelings, and interests. This teacher must honestly like to work with students in this age group and must be prepared to work with them by having an extensive knowledge of educational psychology; theories of learning; goal and objective levels as they influence long-range and daily instructional planning; the organization of structured learning experiences; the importance of conceptual learning as an integral part of the general education of all children; and the structure, literature, and materials of music covering a wide range of styles, forms, periods, cultures, and media. His knowledge of music cannot be confined to the literature he has learned in college music-survey courses. Rather, he must be intimately acquainted with all the basic types of music and well prepared to make himself familiar with any special types (such as regional ethnic music) as the need arises. Since music styles, particularly in the popular fields, are constantly changing, an ongoing program of self-education is a basic requirement for the teacher. This is particularly true if the teacher's familiarity with music is to be wide enough *and* deep enough to be applicable to a concept-oriented program that develops a student's perception for not just in-class experiences but, more important, out-of-school consumption of music, now and in the future.

Such a teacher must also have functional ability with *both* the keyboard and guitar, and have a voice specialist's knowledge of the changing voice. He must be familiar with the available instructional materials on the market, and be imaginative enough to develop his own materials (such as programmed tapes, charts, transparency overlays, and bulletin-board displays) when suitable materials are not available. And he must be able to make *effective use* of a variety of focal devices, including the phonograph, tape recorder, cassettes, overhead projector, and motion-picture projector. Because music education is such a broad field, it is obvious that no one but a specialist in general music could acquire all these characteristic attributes of a successful teacher. As in all other areas of the school curriculum, the success of a general music course will be a direct reflection of the organizational ability, musical excellence, leadership qualities, and personality of the specialist responsible for it.

Time Requirements and Scheduling

There is considerable divergence in practices regarding time allotment and scheduling for general music classes. The Music Educators National Conference has recommended that in the early middle-school grades, the equivalent of three thirty-minute periods per week at a minimum (and more realistically, the equivalent of twenty-five to thirty minutes of instruction daily—125 to 150 minutes weekly) is essential to the maintenance of a program with substance. With heavy curriculum demands on the school day, many schools do not accomplish this goal. It is suggested that in the departmentalized middle school, where classroom teachers do not introduce music at variable but opportune times daily to supplement the music specialist's program, a goal

of two or three periods a week of forty to forty-five minutes should be attempted in grades 5 and 6. In grades 7, 8, and 9, a minimum of two classes a week of forty-five to fifty minutes each is necessary, although three class meetings a week is preferable. (Some schools, with sufficient periods in the day to work with, have been able to schedule *daily* classes.)

In some situations classes meet only once a week, but this makes it difficult to provide a course that builds from one meeting to another and has a reasonable degree of continuity. Other schools schedule classes two or three times a week, but for only one semester or for a block of eight or ten weeks. This, too, is an inadequate plan since the short span of the course does not allow for the gradual development of changing voices, nor does it provide sufficient time to recognize individual needs. Furthermore, cumulative experience, which is necessary for the growth of conceptual understanding, is impossible to achieve with long breaks of musical inactivity, which (considering summer vacations) may extend to as much as eight months. Compared to this type of plan, even one meeting a week would be preferable if the class met for the full year.

At the junior-high level, then, an important goal for the teacher and administration to work for is three meetings a week for the full school year. In the many school systems where such a schedule is still a future goal, the challenge remains for the general music specialist to face the situation realistically and to organize what little time he has with the view that lack of time is not in itself a defeating factor. In the past, too many teachers have used lack of time as an excuse for an inadequate program. Much can be done by the *creative, highly organized* teacher in even one class meeting a week.

Another factor in scheduling is class size. The scheduling administrator in the school may be tempted to enroll large numbers of students in each section of general music. This is very likely based on the common misconceptions that students do nothing in general music but sing songs or listen to recordings, that there is no homework required, and that there is no individualized work. Certainly, if the course is to accomplish goals pertinent to contemporary education, then administrators must be made aware that classes cannot have more than twenty-five to thirty students enrolled in each section; that students should be grouped in terms of stages of learning rather than according to ability as reflected in other courses or by intelligence quotients or results of general testing programs; that outside preparation, though often eliminated in practice, is often as relevant to music classes as to other subject areas; and that the individual cannot be disregarded in *any* phase of education.

Many of the problems commonly encountered in scheduling general music classes are directly related to the formulation of objectives. Planning objectives is not a task for general music specialists and directors of music to tackle in secret. Rather, it should be a cooperative venture that involves the administrative staff. Only when administrators fully understand the needs of students in the area of general music, and are presented with specific, pertinent objectives and a substantial, relevant plan for a program will they take steps to ensure proper scheduling practices in order to realize the stated goals.

Equipment and Facilities

Concomitant with the notion that large music classes are satisfactory is the practice of scheduling these classes in rooms that can accommodate large groups. Auditoriums, stages, cafetoriums, and lecture halls are all sometimes used, and all are unacceptable. The physical arrangements within these "classrooms" do not lend themselves to stimulating music activity, nor to effective communication and intellectual exchange. To be sure, the general music classroom needs to be larger than the ordinary classroom because of space-consuming, special equipment and various types of activity that involve movement and the use of instruments. Nevertheless, the room must also be conducive to optimum communication and must lend itself acoustically to music presentations. Such a room should be situated away from other sound-producing classes in order to permit perceptive listening. It should also be provided with a large amount of storage space for equipment, and with bulletin boards, staff-lined boards, and regular chalkboards. Semicircular, permanent risers may also be desirable to facilitate performance activities.

Equipment and materials should naturally be of the finest quality possible within budgetary limitations. This is true not only in terms of obtaining the very best musical response, but also because of the wear that equipment is subjected to in the active music class. Every general music class should have at least the following equipment:

–A set of up-to-date basic textbooks for each level taught in that particular classroom, and in sufficient quantity to provide one copy to each student.
–Selected supplementary texts, reference books, and scores.
–A quality sound system and basic library of recordings to be supplemented by the school system's central recording library.
–A sound-on-sound, stereo tape recorder, having speeds of 3-3/4 and 7-1/2 ips, a frequency response of at least 30 to 16,000 Hz ± 2 db, output jacks for headphones and speakers, input jacks for microphones, and responsive microphones and speakers.
–Prerecorded and blank tapes.
–A piano.

—A 15-bar Autoharp.

—At least one guitar.

—At least one set of resonator bells.

—Bongo drums, a barrel drum, a tambourine, a triangle, a wood block, claves, maracas, and cymbals.

—Thematic charts and pictures of music subjects.

—Music manuscript paper or staff-lined duplicate masters.

In addition, it would also be desirable to have a few recorders, a screen for projections (preferably suspended), and a listening center equipped with headphones for individual study. Such focal devices as overhead, opaque, motion-picture, slide, and filmstrip projectors should be available from the school's media center, and facilities and equipment for making overhead transparencies would also be desirable.

In some middle schools, where the music specialist travels from classroom to classroom rather than teaching in a music room, this equipment should be available when it is needed. For this purpose, a portable music-equipment cart may be helpful for transporting large equipment or several items at one time.

To teach effectively, the general music specialist must have certain necessary tools of instruction. School administrators may have to be convinced that some of these are essential tools rather than teaching gimmicks, and this is a conviction that will arise only from successful teaching. Instructors who limit their classes to singing a few songs, listening passively to recordings, and occasionally watching a film are, of course, those who find themselves teaching large classes in large rooms with little equipment. General music today is much more. Taught successfully, general music can be stimulating, enjoyable, educative, relevant, and *musical*.

Discussion Questions and Projects

1. Select one of the rhythmic percepts given in this chapter and outline a presentation on three different levels of understanding to develop student perception. Include suggested teaching materials in your outline.

2. Write an outline for a unit of work in any one of the following areas: (a) American folk music; (b) music in the "Top 40"; (c) various types and styles of guitar music; or (d) writing a composition using nonmusical sound sources.

3. Write a course outline for a seventh-grade general music class, and then write course objectives.

4. Write a lesson plan for a general music class following the procedure discussed in this chapter.

5. What is the difference between an organizing element and an organizing center?

6. Write the percepts related to the concept of timbre. Then develop a lesson plan to teach one of these percepts to a seventh-grade general music class.

7. Assuming you are teaching a lesson involving the very basics of music theory, how are you going to involve students who have a good theory background and at the same time involve students who are just beginning to realize the need for understanding music notation?

8. Examine several state and school-system instructional guides for general music classes and evaluate their educational philosophy, goals, objectives, and recommended instructional units.

9. Compare basic music texts for sixth grade and eighth grade in terms of their effectiveness in a concept-oriented curriculum.

Selected References

ANDREWS, FRANCES M. *Junior High School General Music*. Englewood Cliffs, New Jersey: Prentice-Hall, Inc., 1971.

BRAND, MANNY. "Student Teaching: The Emotional Cycle," *Music Educators Journal*, 65:2 (October 1978), pp. 54–55.

COOPER, IRVIN, and KARL O. KUERSTEINER. *Teaching Junior High School Music*. 2d ed. Boston: Allyn & Bacon, Inc., 1970.

HELLER, GEORGE. "Meeting the Challenge of General Music," *Music Educators Journal*, 65:1 (September 1978), pp. 36–38.

HOFFER, CHARLES R. *Teaching Music in the Secondary Schools*. Belmont, California: Wadsworth Publishing Co., 1964. Chapters 12 and 14.

HUGHES, WILLIAM. *Planning for Junior High School General Music*. Belmont, California: Wadsworth Publishing Co., 1967.

LASKER, HENRY. *Teaching Creative Music in Secondary Schools*. Boston: Allyn & Bacon, Inc., 1971.

LEONHARD, CHARLES, and ROBERT W. HOUSE. *Foundations and Principles of Music Education*. 2d ed. New York: McGraw-Hill Book Company, Inc., 1972. Chapters 5 and 6.

MARPLE, HUGO D. *Backgrounds and Approaches to Junior High Music*. Dubuque, Iowa: William C. Brown Company, Publishers, 1975.

MARSH, MARY VAL. *Explore and Discover Music*. New York: The Macmillan Company, 1970.

MC KENZIE, DUNCAN. *Training the Boy's Changing Voice*. New Brunswick, New Jersey: Rutgers University Press, 1956.

MELLALIEU, W. N. *The Boy's Changing Voice*. New York: Oxford University Press, 1957.

MONSOUR, SALLY, and MARGARET PERRY. *A Junior High School Music Handbook*. 2d ed. Englewood Cliffs, New Jersey: Prentice-Hall, Inc., 1970.

REIMER, BENNETT. *A Philosophy of Music Education*. Englewood Cliffs, New Jersey: Prentice-Hall, Inc., 1970. Chapter 8.

WOODRUFF, ASAHEL D. *Basic Concepts of Teaching*. San Francisco: Chandler Publishing Company, 1961. Chapters 5, 6, 7, and 10.

——. "How Music Concepts Are Developed," *Music Educators Journal*, 56:6 (February 1970), pp. 51–54.

ZIMMERMAN, MARILYN PFLEDERER. "Percept and Concept: Implications of Piaget," *Music Educators Journal*, 56:6 (February 1970), pp. 49–50, 147–148.

Music
Listening
Classes

5

The combined efforts of composer and interpreter have meaning only in so far as they go out to an intelligent body of hearers.

AARON COPLAND[1]

People think you got to play music to understand it. That isn't right.

SIDNEY BECHET[2]

In 1923 Karl Gehrkens coined a phrase that has been repeated over and over through the years and has often been mistaken for an official slogan of MENC—"Music for every child, every child for music." Apparently his advice was taken seriously only in terms of the elementary school, for at the secondary level there is a change of focus in most school systems, with programs being offered mainly for a select group of students—those who wish to perform. We have seen, in Chapter 4, how a program for all students in the lower grades can be continued in the middle school and junior high school through a unified structuring of the general music class. Although music may not be required beyond the seventh or eighth grade, there is also a definite need to offer music courses at the senior high level in which the general student, as well as the music student, can continue to develop musicality, refine sensitivity, and expand understanding and enjoyment of the art.

Such classes are occasionally given under the label Advanced General Music. But because of the grade levels involved, the different

[1] Aaron Copland, *What to Listen for in Music*, rev. ed. (New York: Mentor Books, 1957), p. 162.

[2] Sidney Bechet, *Treat It Gentle* (New York: Hill and Wang, 1960).

approaches employed, and the direction toward refinement of experiences and understanding, these courses are more often, and more appropriately, identified by other titles —usually Music Appreciation, Music History, or Music Literature, but sometimes Introduction to Music, Understanding Music, Survey of Music, Advanced Music, or Music Listening. Each title may suggest a different approach and content: "Music History," for example, suggests a course that emphasizes facts, derivations, the evolution of forms, and so on—an emphasis that is more appropriate for a college music major. "Music Literature" implies a concentration on selected compositions or types of composition, but it does not necessarily imply the development of an understanding that would lend itself to subsequent experiences with other works or other styles not studied in class. "Understanding Music" is too general a title since the goal of all music courses, including those in performance, is to foster an understanding of music. And "Introduction to Music" is both a misplaced term (coming this late in the student's education) and another broad term that could be applied to a variety of offerings. The most widely used title has been "Music Appreciation," although the word "appreciation" has fallen into disfavor. As pointed out in Chapter 2, we can teach a student only to perceive, to comprehend, to understand—not to appreciate, since that is a value-laden personal response to what he perceives. Because this course is concerned primarily with developing perceptive listening abilities, the title used here is "Music Listening" (although it is recognized that listening skills are fostered in other courses as well).

It is often thought that this type of course is only for the special music student. While it is true that many of those who enroll are also members of the band, orchestra, or chorus, the music listening class is best organized in a way that will make it of value to *any* student, whether he possesses skills in performance or not. Consider the fact that all students are usually required to take a course in general science, and that this is followed by more specialized senior-high courses such as biology, chemistry, and physics. Rarely do we hear these courses described as being only for future biologists, chemists, or physicists; rather, they are intended to enlarge the general student's understanding of science and the scientific approach to knowledge through more specialized study. As such, they are open to and recommended for many types of students. Similarly, a course in general music should be followed by specific offerings in the areas of music listening and music theory (see Chapter 6 for a discussion of the latter) to serve the needs of the general student in his role as a consumer of music. Through a carefully organized music listening course, the student can enlarge his sense of personal involvement in music and can learn to listen perceptively, which leads successively to greater understanding, increased discrimination, more defined taste, and deeper enjoyment. It can help him develop his ability to reach independent aesthetic judgments as he discovers new types of music experiences throughout his life.

For many years we have heard that music appreciation cannot really be measured. There is truth in this since an individual's response is too personal and too indefinite to be gauged by any objective standard. More recently the term "appreciation" has been attacked from a different standpoint: it is unteachable. Again, this is a valid point, but it would be unfortunate if this should be misconstrued as a reason to abandon the objectives of the music-listening course. It simply suggests the need to recognize what *can* be taught as a foundation from which appreciation may emerge within the individual. Thus, it becomes the music educator's job to place the student in contact and communication with those materials, structures, techniques, and other aspects of music composition and performance that are *measurable, factual,* or *identifiable.* A knowledge and understanding of these factors, passed from teacher to student in and with a setting of enthusiasm, will enlarge the student's capacity to perceive the object of his music experience. The final aesthetic response—the degree or substance of "appreciation," as it were—begins and ends only within the student; this cannot be communicated.

FORMATS FOR ORGANIZING THE COURSE

Music listening classes have been organized in a variety of ways, but most are variations on two basic formats—the historical and the mixed unit. A historical presentation is employed not only in courses called Music History but also often in Music Appreciation or Survey of Music classes. Mixed units are commonly found in courses designated as Music Literature, Advanced Music, or Introduction to Music.

Historical Formats

Many history-oriented courses begin with a study of either Renaissance or baroque music, continuing with sections devoted to the classical era, romanticism, and the twentieth century. Others start with the origins of music and its rise from ancient times through the Middle Ages, before examining the development of Western music during the past four hundred years. Although this straightforward approach allows the student to view the history of music more clearly, its major flaw is that the student is subjected to a long period of relatively unfamiliar sounds before he reaches those styles of music that

are more familiar and easier for him to accept. Another disadvantage is the tendency to condense as the course nears its end in order that everything may be covered; the result is that twentieth-century music is apt to be dealt with superficially. To avoid these problems, occasionally a reverse-chronological format is employed, wherein the class studies contemporary music first, then moves back to the romantic era, and continues backward until it reaches ancient music. With this plan, sufficient time can be assured for contemporary music and the students will hear familiar styles early in the course. However, historical perspective is difficult to achieve through reverse chronology, and as the course continues the students are concerned more and more with periods of music from which they are far removed.

A popular arrangement that is an attempt to reconcile the problems of the other two historical formats is one that begins at a point of high interest—either nineteenth- or twentieth-century music. Then, by moving back and forth in a balance of older and more recent styles, all the major periods of music history are gradually covered. Generally, a second period of relatively high interest is left until the end of the course to assure a psychologically proper conclusion. Again, though, the main purpose of any historical organization is lost by the juggling of chronological sequence. In order to achieve historical understanding, certain basic facts must be repeated at various stages so that styles, forms, and other developments can be related.

A fourth related plan might be called "music history through great works." Here, a few works are singled out from each period for study. They are presented in historical sequence, but the emphasis is on the individual works rather than the over-all styles of the periods in which they were written. This tends to be more of a "literature" class and can easily result in a distorted image of the broad eras of which the selected works are a part.

Mixed-Unit Formats

Those courses that are organized by mixed units are based on the idea that music history is too much a cultural *science* and that it inhibits the study of music as an *art*. Instead, a group of topics is selected and a unit is developed around each one. Often, one major work is examined in each unit, although a few others may also be heard. For example, the Yale Curriculum Development Project proposed a course in music literature consisting of six units: music for the dance, solo instrumental music, chamber music, symphony, concerto, and opera.[3] In each unit major attention is given to an analysis of one work, which must stand, whether intentionally or not, as a representative of all such works in its particular genre. Such a course naturally limits the students' understanding to specific compositions, no matter how representative they may be.

Other courses are based on a study of basic structures and composite forms (opera, oratorio, concerto, symphony, fugue, sonata form, theme and variations), with numerous works being examined in each genre; this type of course is often historically arranged within each unit. Other courses concentrate on performance media (orchestral music including a diversity of styles and forms, band music, solo instrumental music, solo vocal music, and choral music). Still others have units based on an almost random selection of topics (the sonata, opera, folk music, art songs, music in America, tone poems, program music, dance styles, and so

on), with the result that a directionless conglomeration emerges, remindful of the typical junior-high general music class. In courses such as these, the student is seldom able to get a view of music in its totality, and he is often at the mercy of the teacher's own preferences. Even in courses that have a fairly balanced selection of topics, the student comes to know only a few major works, usually in such a way that his knowledge cannot be applied in listening to other compositions.

A Combination Format

Both the historical and mixed-unit types of course by themselves have serious drawbacks. Almost without exception, the history course —no matter how well it is organized—draws only upon music that has developed out of the European concert tradition (or "Western art music," as it is generally called). If we are to provide a music-listening course that recognizes the needs of today's students, as discussed in Chapters 1 and 3, then it is vastly important that all types of music be included in the course. This suggests a unit approach. Most mixed-unit courses, however, lack a central focus and give a too limited view of our music heritage. Rather than opening the door to musical understanding, they merely raise a few window shades that provide a glimpse from the outside of random interiors.

What is needed, then, is a course that has the diversity and interest of the unit format, offers the broader and more systematic perspective of the historical format, and is tied together by the clear direction and singleness of purpose necessary in any good organizational plan. Such a combination plan is proposed in the following section. It is a format that was developed over a period of several years with general high school students, and has been taught successfully as a full-credit, one-year course.

[3] See Kenneth A. Wendrich, "Music Literature in High School: The Yale Curriculum Development Project," *Music Educators Journal*, 53:7 (March 1967), pp. 35–37, 131–132.

A COURSE FOR TODAY'S STUDENTS

If we are to include all types of music in the course, we must have some form of organization that is fairly compact and yet all-inclusive. Since the time factor often requires a decision on what to leave out rather than what to include in a course, a highly organized format is necessary. It will allow the teacher to draw on more resources, involve the students in a wide variety of experiences within a limited time, reduce the time required for understanding important, basic concepts of music as a whole and individual styles in particular, and facilitate the ability to relate learnings acquired in different parts of the course with a minimum of activity designed solely for relationship. Despite the seemingly infinite number of styles heard throughout the world, five basic classifications have proved useful in organizing materials effectively.

The first broad category is *classical music*, embracing not just the "classical period" but developments from early times to the present day. Some might prefer the terms "art music" or "serious music," but these suggest that other styles are not artistic or serious in intent. Thus, "classical" is used here in its widest sense, meaning composed music that has had a tradition of significance prior to modern times and recent music that is an outgrowth of that tradition. A second main category includes *folk and ethnic musics* of the world's cultures. *Jazz* is a third category. Although some think of this as a type of popular music, most jazz—like classical music —appeals to a minority public and is entirely different stylistically from music in the popular field. A fourth basic category is *popular music,* from colonial hymn tunes and early, sentimental ballads to the present-day rock idiom. The fifth category is *music for the theatre,* which, aside from opera, relates to certain popular styles but is sufficiently different to warrant a separate category.

These five categories are the basis of units of various lengths; within all but the folk and ethnic unit, a chronological format may be employed for historical and developmental perspective. However, if the course is to move in a single direction toward perceptive listening and understanding, another unit is required. This would be an opening unit on elements of music and music structure that relate to all styles. Such a unit would need to draw on examples of many types of music to achieve an understanding of concepts that can be applied to the study of each particular style through the remainder of the course. In this way, the student will bring to each new topic a reserve of basic understandings that will simplify his approach to the new and will unify the course regardless of the diversity of materials.

Before examining individually each of these proposed units, or broad organizing centers, it is important to emphasize two points. First, we must keep in mind that in a course like this we are trying to develop the student's musicality to the point that he can function independently as a perceptive consumer of music throughout his life. No one can possibly learn all that might be desirable in approaching each new music experience. Even if it were possible at this point in history, the new styles of the future will require new understandings that are unforeseeable today. Nevertheless, an individual can be prepared to the degree that he can approach any new work or style *intelligently,* with the basic knowledge that will allow him to understand generally what is happening in the music and will allow him to delve deeper if he so wishes. To accomplish this, it is necessary to guide the student first in understanding fundamental concepts of music structure, general stylistic developments, and basic characteristics of different music idioms, from which specific understandings emerge. Psychologist Jerome Bruner has written that "one cannot 'cover' any subject in full, not even in a lifetime, if coverage means visiting all the facts and events and morsels. Subject matter presented so as to emphasize its structure will perforce be of that generative kind that permits reconstruction of the details or, at very least, prepares a place into which the details, when encountered, can be put."[4]

Thus, while it is desirable for the student to become familiar with certain works that we have come to consider as important ones in music history, it is more important to grasp an understanding of the broader period, style, or form of which such a work is a part. Otherwise, what he learns may not allow him to perceive independently the ingredients of other works he hears in the same field.

Certainly great works should be used in class; but the important thing is not to teach only individual works, however great they are. The important thing is to teach an understanding of what happens, has happened, and is happening—an ability to listen with involvement so that the student can meet any work in any style with the basic knowledge needed to come to understand it, judge it, and if it is good, enjoy it. In this sense, the memorization of themes and the college testing technique of dropping the needle in the middle of a record for identification are not useful; they are superficial devices. Similarly, such information as facts of composers' lives and detailed, lengthy analyses of single works should be deemphasized in favor of knowledge of the *principal traits* of baroque music, electronic music, cool jazz, concerto, fugue, or whatever the topic at hand may be. Those factors considered as fundamental elements and concepts in the opening unit will provide

[4] Jerome S. Bruner, *On Knowing: Essays for the Left Hand* (New York: Atheneum Publishers, 1967), p. 121.

the basis for such a characteristic approach (within a historical format) to each of the other units.

Secondly, it is important to consider the selection of music works that will be used for illustration and examination in the class. Within each unit, shall we use only those works that have been widely accepted as "great music"? Some educators feel that only proven works—those found in the standard concert repertoire—should be studied in class. Other works, particularly recent ones, are often avoided because the teacher is supposed to be in no position to evaluate them and make a decision as to their ultimate greatness. What difference does it make, though, what will be accepted in the distant future? We are living *now*, and we hear music *now!* Are we supposed to enjoy only music that is going to last for a hundred or two hundred years? Following this practice would mean that had we been living at the end of Bach's lifetime, we should probably have ignored his music because it was not then fashionable and his greatness was not to be widely recognized for another century. Living today, it would mean that we should not take time to examine a Stockhausen piece, a suite by Piston, an orchestral work by Boulez, or a Havergal Brian symphony, since these works may be considered insignificant a hundred years hence. In line with this thought, it would be well to review what composer Gunther Schuller stated at the Tanglewood Symposium of 1967:

. . . I think we must begin to de-emphasize something which our orchestras and our opera houses, and to some extent even our educational institutions, are overemphasizing: the "masterpiece." . . . If you look at music history in a proper perspective, you must recognize that each period yields very few masterpieces. We tend to expect a masterpiece every time we sit down to a new piece, and this is absurd. Music is constantly growing, constantly in a state of flux (as it should be), and you cannot in this experimental stage expect a masterpiece. We must get away from this masterpiece complex of thinking that everything really should please us in the way that the Schubert's *Unfinished* is able to please us. It leads to the museum approach, which is indulged in by so many of our famous performance institutions around the country.[5]

There is a place, then, for the music of second- and even third-rate composers in the music-listening class, as long as the music communicates something valuable to the student's understanding. If, for example, it is easier to hear a given technique in a certain work by Rossini or Borodin than in a particular work by Brahms, then the Rossini or Borodin should be used for initial exposure to the technique, even though they may not be "great" works. It should not be thought, though, that each new element to be explored requires the use of a new work in which that element alone stands out. Many works can be used over and over to illustrate different percepts, and by repetition of a single work, the student is already one step closer to understanding, since previous familiarity allows more immediate concentration on specific detail.

With these points in mind, let us consider what each of the proposed units might include.

Unit I: The Elements of Music

This unit should be an introduction to the most important concepts needed for an understanding of *any* type of music. Here the ingredients of music can be presented in layman's terms and then related to specific music

terminology, so that as the course progresses the precise music term is used more and more by itself until, in the student's mind, it has clear meaning with all its various shades.

It is important always to build from the simple to the complex, the general to the specific, and the concrete to the abstract. Thus, the unit might begin with an examination of the properties of the smallest building block, musical tone: pitch, duration, volume, and quality. The terms "pitch" and "duration" do not suggest teaching music reading. Reading is not necessary for perceptive listening. Students can still benefit from simple thematic charts and an occasional full score with just the ability to follow contour and *feel* metric organization. Tone can then be expanded into the three basic elements of rhythm, melody, and harmony.

At the outset, rhythm can be examined in terms of beat, accent, pulsation, meter, tempo, syncopation, and repetition. In successive units, as these factors are reexamined in new styles and new works, the student can grasp other concepts, such as polyrhythms, polymeters, irregular meters, specific types of accents, additive rhythms, the rhythmic basis of melody, the rhythmic organization of harmony, the effect of text on rhythmic selection, and so on. The opening unit, however, should examine only the fundamentals of rhythmic understanding. (See page 76 for a definition of basic percepts related to the concept of rhythm.)

Melody can be examined in terms of conjunct and disjunct motion, contour, range, climax, character and expression, sequence, repetition, and mode. Later, in studying certain styles, melody can be studied in terms of its vocal or instrumental idiom, its function and relationship to other parts, its development of material, and other matters. (See pages 232–235 for a definition of basic percepts related to melody.) Harmony, in the first unit, may be considered only in terms of

[5] Gunther Schuller, "Directions in Contemporary Music," in *Documentary Report of the Tanglewood Symposium*, Robert A. Choate, ed. (Washington, D.C.: Music Educators National Conference, 1968), p. 102.

consonance and dissonance, simplicity and complexity, action and resolution, homophony, and polyphony. Throughout the course, it, too, can be reexamined in greater detail. (See pages 259–260 for some percepts related to harmony.)

With a basic grasp of these elements, they can then be combined through principles of unity and variety to form complete works. Concepts of motif, phrase, and period can be studied, leading to understanding of basic structures such as binary, ternary, and rondo forms. (Broader percepts related to form are defined on page 165.) Finally, interpretive factors and principal performance media can be examined to round out the introduction.

The purpose of such a unit is not to make the student a master of basic elements, but simply to lay the groundwork and establish concepts and definitions for more specific explorations. These topics could also comprise a review unit at the end of the course, at which time all the units would be reviewed in terms of common threads rather than as self-contained items. Imagine, for example, returning at the end of the course to the single element of melody and drawing together fundamental concepts after having heard how melody has been handled in baroque music, serial music, jazz, folk music, Indian music, and eighteenth-century music. This is the type of understanding that will enable the student to come to grips with the wide variety of sounds he hears outside the school.

Such a beginning and ending is consistent with what Gerard Knieter has outlined as the four stages in the development of musicality.[6] The first stage is one of receptivity; it arouses response, whether that response is deeply emotional or superficially entertaining. Technical knowledge is not involved at this

point. The second stage is one of understanding. Here, musical intellect is added, and the student acquires the ability to identify elements and principles of structure. The opening unit described above would focus on this second level. Third, according to Knieter, comes explanation. This is a more specific, analytic stage that carries understanding from identification to explanation of what is happening. It is at this point that the student, through comparative listening, develops sensitivity to style and interpretation. This stage would be the principal goal of the following units in our proposed plan. Finally, there is a fourth stage of synthesis, which brings together previous experiences and results in self-directed discovery and intuition. The fourth stage is characterized by the ability to generalize in terms of concepts—an ability that, hopefully, grows throughout the course and is capped by a return at the end in a review of (or really, a new look at) basic ingredients. Robert Glaser, Director of the Learning Research and Development Center, University of Pittsburgh, has underscored the value of this last item by stating, "Generalization is a significant component of concept formation, and the influence of the analysis of subject-matter dimensions can be made most clearly when one considers the teaching of concepts. Many psychologists would agree that the basic procedure for teaching the ability to use concepts involves teaching the student to generalize within classes and to discriminate between classes."[7]

Unit II: Popular Music

Some educators feel that popular music should not be included in the curriculum because it does not require guided listening and

[6] See Gerard L. Knieter, "Musicality Is Universal," *Music Educators Journal*, 54:3 (November 1967), pp. 46–48, 113–116.

[7] Robert Glaser, "The Design of Instruction," in *The Changing American School*, John I. Goodlad, ed. (Chicago: National Society for the Study of Education, 1966), p. 221.

because teen-agers will feel teachers are trespassing on "their" music. We have presented a different attitude and position about this issue on pages 15–16. In addition, however, the teacher must realize there is a great deal happening in good popular music that escapes the ears of even devoted buffs, and teaching efforts *will* be accepted by the class if they are aimed at music analysis rather than useless comparisons with other styles of music. A brief historical survey could examine popular music from the time of William Billings to the emergence of Tin Pan Alley, and major styles of this century, including early and mature developments in the field of rock music. Analysis can relate to elements introduced in the first unit of the course, and might include an examination of song forms, relationship of parts, instrumentation, and the balance between music and lyrics.

The inclusion of a unit that examines rock music prior to units devoted to other styles has two strong points. First, it is psychologically sound because it will involve the students immediately in music that they are familiar with and receptive to. Second, because of familiarity with the idiom and the degree of interest, it is generally easier for students to grasp, early, an understanding of certain concepts than if they had to first discover these concepts in a concerto, aria, or symphony. For example, they can listen for changing meter in the Bee Gees' "Harry Braff" or in the Beatles' "Here Comes the Sun"; for irregular phrase lengths in The Who's "I Can See for Miles"; for bitonality in *Sgt. Pepper's Lonely Hearts Club Band* (which is also an example of a song cycle); for free rhythm in Jane Olivor's "Some Enchanted Evening"; for the use of synthesizers in Jean Michel Jarre's *Oxygène;* or for throughcomposition in the Jefferson Airplane's "Rejoyce."

This section of the course can be kept up to date by the teacher who keeps informed of current pop performers and their music, and who takes the few moments necessary to listen analytically to current recordings. This small investment of time on the teacher's part can pay off well in terms of student motivation, interest, and learning.

Unit III: Classical Music

The unit on classical music will undoubtedly be the longest in the course, consuming perhaps 45 to 50 percent of class time. How much of early music to include in a class for general students is a moot question. Most classical music that the student will hear will be from the baroque period on, although there has been increasing attention (especially through recordings) to Renaissance music, and an understanding of the rise of music in the Middle Ages may also be of some interest. The individual teacher must decide just how much of this is important for his students. If more than a brief sketch of prebaroque music is to be given, it may be worthwhile to break this unit into two parts, covering baroque music to the present immediately and deferring a study of early music through the Renaissance until later in the course. This plan has been used effectively because the division provides greater variety in the sequence of the course and a sufficient block of music history is still retained in each part to allow for historical understanding.

In either case, the section on early music is perhaps best undertaken in terms of large segments of time rather than individual topics. For example, it might be subdivided to include broad views of (1) the origins and functional uses of early music, and music of ancient civilizations; (2) music of the early Christian Church; (3) early polyphonic music; and (4) music of the Renaissance.

The principal part of the classical unit could be divided into (1) the baroque era; (2) the rococo and preclassical period; (3) the

114

Music Education Through Nonperformance Classes

classical period; (4) romanticism and post-romanticism; and (5) music in the twentieth century, with the largest share of time being given to the last period. In each of these areas, attention needs to be given to the contributions of principal composers; general characteristics of period styles; the melodic, rhythmic, and harmonic properties of the music; the treatment of thematic material; main forms and elements of design; instrumentation and orchestration; and interpretation.

There are various ways of organizing materials within each of these time segments. Working on the premise that an understanding of music forms and styles is more important than a study of individual composers, a practical and flexible approach is one based on forms and submovements within a period. Thus, each period could be examined in terms of (1) its general characteristics; (2) a study of common forms and genres; and (3) an introduction to the important composers, whose works will have been used in the first two parts.

Baroque music, then, might include examinations of opera, oratorio, cantata, chorale, and mass, as well as variation forms, fugue, free forms (prelude, toccata), suite, and concerto. The section on rococo and preclassical music would probably be concerned mostly with general stylistic traits, whereas the classical period would focus on sonata form, the symphony, the eighteenth-century concerto, chamber music, and vocal music. Topics for the sections on romanticism and postromanticism include program music; large instrumental forms such as the symphony, tone poem, concert overture, symphonic suite, and concerto; piano music; vocal music including opera and art songs; nationalism; and impressionism. An examination of twentieth-century music should consider the continuation of traditional approaches, such as nationalism, neoclassicism, and neoromanticism; and new approaches and techniques such as expressionism, primitivism, serial music, musique concrète, electronic music, and aleatoric music.

In selecting works to illustrate the trends in twentieth-century music, it would be desirable to avoid the common impression that such works as Stravinsky's *Le Sacre du printemps* or Schoenberg's *Five Pieces for Orchestra* are contemporary compositions. Music such as this from the earlier years in the century is certainly worthy of study, but it would be advisable to limit the number of older compositions and expand as much as possible on the use of "classics" of more recent vintage. Listening time might be devoted, for example, to Lou Harrison's *Symphony on G*, Benjamin Britten's *War Requiem*, Leonard Bernstein's *Mass*, Pierre Boulez' *Le Marteau sans maître* and *Pli selon pli*, George Crumb's *Ancient Voices of Children*, Krzysztof Penderecki's *Passion According to St. Luke*, Luciano Berio's *Sinfonia*, Olivier Messiaen's *Oiseaux Exotiques*, Edgard Varèse's *Deserts*, and Morton Subotnick's *Silver Apples of the Moon*.

A long list of topics such as this makes it appear that much more than one large unit might be needed to cover everything adequately. It must be reemphasized, therefore, that careful organization and planning is the key to the success of this type of course. A listener can function very well with an understanding of just the basic components of these forms and styles, and if topics are arranged in a logical sequence, facts learned about one form can be carried over to an understanding of another form. One does not have to start from scratch in undertaking each new topic. Nor should we underestimate the capacity of today's students to learn quickly and in large doses when the format for learning is well organized and well stocked. To do so results in much more than just a shallow course; it produces shallow students. As Wiley Housewright has pointed out, "Our low level of expectation begets what it sets out to achieve. It reduces aspirations, stifles motivations, and systematically destroys ego and self-concept."[8]

Unit IV: Jazz

Before examining some of the more important schools of jazz, an introduction to the topic could consider elements that are related to all developments in jazz history: jazz rhythm, melody, and harmony; improvisation and composition; instrumentation; and blues tonality and blues form. Rhythmic factors are especially important and include accent, syncopation, the triplet base, the suspended rhythm of the jazz break, and the concept of swing.

From this point, basic elements can be reexamined through a study of the origins of and early influences on jazz (including black religious and secular music, brass bands, and ragtime) and through various jazz styles. Among the jazz styles to consider are classic New Orleans jazz, Dixieland, the later New Orleans style, Chicago style jazz, the classic blues, boogie woogie, the Harlem jazz style including stride piano, New York Dixieland, the jazz of Kansas City and the Southwest, the early big bands, swing and the big bands of the 1930s and early 1940s, jazz of the revival era, bebop, progressive jazz, cool jazz, the West Coast school, hard bop and funky jazz, and the new styles that developed in the 1960s and 1970s, including free-form jazz and the jazz-rock fusion.

Available time will determine how many of these schools can be considered. The most important ones to include in order to give an overview of major developments are classic New Orleans jazz, Chicago-style jazz, swing

[8] Wiley L. Housewright, "Confrontation with Tomorrow," *Music Educators Journal*, 55:9 (May 1969), p. 27.

and the big bands, bebop, cool jazz, and the current movement. In examining the contributions of key figures, the teacher should certainly draw on the recordings of Louis Armstrong, Jelly Roll Morton, Bix Beiderbecke, Duke Ellington, Benny Goodman, Count Basie, Charlie Parker, Dizzy Gillespie, Miles Davis, Thelonious Monk, Ornette Coleman, and John Coltrane. However, a variety of recordings by other jazz musicians should be heard as time permits.

Just as a "basic repertoire" of classical music exists, there are also "classic" recordings of jazz performances that might well serve as the nucleus of class study. These recordings include King Oliver's "Dippermouth Blues," Jelly Roll Morton's "Black Bottom Stomp," Louis Armstrong's "West End Blues," Bix Beiderbecke's "Singin' the Blues," Meade Lux Lewis' "Honky Tonk Train Blues," Coleman Hawkins' "Body and Soul," Count Basie and Lester Young's "Lester Leaps In," Duke Ellington's "Harlem Air Shaft," "Concerto for Cootie," and "Ko-Ko," Dizzy Gillespie's "I Can't Get Started," Charlie Parker's "Ko-Ko" and "Embraceable You," Miles Davis' "Boplicity," Thelonious Monk's "Misterioso," Sonny Rollins' "Blue 7," the Modern Jazz Quartet's "Django," and Ornette Coleman's "Lonely Woman," among others.

Unit V: Folk and Ethnic Music

This unit requires almost entirely a characteristic rather than historical organization. It might begin with a study of the oral tradition and communal re-creation, as well as a concentration on folk and ethnic musics of the United States. This would include the main currents of the British and African traditions, a survey of folk styles around the country, the styles of American Indian music, and possibly the music of other American cultures.

Segments of the unit can also examine general characteristics of the ethnic musics in the following regions of the world: Oceania, Northeast Asia, Southeast Asia, South Asia, West Asia and North Africa, Africa south of the Sahara, Europe, and North, Central, and South America. These categories, though inconsistent with some of the major geographic divisions of the world, are generally accepted by ethnomusicologists as representative of significant regional differences in music. Although ethnic music differs considerably from one small region to another, even within a single country, some general rhythmic, melodic, harmonic, instrumentation, and social characteristics can still be pointed out for each of the eight large areas.

In considering Oceania, the teacher might draw on recordings of the Australian didjeridoo, traditional Hawaiian chant and dance music, or music of the Maori in New Zealand. Northeast Asia could be represented by Japanese koto music, gagaku (Japanese court music), music for the Noh drama and Kabuki theatre, Chinese opera, and kayakeum music of Korea. Southeast Asia offers the sounds of the Javanese gamelan, traditional Thai music, and the music of Balinese shadow plays. The music of India, which has received considerable attention in the United States (both through the travels of Ravi Shankar and through its influence on the Beatles and others), provides the principal literature of South Asia. Here the teacher can use recordings of the sitar, tabla, and tambura; of the two classical traditions—Hindustani music of northern India and Carnatic music of the southern region; and perhaps music from the dance-drama Kathakali.

From the region of West Asia–North Africa, there is the music of the Uzbeks (Afghanistan) and the folk songs and dance music of Arabic countries, including music to accompany the dubka, a common folk dance. Africa south of the Sahara offers a wide range of music, which, contrary to the popular image, involves much more than percussion instruments. There is vocal music with hand clapping and foot stomping from South Africa, xylophone music from many areas, music for the sanza or mbira found throughout Central and East Africa, and the music for membranophones, aerophones, and chordophones from numerous areas.

European folk traditions offer a broad spectrum of styles and instruments. Of particular interest might be music for the bagpipe (found not only in the Scottish highlands but also in many parts of Europe), the eight-stringed (four sympathetic) hardanger fiddle or *hardingfele* of Norway, the struck dulcimer of Eastern Europe and the Balkans, the Irish *ceili* band, and dances from Spain and Greece. In the Americas, besides the strong traditions of Afro-American music, Indian music, and Anglo-American folk song, there is a wealth of interesting material in Peruvian Indian music, the steel drum music of Trinidad, the music of Afro-Bahian cults in Brazil, the Hispanic folk music of Argentina, and the music of the mariarchi orchestras of Mexico.

Recordings of ethnic musics from around the world are plentiful. Probably, the teacher's greatest difficulty is in selecting a few representative styles from all that is available. Since much ethnic music is not easy for Western ears to accept immediately, the receptivity of the particular class to "new sounds" may be a deciding factor. The ethnic population of the local community should also have some bearing on the choice of material. Although it is not expected that students will really get to know the music of Japan or Africa or Oceania during the course of a brief unit, they can learn much from ethnic musics about rhythmic organization, melodic refinement and embellishment, instrumental timbres, and the social significance of music.

Unit VI: Music Theatre

Opera is perhaps best covered in the unit on classical music because of style considerations, its relationship to other classical forms, and the fact that some of the major opera composers also wrote other types of classical music. Principal composers for the popular music theatre, on the other hand, have rarely written music for purposes other than the stage.

A variety of types of musical shows could possibly be presented in this unit, but the important topics are American operetta, musical comedy, and musical play. Operetta would take in the music of Victor Herbert, Sigmund Romberg, and Rudolf Friml, drawing on the scores of such productions as *The Red Mill, Naughty Marietta, The Desert Song, The Student Prince*, and *Rose-Marie*. An examination of musical comedy should certainly include the contributions of George M. Cohan (*Little Johnny Jones, Forty-Five Minutes from Broadway*), Jerome Kern (the Princess Theatre shows, *Roberta*), Richard Rodgers (with Lorenz Hart: *The Garrick Gaieties, A Connecticut Yankee, On Your Toes, Babes in Arms, Pal Joey*), George Gershwin (*Girl Crazy, Of Thee I Sing*), Cole Porter (*Anything Goes, Jubilee, Kiss Me Kate*), Irving Berlin (*Annie Get Your Gun, Call Me Madam*, and scores for the Ziegfeld Follies and Music Box Revues), Frank Loesser (*Guys and Dolls, Where's Charley?*), and Jerry Herman (*Hello, Dolly; Mame*), and possibly the music of Vincent Youmans (*No, No, Nanette*), Arthur Schwartz (*The Band Wagon*), Jule Styne (*High Button Shoes, Bells Are Ringing, Gypsy, Funny Girl*), Harvey Schmidt (*The Fantasticks*), Meredith Willson (*The Music Man*), Burt Bacharach (*Promises, Promises*), Quincy Jones (*The Wiz*), and Cy Coleman (*Annie*).

A study of the musical play, as opposed to musical comedy, would necessarily include Jerome Kern once again (*Showboat*), Richard Rodgers (with Oscar Hammerstein II: *Oklahoma, Carousel, South Pacific, The King and I, The Sound of Music*), Frederick Loewe (*Brigadoon, My Fair Lady, Camelot*), Leonard Bernstein (*On the Town, Wonderful Town, Candide, West Side Story*), Burton Lane (*Finian's Rainbow*), Frank Loesser again (*The Most Happy Fella*), Jerry Bock (*Fiorello, Fiddler on the Roof*), Kurt Weill (*Lady in the Dark, Lost in the Stars*), Galt MacDermott (*Hair*), Stephen Schwartz (*Godspell, Pippin*), Andrew Lloyd Webber (*Jesus Christ, Superstar*), and Marvin Hamlisch (*A Chorus Line*). This section might also include the works of Robert Wright and George Forrest (*Song of Norway, Kismet*), Lionel Bart (*Oliver*), Mitch Leigh (*Man of La Mancha*), John Kender (*Cabaret*), and Stephen Sondheim (*Company, A Little Night Music, Sweeney Todd*).

Since the development of the musical play, this field has been primarily one of theatre and secondarily of music. Attention should be given, then, to the elements of dramatic construction as they relate to musical factors. Distinct melodic and rhythmic styles, and the integration of music and nonmusic aspects, can be compared through examples of each of the main types of musical production.

Thus, one proven format for the music listening class can be summarized by the following outline.

Unit	Approx. Portion of 36-Week Course
I. The Elements of Music	3 weeks
A. Dimensions of tone	
B. Basic elements	
C. Design elements	
D. Performance media and interpretation	

Unit	*Approx. Portion of 36-Week Course*	Unit	*Approx. Portion of 36-Week Course*

II. Popular Music   3 weeks

  A. The rise of popular music in America

  B. Basic styles from Tin Pan Alley to rock

  C. Music analysis of the pop–rock idiom

III. Classical Music   17 weeks

  A. Early music through the Renaissance

  B. Baroque music

  C. Rococo and preclassical music

  D. Music of the classical period

  E. Romanticism and postromanticism

  F. Music of the twentieth century

IV. Jazz   4 weeks

  A. General characteristics

  B. Traditional jazz styles

  C. Big-band-styles

  D. Modern jazz styles

V. Folk and Ethnic Music   4 weeks

  A. The oral tradition

  B. Ethnic musics of the United States

  C. Musics of Oceania

  D. Musics of Northeast Asia

  E. Musics of Southeast Asia

  F. Musics of South Asia

  G. Musics of West Asia-North Africa

  H. Musics of Africa south of the Sahara

  I. Folk musics of Europe

  J. Musics of North, Central, and South America

VI. Music Theatre   2 weeks

  A. Operetta

  B. Musical comedy

  C. Musical play

VII. Synthesis: a Review of Music Materials   3 weeks

  A. Rhythm

  B. Melody

  C. Harmony

  D. Form

  E. Performance media

  F. Interpretation

  G. Style

IMPLEMENTING THE COURSE

Teaching Suggestions

1. At the beginning of the course, students want to know where they are headed —partly out of curiosity and partly out of a desire to know that their destination is worthwhile and relevant. Moreover, they need to have a brief overview so that they will know in advance how each segment of study fits into the whole, and so they will know not only where they are headed but why. It is important, too, to draw relationships as the course progresses, between different styles and between examples of other topics of study. This does not mean comparison in the sense of the old practice of weighing one form against another to see which is better. Each type of music should be examined for its own values. Since each has its own tradition of practice and serves varying functions, it is fruitless to judge one type by the criteria of another. Those factors that make one concerto better than a second concerto are not necessarily the same factors that make one musical play better than another play, or one jazz performance better than another jazz performance. Nevertheless, while evaluative comparisons should be avoided, relationships between the use of materials from style to style and from form to form can be valuable. This is a type of synthesis that can be practiced to advantage *throughout the course.*

2. Students should have some form of reading matter for each unit. If the course has the scope of the one proposed in this chapter, a single textbook will not serve the need. Still, it would be possible to prepare and duplicate for each unit a brief discussion of the important points to be covered, so that students can read in advance about what will be covered in more detail in class and so that they will have some written material for reference and review. The class should also be encouraged to keep notebooks on daily instruction.

3. Class time is best used for listening, discussion, analysis, and synthesis. A good deal of the necessary historical and background information can be given in assigned outside reading, either in textbooks or in the teacher's own duplicated discussion of a subject. This does not mean that such information, along with interesting sidelights, should not be mentioned in class, but it does mean that lengthy discourse should be avoided when the material can be completely introduced by other means.

4. It is valuable to prepare discussion questions that will lead students to discover for themselves what is happening in music examples they hear. Students may also be encouraged to submit their own discussion questions for use at the end of a unit as a means of review.

5. In class discussion, work toward an increasing use of specific music terminology as the course progresses, and encourage students to cite works heard in or out of class as examples of what they are discussing.

6. Each topic—whether it is a unit, a section within a unit, or a specific work—needs to be launched from a point that is of interest and value to the students. There also needs to be some connecting point in moving from the conclusion of one topic to the opening of the next.

7. In examining facts about a style or form, present items one at a time with illustration. Trying to hear several different details simultaneously is difficult and confusing to someone who is not already familiar with them individually. These items can still be pulled together and related after each has been developed by itself. In addition, as new works are introduced, the discovery technique should be employed so that students can analyze the music themselves, perceive elements previously studied in terms of other works and styles, perceive new elements, and draw relationships among all the styles and forms that have been examined.

8. Experiment with programmed tapes on which works for analysis are presented in a sequence of whole, parts, and whole. The portion of a tape containing segments may present recordings of isolated themes, phrases, rhythms, harmonic progressions, developmental techniques, and so on, as they appear in sequence in the complete work, building from a small part to a larger part to a still larger section of the music. Programmed tapes may also be used to compare sections of a work out of sequence, or to relate material in one work to material in another. Such a technique is particularly valuable for an opening unit that draws on many styles of music. For example, programmed tapes may be prepared on such topics as melody, rhythm, and instrumentation. In addition, programmed tapes with commentary can be valuable for individual assigned listening outside of class.

9. In studying a work, it is important to obtain an impression of the whole composition before examining its parts. Then the main point to be illustrated can be focused upon with some familiarity of its setting. If a work is to be heard not just as an example of one point, but because of the importance of the entire composition, specific aspects of it should be presented in a logical sequence of detail. For example, after first hearing the entire composition or a complete movement, the class could focus its attention successively on the medium of performance, melody, melody and rhythm, harmony, form, style, and interpretation. Finally, the entire selection should be heard again as a whole.

10. Music that is heard in class should be available for further examination by interested students. This may be achieved by making the music room or a separate listening room available to students outside of class time. A headphone listening center may be set up within the music facilities or in the school library. Or, students may be allowed to sign out recordings for home listening when those recordings are not immediately required for classroom use. It would also be desirable for the library to include a number of recordings not listened to in class for the purpose of comparative study and free exploration.

11. It is not necessary that each work heard in class be used in more than one class period. To do so would limit the breadth of experiences needed and, most important, would discount those selections that are valuable for clarifying certain points but not worthy of extended examination in terms of the objectives of the class. Nevertheless, a basic list of outstanding selections should be made up and drawn upon over and over

throughout the course so that the class is exposed to important works more than a single time.

12. After directed listening with a new work, try replaying a previously studied selection of a related style or form to see if the students can discover the ways in which a familiar work is similar to or different from a work they have just heard.

13. Many students come into the music-listening class with preconceived ideas of what music should be or what certain types are all about. It is important to develop an open-minded approach to all types of music and to dispel common impressions such as (a) most music tells a story or conveys a literal message; (b) the mood of the selection represents the composer's feelings at the time he wrote it; (c) the listener should assume the same mood as the music; (d) there is a specific way to listen to each type of music; or (e) those elements you listen for in one type of music should be expected in another type if it is good.

14. One way of making class experiences relevant is to use school performing groups whenever possible in place of recordings. These can be heard either live or on tape. Individual students in class may also be called upon for performance to illustrate certain works, forms, and styles.

15. Although full scores may be valuable from time to time for certain members of the class, it is helpful to prepare simple thematic charts for use by the full class. Charts may also be used for other purposes, such as to show the organization of a standard form or to outline the progression of sections in a specific composition. Thematic and diagrammatic materials can also be presented effectively by using an overhead projector and transparent overlays. Such devices help to direct the listening.

16. Students should be encouraged to undertake individual projects in any area of music that is of special interest to them. A course that covers a broad range of styles is likely to include some topic that is especially appealing to the individual student to the degree that he would be willing to do a special investigation on his own. The results may be reported to the class as a whole at various points throughout the year (a more interesting procedure than a series of assigned reports delivered at the same time).

Provisions for the Course

A music-listening course like the one outlined in this chapter needs to be scheduled as a major subject, meeting daily for a full year and offering full credit. It is also desirable, though, whenever it can be managed, to offer a one-semester course meeting two or three times a week for students whose schedules do not permit them to enroll in a larger music class. The one-semester course may be designed as a literature class or as a mixed-unit course that expands upon the proposed first unit of the music-listening class. One plan would be to compile a list of basic works that can be used repeatedly during the semester to illustrate various concepts. This would allow the teacher to develop the course simultaneously as one devoted to important literature and as one devoted to an understanding of broad stylistic elements. It is important, however, to include more than just a basic repertoire of classical works. If the units are organized around such topics as sound sources, rhythm, melody, harmony, form, and performance media, then the listening material for *each* unit can draw on the resources of classical music, rock, jazz, ethnic music, music theatre, and so on.

Sufficient time alone is not the only requisite for a well-organized course. Music-listening classes also require a well-equipped room. Minimum equipment includes a chalkboard and bulletin board, a piano, a quality phonograph, a well-stocked library of recordings, a few basic reference books, and thematic charts. A more complete list of desirable materials would include the following:

–phonograph
–tape recorder
–piano
–headphone listening center
–large, varied record collection
–blank, prerecorded, and programmed reel-to-reel tapes and tape cassettes
–turntable-tape deck for preparation of programmed tapes
–regular chalkboard
–music-lined chalkboard
–bulletin boards
–music scores
–charts of themes, of the relationship of schools, styles, and forms, of seating plans, and so on
–pictures of composers, musicians, music organizations, and instruments
–reference books on music
–supplementary texts and biographies
–current music magazines
–availability of film projector, filmstrip projector, overhead projector, opaque projector, television, and radio

The most important provision for implementing the course is naturally an enthusiastic and qualified teacher. A class that is involved in such a wide range of music materials requires a teacher who feels comfortable with many styles. It is impossible for any teacher to be totally prepared solely by his college training. He must, on his own, extend himself in many musical directions and keep up to date on what is happening. Many teachers assume they are doing this when they rely on standard music literature texts and on special materials produced for the educational market; this is a dangerous practice, however, because of the false information and distorted views most of these sources provide in areas outside of classical music. The teacher must turn to separate authoritative sources in each field. Bennett Reimer has stated that "the subject matter chosen for study must be fundamental to the discipline *as the discipline is conceived by the expert in the discipline.*"[9] And John Goodlad has echoed the fact: "The content used in the organizing center must be authentic and important to the field, *as determined by leading scholars in it.*"[10] Keeping accurately informed can be achieved by attending concerts and music events of various kinds, purchasing an eclectic assortment of record-ings, and reading books, periodicals, and newspapers regularly. In addition to publications in the field of music education, it is valuable to subscribe or have regular access to specialized magazines in the areas of classical music, jazz, ethnic music, popular music and rock, and general music topics.

[9] Bennett Reimer, "The Curriculum Reform Explosion and the Problem of Secondary General Music," *Music Educators Journal,* 52:3 (January 1966), p. 40. (Italics added in quotation.)

[10] John I. Goodlad, "The Curriculum" in *The Changing American School,* John I. Goodlad, ed. (Chicago: National Society for the Study of Education, 1966), p. 40. (Italics added in quotation.)

Projects

1. Draw up a list of fifteen basic compositions, and list as many topics as possible that each may be used to illustrate.
2. Compile a list of important elements, techniques, and concepts that apply in general listening to any style of music.
3. Select one composition and prepare a group of discussion questions that could be used to enable students to discover what happens in that work.
4. Select one element or technique, and prepare a list of materials that could be used in an examination of it. Include a wide variety of types of music, styles, forms, and performance media. Also list appropriate films, still pictures, and charts.
5. Prepare two or three outlines for a one-semester music appreciation course, and determine the advantages and disadvantages of each. Do the same for a two-semester course.
6. Develop some ideas for actively involving students in an examination of aleatoric music, electronic music, communal re-creation in folk music, and jazz improvisation.
7. Research one of the following subjects and determine the principal music concepts that could be illustrated by use of the music in class: gagaku, Chicago-style jazz, musical plays of the 1960s and 1970s, music of the Yoruba peoples of Nigeria, rock of the late 1960s, music of the Pueblos, bebop, musique concrète, black spirituals, ragtime, or the music of Elliott Carter.

Selected References

ABRAHAMS, ROGER D., and GEORGE FOSS. *Anglo-American Folksong Style.* Englewood Cliffs, New Jersey: Prentice-Hall, Inc., 1968.

BELZ, CARL. *The Story of Rock.* New York: Oxford University Press, 1969.

BUGGERT, ROBERT, and CHARLES B. FOWLER. *The Search for Musical Understanding.* Belmont, California: Wadsworth Publishing Company, 1973.

COHN, NIK. *Rock from the Beginning.* New York: Stein & Day Publishers, 1969.

COLLIER, JAMES LINCOLN. *The Making of Jazz.* Boston: Houghton Mifflin Company, 1978.

COPE, DAVID. *New Directions in Music, 1950–1970.* Dubuque, Iowa: William C. Brown Company Publishers, 1970.

ENGEL, LEHMAN. *The American Musical Theater.* New York: CBS Records, 1967.

EWEN, DAVID. *Panorama of American Popular Music.* Englewood Cliffs, New Jersey: Prentice-Hall, Inc., 1957.

GEORGE, LUVENIA A. *Teaching the Music of Six Different Cultures in the Modern Secondary School.* West Nyack, New York: Parker Publishing Company, 1976.

GREEN, STANLEY. *The World of Musical Comedy.* New York: Grosset & Dunlap, Inc., 1962.

GROUT, DONALD J. *A History of Western Music.* Rev. ed. New York: W. W. Norton & Company, Inc., 1973.

HARTSHORN, WILLIAM C. *Music for the Academically Talented Student in the Secondary School.* Washington, D.C.: National Education Association, 1960.

HODEIR, ANDRE. *Jazz: Its Evolution and Essence.* New York: Grove Press, 1956.

JONES, LE ROI. *Blues People.* New York: William Morrow & Co., Inc., 1963.

LA RUE, JAN. *Guidelines for Style Analysis.* New York: W. W. Norton & Company, Inc., 1970.

MALM, WILLIAM P. *Music Cultures of the Pacific, the Near East, and Asia.* Englewood Cliffs, New Jersey: Prentice-Hall, Inc., 1966.

NETTL, BRUNO. *Folk and Traditional Music of the Western Continents.* 2d ed. Englewood Cliffs, New Jersey: Prentice-Hall, Inc., 1973.

REIMER, BENNETT, and EDWARD G. EVANS, JR. *The Experience of Music.* Englewood Cliffs, New Jersey: Prentice-Hall, Inc., 1973.

SALZMAN, ERIC. *Twentieth-Century Music: An Introduction.* Englewood Cliffs, New Jersey: Prentice-Hall, Inc., 1967.

SCHWADRON, ABRAHAM A. *Aesthetics: Dimensions for Music Education.* Washington, D.C.: Music Educators National Conference, 1967. Chapters 3 and 4.

SCHWARTZ, ELLIOTT. *Electronic Music: A Listener's Guide.* New York: Holt, Rinehart and Winston, 1975.

SMITH, BARBARA B., ed. *Music in World Cultures.* Washington, D.C.: Music Educators National Conference, 1972.

SOUTHERN, EILEEN. *The Music of Black Americans.* New York: W. W. Norton & Company, Inc., 1971.

THOMSON, WILLIAM. *Introduction to Music as Structure.* Reading, Massachusetts: Addison-Wesley Publishing Co., 1971.

WILDER, ALEC. *American Popular Song: The Great Innovators, 1900–1950.* New York: Oxford University Press, 1972.

WILLIAMS, MARTIN T. *The Jazz Tradition.* New York: Oxford University Press, 1970.

YATES, PETER. *Twentieth-Century Music.* New York: Pantheon Books, Inc., 1966.

Music
Theory
Classes

It is possible to look at music, theorize about it, philosophize over it,
but until the mind through the ear can perceive, comprehend, and remember
the sound itself, little is accomplished, for music must be realized
in the ear of the listener.

HOWARD HANSON[1]

CLASSES DEALING with the manipulation and organization of the basic
components of musical sound (pitch, duration, intensity, timbre), and
with their related concepts, percepts, and symbolic representations (notation), appear in the curriculums of many high schools. Such courses are
offered under a variety of titles: Harmony, Theory of Music, Elements of
Music. Music Fundamentals, Essentials of Music, Basic Musicianship,
Comprehensive Musicianship, and occasionally, Composition. For many
years, music educators and administrators held that the instruction given
in these theory courses should be reserved for the musically talented.
This view has been negated, however, by current success in working with
general students at various grade levels in the development of conceptual
understanding through theory instruction—especially through compositional activities. The theory teacher with insight and an understanding of
the multiplicity of music needs within one student body finds it necessary to abandon the monolithic, one-track approach to teaching theory
and provide for the musical growth of both those students who are planning to become professional musicians and those whose interests are
strictly avocational. Whether or not the latter become dabblers in composing music or in playing in a community symphony or rock group, they

---

[1] Used by permission of Mr. Hanson.

can all become better listeners through a theory course. The musical insight, understanding, and independence gained can contribute greatly to raising the level of their musicality and aesthetic sensitivity.

Regrettably, what is presented in the typical high school theory course is often limited in scope to the techniques of what is called the "common practice" period—the seventeenth, eighteenth, and nineteenth centuries. This is limiting because, as John R. Fitch has noted:

> "Common practice" has not been the common practice of the majority of serious composers for at least seventy years. Each year the practices of living composers push the common-practice period further into the past; each year the distance between theory instruction and current practice becomes greater. By standing still, theory instruction moves backward.[2]

In a first-year harmony class, for example, considerable time and effort is often devoted to teaching conventional notation, the tonal organization of major and minor scales, a little sight-singing skill, facility in traditional four-part choral writing, and some aural skill through rhythmic, melodic, and possibly harmonic dictation. Although such an approach has validity in terms of its contribution to the individual student's musical growth, it is nevertheless quite restrictive. It neglects (1) nontraditional notation associated with electronic and aleatoric music; (2) other tonal systems, including twelve-tone, pentatonic, and whole-tone scales, European modes, Oriental modes, and some of the unique scales devised by composers; (3) chords that are not tertian in structure but are built on seconds, fourths, or fifths; (4) multimetric change, polyrhythm, free rhythm, and addi-

tive rhythm; (5) the relationship of harmonic practices studied in class to musics of the present era; (6) opportunities for creative composition within the framework of the harmonies being studied in class; (7) opportunities for free composition, extending beyond class studies; (8) improvisational techniques that are applicable to the student's major instrument or to vocal performance; and (9) opportunities to write for instruments and to deal with their range and transpositional problems.

The limited scope of the harmony course seems to be perpetuated by the belief of some teachers that a strong "traditional" background is necessary before a student should be introduced to more contemporary practices. Another factor is undoubtedly teacher timidity in digressing and exploring beyond the traditional approach to which they themselves have been exposed. Still, it is possible to expand the content of the course, even with beginning theory students. For example, a unit on melodic writing, generally limited to major and minor modes, can easily be expanded to include experiences with twelve-tone serialization; church modes; pentatonic melodic construction; some of the modes of the Near East, such as the Ahavch Rabboht (see Figure 6-1); whole-tone melodies; and

FIGURE 6-1

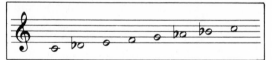

unique scales devised by composers, such as the half-step, whole-step structure created by Olivier Messiaen (see Figure 6-2).

The teacher who wants to extend his harmony class beyond conventional bounds will necessarily have to plan his work beyond the confines of one harmony textbook. Similarly,

[2] John R. Fitch, "Twentieth-Century Students Should Start with Twentieth-Century Techniques," *Music Educators Journal*, 59:8 (April 1973), p. 46.

FIGURE 6-2

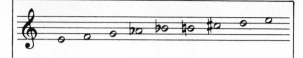

the student who is to work creatively with the variety of available techniques will have to be provided with recordings, scores, and books related to the particular tonal system and harmonic practices within which he will compose. Such an approach will involve much more preparation on the part of the teacher and increased expenditures for materials, but the differences are certainly worthwhile in terms of involvement, relevancy, and personal growth. The theory teacher, who works with the very materials used by the composer for creative expression, must not hesitate to be equally creative in developing new approaches to organizing theory for learning.

ORGANIZING THEORY FOR LEARNING

To plan theory instruction in the high school involves a number of fundamental considerations: (1) the use of basic principles such as providing a creative atmosphere, basing theory in concrete experiences, and making instruction functional; (2) the outlining of course content and its scope; (3) the development of a sequence of instruction; (4) the planning of multilevel instruction; and (5) the provision for individual projects.

Basic Considerations

Many musically talented students have difficulty in their initial encounter with music theory. One of the main reasons has been pointed out by theory professor Robert W. Sherman:

. . . they have been placed under the yoke of a dominating teacher who envisions himself as a crusading taste maker. Such a teacher insists on having the student compose, perform, or even listen according to the manner in which he or others of authority do. Such students are never allowed to work out solutions of their own. By contrast, the teacher who stimulates the student's imagination through creative problem solving is the teacher who prepares the student for a life of continued growth and accomplishment.[3]

Theory often becomes what Sherman has called "a kind of activity related to the idea of painting by numbers."[4] Students are encouraged to work only within the framework of techniques devised by recognized composers, and have little opportunity to use their own imaginations. Although the study of these techniques is important, it can stifle creativity unless it is used as a cornerstone upon which the student can build and develop his own ideas.

Creativity is a basic consideration and ought to be one of the prime outcomes of the theory class. If the student's creative imagination is to be developed, he needs to have many opportunities to compose freely, *prior* to studying how others compose. He must learn to select and manipulate music materials without outside influence. By becoming aware of problems involved in composition through personal experience, and by working out his own solutions, his subsequent study of traditional and contemporary compositional practices will be more meaningful, for they will relate directly to his own work.

A second basic consideration in teaching theory is that instruction should be based

[3] Robert W. Sherman, "Creativity and the Condition of Knowing in Music," *Music Educators Journal,* 58:2 (October 1971), p. 22.

[4] *Ibid.*

upon practices found in music literature. That is, the point of departure should be an analysis of specific works of music that contain the particular theoretic concept to be examined, rather than a presentation of a series of meaningless rules and regulations, introduced abstractly and reinforced through artificial and contrived exercises. In the study of cadences, for example, the student will find it more meaningful to hear and analyze standard as well as pop literature to discover how, when, where, and why cadences are used than to merely memorize the chord progressions that make up familiar cadences. The student can gain further understanding by finding and analyzing cadences in the music he performs in band, orchestra, or chorus, and by harmonizing related exercises or creating original compositions.

Another consideration is that theory instruction must be relevant and functional. The danger here is in viewing relevancy and functionability only in terms of twentieth-century music practices. Although these practices should receive *increased* attention, we must consider relevancy and functionability as they relate to the totality of music practice. The present inequity caused by concentrating theoretic study upon eighteenth- and nineteenth-century practices would not be removed if, instead, the same amount of time was spent exclusively on twentieth-century techniques. The result would be just another inequity. Relevancy and functionability must be viewed in terms of what particular knowledge, understanding, and skill the student needs to solve his particular music problem; this relates not only to contemporary music, but also to music of the past, which is still a part of the music culture of the present era. The teaching of traditional harmony should be continued, as Hindemith said, because it has not been replaced by any other system that has been more universally recognized and adopted. But in presenting this material,

the teacher must "give the student what he needs in *condensed* form and with constant emphasis on the purely historical basis and only relative practical value of his study of harmony, and then try to make him acquainted with more far-reaching methods of harmony. Instruction should be speedy; but . . . not careless. . . ."[5]

The course content suggested in the following list includes both traditional and contemporary techniques. The list is presented here simply as a checklist and does not represent a sequence of instruction. Using this as a guide, the teacher can work out his own plan for first- and second-year theory courses, beginning with either current or past practices, or a combination, and balancing the traditional with the contemporary in a sequence that will best fit the educational scheme of his particular school and also meet the specific needs of each student.

Content of the Theory Curriculum

I. Basics

Clefs, staves, note and rest values, meter signatures, measure and bar lines, key signatures, major scales, forms of minor scales, major-minor relationships, dynamic and tempo marks, structural symbols, accidentals, transposition, traditional sound sources (ranges and timbres of voices and instruments).

II. Traditional Practices

Triadic harmony: primary triads (I, IV, V) and inversions; the dominant seventh, its inversions, and resolutions; cadences; secondary triads (ii, iii, vi), the leading-tone triad (vii°), and their inversions; nonharmonic tones; aug-

[5] Paul Hindemith, *Traditional Harmony*, book 1, rev. ed. (Rockville Centre, New York: Belwin-Mills Publishing Co., 1968), p. 3.

mented triads; nondominant seventh chords; secondary dominants; modulation; diminished-seventh chords; modal interchange; chords of the ninth, eleventh, and thirteenth; the Neapolitan chord; chords of the augmented sixth; altered chords; two- and three-part counterpoint; melodic and rhythmic style.

III. Contemporary Practices

Whole-tone, pentatonic, and original scales; modes; chord scales; microtonal systems; secondal (tone clusters), quartal, and quintal chords; polychords; atonality; serialization; pandiatonicism; bitonality and polytonality; polyrhythm, polymeter, and alternating meter; free counterpoint; pointillism; new sound sources; techniques and notational systems of musique concrète, electronic music, aleatoric music, and chance music; melodic and rhythmic styles.

Sequential Courses

In determining the content and organization of a first-year theory class, the teacher will be influenced by such factors as the number and availability of interested students, the number of years of theory to be offered, the flexibility of the school schedule, the availability of time in the teacher's schedule, and the attitude of the administration toward music electives. Ideally, Theory I should be offered in two sections—one class for students with a high degree of musical competency who may be interested in music as a career, and a second, parallel class for those whose interest may be avocational and whose music backgrounds are limited. However, in many school situations it is impossible to organize the course into two separate sections, and the teacher must either limit membership to the musically proficient or work with students on several ability levels within one class. The second alternative—a dual-, triple-, or even quadruple-track course—is highly recommended.

Whatever organizational plan is adopted for the first-year course, it is advisable for the teacher to meet with all prospective students prior to the closing of school in June for planning purposes. At that time, he can determine the level of each student's musical competency. This may be accomplished by administering a teacher-made written test related to such basics as key signatures, note values, meter signatures, scale construction, and so on; through a tool such as the Colwell *Music Achievement Test*[6] to measure auditory discrimination; and perhaps through some graded material for sight-singing. The teacher should also determine what instruments, if any, are played by each student, the number of years of study, and the level of his technical proficiency. Finally, the student's personal reasons for electing the theory course can be solicited. Having this information prior to the summer vacation will give the teacher sufficient time to assign students to the proper theory section, or if only one class is offered, to organize it on more than one ability level.

A second-year theory course is a necessity if the students are (1) to be offered the full range of the curriculum outlined above; (2) to have sufficient opportunities for creative work in composition; (3) to become familiar with both traditional and contemporary practices in music literature through analysis, performance, and listening; and (4) to learn the basics of improvising either vocally or on their instruments. The students who are usually interested in continuing their

[6] Richard Colwell, *Music Achievement Test* (Chicago: Follett Educational Corporation, 1969).

Table 6-1. THEORY II—STUDY OUTLINE

Unit 2: Six-week Assignment, November 1–December 18

Traditional Practices

DOMINANT SEVENTH CHORD

Structure	page _____	(Teacher would
Regular resolution	page _____	indicate here the pages of the student's
ii V⁷ progression	page _____	text where these
ii⁶ V⁷ progression	page _____	subjects are covered.)
IV V⁷ progression	page _____	
IV⁶ V⁷ progression	page _____	

NOTE:

Familiarity with the above material is necessary before you can complete the work in this section.

ASSIGNMENT:

Complete the exercises on pages _____. Continue to use the nonharmonic tones covered in the previous unit.

Contemporary Practices

QUARTAL HARMONIES

Read Chapter 4 in *Twentieth Century Harmony* by Vincent Persichetti (on reserve in the library).

ASSIGNMENT:

Complete exercises 5, 7, and 8 on page 107. Study the following material. Scores and recordings are on reserve in the library: Webern, *Piano Variations*, Op. 27, pages 5–6 of score; Copland, *Piano Fantasy*, page 2 of score.

Original Compositions

Compose two short compositions for piano and bassoon—one in traditional style and the other using quartal harmonies. Refer to pages 87-90, on the bassoon, in *The Technique of Orchestration* by Kent Kennan (second edition on reserve in library). Prior to writing, listen to recorded excerpts of music for bassoon (check in music office for available recordings).

Introductory sessions will be held after school from 2:45 to 3:45. Traditional practices, November 1; contemporary practices, November 18.

theoretic studies are those who have had significant success and satisfaction during their first year. Even though there may be a small number of students who wish to continue, some provision should be made for them. If the main problem lies in finding time in the teacher's schedule, then the use of multilevel planning will make it possible either to group all of the second-year students together (those with both vocational and avocational interests in music) or to schedule the interested second-year students in the same class with the beginners. If neither of these plans is possible, the teacher could probably still meet with these students periodically and make long-range detailed assignments. Once a student has completed an assignment and his progress has been evaluated, another long-range assignment can be made. Whenever necessary, the teacher may arrange for individual or group meetings during study periods, before school, or after school. Although this procedure is not entirely satisfactory, it does provide the continuing students with the opportunity to gain new theoretic knowledge, understanding, and skill, and to retain those concepts learned during the first year. An example of the type of long-range assignment that could be organized for several musically talented students is given in Table 6-1.

Finally, provision must be made to assist the most advanced and talented students in individual theory projects oriented toward creative composition. Such projects, determined by student interest, might include (1) arranging for a stage band, rock band, orchestra, wind ensemble, or a variety of instrumental combinations in small ensembles; (2) composing a work in sonata form for selected instruments; (3) composing a theme and variations for one or more instruments; (4) composing songs for various vocal combinations, as well as solos with piano or other instrumental accompaniments; (5) creating electronic music, when suitable equipment is available; and (6) writing a short music drama, opera, or Broadway type of musical.

To support a theory program of this scope, well-furnished facilities are needed. The music room should be furnished with a piano, phonograph, tape recorder, overhead projector, staff-lined chalkboards, and regular chalkboards. Facilities should be available for making transparencies and programmed tapes. An adjacent listening room with phonographs and tape recorders would be desirable, as well as practice rooms with pianos. Necessary materials include a well-stocked library of tape and disc recordings, blank tapes, manuscript paper, scores, a basic textbook, and supplementary reference materials.

Multilevel Planning

Theory classes should be limited to no more than fifteen members, and should meet as often as other academic subjects for full credit. Even with such a small and seemingly select group, the teacher must be prepared, after the first few weeks, to organize the class on more than one ability level in order that each student may have the opportunity to grow musically at his own rate. Since students who enter a high school theory class will have diverse music backgrounds and ability levels, it is inconceivable for them all to progress uniformly. The student who has studied flute for seven years and piano for four years and the rock guitar player who is creative in his own right but cannot read music should both have equal opportunity for musical growth as a result of the theory class. But if there is only one set class pace, it cannot serve both of these students equally well. On the high school level particularly the theory teacher must organize his class with room for considerable flexibility.

In organizing a multilevel theory class, the main problem is in keeping all levels involved in learning during the regular class period, especially when the teacher must devote a large segment of class time to the instruction of a particular level. Table 6-2 is a page from the weekly plan book of a teacher who seems to have solved the problem. He has organized his class on three levels, using programmed materials, annotated listening lessons, a staggered exam schedule, and dictation and sight-reading activities that include all the students but on their respective levels.

Behavioral objectives for level I of the week's plan shown in Table 6-2 might be stated as follows:

As a result of this week's work in Theory I, the student will:

(1) Harmonize an eight-measure soprano melody in the key of G minor, using the tonic, subdominant, and dominant chords in root position; only the root or

Table 6-2. MULTILEVEL PLANNING

		THEORY CLASS LESSON PLANS – THREE LEVELS			
LEVEL	MONDAY	TUESDAY	WEDNESDAY	THURSDAY	FRIDAY
I, II, III:	Remind all levels that original, free composition is due on Friday.				
I 2 Students	1. Return homework, make corrections. 2. Chordal dictation (I, IV, V) in Listening Room A (piano). Material prepared by teacher, played by students.	Full-period written exam on i, iv, V. Soprano given. Use passing and auxiliary tones.	1. Return exam. 2. Review modes on piano and at board. 3. Write and play modes in class.	1. Planned listening to simple modal compositions with annotated scores. 2. Collect homework.	1. Collect original compositions. 2. Melodic dictation: correct rhythms and pitches. 3. Sight-reading: all skips, major and minor, pp. 45–60.
Homework:	Review sheet and exercise for exam.	Read chapter on modes.	Workbook: Original melodies (8 measure). All modes.	Complete original compositions.	Prepare to perform original compositions in class.
II 4 Students	Return originals for final changes. Make revisions in class.	1. Exchange homework for analysis of chord connection. 2. Check final progress on originals.	Full-period written exam on I, IV, V. Given bass.	1. Return exam. 2. Review harmonization of melodic line. 3. Work out exercises in class. Pass in.	1. Collect original compositions. 2. Melodic dictation: correct pitches only. 3. Sight-reading: scale, tonic skips. Major and minor, pp. 29–39.
Homework:	Exercise: Given bass, i, iv, V in root positions.	Review sheet and exercise for exam.	Read section on harmonization of melodies.	Complete original compositions.	Prepare to perform original compositions in class.
III 1 Student	Review of minor scales. Use transparencies in Listening Room B. Record player needed.	1. Check original. 2. Analyze melodies to determine, both visually and aurally, whether major or minor tonality.	1. Write homework on board. Needs manuscript writing experience. 2. Have Level I student play while Level III student listens for accuracy.	Full-period written exam on major and minor scales. Aural and written.	1. Collect original composition. 2. Dictation: determine if meter is duple or triple; also rhythmic pattern of melodic line. 3. Sight-reading: Scale progressions, major and minor, pp. 9–12.
Homework:	Work on original. Clean up rhythmic problems.	Compose 8-measure melodies, beginning on G in major and minor.	Review sheet for exam.	Complete original composition.	Prepare to perform original composition in class

fifth of each chord may be doubled, and common tones are to be carried over whenever possible; three passing tones and three auxiliary tones are to be used in the soprano, alto, or tenor parts; and contrary motion between the bass and the three upper parts is to be used in a subdominant-dominant progression, avoiding parallel fifths and octaves. No more than forty-five minutes will be allowed to complete the harmonization, and five mistakes or fewer will be considered passing.

(2) Aurally identify chord progressions consisting of tonic, subdominant, and dominant triads in major keys. Fifteen examples will be played and discussed, after which twenty more examples will be played, each twice, for identification. All examples will be played on the piano. Four mistakes or fewer will be considered passing.

(3) Sing at sight (using movable "do") melodies in major keys that move by step and by skips within the tonic chord, that are in $\frac{2}{4}$, $\frac{3}{4}$, $\frac{4}{4}$, and $\mathۃ{C}$ meters, and that are notated in both bass and treble clefs. The note values to be used will be 𝅝 𝅗𝅥 𝅗𝅥. 𝅘𝅥 𝅘𝅥. 𝅘𝅥𝅮 𝅘𝅥𝅮. 𝅘𝅥𝅯 and their equivalent rest values. The student will identify the key and the syllable on which each melody begins. The tonic chord will then be played for him, the tempo will be established, and he will begin when ready. All melodies must be sung without rhythmic or melodic mistakes.

(4) Aurally-visually identify modal melodies heard on tape and analyzed by score, by writing the name of the mode (for example, "Dorian on C"), notating its scale, and indicating the intervallic structure of the scale. Fifteen examples will be played, and four mistakes or fewer will be considered passing.

The success or failure of multilevel planning depends entirely on the teacher's theory background, knowledge of materials, creativity in developing his own materials, and most important of all, ability and flexibility to organize and implement preplanned activities that operate on several tracks in one class at the same time. Students who are members of such a class must understand that their musical growth in theory will be evaluated in terms of their own individual growth as it relates to the increased degree of knowledge, understanding, and skill that has been acquired. They are not in competition with other students, and they are not expected to cover the work in the same depth nor to achieve on the same level.

Individual Theory Projects

A third-year theory course should be devoted entirely to creative composition. Since the number of students who reach this level will be relatively small, a daily scheduled class is unnecessary. Instead, student-teacher conferences may be arranged during study periods or before and after school. After working with each student for a short period of time, the teacher will quickly determine which students can work without much direction and which will need a more detailed, structured type of program to follow.

To ensure success, a procedure similar to the following needs to be established: (1) The students should be allowed to determine the type, style, form, and length of each composition they create, with the teacher making suggestions only to effect a balance in the year's work. (2) Periodic check-up sessions need to be scheduled in order to evaluate each student's progress and to help with problems that arise. (3) The teacher should be specific in assigning the minimum amount of work to be accomplished between check-up sessions.

(4) Students should know that the teacher is available any time help is needed. (5) Necessary scores and recordings should be available in the school library for reference and assigned study. (6) All compositions should be performed. Therefore, it may be advisable to write for those groups that are available within the school and to schedule a program for their presentation.

Once the student has identified his area of interest, the teacher will want to provide additional impetus. For example, a student who is a baritone and is interested in vocal performance may choose to compose a group of songs for himself with piano accompaniment (or with possible expansion to other instrumental accompaniment if time permits). In such a case, it would be desirable for the student to learn how composers from various stylistic eras have handled this type of composition. He could be given listening and analysis assignments involving such works as Franz Schubert's *Die Winterreise*, Op. 89, Robert Schumann's *Dichterliebe*, Op. 48, Antonín Dvořák's *Gypsy Songs*, Op. 55, Ralph Vaughan Williams' *Five Mystical Songs*, Irving Fine's *Childhood Fables for Grownups*, and Carlisle Floyd's *Pilgrimage*. Recordings or scores for these works must be made available to the student.

As a result of this type of assignment, the student should become familiar with each composer's stylistic techniques as they relate to melodic and harmonic structure, rhythmic patterns, motivic material and development, key relationships within and between songs, the synthesis of words and music, the form of each song and of the entire cycle, the suitability of text relationships among the songs, the style and function of the accompaniment, the relation of the vocal line to the accompaniment, and the suitability of the vocal range. During the check-up sessions scheduled during the listening-analysis period, the student should be encouraged to peruse various library sources for lyrics suitable for music settings. The amount of time taken to complete this initial assignment will depend entirely on the student, who may listen to one or two suggestions and then make his decision, or may listen to all the suggested works, reject them, and set out on something completely different and completely personal in style. The student who wants to try his own "thing" ought to be encouraged, unless the teacher discovers after a few sessions that little or no progress is being made. At this point, and especially if the student is getting discouraged, the teacher will have to provide specific, well-structured directions.

The success of this type of flexibly organized individual project depends, first, on the teacher's background in music theory, composition, and orchestration, and on his knowledge of music literature, recordings, and standard reference materials. Secondly, it depends on the availability of scores, recordings, and various source materials in the school or public library. Finally, and most important of all, it depends on students who have talent and creative potential (much more plentiful than is generally expected on the high school level), and who have received opportunities for creative expression as well as suitable theoretic experience and background during their previous two years of study.

TRADITIONAL MODES OF LEARNING

The traditional modes of learning in the theory class have been experiences in harmonization, dictation, analysis, and performance. The degree of involvement in each of these areas will be determined by the teacher as he works with his class. Although each is discussed separately in the following sections for clarity, it should be realized that these areas are interrelated and need to be integrated in class.

Harmonization

Learning the skill of four-part harmonization should foster musical values rather than simply an accumulation of routine techniques. This requires beginning with *music* rather than with a set of rules; aural experiences should precede the establishment of "common practices." Because the conventional approach to harmonic writing is so firmly established, emphasis needs to be placed on understanding the nature of the so-called rules of four-part harmonization. Actually, there are no such things as "rules" of harmonic writing; rather, there are a number of procedures or common practices that established composers have used in their music down through the years, and which are worth noting while one is developing a foundation in harmony. It is best to refer to these procedures as "practices" or "principles"; alert students can find examples by the most eminent composers to illustrate how rules have been broken. Regardless of the number of semesters or years a theory course is offered in the high school, students should be introduced to contemporary practices along with those of the seventeenth, eighteenth, and nineteenth centuries. It is not necessary to teach harmonic practices in their chronological order, thus leaving contemporary procedures to the end of, say, a second-year course. Both traditional and contemporary idioms can be learned simultaneously.

The conventional practice of learning part writing through the study of figured bass actually has little value for theory students today. Historically, its only functional value was to enable a keyboard performer to realize the inner voices of an accompaniment.

The student should be given a certain amount of instruction in the use of figured bass; he should have an opportunity to create the inner voices when soprano and bass lines are given; and he should be directed to give attention to developing a strong bass line in support of a melody. Beyond this, there is little value in working with figured bass. Much more attention needs to be given to the creation of melodies and their harmonization.

In teaching harmonic practices, the teacher may wish to give thought to using programmed instructional materials (see Chapter 8). Considerable class time can be saved by the use of programmed texts or even computer-assisted instruction, especially in teaching traditional practices. This can leave the teacher free to concentrate on and plan more thoroughly for experiences with contemporary practices, harmonic usage in rock and jazz styles, and integrating harmonic writing with other areas of the course.

Listening

An important form of listening experience in the theory class is ear-training through dictation. Planning appropriate instructional strategies in this area should involve the following considerations: (1) The teacher should use dictation materials that parallel the particular aspect of theory being studied in class. That is, if the class is studying the natural, harmonic, and melodic forms of minor scales, then melodic dictation based on minor scales would not only be logical but would act as a reinforcing agent. (2) As much as possible, dictation materials should be selected from practices found in music literature. However, the teacher should not hesitate to create his own material if it will help students solve a particular problem in perceiving certain rhythmic, melodic, or chordal factors. (3) If it is to be effective, the ear-training portion of the class must be planned as a regular occurrence, not as a filler for the last few remaining minutes of a class session or when nothing else has been planned. (4) To ensure that the desired aural skills are organized sequentially, the teacher should arrange his materials in a simple to complex progression. In melodic dictation, for example, scalar passages could eventually be coupled with tonic chord skips, then with skips of a third outside the tonic chord, and so on.

Some theory teachers believe that all material used for dictation should be presented as a unified whole, without separating the elements. Those who have worked extensively with high school students, though, realize that such an inflexible approach can actually hamper aural perception. For example, in beginning experiences in chordal dictation for a written response, the student is faced with the multiple problem of making specific identification of each chord, its voicing, and its rhythmic designation. In this case, it might be more advisable to present the chord progression without a definite rhythmic pattern, so that students with limited experience can concentrate on the task of classifying the multiple tones they perceive. Another possible procedure is to achieve a balance in the difficulty of the dictated pitches and rhythms; that is, if the major difficulty lies in the identity of pitches, then the level of rhythmic complexity should be reduced, or vice versa.

Developing aural awareness of music structure is at the root of all theoretic learning. Dictation, however, is sometimes thought of as an end in itself, rather than as one means toward perceptive listening in all music experiences. Whenever possible, listening experiences should be integrated with other theory instruction—at the piano, through live ensemble performances, or by use of recorded materials. It is a natural process, for example, to introduce listening experiences in conjunction with the study of certain chords, instrumen-

tation, or forms. Music on paper is nothing but symbols; the development of the "hearing ear" is much more. Haydn stated it aptly when he said, "The only arbiter of music is the trained ear." Schumann put it even more positively: "The training of the ear is the most important of all."

Analysis

All study of music is, in a sense, analytical. The student of music, the listener, the performer, and the composer are all involved in analysis as they search for musical insight and understanding. Theoretic analysis is a very exacting activity in which the eye, ear, and mind focus collectively on specific relationships in the music under consideration. This activity is given little attention in high school theory courses. Yet, when theoretic instruction evolves from the study of actual music, rather than from a series of exercises, analysis of music literature becomes a major part of the learning process.

Analyzing music by eye is an obvious path to pursue because notated music is tangible. One can see all the "tones" (notes), dwell on certain aspects, and bring the flow of music to a halt in order to resolve an analytical problem. The more challenging approach, though, and the real proof of music perception, is analysis by ear. All analysis should be closely allied with aural impressions, even if the eye is making the initial contact with the music. The best results are obtained through a combination of ear and eye. For example, analysis by reading the score during a performance is ideal.

Melodic and rhythmic analyses are means by which one can develop a facility for music reading and listening, and at the same time gain insight regarding the structure of music. Melodic contour, phrasing, scales, accidentals, intervals, and many other aspects of music structure can be observed by analyzing the melodic content of a composition. Concepts of beat, meter, durational relationships, rhythmic groupings, and so on can be developed through analysis of the rhythmic properties of a work.

This phase of the program makes its greatest impact in the area of harmonic analysis, including both the structure and function of chords. Harmonic classification is presented in a variety of ways by authors of textbooks. There is some variance in the manner of labeling chords, although identification by Roman numerals, figured bass, or letter names is somewhat standardized, with only minor self-styled adaptations that are not difficult to understand. In the area of the function and relationship of chords, however, authorities go their divergent ways. The theory teacher would be wise to select a particular approach in which he feels secure and to use that approach consistently throughout the course.

Recognition of form or design is another area to which analysis can contribute. Form is the "glue" of music. The longer the composition, the more important it becomes that it be based on a definite design; otherwise, the work will fall apart aesthetically. For heightened awareness and sensitivity to music, the theory student should become familiar with the basic elements of form (unity, variety, balance), elements of formal development (motif, phrase, sentence, sequence, inversion, transposition, and so on), and with selected standardized forms (binary, ternary, rondo, sonata, and variations). The astute musician does not listen to music for the specific purpose of discerning its form or structure, but he is sensitive to form and allows it to affect his musical responsiveness. Through analysis the student can gain understanding that will sharpen his perception in listening.

Analysis should also be extended into the consideration of style. Style may be viewed as the product of the collective efforts of a group of people at a particular time in history; music has a number of general stylistic properties that enable us to place a composition into a certain historical period. Style may also be viewed in terms of a number of individual or personal aspects that allow us to identify a particular creator of music. In addition, there are qualities and characteristics of music that lead us to define style in relation to regions (the Viennese style), techniques (the fugal idiom), genres (an operatic style), or media (a pianistic style). Response to style can begin with broad generalities and be refined to specific aspects of the manner in which the elements of music are handled. Through aural and visual analysis of music, students can learn to identify particular schools of composition. The truly astute musician is one who can stylistically analyze a composition down to the point of naming the person who created it.

Performance

Every possible resource for the performance of materials prepared or studied in class should be used, for theoretic study is a "dead experience" unless it is related to actual musical sounds. Students should sing music examples and exercises in four-part vocal writing, rather than have them played regularly on the piano. (Common sense tells us that music conceived for voices should be reproduced in the medium for which it was intended.) In addition, students who play instruments should be asked to perform class work whenever the material being studied is appropriate to performance on available instruments.

The piano is an especially valuable tool in the theory classroom, and ought not to be restricted to use by the instructor. Keyboard experiences provide students with a means for reinforcing music understandings gained in other areas of class activity. The piano is also an excellent resource for general creative exploration, as well as for the realization of composed music. Of all the instruments available, the piano is certainly the most versatile for use in the theory class: a student can play melody, harmony, or both; he can use it to search for sounds that he hears in his mind but somehow has been unable to write; he can use it as a graphic tool for visualizing music relationships; and he can employ the keyboard for improvisational work. Furthermore, he can do this with a minimal amount of playing technique. Viewed in this way, experiences at the piano become much more than is suggested by the common nomenclature for such theory-class activities—"keyboard harmony."

Harmonization at the keyboard offers an interesting departure from the written approach, and is not beyond the capabilities of many high school students, even if they have limited piano backgrounds. This type of performance activity is essentially a mental rather than a physical one; thus, technique and finger dexterity are unimportant in comparison with harmonic understanding. Students should attempt to "think" a harmonization before striking it. Those who approach keyboard harmonization through a trial-and-error process are explorers who must strive to relate their explorations to theoretic concepts. Opportunities must be allowed both for the student who hears something but is not able to think accurately of what is needed theoretically, and for the student who wants to explore sounds freely without any preconceived concepts of what to expect.

Keyboard work can begin with the performance of given chords in selected keys and with certain stylized chord progressions. From there, attempts should be made to cultivate skill in harmonizing melodies at the piano, and finally work can extend to improvisation.

Sight-singing experiences are another as-pect of performance. It is particularly important that activities related to and emphasizing music-reading skills not be approached as monotonous drill work. Rather, they should be integrated with experiences of all types. For example, written exercises that have been put on the board for analysis can be sight-read; student compositions or melodies from standard literature being examined for style can be used for reading material; and other excerpts from listening, writing, and analyzing experiences can be adapted to improve reading skills. Enjoyment and personal satisfaction should be inherent properties of a good sight-singing program.

Integrated Experiences

As the student works to develop his theoretic knowledge, understanding, and skill, the teacher must also work to integrate the opportunities for writing, analyzing, listening, composing, reading, and performing. Learning is reinforced as these activities are brought together. If, for example, the topic of study is the dominant thirteenth chord, pupils should have the opportunity to hear it used in selected recorded works, write it in harmonic exercises, identify it visually in reading scores, identify it aurally in brief passages being performed, employ it in original compositions, and play it at the keyboard in various keys and within various progressions. Or if the topic is melodic structure, the students can analyze melodies in scores, listen to works in several styles by master melodists, write harmonic exercises in which the melody is not given, compose melodic variations on an original theme in various styles, and improvise melodies vocally or instrumentally. Through a combination of activities, knowledge of a particular topic will be solidified and retained, understanding will be deepened, and skill in employing the principles that have been learned will be broadened. Numerous techniques are available to the teacher who thinks in terms of a comprehensive, varied program of theoretic studies.

It is advisable to use a basic textbook as a point of departure and as a reference source for the students. However, many theory courses are constricted because the teacher never deviates from the sequence of the assignments in the book. In order to balance the course, he must determine what other learning materials he and his students will need and make them available in the classroom or school library.

LEARNING BY COMPOSING

Composer Paul Creston wrote that ". . . musical composition is not for the chosen few, but for every normal person; . . . it should be as much a part of academic studies as literary composition—not necessarily to make professional composers of everyone, as we do not intend to make authors of every student of literature, but for the joy of individual creation."[7] Creative ability is a universal quality, one that all people possess, only in varying degrees. Creativity is the main function of self-expression.

The use of compositional activities to develop music understanding has been especially successful in classes for those with little musical competency. It has been proven that students need not wait until they have acquired "enough" skill with traditional notation before they are given the opportunity to compose. With the compositional approach, students are assigned a composition after the very first class. These initial experiences may begin with the creation of compositions for

"nonmusical" objects or vocal sounds, or with the scanning of a given set of words (to discover accents and implied rhythmic patterns), after which students are encouraged to improvise a melody vocally to fit the words. From these very first assignments, it is important to require students to notate all their compositions, even if they have to invent their own notation systems. In this way they will quickly discover the necessity and value of a standard system of notation so that compositions may be played by all performers, not just by the composer. At this point, concepts related to traditional notation can be presented in a more meaningful frame of reference.

The teacher who uses the compositional approach must be ready to provide each student with a variety of creative problems that will necessitate acquisition of additional theoretic knowledge, understanding, and skill in order to be solved. A number of simple procedures may be used to get students involved in composition immediately. Vocal improvisation to a given lyric is one way. Another is an extension of this idea: group improvisation based on a general plot idea for a scene, but without predetermined words. The result will be a sort of mini-opera, conceived through an improvisatory theatre experience. In addition to the creative activity itself, this type of episode can help beginners overcome their initial hesitancy in creating freely without restrictions. Other possibilities for initiating composition are to have the students begin with:

1. *a rhythmic or melodic motif*. Once the opening idea has been set forth, most students are eager to try to elaborate on the idea, expanding and developing it into a full-fledged composition. They may work on a rhythmic score alone, or they may attempt to develop their work melodically as well.

[7] Paul Creston, "A Composer's Creed," *Music Educators Journal*, 57:7 (March 1971), p. 36.

2. *a tone row.* Starting with a random arrangement of a half-dozen or more pitches, without any rhythmic pattern, students can experiment with setting the tones to various rhythms, and then develop these into phrases, sections, and a complete work.

3. *a chordal sequence.* Using a brief, predetermined sequence of chords (as simple as I-V-I or I-IV-V-I), the students can explore the tonal possibilities to determine what melody tones can be used with each chord. Through a process of selection, trial, error, selection, and evaluation, a composition can be developed.

4. *a scale.* Beginning with a major, minor, or modal scale (and not necessarily with the scale of C major), students can experiment at the piano or on bells in putting together interesting tonal and rhythmic patterns from the available pitches.

5. *a stylistic concept.* Through listening to recordings of music in a selected style, the rhythmic, melodic, harmonic, and formal characteristics of that style can be discovered. Then, the students can experiment to try to capture similar sounds and designs. From this, ideas may emerge for a number of original compositions.

6. *a sound source.* By exploring the possibilities of a selected sound source—either musical or nonmusical—ideas for a composition may be generated.

If the teacher desires a less structured approach, he can encourage class members to experiment freely at the keyboard with various melodic and harmonic sound combinations. It does not matter at this point that the students may not be able to identify these sounds as specific tones or chords. They should be allowed to try anything, explore numerous possibilities, test them, make the best

selection, and then write down what they have selected in any form possible.[8]

The compositional approach can also be expanded to include experiences with electronic music. Response has been very positive and stimulating from secondary school students who have been involved in creating in this medium. Some schools now are equipped with complete electronic labs, which permit the students to attain a higher level of sophistication in their works, but simple equipment can also be used quite effectively for initial experiences in manipulating electronic sounds. Two stereo tape recorders, for example, are the only equipment necessary to work in the medium of musique concrète. On one recorder, the students can tape a variety of sounds—vocal and instrumental sounds, humming, whispering, crackling paper, timpani mallets on guitar strings, crashing cymbals, scraped sandpaper, street noises, tapped water glasses, the sounds of nonmusical objects around the classroom, and so on. The possibilities are closed only by the imagination. Then, using the second machine, these sounds can be re-recorded and altered. They can be recorded twice as fast to raise the pitch an octave or twice as slow to lower the pitch. They can be recorded in succession or simultaneously (by overdubbing with a sound-on-sound switch). The quality of the sounds can be altered by adjusting the treble, bass, and volume controls. By recording backwards, a decaying sound, such as a cymbal noise dying away, can be caused to crescendo. The students might also create an ostinato pattern

[8] For numerous suggestions on involving students in composition, see Henry Lasker, *Teaching Creative Music in Secondary Schools* (Boston: Allyn & Bacon, Inc., 1971). See also Warren Benson, *Creative Projects in Musicianship* (Washington, D.C.: Contemporary Music Project/Music Educators National Conference, 1967), and *Experiments in Musical Creativity* (Washington, D.C.: Contemporary Music Project/Music Educators National Conference, 1966).

by using a tape loop, a short piece of tape spliced end to end and threaded around both reels on the machine so that the taped sound is played over and over. Purely electronic sounds can also be recorded. For example, patchchords between the two machines can be used to cause feedback, or a shortwave radio can contribute the roar of "jamming" equipment and the rush of white noise. When all the desired sounds have been collected, manipulated, and altered, they can be combined in patterns, and sections can be repeated at a later point to give the composition a particular form.[9]

Theoretical concepts are more meaningful and more easily learned when they are introduced by the teacher or discovered by the student at a time when they are needed to solve a particular problem. Because of this, the compositional approach to learning is useful both with students having a low level of musical competency and with those having a higher degree of understanding. At whatever level the student is when composing, he will find himself involved in creative problems that require additional knowledge and understanding before solutions can be reached. At this point, he can be introduced to concepts in greater depth, can be given guided instructions for listening experiences that will expose him to new techniques, and can be led into further experimentation to discover solutions for himself.

Robert Sherman, who recommends the compositional approach to foster greater creativity, suggests that class procedures be based on the following premises:

(1) learning is best effected when a genuine need to know is present; (2) the exercise of imagination and originality by the inexperienced student is best achieved through his un-

fettered manipulation of unfamiliar materials; (3) technique as such is a natural consequence of experience gained in doing the very things for which the technique is needed; and (4) a genuine sense of proportion, artistry, and creative fulfillment requires that all problems in composition be complete and musically self-sufficient.[10]

Sherman also recommends that initial compositional experiences involve the manipulation of nonconventional sound sources, in order to help the student develop a new consciousness of sound. Thus, the first assignment might be as follows: (1) Create a two-minute composition using two wooden objects found in your home. (2) Write the composition for two performers. Notate it, but do not use conventional notation; make up your own system. (3) Be prepared to perform the composition in class.

Such an assignment is simple, easily completed, fun to write, and enjoyable to perform in class. Moreover, it requires that the student make many of the decisions every composer makes in the process of creating a work: He must find and decide upon his sound sources, explore their sound-making possibilities and select the sounds he wants to make, determine the mood to convey, the tempo, and dynamic changes, and work out a means of notating the sounds. The use of nonconventional sound sources rather than commonly accepted musical sounds makes it less likely that the student will be influenced by anything that is not directly related to solving his problem. When an assignment using conventional sound sources is made, it is difficult for the student not to be influenced by the instrument he plays, how well he plays it, the music he is currently studying, and so on. His imagination and originality are apt

[9] Many similar techniques are offered in articles in the November 1968 issue of *Music Educators Journal*, vol. 55, no. 3.

[10] Robert W. Sherman, "Creativity and the Condition of Knowing in Music, part 3," *Music Educators Journal*, 58:4 (December 1971), p. 48.

to be less free. As a result, the student who plays the piano often writes pianistic pieces, and the one who is studying baroque music tries to write music that imitates the baroque style.

The educational worth of learning through creating should not be underestimated. Creative expression provides an opportunity for the student to internalize and personalize knowledge. It is a valuable tool for promoting music insight because it emphasizes an element that should be part of every learning experience—*personal discovery.*

When composition becomes a central activity in the theory course, the old adage "necessity is the mother of invention" is clearly applicable. In order to solve problems in composition, certain theoretic knowledge must be learned; as new problems arise, unique to the individual's work, new knowledge is acquired. Given the opportunity, a student will assimilate all of his training and develop a personal bundle of creative technique. He is learning music theory in the sense that he is taking the materials and tools of class experiences and demonstrating his comprehension of them by restating or manipulating them in his own creations.

Creative writing also offers the instructor a valuable means for evaluating a student's understanding. Many examinations in the classroom test ability to respond academically to prepared music. The reverse procedure, however—composition by the student—is recommended for an alternative profile of understanding.

An essential part of compositional experiences is having the works performed so that the student composer and his classmates can actually hear the results and be able to evaluate them. With this in mind, assignments may be made occasionally to write for instruments available in the theory class or for school performing groups. Performance of the works provides further opportunity for teaching and learning. The compositions should be examined in terms of technique for total effect, with suggestions being made to help each student improve his means of expressing himself. In the simplest of terms, creative efforts involve self-expression and imagination on the part of a developing musician, as compared with noncreative work in which observation and memorization are the main products of the learning experience. Naturally there is a close relationship between the two, but this does not mean that students should be restricted in their creative activities to the application of only that knowledge that has been gained in the theory class. Rather, the students should be encouraged to experiment freely with sounds and techniques, extending themselves beyond what has been covered formally in class work.

The opportunities for creative musical expression are almost endless in the sense that there is no limit to the number of original or personal ideas that both the students and the teacher can conceive. Similarly, there is no limit to the validity of a specific technique, considering the variety of personal ideas and styles that may be developed. A theory instructor working with novice composers may often be tempted to pass judgment on a student's work in terms of his own very personal feelings, beliefs, and practices, but that teacher would do well to take his cue from Anton Webern, one of the most perceptive teachers of composers. "He fervently believed that the greatest freedom of expression arose from the greatest exercise of exactitude and rigorous control over the imagination," wrote one of Webern's pupils. "Only on the rarest occasions did Webern attempt to amend what [had been written by his students], . . . for he knew that this amounted to the intrusion of a foreign aesthetic sensibility, and that somehow it constituted an act of violence to the student's own sensibility. . . . Essentially, Webern's scrupulous care not to influence the student in his choice of style showed his deep respect for the innate capacity of the student to discover himself, and this quest for the authentic musical self . . . eventually led far beyond one's efforts at acquiring an adequate technique."[11] Another of his students has written that "his extraordinary perceptiveness enabled him to realize what we actually had intended to say. A brief suggestion, 'Was this not what you really had meant?' would help a basically good idea toward its appropriately clear and understandable formulation. He was always right, but his teaching was never authoritarian. The personality of each pupil was respected."[12]

LEARNING BY IMPROVISING

Improvisation is a form of creative musical expression that has been largely neglected in the high school because it has been considered too difficult a skill to acquire and possibly an unteachable one as well. Neither view is correct. To be sure, improvisatory skill does not come easily, but it *is* possible to teach it to high school students, and even beginning levels of improvisation can contribute a great deal to music learning.

According to jazz musician-educator Jerry Coker, five factors contribute to the jazz performer's ability to improvise. (Actually, these are factors that apply to improvisatory skills in nonjazz idioms as well.) They are

> . . . intuition, intellect, emotion, sense of pitch, and habit. His intuition is responsible for the bulk of his originality; his emotion determines the mood; his intellect helps him to plan the technical problems and, with intuition, to develop the melodic form; his sense of pitch transforms heard or imagined pitches into let-

ter names and fingerings; his playing habits enable his fingers to quickly find certain established pitch patterns. Four of these elements of his thinking—intuition, emotion, sense of pitch, and habit—are largely subconscious. Consequently, any control over his improvisation must originate in the intellect.[13]

Thus, the teacher's approach to instruction in this area must be in terms of those factors that contribute to the performer's intellectual control. Artistic improvisation is not just "leting your feelings run free and playing anything that comes to mind," as some people seem to believe. Rather, the student must know precisely what he is doing while he is improvising. He must be at ease with chords, scales, and rhythms in order to be capable of making instant decisions within a given framework.

Most improvisation is based on harmonic structures and related tonal systems. It follows, then, that the student who does not yet have a firm grasp on chords and progressions is going to be limited in improvisatory skill. However, while he is increasing his harmonic understanding, he can still be involved in improvisation on the simpler level of melodic embellishment, alteration, and paraphrase, free of harmonic considerations. Or, he can improvise within the framework of the harmonic knowledge he does possess. For example, if he is familiar with the primary chords, he can improvise melodically around the tones of the tonic, subdominant, and dominant chords, using simple passing tones, auxiliary tones, changing tones, anticipations, and appoggiaturas, without reference to related chord scales that he will come to work with at a higher level. As soon as possible, however, he needs to move beyond this dimension of improvisation and base his mel-

[11] Quoted in Hans Moldenhauer, "Webern as Teacher," *Music Educators Journal*, 57:3 (November 1970), pp. 32–33.
[12] *Ibid.*, p. 31.

[13] Jerry Coker, *Improvising Jazz* (Englewood Cliffs, New Jersey: Prentice-Hall, Inc., 1964), p. 3. Reprinted by permission of Prentice-Hall, Inc., © 1964.

odic creativity on a much broader harmonic scheme.

In addition to understanding the formation of chords of different types, their relationships within and between a variety of keys, and basic chord progressions, the student should become familiar with common chord substitutions. For example, in improvising, the following substitutions are often made for specified chords: (1) A dominant seventh chord may be replaced by any augmented chord on the same root or by a seventh chord on the same root with a flatted fifth. (2) A dominant seventh chord may be replaced by another dominant seventh, or an extension, constructed on the flatted fifth of the original chord (such as the substitution of D♭7 for G7 in the key of C). (3) A tonic major triad may be replaced by a minor seventh chord on the third degree of the scale. And (4) a subdominant minor triad in a major key (itself an alteration, in the form of modal interchange) may be replaced by a dominant seventh or major ninth chord constructed on the lowered seventh degree of the scale (for example, B♭9 instead of Fm in the key of C).

Understanding substitutions such as these, as well as understanding chord extensions or superimpositions and possible alterations to specific tones within these chords, needs to be developed to the point where usage by the performer becomes automatic. The degree of the student's facility in working with these elements is affected, of course, not only by his knowledge of chords and his practice with them, but also by his technical skill, instrumental or vocal.

Beyond these considerations, the student needs to become familiar with chord scales.[14]

<hr />

[14] Portions of the material on chord scales and improvisation in this section are derived from an outline of a course prepared by David Dubinsky and offered by him to members of the Danvers (Massachusetts) High School Stage Band.

In the jazz, blues, and rock idioms, improvisation revolves around the careful discrimination and usage of harmonic and nonharmonic tones, and the avoidance of certain tones. For all practical purposes, chord scales, derived primarily from medieval modes, are used as guidelines for improvisation. A chord scale is simply a tonal system that is implied by a given chord; it has its own structure and tonal center and is used temporarily instead of the scale related to the main key in which the chord is functioning. This approach is not a new one; it has been used by jazz artists for decades. Table 6-3 shows the modal chord scales implied by chords in the key of C major.

With the exception of the Lydian and Aeolian, each of the scales in Table 6-3 includes a blackened note. The black notes represent tones to be avoided; they should not be used as tonal centers or target tones because of their nonchordal sound (for example, the sixth in the Dorian can create a tritone in relation to the chord), although they may be used as passing tones. The numbers above the nonchord tones in the table indicate color tones—the ninths, elevenths, and thirteenths in traditional harmony. These can provide a much richer sound than the chord tones and may be used just as freely either as target tones or to develop areas of concentration.

In addition to these modes, other tonal systems should be introduced to the student improviser, including pentatonic scales, the whole-tone scale, the various forms of minor scales, the blues scale, and altered forms of the modes (such as the Lydian scale with a flatted seventh degree). The student should also understand that these scales are not limited to use with a chord on only a certain degree of the original key scale; rather they are related to certain *types* of chords, wherever they appear, and thus may be transposed. For example, the Mixolydian scale is

Table 6-3. MODAL CHORD SCALES

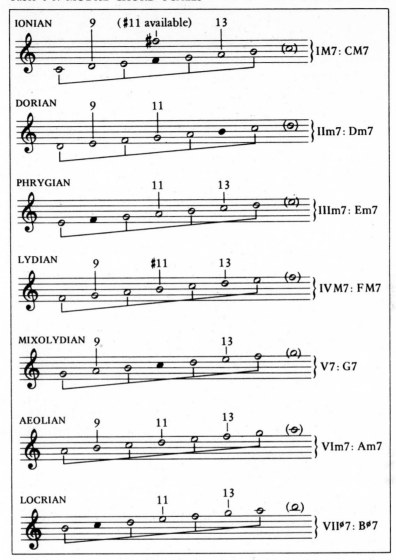

The brace below each chord scale indicates the four-tone chord structure to which the chord relates. Black noteheads represent tones to be
avoided as "targets" in improvisation.

related primarily to the dominant seventh
chord, and it may be used whether the chord
is employed on the fifth degree of the original
scale or whether it is constructed on, say,
the second degree as a secondary dominant.

The basic principle underlying the use of
chord scales in improvisation is that any scale
may be used with a given chord as long as
that scale (1) is based on the root of the
chord and (2) includes all or a majority of

Table 6-4. CHORD EXTENSIONS AND SCALES

	Symbol	Example	Possible Extensions	Principal Related Chord Scale	Other Related Chord Scales
MAJOR	...	C	min. 7, maj. 7, min. 9, maj. 9, perf. 11, maj. 13	major	Lydian, Mixolydian (blues scale, pentatonic)
	... 6	C6	maj. 9, aug. 11	major	Lydian, Mixolydian (blues scale, pentatonic)
	M7 (♮7)	CM7	maj. 9, aug. 11, maj. 13	major	Lydian (pentatonic)
MINOR	m	Cm	min. 7, maj. 7, maj. 9, perf. 11, maj. 13	melodic minor (natural minor, harmonic minor)	Dorian, Phrygian, blues scale (pentatonic)
	m6	Cm6	maj. 9, perf. 11	ascending melodic minor	Dorian, blues scale (pentatonic)
	m7	Cm7	maj. 9, perf. 11	Dorian	natural minor, Phrygian, blues scale
	m M7 (m ♮7)	CmM7	maj. 9, perf. 11	melodic minor (harmonic minor)	

	Symbol	Example	Possible Extensions	Principal Related Chord Scale	Other Related Chord Scales
DOMINANT	. . . 7	C7	min. 9, maj 9, aug. 9, aug. 11, maj. 13	Mixolydian	(Dorian, blues scale, whole tone)
	+7	C+7	min. 9, maj. 9, aug. 9, aug. 11	whole tone	
	7(♭5)	C7(♭5)	min. 9, maj. 9, aug. 9, maj. 13	whole tone	blues scale
DIMINISHED	°7	C°7	min. 9, perf. 11, min. 13	blues scale	(melodic minor)
	⌀7	C⌀7	min. 9, perf. 11	Locrian	blues scale

the tones in that chord. Table 6-4 shows the types of chord scales that may be used in conjunction with different types of chords.

Students need to have many opportunities to write, analyze, and experiment with these chord scales on their instruments in order to develop functional understanding and skill in manipulating them. Following basic experimentation, the use of a twelve-measure blues progression is a practical vehicle for putting the scales into use. In its simplest form, the blues progression employs only three chords in expansive phrases and thus permits application of chord scales within a delimited format. Variations on the twelve-measure blues that employ a wider variety of chords can be introduced next, and once students have had sufficient experience and are comfortably familiar with the scales, standards and pop tunes can be introduced. It is best to use compositions that stay within one key (except for the modulation at the bridge) until the student is relating and manipulating chords and scales with general facility.

While building the student's theoretic

knowledge and understanding for improvisation, the teacher needs to encourage the development of technical skill on his instrument. Although the fair player is capable of experiencing the joys of improvisation, he cannot pursue this type of performance very far without advancing his instrumental technique.

It is also important to provide opportunities for the student to listen to recordings of outstanding improvisers such as John Coltrane, Miles Davis, Bill Evans, Charlie Parker, Dizzy Gillespie, Cannonball Adderley, and Ornette Coleman. Recordings of Ella Fitzgerald and Sarah Vaughan would be appropriate reference materials for the vocal improviser. As the student progresses, he may need to be reminded that his goal is originality and *self-*expression in improvisation; therefore, while picking up a few "cliches" from recordings may be acceptable at the outset, they should

be avoided as he develops his improvisatory skills.

Obviously, a considerable amount of time is required on a regular basis in order for students to develop more than surface skills in this area. Although some improvisational experiences can be incorporated into the regular theory course, it is desirable that improvisational sessions be held in conjunction with school performance groups. For example, a session might be held once a week for members of the band and stage band during an activity period or after school. In some high schools, separate courses in improvisation are now being offered. A variety of instructional materials are on the market for the development of improvisatory skills on various instruments. Valuable sources, applicable to any instrument, are the books by Jamey Aebersold, David Baker, and Jerry Coker (cited in the selected references for this chapter).

Discussion Questions and Projects

1. Using the curriculum content suggested on pages 128–129, outline a first-year theory course and select a suitable textbook for (a) students of limited music competencies, and b) students with a high level of music competencies.
2. Investigate the theory programs in several high schools in your area to determine the number of years theory instruction is offered, the types of theory curriculums, and the approaches that are used (such as harmony study only; a compositional approach; traditional usage only; multidimensional experiences; dual- or triple-track planning). Compare findings in class and make realistic suggestions for improvement.
3. Behavioral objectives are presented on pages 132–133 for level I of a multilevel theory class. Consult Table 6-2 and write behavioral objectives for the other two levels.
4. Organize a Theory I class around the development of improvisational skills. Select suitable text materials, develop a sequential curriculum, choose a required discography, and develop *course* objectives.
5. Develop a long-range lesson plan for teaching a specific rhythmic concept in an introductory theory class. In your plan, include experiences in harmonization, listening, dictation, sight-singing, analysis, composition, and performance.
6. What music knowledge, understanding, and skill can a student gain by writing a composition using nonmusic sound sources?

7. What kinds of theoretic knowledge can be imparted by having a student who plays a wind instrument, or one who sings, improvise a blues along with a student who plays the piano?

8. Discuss the advantages and disadvantages of (a) multilevel planning, (b) the compositional approach, (c) individual theory projects, (d) a high school theory course for the musically talented only, and (e) a high school theory course for students with strictly avocational interests in music.

Selected References

AEBERSOLD, JAMEY. *A New Approach to Jazz Improvisation.* New Albany, Indiana: Aebersold, 1967.

BAKER, DAVID. *Arranging and Composing.* Chicago: Down Beat Music Workshop Publications, 1970.

————. *Jazz Improvisation.* Chicago: Down Beat Music Workshop Publications, 1971.

————. *A Jazz Improvisation Method for Stringed Instruments.* 2 vols. Chicago: Down Beat Music Workshop Publications, 1978.

————. *Techniques of Improvisation.* 4 vols. Chicago: Down Beat Music Workshop Publications, 1969–1974.

BENSON, WARREN. *Creative Projects in Musicianship.* Washington, D.C.: Contemporary Music Project/Music Educators National Conference, 1967.

BERRY, WALLACE. *Form in Music.* Englewood Cliffs, New Jersey: Prentice-Hall, Inc., 1966.

BOBBITT, RICHARD. *Harmonic Technique in the Rock Idiom.* Belmont, California: Wadsworth Publishing Company, 1976.

BORETZ, BENJAMIN, and EDWARD T. CONE. *Perspectives on Contemporary Music Theory.* New York: W. W. Norton & Company, Inc., 1972.

CHASTEK, WINIFRED K. *Keyboard Skills: Sight Reading, Transposition, Harmonization, Improvisation.* Belmont, California: Wadsworth Publishing Company, 1967.

COKER, JERRY. *Improvising Jazz.* Englewood Cliffs, New Jersey: Prentice-Hall, 1964.

————. *Patterns for Jazz.* Lebanon, Indiana: Studio Publications and Recordings, Inc., 1970.

Comprehensive Musicianship: The Foundation for College Education in Music. Washington, D.C.: Contemporary Music Project/Music Educators National Conference, 1965.

DELAMONT, GORDON. *Modern Harmonic Technique.* 2 vols. Delevan, New York: Kendor Music, Inc., 1965.

DONATO, ANTHONY. *Preparing Music Manuscript.* Englewood Cliffs, New Jersey: Prentice-Hall, 1963.

ERNST, DAVID. *Musique Concrète.* Boston: Crescendo Publishing Company, 1972.

Experiments in Musical Creativity. Washington, D.C.: Contemporary Music Project/Music Educators National Conference, 1966.

FITCH, JOHN R. "Twentieth-Century Students Should Start with Twentieth-Century Techniques," *Music Educators Journal,* 59:8 (April 1973), pp. 46–47.

FOWLER, CHARLES B., ed. *Electronic Music.* Washington, D.C.: Music Educators National Conference, 1968.

GARCIA, RUSS. *The Professional Arranger-Composer*. New York: Criterion Music.

GROVE, DICK. *Arranging Concepts: A Guide to Writing Arrangements for Stage Band Ensembles*. Studio City, California: First Place Music Publications, Inc., 1972.

HARDER, PAUL O. *Bridge to 20th-Century Music*. Boston: Allyn & Bacon, Inc., 1973.

———. *Harmonic Materials in Tonal Music*. 2 vols. Boston: Allyn & Bacon, Inc., 1968.

HINDEMITH, PAUL. *Traditional Harmony*, rev. ed. 2 vols. Rockville Centre, New York: Belwin-Mills Publishing Co., 1968.

HUTCHESON, JERE T. *Music Form and Analysis*. 2 vols. Boston: Allyn & Bacon, Inc., 1972.

JOYCE, JIMMY. *A Guide to Writing Vocal Arrangements*. Studio City, California: First Place Music Publications, 1977.

KENNAN, KENT WHEELER. *The Technique of Orchestration*. 2nd ed. Englewood Cliffs, New Jersey: Prentice-Hall, 1970.

LA RUE, JAN. *Guidelines for Style Analysis*. New York: W. W. Norton & Company, Inc., 1970.

LASKER, HENRY. *Teaching Creative Music in Secondary Schools*. Boston: Allyn & Bacon, Inc., 1971.

———. "Why Can't They Compose?" *Music Educators Journal*, 59:8 (April 1973), pp. 41–45.

LEVEY, JOSEPH. *Basic Jazz Improvisation*. Delaware Water Gap, Pennsylvania: Shawnee Press, 1971.

MANKIN, LINDA R., MARYCLAIRE WELLMAN, and ANGELA M. OWEN. *Prelude to Musicianship: Fundamental Concepts and Skills*. New York: Holt, Rinehart and Winston, 1979.

MARQUIS, G. WELTON. *Twentieth-Century Music Idioms*. Englewood Cliffs, New Jersey: Prentice-Hall, 1964.

PERLE, GEORGE. *Twelve-Tone Tonality*. Los Angeles: University of California Press, 1977.

PERSICHETTI, VINCENT. *Twentieth-Century Harmony*. New York: W. W. Norton & Company, Inc., 1961.

PISTON, WALTER. *Harmony*. New York: W. W. Norton & Company, Inc., 1947.

READ, GARDNER. *Music Notation: A Manual of Modern Practice*. New York: Crescendo Publishing Company, 1969.

ROBINSON, RAYMOND C. *Progressive Harmony*. Boston: Bruce Humphries Publishers, 1962.

SEBESKY, DON. *The Contemporary Arranger*. Sherman Oaks, California: Alfred Publishing Company, 1975.

SHERMAN, ROBERT W. "As Taught, Music Theory Is an Anachronism," *Music Educators Journal*, 56:2 (October 1969), pp. 39–41.

———. "Creativity and the Condition of Knowing in Music," *Music Educators Journal*, 58:2–4 (October, November, December 1971).

SIEGMEISTER, ELIE. *Harmony and Melody* (vol. 1: *The Diatonic Style*; vol. 2: *Modulation, Chromatic and Modern Styles*). Belmont, California: Wadsworth Publishing Company, 1965.

SMALLEY, JACK. *A Simplified Guide to Writing and Arranging Songs for Swing and Show Choirs and Small Instrumental Groups*. Studio City, California: First Place Music Publications, 1972.

STONE, KURT. "New Notation for New Music," *Music Educators Journal*, 63:2–3 (October-November 1976).

THOMAS, RONALD B. *MMCP Synthesis*. Elnora, New York: Media, Inc., 1972.

THOMSON, WILLIAM E., and RICHARD P. DE LONE. *Introduction to Ear Training*. Belmont, California: Wadsworth Publishing Company, 1967.

VELLEMAN, BARRY. "Speaking of Jazz: Jazz Improvisation Through Linguistic Methods," *Music Educators Journal*, 65:2 (October 1978), pp. 28–31.

WALTON, CHARLES W. "Analyzing Analysis," *Music Educators Journal*, 55:6 (February 1969), pp. 57–59, 139.

Music Among the Arts and Humanities

7

There are very few principles governing how things are associated. . . .
No generalized principle ever contradicts another because none is specialized.
. . . If you know your generalized principles, you can go in any direction.
BUCKMINSTER FULLER[1]

EDUCATION AMOUNTS TO LITTLE if it does not encourage the individual to exercise his innate power to shape himself, if it does not provide experiences that release the student's potential and help him to build his self-awareness. The late psychologist Abraham Maslow stated that "the goal of education . . . is ultimately the 'self-actualization' of a person, the becoming fully human. . . ."[2] The process of learning to be a human being is what he referred to as "intrinsic education." Maslow also believed that

> . . . effective education in music, education in art, education in dancing and rhythm, is intrinsically far closer than the core curriculum to intrinsic education of the kind that I am talking about, of learning one's identity as an essential part of education. If education doesn't do that, it is useless. Educa-

---

[1] Buckminster Fuller, in a speech before a general session of the North Central Division convention, Music Educators National Conference, in Cincinnati, March 11, 1971.

[2] Abraham H. Maslow, "Music, Education, and Peak Experiences," in *Documentary Report of the Tanglewood Symposium*, Robert A. Choate, ed. (Washington, D.C.: Music Educators National Conference, 1968), p. 70.

tion is learning to grow, learning what to grow toward, learning what is good and bad, learning what is desirable and undesirable, learning what to choose and what not to choose. In this realm of intrinsic learning, intrinsic teaching, and intrinsic education I think that the arts . . . are so close to our psychological and biological core, so close to this identity, this biological identity, that rather than think of these courses as a sort of whipped or luxury cream, they must become basic experiences in education.[3]

Maslow's beliefs about personalizing the curriculum have pertinent application to the teaching of music as an individual discipline, and in the various courses of music instruction, efforts need to focus on involving the student more as an individual for the purpose of self-realization through music. But there should also be application on another plane—that of the full gamut of education, in which music is just one aspect. In building a curriculum that can promote personal identity, it is necessary to initiate a process by which learning experiences of different types and in different fields are ultimately brought together and synthesized in terms of, for, and by the individual.

One approach toward unification and enrichment of the curriculum is a movement known as "arts in general education" (AGE) or sometimes as "comprehensive arts." The purpose of an AGE program is to allow the arts to filter through the entire curriculum, using them to teach other subjects. Music and drama, for example, might be used in a United States history class to establish the cultural climate of a certain period and to act out some historic event. Dance might be used in a mathematics class to study geometric shapes or in an English class to examine mood and rhythm in poetry. Songs might be composed in a reading class to make use of new vocabulary. The arts can be put to use in all types of

classes at all levels, both to create an exciting learning environment and to provide alternate ways of studying, perceiving, and experiencing a concept, form, event, language, and so on.

In many schools around the country, music educators have participated in AGE programs as teachers and resource persons, and they have found that such programs have heightened interest in the arts and strengthened separate music curriculums. Quite often, in AGE schools, the learning environment has become more vibrant, teacher and student attitudes have improved, absenteeism has dropped, vandalism has declined, exceptional students have been better served, community support has increased, and both verbal and nonverbal skills have increased. The use of the arts throughout the general curriculum (in addition to distinct music and arts programs) could provide one of the most easily understood and accepted justifications for arts education in the public schools.

Although AGE is applicable at any instructional level, it has made its strongest inroads in elementary and middle schools. The unification of subjects in upper grades has taken a different turn in most instances. Until recent years, pupils have studied secondary school subjects largely in isolation, with the result that they have gained little perspective on how one field of inquiry relates to another. More important, the isolational curriculum offers little opportunity for students to relate subjects to their own lives and their own identities. Aside from the open education movement (discussed in Chapter 8), attempts to unify the curriculum, to bring together segmented studies into a whole, have resulted in two general types of courses of interest to the music educator—the humanities course and the related arts course. Contrary to some misconceived attitudes in the field, neither of these two types of courses should be thought of as a substitute for basic music courses, neither should be construed as "frosting on

[3] *Ibid.*, p. 73.

the cake," and neither should be considered better than the other.

First, it is important to realize that as projects have been formulated during the curriculum reform movement, there has been agreement throughout the various fields that the integrity of the individual discipline must be maintained. This must precede any attempt at the integration of subject matter. Some educators, for example, have suggested a humanities base for the junior high general music class, but this is not the place for humanities. Such an approach is more an indication that some teachers are in a quandary over what to do with general music, rather than an indication of insight regarding student needs. It is essential for students at each level to be provided with the fundamental courses in a given field before they are introduced to interdisciplinary courses. Without a basic foundation in each of the subjects involved, it is difficult for students to synthesize any meaningful knowledge in a personal manner. Neither the humanities nor the related arts course should be a substitute for any basic course in music, art, literature, or any other field. Rather, it should be a complement to the basic curriculum.

Secondly, educators must understand that a complementary course is a "completing" course, not a supplementary item of nonessential nature. The directions taken in recent years by humanities and arts courses have been toward the *humanization of the curriculum*—a matter that is perhaps the most important concern of education today. When these courses are well planned and well taught, they allow the student to identify personally with his educational experiences on a level that is often difficult to attain in other areas of the curriculum.

Third, music educators should not bewail —as many do—the fact that these courses are not music-centered. Some of us, it seems, have become so involved in our work that

we cannot view any other area of the curriculum except in terms of music. One prominent educator in the related arts field denounced most humanities programs on the basis that music and art get short-changed, that they are forced to conform to the selected themes of the humanities program.[4] Although there is some validity to this view, it derives largely from a music-oriented or art-oriented approach to the humanities. If a humanities course is to serve its purpose well, it cannot be music-centered, art-centered, literature-centered, or history-centered; it must be man-centered. Similarly, the related arts course must be *aesthetics*-centered. To focus either course in any other direction would distort the very reasons for its being.

Finally, it is essential that these integrated courses be made available to all students, not merely to a select, elite group. In many high schools, such courses are open only to seniors, to honor students, or to those in a college preparatory program. Such an exclusive enrollment is foreign to the spirit of the humanities and aesthetics. *All* students need to be involved in humanistic studies, and all can be if course content and procedure are adjusted to the abilities and backgrounds of the students enrolled in a particular class.

In keeping with the nature and goals of these offerings, it is also fitting that examinations be eliminated and that no marks be given other than perhaps "Pass" and "Fail." Mark Freeman, of Glens Falls (New York) High School, has summarized this matter precisely: "It would be ridiculous and presumptuous to evaluate a student as A, B, C, D, or E in heightened awareness of himself as a human being."[5]

[4] See Gene C. Wenner, "The Use and Abuse of Interdisciplinary Arts Courses," *Music Educators Journal*, 56:9 (May 1970), pp. 63–66.

[5] *Humanities Is . . .* (Albany, N.Y.: The University of New York/The State Education Department, 1969), p. 7.

154

Keeping these general principles in mind, let's examine each type of course more closely.

HUMANITIES COURSES

The study of self is in large part the study of man—of his thoughts, goals, methods, actions, perceptions, expressions, and everything that makes man human. Developing a sense of personal identity is naturally, and most directly, a matter of examining man today, but it also requires something of a feeling of oneness or continuity through the span of many eras and many fields of knowledge, belief, feeling, and sensitivity. The humanities course, therefore, is concerned with man (and the individual self) in all of society —man past, present, and future, man with himself and man in action with others.

Lee Streiff has stated the guiding premise of such courses in this way:

> The underlying assumption of a study of the Humanities is that a man faces the same basic problems, whether he lives in ancient Babylon or twentieth-century America.
>
> Fundamentally, it is the assumption that there is a human nature and a human condition with which each man, in his own way, must deal. Because of the universality of man's nature and condition, the problems and emotions of any man are comprehensible to all men, and the way in which any man goes about solving the unique problems of "being" is meaningful to all other men. It is through seeing what other men have been and done that we may see what we may be and do. In this sense, the cultural materials that are studied in Humanities are an illumination of a common nature, and provide the means by which we can understand what it means to live and to be human; what it means not only to live, but to live well.[6]

[6] Lee Streiff, "Humanities in the High School," *Kansas Music Review*, vol. 29, no. 1 (February 1967), p. 35.

The purpose of a humanities program is essentially to promote self-awareness, self-expression, and self-fulfillment by enriching the student's daily life and relating the individual to the realities and potentialities of his immediate environment. This type of program encourages students to have recourse not only to the thoughts, ideals, and creations of other men through the ages, but also to their own unique powers. It can serve to explore ideas and synthesize experiences; to orient students to the process of seeking answers; to foster individual, creative thinking; to enable students to see relationships in various areas of human activity; to help students understand man's heritage and his multi-images; to develop one's own system of values; to promote an awareness of man's potential and the reasons and methods of his creative acts; and to consider from many angles the quality of life.

When the subject is man, there are obviously unlimited approaches to the study, and every discipline can have some bearing on the course. At the same time, though, there is no single aspect of man's past or present being that should be dwelled on at length, for the study should analyze man in his *total* complexity. Similarly, there are no specific conclusions that need to be reached. As Carl Ladensock, chairman of the humanities program at Scarsdale (New York) High School, said in a speech before the National Council of Teachers of English, "Humanities courses inevitably suggest more questions rather than give tidy answers. Therefore, each subject becomes a jumping-off place for the next one and hopefully the student's mind will never come to a final stopping-off place." Humanities programs vary considerably from school to school; nevertheless, there are several common approaches: (1) the chronological, historical approach that views man in the setting of several selected cultures and eras; (2) a philosophical organization that considers man in relation to rather abstract topics, such as religion, war, nature, love, order, and art; (3) a categorical approach that concentrates on more concrete, documentable topics, styles, functions, and elements of living; (4) a "mini-course" program that consists of a series of brief, generally unrelated courses in literature, science, sociology, anthropology, music, art, and other subjects; and (5) a combination of two or more of the preceding course structures.

Discussion of the "mini-course" approach can be dispensed with immediately. If the purpose of the course is to be realized, a humanities program must be more than a quick survey of one discipline after another. Even if the selected subjects are related in some way, humanistic study does not begin until each of these subjects is tied to the central core of man and the student begins to ask questions such as "How does man change?" "What is love?" "Who am I?" "What is my environment?" Of the other approaches, the first two are the most common.

Representative Courses

The various possibilities for organization can best be understood, perhaps, by considering some of the humanities courses that have been developed in recent years. For example, at Oak Park and River Forest High School in Oak Park, Illinois, a course in world civilization has been offered that incorporates history, literature, art works, music, and creative projects. It begins with a discussion of student life and values, the impact of society on the individual, and the balance between individual perception and mass consensus. The initial understandings are then broadened through a study of Egypt, Greece, Medieval times, the Renaissance and Reformation, and the contemporary period. The organization is thus chronological; however, a second-year course continues with a study

of the world in 1780; political and social revolution; nationalism, socialism, and racism; mass society and industrialism; war and catastrophe; and new images of man and the universe.

A different chronological approach has been tried in a Wichita, Kansas, humanities program that combines art, music, anthropology, history, literature, philosophy, and political science. Employing a team of three teachers—one in the fine arts, one in social studies, and one in the language arts—the program focuses on case studies through visual, auditory, and conceptual methods. Seven ages of man are examined: the prehistoric period; early civilizations; the period of Crete, Greece, and Rome; the Middle Ages; the Renaissance; the Age of Reason and Industry; and the twentieth century. After each case study, certain elements are traced forward and backward in time and related to other cultures. (This is somewhat akin to the technique used by Willis Wager in his two-volume history of the arts, *From the Hand of Man.*[7])

A "post-hole" chronological approach has been employed at Ann Arbor (Michigan) High School. There, selected ideas and art works from various periods are given intensive study, but the eras themselves are not examined as such. A team of six teachers (one in music, one in art, two in English, and two in history) presents individual weekly lectures, supplemented by four weekly seminars. Time is also set aside each week for special presentations, such as field trips.

At the Loomis School in Windsor, Connecticut, the seniors meet twice a week for lectures on philosophy, science, literature, and the fine arts. The lectures are supplemented by discussion periods. Each student is assigned to a faculty adviser and has two major projects for research on humanities topics of his own choosing. Typical projects have

[7] Published in 1965 by Boston University Press.

included the mathematics of musical sound illustrated on tape; cubism in painting, with an original student work; an original music composition recorded on tape; and personal philosophical essays. The actual course work is presented chronologically.

A number of schools offer a humanities course based on one that was developed at the Carnegie Institute of Technology. The Carnegie program, called "The Humanities in Three Cities," focuses on ancient Athens, Renaissance Florence, and present-day New York. Through a study of these cities at three points in history, attention is given to three primary questions: "What is the good man?" "What is the good life?" "What is the good society?" In the Fairfield, Connecticut, Public Schools, this approach has become part of a four-course sequence in the humanities. The sequence begins in the sixth grade with a six-week unit entitled "Discovering Who I Am," which integrates literature, music, art, social studies, and semantics. It continues with a transitional course in the junior high school that leads to two courses in the senior high school—"Humanities for the World Bound," offered to noncollege students, and "A Tale of Three Cities," offered to college-bound seniors.

The Carnegie program has been adapted in a different way at the David Douglas Public Schools in Portland, Oregon. Prior to the focus on cities, there is a six-week introduction, "What Are the Humanities?" In this, the students examine style, form, photography, ideas, and society. There is also a section on urban environment. The remainder of the course expands the Carnegie concept to six cities, with related questions: Classical Athens ("What is justice?"), medieval London ("What is truth?"), Renaissance Florence ("What is beauty?"), nineteenth-century Paris and St. Petersburg ("Does man have an identity?"), twentieth-century New York and Nairobi ("What is freedom?"), and twenty-first-century Portland ("Are there still questions?"). Throughout the course, the students keep diaries in which they enter answers to the three original questions regarding the Good Man, the Good Life, and the Good Society.

Each of the programs described so far has basically been chronologically structured. Nonchronological courses are built on a variety of topics. In Garden City, New Jersey, for example, there is a course organized around geographical cultures, with an emphasis on non-Western cultures and their impact on the West. Spiritual, moral, and artistic developments are considered, and the class explores man's expressions of feeling and his search for meaning in life.

Northern High School in Baltimore has offered a course that covers five diverse themes: man's search for identity, the study of an opera, man's responsibility to man, the study of an artist, and the Renaissance. The Board of Education of the City of New York, Brooklyn, approved the following themes for its humanities program: man has a need to express himself; man is gregarious; man continually seeks to interpret his environment; man seeks to create order in his environment; and man is unalterably bound to a cultural heritage. At Sewanhaka High School, District 2, Nassau County, New York, four themes were selected for the program: man alone, man in contention, man together, and the brave new world. A similar sequence was devised at Hunter College High School in New York City: public man, private man, man and woman, man's relation to society, and society's relationship to man. Finally, the State Department of Education in New Jersey prepared a humanities course consisting of these six units: the exploration of human emotions, means of expression, types of experience, experiencing a work of art, experience through oral expression, and experiencing through painting.

157

Organizational Steps

A review of course offerings around the country reveals that there is no standard structure for the humanities course. Certain courses share similar ideas, but each school seems to provide something different. This is as it should be. Although no specific content will be recommended here, several steps in organizing a course can be suggested.

It should be obvious that with the integration of so many different subjects in a humanities program, no one teacher would have sufficient knowledge to teach the course alone. The first step, then, is to bring together a team of teachers to plan and carry out the program. A minimum would include one specialist in the arts, one in social studies, and one in literature. It would be desirable, though, to include one in music, one in visual arts, one in literature and drama, one in history, and one in science. Other teachers might serve as consultants to the team in more specific areas. It is most important that the chosen instructors have a desire to teach with a team and that they have compatible personalities; some do not or are unable to function well as part of a group (although they may be excellent teachers when they are in sole command of a classroom). In addition, the teachers must recognize that they need to work *together* in the teaching process, not only in planning. "Turn teaching" is not team teaching; each teacher must be present at each class meeting to contribute when class activity turns to an area in which he can offer his unique talents.

The instructors need to be released from an adequate portion of their teaching responsibilities in order to have sufficient time to plan the course. It may be advisable to bring the group together for a couple of weeks after the closing of school in the summer to complete their plans for the following year. Group planning time must also be provided by the school during the time when the course is actually being taught.

Initial planning might begin by examining the meaning of the term "humanities," and by listing as many topics as possible that represent broad circumstances in man's existence. The following topics, for example, might help to organize the team's thinking:

–Man by himself
–Man with others
–Man and his natural environment
–Man and his manufactured environment
–Man shapes (adjusts to, destroys) his world
–Man and his several communities
–Man and the universe
–Man as creator (explorer, pretender, dreamer, realist, pragmatist)
–Man the introvert (extrovert)
–Man in search of order (beauty, meaning, change, improvement)
–Man and his freedom (containment)
–Man the ruler (the ruled)
–Man at war (in peace)
–Man and the unknown
–Man and the aesthetic
–Man and his mind (senses, emotions, beliefs, loves, hates)
–Man and understanding
–Man and communication
–Man and humanity (inhumanity)
–Man and his values
–Man and his identity

Another approach is to consider what each subject area can contribute to an understanding of man: history, literature, drama, dance, music, art, architecture, sociology, anthropology, psychology, natural sciences, philosophy, and so on.

With this beginning, the team can probably determine several main ideas that will suggest a focus and an organization for the course. In deciding on the focus, thought will also have to be given to the group of students to be taught (their number, backgrounds, interests, and abilities), to the faculty (their areas of specialization, strengths and weaknesses, and expertise in various teaching methods), and to the available resources (including facilities, materials, equipment, budget, and time). It may be decided that classes should be arranged for one, two, or three general meetings a week, with smaller, more specialized seminars or discussion groups intervening. If scheduling is flexible (or modular), double time blocks might be used for the larger group meetings, and depending upon the number of students involved, time might be allotted for individual conferences. Efforts should be made to allow for at least small seminars of five to ten students.

Before specific content is planned, the team should consider the variety of learning situations that might be used. The lecture approach should be kept to a minimum. Instead, plans should be made to involve students through creative projects, multimedia presentations, films, recordings, field trips, keeping a diary of thoughts, individual projects, and other means. Lists of resources can be drawn up, including resources outside the school. It is possible that members of the local and surrounding communities may be called on as guest lecturers, demonstrators, or performers. In this regard, the team might look for an actor, anthropologist, archeologist, architect, art historian, artist, city planner, composer, dancer, drama critic, fashion designer, filmmaker, graphics designer, museum curator, music critic, musician, novelist, photographer, playwright, poet, psychologist, sculptor, sociologist, television director, or theatre designer.

In following a "systems approach," such as this, the team would next select an instructional pattern and materials, and weigh the possible methods of evaluation. Inaugurating a humanities course or redesigning one in existence can be a long and difficult task. If it is well planned and well taught, however, it can be one of the most stimulating and significant courses in the curriculum.

RELATED ARTS COURSES

The music teacher will most likely feel more at home in the related arts course than in the humanities course, for here the focus is on aesthetics rather than man. The over-all goal, as in the strictly music courses, is to develop aesthetic sensitivity. In support of this, the related arts program has several primary operational objectives: (1) To develop auditory and visual perception. (2) To develop an awareness of the aesthetic environment. (3) To foster an understanding of artistic forms of expression. (4) To encourage a sense of artistic self-discovery. (5) To develop an understanding of the uniqueness of each art. (6) To develop an understanding of how the arts are related. (7) To extend knowledge of art forms, structures, and modes of expression. (8) To encourage participation in and self-expression through the arts. (9) To promote an understanding of the world's cultures and our own artistic and cultural heritage; and (10) to develop the ability to analyze, form independent critical judgments based on a personal set of values, and make rewarding aesthetic discriminations.

The materials to be used will obviously be works of art, but which artworks—indeed, which arts—should be included? Those works whose values transcend time should naturally be at the center of class study, but contemporary artworks, including the students' own creations, must also be explored. Moreover, there should be no limit on the form of art that is examined; all kinds of music, painting, sculpture, architecture, drama, literature, poetry, and dance are valid in this class. So, too, are photography, filmmaking, fashion design, city planning, graphic design, product design, and decorative arts and crafts. Guy Hubbard, professor of art education at Indiana University, has said that "the sights and sounds that surround us in our daily lives are probably more important in an education than learning directed toward more remote phenomena."[8] This is quite true, and although our surroundings today include both ancient and contemporary arts, Hubbard's statement makes evident the relevancy of even automobile design and interior decorating to the related-arts class.

Relating the Arts

Speaking at the Tanglewood Symposium in 1967, Gunther Schuller remarked that relating music to the other arts tends to neglect music as a distinct or separate art. It promotes, he said, "a general sort of liberal arts view . . . which results too often in what Oscar Levant so brilliantly called 'a smattering of ignorance.' "[9] This view is certainly a valid one in cases where the related-arts course, no matter how well organized, is a substitute in the curriculum. When it is a supplement to a separate and comprehensive music program, however, many are likely to think that the integrity of music as a distinct art is being upheld. Yet, the problem still exists. For the unique qualities of music—and of each other art—must still be emphasized in the related arts class. The differences among the arts are strong and a healthy factor in the significance and advancement of each of the arts. Similarities are few, and attempts to relate the arts are often contrived. There are perhaps three common ways of bringing together the separate arts: (1) through thematic relationships, (2) through shared means of experience, and (3) through related elements in perception.

The thematic or topical approach is the least aesthetic for an introduction to related arts. It is represented by such tactics as listening to a piece of programmatic music and then viewing a painting or reading a story that has a similar topic; studying Debussy, Monet, and Mallarmé because the work of each is in some way connected with the term "impressionism"; or reading passages from Shakespeare's *Romeo and Juliet*, followed by a study of Tchaikovsky's overture on the same subject or Bernstein's modernization in *West Side Story*. This is essentially a topical approach, which works in the humanities course but not in the arts course. In the former, the arts are used only as they have bearing on understanding man. In the latter, however, the topical approach confines art to commentary—to the expression of ideas and attitudes. It limits aesthetic education. This is not to negate the value that does exist in exploring such relationships. It is interesting, for example, to see how artists in different media have treated the same theme or expressed the same attitude; it can also be enlightening. Nevertheless, this type of understanding is supplementary to the core of aesthetic structure and should not become the central approach in an introduction to the arts.

The second approach—the experiential relationship—has much validity. It is represented by Max Kaplan's statement that "you cannot deal with the arts alone; and even if you are dealing with integration between them you do not start with a close look at any of the arts. Rather you begin to integrate all of them together on the broadest level in relationship to other forms of human experience."[10] Kap-

<hr/>

[8] See Gene C. Wenner, comp. *Conversations on the Arts* (Harrisburg: Commonwealth of Pennsylvania Department of Public Instruction, 1967), p. 42.

[9] Gunther Schuller, "Directions in Contemporary Music," in *A Documentary Report of the Tanglewood Symposium*, Robert A. Choate, ed. (Washington, D.C.: Music Educators National Conference, 1968), p. 102.

[10] See Wenner, *op. cit.*, p. 53.

lan has developed an approach to the arts that divides concepts about them into four basic groups, which he has called "awareness in experience," "functions and organization," "relations and variables," and "social roles in art."[11] His first category includes concepts regarding elements, materials, styles, and media. The next relates aesthetic functions to social structure. In his third category, the concepts are those that relate the arts to industrialization, social class, leisure, science, religion, and so on. The final group deals with the roles of artists, critic, patron, educator, and audience. This is clearly a sociologist's approach, but since art is a social force it is justified and realistic. It can also be a flexible and comprehensive organization for the teacher to employ.

Within this approach of shared means of experience, we can also classify Malcolm Tait's viewpoint that art "springs from the life process itself. The facts of art are life, and the feelings about those facts are our feelings about life. . . . While it is clearly possible to describe our response to an art object or a series of artistic events in a vocabulary that is unique to each art form, it is also possible to describe our response in a vocabulary of concepts drawn from the living process."[12] As principles for an interdisciplinary study of the arts, he has suggested such concepts as "action," "anticipation," "balance," "climax," "conclusion," "continuity," "decline," "dimension," "direction," "energy," "fulfillment," "gravitation," "growth," "intensity," "modification," "pattern," "relativity," "repetition," "resolution," "stability," "stress," "unity," "variety," and "vitality," among others. These shared concepts, Tait believes, are important in shaping aesthetic experiences, regardless of the art form.

[11] Ibid., p. 57.

[12] Malcolm Tait, "The Facts of Art Are Life," Music Educators Journal, 59:7 (March 1973), p. 34.

The third common form of relating the arts, in addition to thematic relationships and shared experiences, is through their elements. This is a somewhat controversial means. Such terms as "line," "color," "rhythm," and "texture" are used in a number of different arts. One group of educators, therefore, has seized the terminology and attempted to show that "line" in music is like "line" in painting is like "line" in poetry. Or—a very familiar technique—the three-part form of a minuet is like the three-part form of Notre Dame Cathedral. An opposing group of educators, however, claims that this is not so; the terms may be the same, but they have different meanings in music than they do in painting or drama or architecture.

Certainly the differences here are obvious, but that does not negate the value of a structural approach. It has been stated previously that the differences in the arts are a healthy factor, and these should be emphasized in the course. Even so, there are ways to experience the arts, to think about them, to analyze them, and to understand them that are—if not the same—very similar. The organization of the arts course around elements can work if each element is used to demonstrate both similarities and differences. When we are dealing with similarities, we need to speak of structural elements in terms of the process of conceptualization—in terms of the beholder rather than the beheld. When we are concentrating on the artworks themselves, though, we should be concerned more with their unique qualities. In the first instance, we are asking, "What is similar in one's approach to thinking about rhythm in music, rhythm in painting, or rhythm in drama?" In the second instance, we are asking, "How is line in music different from line in sculpture or line in drama?" The similarity is in the thought process, not in the thought-object.

A few examples based on different elements may serve to clarify this point. Consider, for instance, the term "color." Combinations of color have a similarity in the visual and aural arts in their relation to saturation (the degree of purity). A pure color in the visual arts is that of a single wavelength. This is hardly realized, although low saturation is achieved by a combination of colors that add up to gray. The greater the number of wavelengths, the greater the saturation. In music, a pure color is also one of a single wavelength; this, again, is rarely produced, although blowing across the top of a soda bottle or hollow shoot comes close. The degree of color of a musical tone depends on the combination of a number of different wavelengths of different tones. Visually, a combination of all the colors of the spectrum produces white, which is both completeness and nothingness. (It is, as psychologist Rudolf Arnheim once said, "as complete and empty as the circle.") The "visual white," produced from all colors in the spectrum, can be likened to the "white sound" technique of electronic music, in which a generator emits simultaneously all audible frequencies—a block of sound in which no single tone predominates. White sound is everything, and yet it is nothing. What can we conclude from these facts? It is evident that the terms "color" and "white" are both being used here in reference to different elements. Color in painting is surely not identical to color in music. We perceive each in a different way, by different senses. Still, in intellectualizing about these elements, there is definitely a similarity; we can think about and conceptualize color in both the visual and aural arts in much the same way.

A second example can be based on the principle of "value," which in the visual arts refers to the range of tones from white through gray to black—in a sense, the amount of "lightness" or "darkness." The value of a tone of color has no meaning unless it is related to a particular background. In Figure 7-1, for example, the small squares of gray in the centers of the boxes are all equal in value to the small square of gray above the row. Yet, as the value of the background changes from left to right, the small square seems to change as well. Again, there is a relationship to music. Imagine the tone of a trumpet sounded several times, and each time with constant pitch, intensity, and tone quality. If background sounds were added, but changed each time the trumpet tone was heard—say, violins at first, then clarinets, then an oboe, and then a full brass section—the successive trumpet tones would sound different to the listener. Depending on the orchestration, the quality of the tone—its value, its "lightness" or "darkness," its total effect—would be changed. Here, then, is another way in which the components of two arts can be similar but different.

One final example can be drawn from the concept of planes (backgrounds and foregrounds) in a work. Planes in music may exist between the various sections of an orchestra or in the use of selected instruments. One group of instruments may be in the background while another is in the foreground of sound. These "distance planes" are determined by timbre, intensity, and so on. There are also "directional planes" in music, which are determined primarily by melodic contour and formal structure. Now consider a work of literature: a story may also be developed on two or more planes, with dominant and subordinate themes, dominant and subordinate characters, or dominant and subordinate locales. The directional plane in literature is established through plot and formal structure. Both types of planes are brought into

FIGURE 7-1

varying relationships in both music and literature through rhythm, contrast, variation, repetition, and similar elements. It is the resulting relationship that provides movement, unity, and meaning. Here again are two different types of art that make use of similar structural ideas.

It should be reiterated that in each of these three examples, regarding color, value, and planes, there is no similarity between the pretended art objects themselves. Each is different, and each is perceived differently. But there is a similarity in the way the listener or observer develops his thinking about the elements and their treatment. As stated earlier, we need to speak of the similarities in structural elements *in terms of the beholder rather than the beheld.*

Organizing the Arts Course

Bringing all the arts together in one course requires the knowledge and efforts of several teachers, preferably a team consisting of one specialist each in music, the visual and plastic arts, dance, drama, and literature. Consultants may be called on to develop class experiences in the other arts. Since several universities are now building curriculums to prepare future teachers of the interdisciplinary arts course, it is possible that there will be instructors entering the field in coming years who will be qualified to teach such a class individually or at least with a smaller team. Considerable study beyond an undergraduate degree would undoubtedly be necessary, however.

In planning the course, the team should first consider the students who will be involved and the over-all approach to developing their aesthetic sensitivity. Richard M. Jones has stated that "a credible psychology of instruction must at the very least be suggestive in respect to three types of students: those who are predisposed to lead with their thoughts; those who are predisposed to lead with their feelings; and those who are predisposed to lead with their fantasies."[13] Applying his statement to a related arts course, three types of experience should obviously be provided. First, actual experience in working with the arts—in creating artworks—needs to be included for all students; these creative projects also must be provided to the degree that those who "lead with their fantasies" will find sufficient activities to keep them interested and involved. Second, broad experiences in listening to and observing the arts must be included. Once again, this should be for all students, but gauging the extent and depth of these experiences against those students who "lead with their feelings" would be an appropriate measure. Third, there must be experiences for all students in analyzing the arts, and this must be to a degree that will evoke continued involvement by even those students who "lead with their thoughts."

These three basic forms of experience relate closely to what Malcolm Tait has outlined as the structure of aesthetics, although he takes the process a step further:

. . . aesthetics has a tripartite structure of process, product, and rationale. The sequence of aesthetic development in education might therefore be stated in the following way. The first step would be practical involvement with the artistic process. . . . The second stage will develop from practical involvement, but will also emphasize conceptual growth derived from analysis of artistic products. . . . The third stage in aesthetic growth is the study of artistic rationale where rationale refers to the whole history of art; its characteristics are seen through studies in anthropology, history, so-

13 Richard M. Jones, *Fantasy and Feeling in Education* (New York: New York University Press, 1968), p. 197.

ciology, theology, philosophy, psychology, and technology.[14]

Let us assume that the team of teachers has established the basic content of the course. The organization might be similar to this plan:

I. *The Nature of Art and Aesthetic Experience*

A. What is art?
B. The creative process
C. Social foundations of art
D. Meaning in art
E. Forms of perception
F. Forms of response
G. Value, judgment, and taste

II. *Media, Methods, and Materials of Artistic Expression*

A. Music
B. Painting
C. Sculpture
D. Other graphic and plastic arts
E. Architecture
F. Drama
G. Literature
H. Dance
I. Photography and cinema
J. Industrial, product, and fashion design
K. Decorative arts
L. Community planning

III. *Style and Form in the Arts*

A. Themes
B. Symbolism
C. Line
D. Rhythm
E. Color
F. Texture
G. Size
H. Closed and open structures

I. Form
J. Cyclical development

IV. *The Arts in History*

A. Prehistoric art
B. Ancient art
C. Middle Ages
D. Renaissance
E. Modern (or post-Renaissance)
F. Primitive art
G. Eastern art
H. Art in America

In each of these four sections, but especially in the first, an appropriate starting point is to expose the students to a variety of artworks in different media, forms, and styles. Let them explore art that has already been created and let them create artworks themselves. By applying a *heuristic* approach—that is, motivating the students to search and make their own discoveries—many basic principles can be uncovered. They will immediately make generalizations about the arts, which can later be analyzed, and still later synthesized into other general concepts. The important thing is to allow each individual freedom of thought and movement in regard to the arts. Ryland W. Crary has written:

> Aesthetic theory must come to school as the stuff of curriculum, but the school must never arrogate to itself an aesthetic by which to select and reject, by which to judge, or by which to praise and condemn. . . . The work of the school is to explore and to release creativity, not to define and surely not to capture it.[15]

After examining the nature of art, the ingredients of aesthetic experience, and the various media employed in creating art, attention might turn to the stylistic and structural elements involved. The preceding list suggests

---

[14] M. Tait, "Music and Aesthetic Education," *New Zealand Journal of Educational Studies*, vol. 2, no. 2 (1967), pp. 161–162.

[15] Ryland W. Crary, *Humanizing the School: Curriculum Development and Theory* (New York: Alfred A. Knopf, Inc., 1969), p. 299.

a few broad categories of this sort in the third section; the teachers, however, should construct a more detailed outline. For example, the element of form might be broken down in the following manner:

1. *Concept:* The internal–external design of a work of art, in terms of both the interactivity of structural units (the logical succession of phrase after phrase in music, sentence after sentence in literature, section after section in architecture, shape against shape in painting) and the over-all pattern of the entire work (the total effect of a particular grouping of parts), is referred to as *form.*

2. *Percepts:*

a. BALANCE—Good form in art demands a controlled ordering of components of varying dimensions, so that each part has an essential function and contributes in proper proportion to the essence of the whole work.

b. PROPORTION—Each part of an artwork may vary from the next part in size, shape, texture, weight, movement, emphasis, and so on, but each must, in its variation, maintain an appropriate relationship to the other parts and to the whole.

c. VARIETY—Interest is maintained and movement (even in the graphic and plastic arts) is achieved when change is introduced in an artwork.

d. CONTRAST—Change carries the greatest force when it creates contrast—the use of opposite or at least significantly different effects in proximity.

e. UNITY—Good form in art demands a homogeneous sum of all the parts, a balanced assemblage of repetitive elements, varied arrangements of basically similar material, and changes that are complementary digressions—all joined in a logical progression or pattern with a singularity of purpose or function.

f. MOVEMENT AND CONTINUITY—An arrangement of parts that carries the eye or ear onward from section to section in a logical and seemingly necessary manner gives movement and continuity to an artwork.

g. TENSION AND RESOLUTION—The interplay between elements that exhibit stability, consonance, restfulness, or unity and those that exhibit instability, dissonance, activity, or variety establishes points of tension and resolution in an artwork that give it movement and interest.

h. MOTIF—A small structural unit or idea that generates a larger section of an artwork, or even the entire work, is known as a motif.

i. REPETITION—Unity, balance, and continuity in art are often achieved through the recurrence of a single idea, structural element, or pattern.

j. PLANES—Despite a central point of focus, activity and movement in an artwork may take place on several planes simultaneously—for example, in the foreground, middleground, and background, or on both literal and symbolic or philosophical planes.

The music teacher might also wish to deal with other percepts related to both form *in* music (such as phrase, sentence, and period) and forms *of* music (such as binary, ternary, and rondo). The percepts listed above, however, are those that generally apply to all the arts.

With an outline similar to this, the team can then proceed to the selection of materials for study. Continuing for a moment with the same area for the purpose of illustration, there are many ways in which artworks of different types can be brought together to examine various aspects of form. In considering balance and variety, for instance, music selections with clearly defined A and B sections (in various patterns) could be juxtaposed with an analysis of the line-by-line balance in a sonnet (ABBA, ABBA, CDE, CDE), with the type of directional balance found in a three-act play (Act I ↗ ; Act II ↘ ; Act III ↗), or with the type of balance found in a typical mystery novel:

FIGURE 7-2

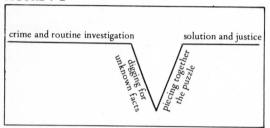

Another example of how different arts can be juxtaposed in an analysis of formal elements can be seen in dealing with repetition: In music, the class could examine the recurrence of one rhythmic, melodic, or harmonic pattern to tie a work or a section of a work together. Then, attention might be focused on the use of rhyme, alliteration, and assonance in poetry—all repetitive elements. In literature and drama, the class might look for the recurrence of a particular setting, a mannerism in a character's speech, a particular word, or a structural element in the plot.

Specific forms can also be examined through several arts. For example, listening to a music composition in binary form might be followed by a study of J. D. Salinger's novel *Franny and Zooey*, which is in two parts, each complete in itself although the two are connected by characters. Or, music in ternary form might be juxtaposed with poetry in ABA form (for example, Edgar Allan Poe's "Dream Land," Alfred Noyes' "The Highwayman," or William Blake's "The Tiger") and with a painting done in a three-part symmetrical design (such as Leonardo da Vinci's *The Last Supper* or Raphael's *Sistine Madonna*). Similarly, rondo form can be found not only in music but also in many Eliza-bethan poems, in Robert Burns' "Green Grow the Rashes, O," or in the anonymous "Fair Would I Have a Pretty Thing." One might also look beyond music for examples of theme and variations—such as magazine formula stories or Chaucer's and Boccaccio's tales in literature; or the Pont du Gord in southern France or even housing developments in the field of architecture.

Whatever approach is used, it is important not to isolate the elements from the artworks that embody them. Otherwise, the analysis can become cold and clinical. A few other general guidelines might be offered in conclusion: (1) Permit the students to experience the artwork as it was intended to be experienced (that is, attend or perform a play instead of reading it; listen to the music instead of reading about it). (2) Present the artwork first without any description, and let the students react affectively, cognitively, physically—in any manner they wish. (3) In analyzing an artwork, help the students apply a *noetic* process—the mental activity involved in intellectually knowing an object and being able to make some judgment about it. Synthesize their reactions and analyses, and compare them to previous experiences. Then, following analysis, present the entire work again for continued response and new involvement. (4) Select a small number of works for insight into the specific elements, issues, or values involved, and examine them carefully. Then select a large number of other works for the pure effect of experiencing them. (5) Get involved in as many different arts as possible, and try to employ multimedia. (6) Make use of the past as a part of the present. Introduce art from out of history in terms of its place in life *today*. (7) Provide numerous opportunities for the students to *participate* themselves, through the application of their own discriminatory powers, through creative projects, and through other means.

166

Music Education Through Nonperformance Classes

Projects

1. Select some teaching materials and determine how you would use them to show that (a) rhythm in several different arts may be conceptualized in much the same way, and (b) rhythm in the same several arts is perceived differently from one art to the other.
2. Assume you are on a team of teachers conducting a related arts course. The English teacher has prepared several lessons to show that (a) two themes or plots may be developed within the course of a single story; (b) in the use of a pun, an author may say two things simultaneously; and (c) in a crowd scene in a play, two dialogues may be carried on at the same time. Select some contrapuntal music and determine how you would present it to show that the texture of the music selections is both similar to and different from the ideas presented by the English teacher.
3. In a humanities course, the teachers are preparing a two-week unit on "man and communication." Plan how you would make use of music in this unit.
4. Consider the three questions explored in the humanities program developed at the Carnegie Institute of Technology: "What is the good man?" "What is the good life?" "What is the good society?" Discuss the role of music in terms of these three ideal conditions, and discuss the function of the school in promoting music for the Good Man, Good Life, and Good Society.
5. List as many creative projects as you can think of that would involve the individual student personally in music in a related arts course.
6. Plan a lesson on form and its related percepts as described in this chapter, using material in a current basic music book series for grades 5 through 8 as well as the resources of your community.
7. Begin a permanent reference file by going to your school library and compiling a bibliography of reference books that would be useful in developing a humanities course and a related arts course.

Selected References

ANDREWS, MICHAEL F., ed. *Aesthetic Form and Education.* Syracuse: Syracuse University Press, 1958.

AQUINO, JOHN T. *Artists as Teachers.* Bloomington, Indiana: Phi Delta Kappa Educational Foundation, 1978.

ARTS, EDUCATION AND AMERICANS PANEL. *Coming to Our Senses: The Significance of the Arts for American Education.* New York: McGraw-Hill Book Company, 1977.

Arts Impact: Curriculum for Change, A Summary Report. University Park: The Pennsylvania State University Press, 1973.

"The Arts in General Education," a special issue of *Music Educators Journal,* 64:5 (January 1978).

BAIR, MEDILL, and RICHARD G. WOODWARD. *Team Teaching in Action.* Boston: Houghton Mifflin Company, 1964.

BEARDSLEY, MONROE C. *Aesthetics from Classical Greece to the Present.* New York: The Macmillan Company, 1966.

BEGGS, DAVID W., ed. *Team Teaching—Bold New Venture.* Indianapolis: Unified College Press, Inc., 1964.

Comprehensive Arts Planning. New York: Ad Hoc Coalition of States for the Arts in Education, 1977.

DEWEY, JOHN. *Art as Experience.* New York: Capricorn Books, 1958.

DUDLEY, LOUISE, and AUSTIN FARICY. *The Humanities: Applied Aesthetics.* 4th ed. New York: McGraw-Hill Book Co., 1968.

Forum on the Humanities. Albany: The University of New York/The State Education Department, 1969.

GHISELIN, BREWSTER, ed. *The Creative Process.* Berkeley: University of California Press, 1952.

HIPPLE, WALTER J., JR. "Humanities in the Secondary Schools," *Music Educators Journal,* 54:6 (February 1968), pp. 85–88, 155–159, 161.

HOSPERS, JOHN, ed. *Introductory Readings in Aesthetics.* New York: The Free Press, 1969.

Humanities Is . . . Albany: The University of New York/The State Education Department, 1969.

KAREL, LEON C. *Avenues to the Arts.* Kirksville, Missouri: Simpson Publishing Co., 1966.

————. *Setting the Stage for Learning: Humanistic Education; How and Why.* Kirksville, Missouri: Simpson Publishing Company, 1978.

LANDIS, BETH. *Man and His Arts. Exploring Music* series, senior book. New York: Holt, Rinehart and Winston, 1969.

LANGER, SUZANNE K. *Feeling and Form.* New York: Charles Scribner's Sons, 1953.

————. *Philosophy in a New Key.* New York: Mentor Books, 1942.

————. *Problems of Art.* New York: Charles Scribner's Sons, 1957.

————. *Reflections on Art.* New York: Oxford University Press, 1961.

MADEJA, STANLEY S., ed. *Arts and Aesthetics: An Agenda for the Future.* St. Louis: CEMREL, Inc., 1977.

MEYER, LEONARD B. *Emotion and Meaning in Music.* Chicago: The University of Chicago Press, 1956.

————. *Music, the Arts, and Ideas.* Chicago: The University of Chicago Press, 1967.

MUNRO, THOMAS. *The Arts and Their Interrelations.* 2d ed. Cleveland: The Press of Western Reserve University, 1969.

————. *Form and Style in the Arts.* Cleveland: The Press of Western Reserve Unisity, 1970.

Programs That Work. Washington, D.C.: Alliance for Arts Education, 1978.

RADER, MELVIN, ed. *A Modern Book of Esthetics.* New York: Holt, Rinehart and Winston, Inc., 1962.

REIMER, BENNETT. *A Philosophy of Music Education.* Englewood Cliffs, New Jersey: Prentice-Hall, Inc., 1970. Chapter 10.

SACHS, CURT. *The Commonwealth of Art.* New York: W. W. Norton & Company, Inc., 1946.

SCHWADRON, ABRAHAM A. *Aesthetics: Dimensions for Music Education.* Washington, D.C.: Music Educators National Conference, 1967.

SHAPLIN, JUDSON T., and HENRY F. OLDS, JR., eds. *Team Teaching.* New York: Harper & Row, Publishers, 1964.

SMITH, R. A., ed. *Aesthetic Concepts and Education.* Urbana: University of Illinois Press, 1970.

STERLING, ALFRED M., and LEON C. KAREL. *The Allied Arts*. Jefferson City, Missouri: State Department of Education, 1963.

Toward an Aesthetic Education. Washington, D.C.: Music Educators National Conference, 1970.

WAGER, WILLIS J. *From the Hand of Man*. 2 vols. Boston: Boston University Press, 1965.

WENNER, GENE C. "Arts in the Mainstream of Education," *Music Educators Journal*, 62:8 (April 1976), pp. 28–36.

————, comp. *Conversations on the Arts*. A Report of the Fine Arts Project, Title 5, ESEA. Harrisburg: Commonwealth of Pennsylvania Department of Public Instruction, 1967.

Music and the Individual Student

The school's function is to expand the differences between individuals and create a respect for those differences.

VERMONT DESIGN FOR EDUCATION[1]

FREEDOM TO LEARN is a fundamental and cherished principle in our society. In many ways, however, it is a difficult one to realize if a school has become so structured that the individual student is locked in place (or locked out of *his* place) by a rigid curriculum, standardized procedure, restrictive schedule, confining facilities, and dehumanized routine—all symbolized by the dominating figure of the teacher-authority, who may make little effort to recognize each student as an individual. The problem is especially apparent in dealing with students who are physically, mentally, or emotionally handicapped, and with those who are handicapped "in the system" by being gifted. It is also a problem, however, in teaching the "normal" child, who differs in many respects from the "normal" youngster sitting next to him in class.

It is widely accepted that students at any given age have different interests, different backgrounds, different problems, different needs, different emotional characters, different potentials intellectually and physically, different outlooks and goals, different responses to social forces, different capacities for adjusting to alternative learning procedures, and

[1] *Vermont Design for Education* (Montpelier: State of Vermont, Department of Education, 1968), p. 6.

different rates for learning in different subject areas. Yet, fully cognizant of these factors, most schools place students in learning situations that demand a basic uniformity in subject matter to be taught, uniformity in the learning process, uniformity in the time allotted to master a subject, and uniformity in the methods of evaluating progress. As David E. Armington has said, " 'Meeting the needs of the individual' is standard idiom among schoolmen, yet . . . competition, pass and fail, prescribed curricula, minimum requirements, all these continue as hallmarks of the system, dramatic evidence of the persistent contradiction between our practices and our ideas."[2]

INDIVIDUALIZED INSTRUCTION

We have all been familiar, surely, with situations in which the student, expressing himself as an individual thinker, creator, or feeler, has been put down by a teacher who plays his classroom role in an authoritative *and* authoritarian manner. Recognition of the inherent problems in the traditional relationship of teacher and student is nothing new: Two thousand years ago, writing in *De natura deorum*, the Roman statesman and orator Cicero said, "Most commonly, the authority of those who teach hinders those who would learn"; and more than a hundred years ago Louisa May Alcott's father, Amos Bronson Alcott, wrote, "The true teacher defends his pupils against his own personal influence." What *is* new is the dynamic effort made by educators in recent years to serve the individuality of the student—to recognize that each student not only has different needs

and interests, but actually learns in different ways and at different rates, and responds best to different materials and different approaches. As a result, a variety of instructional approaches have been devised: programmed instruction, teaching machines, computer-assisted instruction, independent study, individually prescribed instruction, and individualized learning packets.

Individualized instruction does not mean that there is a ratio of one teacher to one student. In simple but general terms, it means that the teacher approaches a class of thirty students as though it were actually thirty classes. He does not formulate a composite profile of the class to determine needs and interests, but instead constructs thirty profiles. He does not prepare one lesson plan to teach a given concept, but develops a number of plans for the same concept to allow each student to experience it in the manner that is easiest, most interesting, and most meaningful to him. He does not select one recording to illustrate a particular point, but makes available a variety of recordings, reading materials, vocal and instrumental experiences, and creative activities to get that point across. And he does not determine a set curriculum of concepts and experiences to be "covered" in a certain amount of time, but allows each student a voice in what, when, and how he will become involved with music.

Mastery Learning

Advocates of mastery learning believe that most students, possibly over 90 percent of them, can master what is taught.[3] All the teaching strategies designed for mastery learning are concerned with individual differences among learners and ways to promote each

[2] Quoted in Ewald B. Nyquist and Gene R. Hawes, eds., *Open Education: A Sourcebook for Parents and Teachers* (New York: Bantam Books, Inc., 1972), p. 64.

[3] See Benjamin S. Bloom, "Mastery Learning," in James H. Bloch, ed., *Mastery Learning Theory and Practice* (New York: Holt, Rinehart and Winston, 1971), p. 48.

student's cognitive and affective development. Mastery advocates do not view the individual's aptitude in a particular subject area as an index of the level of possible achievement. Instead, aptitude is considered an index of the *amount of time* it will take to learn a particular task to a given criterion level under ideal teaching conditions. Traditionally, the element of time was considered the constant, and student achievement, the variable. All students, for example, were required to attend school for 180 days (constant), and their achievement differed depending on aptitude (variable). In mastery learning, however, the constant is achievement—at least 90 percent of the students are expected to achieve on the same level with the best students—and the variable elements are time (how long will it take?) and methodology (how will the learner be instructed?).[4]

Most individualized programs have a problem when a student does not do well at a particular point; the teacher generally assumes that what is needed is more practice with the problematic material, and so the same material that was initially presented to the student is used again for remedial purposes. Mastery advocates, on the other hand, recommend that when the student does not complete a task with expected success, the supplementary material used for remediation should differ from that used initially. Although the content remains the same, the method of presentation differs.

Any successful program of individualized instruction based upon mastery principles requires two kinds of evaluation procedures. The first, *formative evaluation*, is evaluation of day-to-day learning. These diagnostic tools test those particular skills students are expected to have achieved at the end of a unit or even at a point within the unit. Such tests provide the teacher with data that suggest directions for subsequent lessons or for corrective lessons. The second procedure is *summative evaluation*. This testing process is usually administered at the end of a large block of work to grade students in their achievement of the course objectives.[5] Table 8-1 diagrams a model for an individualized class that follows the principles of mastery learning. As shown in the diagram, the formative testing cycle is repeated until the student is ready for the summative test.

Management Systems

The music teacher faced with organizing individualized instruction will find it neces-

Table 8-1. MODEL FOR AN INDIVIDUALIZED CLASS FOLLOWING THE PRINCIPLES OF MASTERY LEARNING

Shaded boxes show the formative testing cycle.

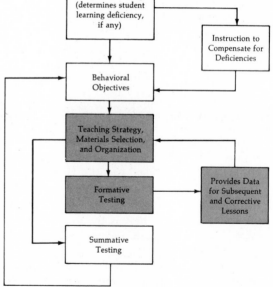

[4] See James H. Bloch, "Introduction," *op. cit.*, pp. 2–11.

[5] See Peter W. Airasian, "The Role of Evaluation in Mastery Learning," in James H. Bloch, *op. cit.*, pp. 78–87.

sary to develop a management system for instructional procedures and another management system for the wide variety of instructional materials such a program requires. An instructional management system can be as simple as a programmed workbook or as sophisticated as computer-assisted instruction. A system can be devised that will provide the necessary organization and direction for a year-long instructional program or for a smaller unit of instruction. Regardless of the extent or type of system the teacher employs, the following parts (see Table 8-2) should be included:

1. *Diagnostic pretesting procedure:* To avoid having students cover material they already know, a diagnostic placement test is necessary.

2. *Instructional objectives:* Behavioral objectives will ensure that both the teacher and student know the desired instructional outcomes.

3. *Task-analysis procedure:* Here the teacher lists the sequential tasks that the learner must complete to achieve the outcomes set forth in the instructional objectives. This analysis will assist the teacher in choosing instructional materials and teaching strategies.

4. *Criterion-referenced test:* This test is directly related to the instructional objectives (see Chapter 15 for a detailed discussion).

5. *Method of recording learning progress:* A system has to be devised to minimize the teacher's clerical tasks and yet provide the necessary data on each learner's progress toward achievement of the instructional objectives.

Any successful music course that is geared to individual style and rate of learning will, of necessity, use a wide variety of instructional materials. To ensure that the right materials get into the hands of the right learner at the right time and then are returned intact

Table 8-2. AN INSTRUCTIONAL MANAGEMENT SYSTEM

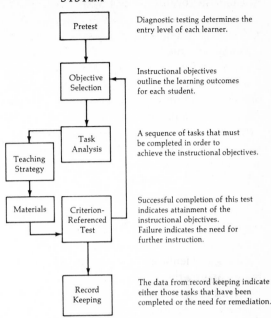

Pretest — Diagnostic testing determines the entry level of each learner.

Objective Selection — Instructional objectives outline the learning outcomes for each student.

Task Analysis — A sequence of tasks that must be completed in order to achieve the instructional objectives.

Criterion-Referenced Test — Successful completion of this test indicates attainment of the instructional objectives. Failure indicates the need for further instruction.

Record Keeping — The data from record keeping indicate either those tasks that have been completed or the need for remediation.

to a designated place for future use, requires a management system for materials. One method of distributing and collecting is strictly teacher-centered, with little responsibility given to the students. Although such a system is less complicated to maintain, it places the teacher in the role of a *manager of materials* rather than a *manager of learning*. A system that is student/teacher-oriented leaves the teacher enough time to facilitate learning. No single system is applicable to all individualized learning situations. Each management system must be unique to fit a particular materials problem, a particular instructional setting, and a particular teacher's needs. The following are some basic considerations to use as organizing guidelines:

1. All students should receive hands-on instruction in the operation of audiovisual hardware to be used.

2. An audiovisual center should be established in the classroom for individualized instruction. The teacher must be sure that backup hardware is available from the school's media center in case of a malfunction.

3. All print and nonprint software (books, pamphlets, magazines, cassette audiotapes, cassette videotapes, reel-to-reel audiotapes, overhead transparencies, films, film loops, and so on) should be labeled with the *objective number* and stored systematically.

4. All the materials used in a learning activity package should be labeled and boxed together.

5. A student checkout system should be devised that allows for daily monitoring by the teacher, to ensure that all learning materials are returned to their designated places.

6. The teacher should be familiar with supplementary print and nonprint materials available in the school's media center.

Programmed Learning

Current programmed learning can be traced back to an article written by B. F. Skinner for the *Harvard Educational Review* in 1954.[6] That article, referring to learning theory and instructional procedure, evoked many other articles in support. Skinner, however, was not the inventor of programmed instruction. In 1963, Harry S. Broudy pointed out that some of the principles and characteristics of programmed learning were present in the teaching of Socrates.[7] Still, it is to Skinner that credit must be given for formulating the principles governing programmed instruction as it is understood and practiced today.

Some of the operating principles of pro-

grammed instruction have been cited by E. G. Fry:

1. Subject matter is broken up into small units called frames. [Boxed information or questions.]
2. At least part of the frame requires some type of response from the student.
3. The student is provided immediate feedback reinforcement. [Correct responses are indicated in the same frame or the next.]
4. The frames are arranged in careful sequence.
5. Programs are aimed at specific goals.
6. Revisions are made on student responses. [A student whose response is incorrect may be directed to frames out of the normal sequence for remedial instruction.]
7. The student is usually free to vary his own rate of learning.[8]

There are three types of programs: (1) linear, (2) branching, and (3) adjunct autoinstructional. Linear and branching programs are recommended when students have little understanding of the material to be learned. Linear programs require the learner to proceed in small steps through all the frames, whereas branching programs provide some latitude to the learner by offering alternative learning paths when known or unknown material is encountered. That is, the student, according to a response, may be referred back or forward to other frames out of the normal sequence. Adjunct autoinstructional programs are used most effectively when the learner has previous familiarity with the programmed material; they reinforce material that was first presented in a class lecture or a textbook. Table 8-3 shows a few pages from a programmed workbook that is used with an accompanying audiotape.

One current form of programmed instruction is the *learning activity package* (LAP). Each package deals with a single concept or a

[6] B. F. Skinner, "The Science of Learning and the Art of Teaching," *Harvard Educational Review*, 24 (1954), pp. 99–133.

[7] See Harry S. Broudy, "Socrates and the Teaching Machine," *Phi Delta Kappan*, 64 (1963), pp. 234–235.

[8] E. G. Fry, *Teaching Machines and Programed Instruction* (New York: McGraw-Hill Book Company, Inc., 1963), p. 2.

Table 8-3. A PROGRAMMED LEARNING SEQUENCE

TURN ON THE TAPE DECK. **PUT ON TAPE NO. 2.2.** **START THE TAPE.**	

1.0 As you go through this detailed learning sequence, check the answer of any multiple-choice question you think is correct by putting a mark next to the letter of your choice. In some cases, only one answer will be correct, whereas in others more than one answer will be correct. In those questions containing blanks, write out your answer. Be sure that you check your answer each time you complete a frame. Keep the Expected Answers section covered until you have completed the frame.

TURN OFF THE TAPE DECK.
YOU WILL NOT NEED IT FOR
THE FIRST THREE FRAMES.

	EXPECTED ANSWERS
1.1 This unit is concerned with FORM, and form has been defined as the shape, the order, or the plan of a piece of music; it is the way a composer organizes and puts together the musical sounds we hear. Which of the following statements defines FORM? _____ a. The shape of a piece of music _____ b. The order of a piece of music _____ c. The way a composer organizes musical sounds	All three

1.2 The sectional forms you will study in this unit are BINARY and TERNARY.
BINARY FORM is sometimes called TWO-PART FORM because it is made up of TWO musical ideas.
TERNARY or THREE-PART FORM also has only two musical ideas; however, it is organized into three sections: The first and third are the same, whereas the middle section is different.
As you continue in this frame, decide which of the following statements are TRUE or FALSE. Be sure to circle the answer you feel is right.
a. Both BINARY and TERNARY FORM have two musical ideas.
    T   F
b. BINARY FORM contains two sections.
    T   F
c. TERNARY FORM is made up of three sections.
    T   F
d. Two sections of TERNARY FORM are the same.
    T   F
e. Another name for two-part form is BINARY.
    T   F
	
	T
	
	T
	
	T
	
	T
	
	T

Table 8-3. A PROGRAMMED LEARNING SEQUENCE (continued)

1.3 Capital letters are used to identify the different sections of BINARY and TERNARY FORM. For example, AB indicates the two different sections of BINARY FORM. ABA indicates the three sections of TERNARY FORM, showing that the first and third sections are the same. What capital letters are used to indicate BINARY FORM? ———— What capital letters are used to indicate TERNARY FORM? ———— <div align="center">TURN ON THE TAPE DECK.</div>	AB ABA
1.4 The music example you are about to hear, "Summer Breeze" by the Main Ingredient, is in BINARY FORM—AB. Listen. (Music Example 1) Let's listen to the same example once again; only this time, let's hear just the A section. (Music Example 1A) And now let's hear the B section. (Music Example 1B) Once again, here are the two sections put together. Listen. (Music Example 1C)	Go on to the next frame.
1.5 The next music example you will hear is in TERNARY or three-part form, and the following capital letters describe its overall design: ABA These letters tell us that the first and third sections will be the same and the second or middle section is different. Listen. (Music Example 2) Let's listen to the different sections of the same example. Here is section A. Listen. (Music Example 2A) Now listen to section B. (Music Example 2B) And once again, here is the complete music example—ABA. Listen. (Music Example 2C) You will now hear two music examples; each will be played twice. As you listen, determine which is written in BINARY FORM and which is written in TERNARY FORM. Be sure to circle your answers below. (Music Examples 3 and 4) Example 3: Binary Ternary Example 4: Binary Ternary	Binary Ternary

single skill and includes a variety of teacher-prepared materials that will accommodate the diverse needs of students. In a LAP, which is labeled with a number and title, the concept or skill is identified along with behavioral objectives and a criterion level by which the teacher can determine whether the student accomplishes the task successfully. Directions for using the materials and for completing the LAP are provided; they must be easily understood and easily followed. A time allotment is also generally given, although a package is self-pacing. The materials must be devised in such a way as to be self-instructing, requiring little or no monitoring by the teacher. A learning activity package also contains concluding information for the student—that is, a follow-up activity, enrichment activity, or test. A well-prepared LAP is an excellent means of offering appropriate, self-teaching activities to students who perform on approximately the same level. Multiple LAPs, of course, can accommodate a variety of performance levels.[9]

Technological Aids

Recent technology has yielded a number of goods to aid the teacher in individualizing instruction. Many schools, for example, now either have *computers*, are part of a regional consortium that provides computer services to several schools in an area, or are involved in computer time-sharing by means of a teletype machine that is connected by telephone line to an installation that may be hundreds of miles away. Although the computer is most often used for instruction in mathematics, science, and languages, there is no reason why it cannot be utilized in certain areas of music education. For example, it can be used by an individual in problem-solving ex-periences. In theory instruction a student may use a computer program to work out a harmonic progression. From a variety of starting points, the student would select the next chord or a particular voicing of a given chord, and the computer would either verify his selection or provide a printout that explains his error and recycles him back to the appropriate spot. This immediate reinforcement in terms of acceptance or rejection of his responses is an important factor in B. F. Skinner's theory of operant conditioning (see pages 26–27).

At the Artificial Intelligence Laboratory at the Massachusetts Institute of Technology, an experiment was carried out that provided the student with several phrases of a theme; using the computer, the student was able to combine them in various sequences by directing the computer to play them back in the particular order he had arranged. Through application of a discovery technique, he not only was able to hear the results of each of his choices but also was able to discern certain principles of form in music.[10]

Some computer systems make use of a cathode-ray tube on which material is presented visually; the student then uses a light pen to mark selections or corrections directly on the tube and awaits the computer's programmed response to what he has marked. Music games can be worked out so that depending on the answer or response given by the student, the computer will either move ahead to the next item or direct the student to alternate questions or go back to a previous point to try again. The game progresses until the student provides the "ultimate answer" and wins.

Computer-assisted instruction (or CAI) can be used for tutorial purposes, providing drill

[9] See Joseph W. Landon, *How to Write Learning Activity Packages for Music Education* (Costa Mesa, California: Educational Media Press, 1973), p. 2.

[10] See Jeanne Bamberger, "Learning to Think Musically," *Music Educators Journal*, 59:7 (March 1973), pp. 53–57.

and practice in theoretical aspects of music instruction that might not be necessary for an entire class, or that would require varying lengths of time spent by different members of the class. CAI, then, can relieve the teacher of routine work and can relieve the class as a whole of study that might be unnecessary or boring for some. It also can intensify interest on the part of many students. As comedian-educator Bill Cosby has said, "Some kids relate to a machine more than to a teacher, simply because a machine does not give out emotion."[11] In addition, computer-managed instruction (known as CMI) can keep a record of each student's progress and provide individual instructional diagnoses. Thus, the student's responses on the computer will advise both the student and the teacher of readiness for the next unit of instruction or will indicate the need for remedial work.

Other examples of recent technological aids are the *videotape*, which allows a student to immediately play back his performance so that he can both see and hear what he has done and make a self-evaluation; *videotape cassettes*, which permit the student to view at his own chosen time a commercially prepared or school-made program on any of a variety of music subjects; *film loops*, which offer five- to seven-minute experiences with a single concept and can be viewed as many times as desired by the student in an individual study carrel without bothering other members of the class; *synthesizers*, on which students can manipulate sounds and create compositions; *listening centers* that feature headphones for individual listening to discs and tapes; and an *electronic staff* that visually depicts pitches as the student produces them, thus relating the senses of the eye and ear and serving as an aid in learning music notation.

[11] From dialogue on *The Tonight Show*, NBC-TV, December 4, 1978.

Music Labs

One means of providing a number of possible approaches to individualized instruction is the *music laboratory*, which has been established in many general music classrooms. In the music lab the student is given a number of alternatives. He is able to select a particular area of music that he wishes to study as well as the type of experience he wants to become involved with to study that area. Janet C. Earl has stated the rationale in these terms: "If one accepts the validity of music experience evaluated in terms of individual value formation, why is it necessary for all students to have the same music experiences?"[12] For instance, an eighth-grade music lab may offer the student a selection of study areas such as beginning guitar instruction, advanced guitar instruction, the male/female voice, music of the romantic era, contemporary jazz styles, music on Broadway, African music south of the Sahara, rock music, beginning harmony, theme and variations, understanding rhythmic notation, vocal improvisation, and operatic arias. The student chooses an area of study and enters into a "contract" with the teacher. He then pursues that area of study until he has achieved certain stated objectives, at which time he is allowed to select another area. When he chooses a topic, he is provided with a guide to various study materials; these may include a study packet of written material, records, tapes, filmstrips, film loops, suggestions for creative activities, performance material, programmed listening guides, and so on. He may pick any one or a combination of these materials to work with until he can demonstrate the behaviors specified in the objectives for that area. In pursuing his selected topic, the stu-

[12] Janet C. Earl, "Recognizing the Individual: It's Important in Music, Too," *Music Educators Journal*, 59:3 (November 1972), p. 23.

dent may work at a listening center equipped with headphones, in an individual study carrel, in a studio with electronic sound equipment, or in an enclosed, sound-proof performance room. In some instances, a special course of study may be prescribed by the teacher to fit his needs, or the student may be permitted to follow his own line of independent study with regular student-teacher consultations.

Whether traditional or new technological materials are used, the student can be provided with means of meeting his own needs and interests, of progressing at his own rate, and of selecting the approach that makes the most sense to him. Usually, in music programs of this type, there is a certain body of material that is still presented to the class as a whole; however, a variety of opportunities are then offered to involve each student on an individual basis in specific experiences to expand upon and reinforce the understanding of concepts that are presented to the entire class.

Even when a lesson is presented to the whole group, there are numerous opportunities to develop individual potentials. Suppose, for example, that the lesson is on sacred music. An English translation of the text from one section of the mass could be given to the class, and an assignment could be made for each student to create his own melodic setting of the text. Each student would determine individually the style of the melody, the meter, rhythmic patterns to be used, tempo, dynamics, and so on, notating his melody by any means he saw fit. One student might prefer to write an arrangement for instruments played by his classmates, to be performed as an accompaniment to a recitation of the text. Another might wish to allow for an improvisatory passage in his melody, and still another might write snatches of melodies for various lines to be rearranged in performance according to chance. The melodies would

then be performed, discussed, and analyzed by the class, *after* which the teacher could reveal how other composers in the past have set the same text to music, presenting at this point whatever concepts he wishes to teach. To follow this up, the students could undertake individual listening assignments based on their particular interests. One might want to listen to a portion of Beethoven's *Missa Solemnis* and another to Bach's *Mass in B Minor*, while still another might select the Poulenc *Mass in G*, the Stravinsky *Mass*, or the improvised Congolese *Missa Luba*. In addition, the listening assignment could be expanded to include other forms of sacred and spiritual music, so that students could select from such a variety as Bach's *St. Matthew Passion*, Penderecki's *Passion According to St. Luke*, Brubeck's *Light in the Wilderness*, Ellington's jazz-styled *Sacred Concert*, or perhaps a gospel recording by Mahalia Jackson or the Clara Ward Singers. Thus, the instruction would be individualized in terms of the beginning creative activity and in terms of each student's interest in listening material, with the teacher's lesson on specific concepts sandwiched between as a prelude to identifying those concepts in the subsequent listening assignments. Moreover, the assignment could branch from there into independent projects dealing with the mass, choral music, jazz, gospel singing, the baroque era, film scores, composition, and numerous other topics—each of which can be guided by the teacher but shaped to the individual's interests and his needs within a larger framework.

OPEN EDUCATION

Among developments to meet individual needs, one movement that has generated considerable enthusiasm is the one toward open education. Since the mid-1960s, it has introduced a number of new terms to our educational patter: informal classroom, integrated day, free day, open corridors, Leicestershire method, and open classroom. (See Chapter 3, pages 51–53, for historical information on the emergence of open education.) Basically, the term "open education" refers to a school environment in which (1) the teacher functions as a resource person, facilitator, and guide rather than authoritarian fount of knowledge; (2) a student is relatively free to move and to pursue what interests him at a particular moment, at his own rate and in his own manner; (3) the self-contained classroom is replaced by multiple learning centers with a wide range of resources and alternative study materials; and (4) there is interaction among students and among areas of the curriculum. In addition to these four basic principles, a variety of other concepts related to the uniqueness of the student underlie the philosophy of open education. Seventeen such concepts were set down by the State of Vermont Department of Education in the *Vermont Design for Education* (1968). Although that document does not mention open education at all and was prepared simply as a basic philosophy of the education process, its contents are applicable to the open movement. (It may be noted that schools in Vermont have actively moved toward open education since the statement was released.) The seventeen concepts are given in Table 8-4.

The Nature of the Open Classroom

To the casual observer it might appear that there is no specified curriculum in an open classroom. This is true only if one thinks of "curriculum" in the traditional sense of a set amount of content to be learned in a given amount of time through a predetermined sequence of activities and experiences. Goals and objectives are still extremely important in the open classroom, as is the working out of strategies to achieve objectives. The differ-

ence is that the strategies are worked out to meet the needs of students on an individual basis rather than as a class. Instead of employing one set of curriculum materials, there is a variety of materials available. Instead of conceiving one means of reaching an objective, numerous means are used. And instead of molding the child to the curriculum, the curriculum is shaped to the needs of the child.

The traditional approach to learning in America has been a Pavlovian one of stimulus and response. Such an approach is not necessarily outdated; it is manifested, in fact, in the recent writings of B. F. Skinner and in the experiments of the 1970s in biological feedback. In the classroom, however, it has often resulted in situations that are no more stimulating or creative than the teacher's asking a series of questions that lead students on until the sought-after answer is given. In contrast to this, the approach employed in the informal classrooms of Great Britain, from which open education was derived, draws on the thinking of John Dewey, Maria Montessori, and Jean Piaget, and is based on theories of child development. Here it is realized that children respond in alternative ways to a given situation, and that their interests, needs, ways of thinking, and styles of involvement will affect how they learn, when they learn, and what they learn. This has considerable bearing on whether or not a student is considered "successful" in school. Robert B. Howsan has written:

For many years it was assumed that the capacity to learn was normally distributed among the population of learners. Thus some could be expected to achieve while others could not. In recent years a counter hypothesis has been proposed and widely accepted. The mastery learning theory holds that a high proportion of children can reach a mastery level of learning if given the time needed. Research in support of this contention has grown. Given pre-

Table 8-4. VERMONT DESIGN FOR EDUCATION[13]

1. The emphasis must be on learning, rather than teaching.
2. A student must be accepted as a person. ["His feelings and ideas deserve consideration and his inquiries an honest response."]
3. Education should be based upon the individual's strong, inherent desire to learn and to make sense of his environment. ["... in the process of growing up, the better part of learning is done independently."]
4. All people need success to prosper.
5. Education should strive to maintain the individuality and originality of the learner. ["The school's function is to expand the difference between individuals and create a respect for those differences."]
6. Emphasis should be upon a child's own way of learning—through discovery and exploration—through real rather than abstract experiences.
7. The development of an individual's thought process should be primary. ["Rote learning of facts should be de-emphasized—facts should become the building blocks for generalities and processes."]
8. People should perceive the learning process as related to their own sense of reality.
9. An individual must be allowed to work according to his own abilities. ["... schools must allow and encourage students to work at their own rate, to develop their own unique style of learning. ..."]
10. The teacher's role must be that of a partner and guide in the learning process.
11. The development of a personal philosophy, a basic set of values, is perhaps one of the most important of human achievements. ["The teacher must not dictate a particular set of values or try to impose his own, but rather must help each person sort out his own experiences and seek a set of truths which can provide a tentative philosophy. ..."]
12. We must seek to individualize our expectations of a person's progress as we strive to individualize the learning experiences for each person. ["... the ultimate purpose of evaluation is to strengthen the learning process."]
13. The environment within which students are encouraged to learn must be greatly expanded. ["The wealth of personal talent in the community should be utilized."]
14. The school should provide a structure in which students can learn from each other.
15. To provide a maximum learning experience for all students requires the involvement and support of the entire community.
16. Schools should be compatible with reality. Learning which is compartmentalized into artificial subject fields by teachers and administrators is contrary to what is known about the learning process. ["It is unrealistic that ... any subject be limited to a certain period during the day, to be turned on and off by a bell."]
17. Individuals should be encouraged to develop a sense of responsibility.

---

cise objectives, formative evaluation, and adequate time, 75 percent of the learners have reached mastery levels equal to that of the highest 25 percent under conventional instruction and assumptions.[14]

[13] Concepts, and excerpts from supporting comments, from *Vermont Design for Education* (Montpelier: State of Vermont, Department of Education, 1968).

[14] Robert B. Howsan, "Current Issues in Evaluation," *The National Elementary Principal*, 52:5 (February 1973), p. 16. Copyright 1973, National Association of Elementary School Principals. All rights reserved.

As noted earlier, formative evaluation takes place during the process of learning; it allows for varying time periods to learn, accommodates individual differences, places the student in competition with himself, and at any given moment, permits an evaluation of the student's achievement in terms of expected performance. Instead of being constants, as in traditional approaches, time is flexible, the means are adaptable, and the student is a variable.

To facilitate the freedom of choice and response that students need, the open classroom employs a new physical arrangement. Instead of rows of desks and chairs, a variety of learning centers are set up. These consist of separate areas in the classroom for the study of math, science, social studies, reading, music, art, and crafts. These learning centers are relatively small areas sprinkled throughout a large "classroom," sometimes separated by dividers or partitions. Ordinarily, large tables replace desks in each area, and each center is stocked with a wide array of materials related to the subject. As the students' interests develop and as new challenges are required, the materials are changed regularly. Very often, the room will also contain a couple of private areas—nooks where one or two students can go, away from any learning center—either to relax or to work separately. During the course of a day, a student may spend most of his time at one learning center or may work in several areas, depending on his interests and the teacher's suggestions (based on observation of the student's needs).

Open education is not achieved, as some have thought, when only one area of the classroom is stocked with resource materials and when the children go there if they have time or when time is arranged for them as a group. Rather, it involves a free use of all areas and all resources, with interaction among the children, between the children and

teacher, and among areas of the curriculum. However, this does not mean that an open classroom is nothing more than a large one-room facility with a variety of areas and resources. It is much more than this. Open education is a philosophy, an approach (but not a "method"), a means of operation that may or may not be connected with a particular type of physical facility. Open education is not synonymous with any architectural design. It is more a condition of the mind. The resources, the learning centers, the interactivity, the individualization, the "openness" can also be found in what otherwise looks like a traditional classroom. And sometimes, the community at large becomes the "classroom."

Since integration of learning experiences and freedom of movement are basic to this type of environment, some music teachers have found it difficult to work in an open classroom. In fact, in some schools where open education is practiced, music is still taught only in a separate room at a given time because music educators have a tendency to be set on the idea that students must come together at the same time, be seated in rows, and remain seated so that the old backbone of general music—singing—can continue to support music learning. In such cases, music is not functioning as a part of open education and is not contributing to individual needs. In an open learning environment, music must be integrated with all the other subjects or it will not be effective. The fear of music educators that students will then not become involved in music is largely unfounded, as one can see by looking at Britain's informal classrooms. A good description of music's integration there has been offered by Alvin Hertzberg and Edward F. Stone:

> Music is a natural and often quite spontaneous means of expression for the British primary school child. The teacher helps the child to find

joy in music, to see it as a source of satisfaction, to approach it creatively, and to participate in a wide range of musical experiences. There is little self-consciousness about music, and except for those times when an assembly is held, music is approached freely, without the formality of a scheduled music period. There is almost no fragmenting or departmentalizing of music, and it is not thought of as a separate subject of the curriculum. Music is more than just sound. Music is movement, feeling, expressing, being, and listening. It spills over into dance, drama, art, reading, writing, mathematics, and science.[15]

Naturally, music teachers will wonder whether certain music experiences that they believe to be essential will be bypassed in this situation. This has also been a concern of teachers of other subjects, particularly of some early opponents of open education who suggested that the movement was nothing more than progressive education of the 1920s warmed over. Although open education shares basic tenets of progressivism, there is a significant difference. Progressive education never got off the ground because the important role of the teacher—as planner, organizer, and guide—was not developed. Open education is not a laissez-faire approach to learning; it is neither the same as progressivism nor the same as free education, such as was practiced for so many years at A. S. Neill's famed Summerhill. Rather, in the true open classroom, the teacher is in definite control of what takes place; he maintains full authority and responsibility. Whether there is a music or fine arts teacher in residence, working as part of a team in the classroom, or whether the job is handled by a single classroom teacher, aided by a music specialist, the teacher can comment on what the student is doing musically, raise questions, offer suggestions, guide him into a different aspect of music learning, build on spontaneous music happenings as they occur, provide feedback to the student, and assist him in maintaining a balance in his music experiences. The teacher thus functions as a resource person and facilitator of learning—not simply as a "consultant" who is there when the student wants him, but as a constant, active participator in the learning process.

In this way, then, the seemingly unstructured open classroom takes on structure. To be sure, the teacher does not prepare a lesson plan in the conventional sense of a single plan to cover thirty-odd children. But he *does* plan, and in a more precise manner. While the students have considerable freedom in movement and choice of activity, it is freedom within order. First of all, there is structure imposed in the teacher's selection, arrangement, and substitution or replenishment of learning materials. Secondly, structure is provided as the teacher moves in and out of the children's activities. The typical physical arrangement of the open classroom in itself helps the teacher to keep visual watch on which areas are being neglected or extensively used by certain students. Third, there is structure in the teacher's feedback to students to help them achieve a balance in their activities. And fourth, there is structure on the most personal and significant level as the teacher helps each student to find meaningful experiences in music in terms of himself. "The properly managed informal classroom is well-structured, albeit in its own way. . . . The atmosphere . . . can best be described as controlled but not regulated. Extensive planning and meticulous records are part and parcel of informal education."[16]

[15] Reprinted by permission of Schocken Books Inc. from *Schools Are for Children* by Alvin Hertzberg and Edward F. Stone. Copyright © 1971 by Alvin Hertzberg and Edward F. Stone. P. 53.

[16] *The Open Classroom: Informal Education in America* (Dayton, Ohio: Institute for Development of Educational Activities, Inc., 1972), p. 15.

The true nature of the open or informal classroom, including the careful planning and structuring, is not readily apparent to a classroom visitor. In fact, the visitor might very well feel that the open classroom wastes time —that the children are just playing freely, without direction. Actually, play is an important component of the classroom's activities. The very young child does not distinguish between play and work, and as he gets older—into middle school and junior high school age—the distinction is still not the same as for adults. Charles Hoole, in *A Sixteenth-Century Schoolmaster*, appropriately wrote, "He shall do his work playing and play working. He shall seem idle and think he is in sport when he is indeed seriously and well employed." This thought is well supported by Britain's Plowden Report, which might be called the "Bible" of the open education movement:

> The school sets out deliberately to devise the right environment for children, to allow them to be themselves and to develop in the way and at the pace appropriate to them. . . . It lays special stress on individual discovery, on first hand experience and on opportunities for creative work. It insists that knowledge does not fall into neatly separate compartments, and that work and play are not opposite but complementary.[17]

The same visitor might also wonder how any learning can take place when the variety and simultaneity of activity and sound result in so much noise and chaos. This is a view that misinterprets what is actually happening; the seeming confusion is often only in the eyes of the observer who is himself locked into time schedules, uniformity, formality,

[17] Plowden, Lady Bridget, et al., *Children and Their Primary Schools: A Report of the Central Advisory Council for Education*, vol. 1 (London: Her Majesty's Stationery Office, 1967), p. 187.

and routine. There is no chaos from the standpoint of the students, who are largely oblivious of other sounds when they are absorbed in their own projects, nor from the standpoint of the teacher, who knows what is going on and is in control of it. Learning is obstructed more when students are tied down to a single lesson presented to everyone at the same time and expected to be digested by all at the same rate.

Music in an Informal Environment

What, then, is the nature of music experiences in the open or informal classroom? The best descriptions can be offered through the words of close observers or of teachers who have been involved in this movement. Two American elementary school principals, Alvin Hertzberg and Edward F. Stone, visited British schools and made the following observations about music experiences:

> When children want to sing, they sing. . . . Where appropriate, children are helped to identify pitch and timbre and to become familiar with qualities of sound.
> Playing instruments is encouraged. . . .
> Children are encouraged to find rhythmic patterns everywhere, in games, in counting, in their own bodies. . . . They are encouraged to interpret sounds, rhythms, and music in spontaneous and free movement. . . .
> A natural part of the music program, indeed of the integrated day, is listening to music. . . . No matter whether the child is singing or listening, . . . or is dancing, moving, creating rhythms, composing, or playing an instrument, he is respected for his efforts and given time to pursue his interests. . . .
> Despite the emphasis on free expression and a wide range of musical experience, there is no lack of "artistic" discipline, especially for those children who are seriously learning to play instruments and to compose simple tunes.

The children learn to use the important symbols of notation as needed.[18]

This range of experiences is very much like the scope of many *prescribed* music curriculums in the United States. Marie Westervelt, an American music educator who visited twenty-nine English schools, noted the variety of performance activities:

In the schools I visited, the emphasis was on active involvement in singing, playing instruments, and creative music making. Singing was the basic musical activity in which everyone took part in the classroom and at the daily assemblies. . . .

Vocal and instrumental ensemble work was encouraged; it began very early with children playing and singing together informally in the classroom. I saw many vocal and instrumental performing groups in which everyone was allowed to participate. The aim was to accommodate the different interests and abilities of the children. Some children played recorders, guitars, and Orff instruments; others played the traditional orchestral instruments. Some played by note; others by rote. The emphasis was on cooperation, not competition; on a child's best effort, not the achievement of a set norm or standard. I was impressed with the variety of performing groups, the number of students who participated, and the quality of performance which many of them achieved.[19]

Creative experiences with music occur naturally and spontaneously in this type of learning environment. For example, Lorna Ridgway and Irene Lawton, both British educators,

have described how a trio of classmates came to write two compositions:

Three boys came to their teacher one day with a wooden xylophone, a triangle and a pair of cymbals which were being played by placing them flat together and gently rotating them. They said, "Will you hear our thing? It's called 'The Oodly Door.'" The children played a rather mysterious, chilling little piece, with soft tinkling sounds against the rubbing of the cymbals, and a hesitant, meandering tune on the wooden xylophone. They explained, "We was in the library and the door kept coming open, so we made 'The Oodly Door.'" . . .

The same three boys, who often played together, came to play a piece which they called 'Ot Rice.' It consisted of a series of rising and falling passages on the chime bars, interspersed with the chatter of a castanet and a shake or two from the tambourine. To the mystified teacher the children explained, "The rice at dinner time was 'ot, so we made 'Ot Rice.'"[20]

Sister M. Tobias Hagan and Frances S. Redding, both American music educators, have described not only types of experiences but also how the music specialist functions in an open classroom. Sister Tobias has written:

Sometimes there is a music space, which may be a specific room or just a certain area within a larger space. . . . Activities may be scheduled at different hours—for example, Listening to Music at 9 A.M., Guitar Lessons at 10 A.M., and so on. Students are aware of the schedule and may choose the music activity they want. Large blocks of free time are also included in which the music teacher is available to an individual or small group for whatever the student or group wants to do. This free time is valuable for providing guidance in individual skills, such

[18] Reprinted by permission of Schocken Books Inc. from *Schools Are for Children* by Alvin Hertzberg and Edward F. Stone. Copyright © 1971 by Alvin Hertzberg and Edward F. Stone. Pp. 53–55.

[19] Marie Westervelt, "Open Education; Music in Isolation or Integration—That Is the Question," *The School Music News* (New York State), 36:7 (March 1973), pp. 30–31.

[20] Lorna Ridgway and Irene Lawton, *Family Grouping in the Primary School* (New York: Agathon Press, Inc., 1969), pp. 124–125.

as learning to write notation or to play the piano.[21]

These activities with the music teacher *supplement* the music experiences that arise naturally during the school day under the supervision of the classroom teacher, for which various resource materials (including recordings, instruments, and books) are left in the classroom.

Frances Redding has described a modified open environment in which music activities are available in a separate room of the school:

> . . . the music schedule is divided into hour-long blocks. . . . By looking at the schedule the child may discover what the music program has to offer him. He may chose, or will be invited to choose, one of the following: (1) exploring percussion instruments, (2) exploring other instruments, (3) vocal experiences, (4) guitar class, (5) reading music, (6) listening, (7) rock music, or (8) playing mallet keyboard instruments. . . .
>
> The music room has its own centers of learning. There are interesting signs to indicate the type of activities in each center. . . .
>
> Each learning center has directions prepared by the teacher. They are either written or recorded on a cassette tape. The directions, which may be stored for future use, are developed by the teacher to correlate with certain concepts in the whole curriculum, to relate to particular individual needs, to direct the child toward a specific music concept or skill, or to provide for enjoyment.[22]

Marvin S. Adler has also worked in a modified open music classroom:

> . . . I planned the following strategies: (1) marimbas, dinner chimes, and bell lyres were hung on the walls for optimum visual effect

and utilization of space; (2) overhead-projector transparencies of both popular and classical songs were created so that students could work independently without getting bored quickly; (3) a listening booth was organized with phonographs and cassette players equipped with multiple inputs and headphones; (4) a variety of cassettes were recorded dealing with single concepts, each a mini-lesson for interested students so that those who did not want to sing, dance, or play instruments could be actively involved; and (5) musical games were prepared through which the students could acquire musical skills —games involving children being "out" if they didn't produce the correct response, games involving competition between two or more teams, and games involving rewards for accumulating points.[23]

It can be seen that the scope of music activities in an open environment can be extensive, and that the philosophy of open education can be applied not only in those middle schools where all the subjects are taught in one room, but also in departmentalized junior and senior high schools. There are opportunities for the music teacher to work cooperatively with classroom teachers in arranging an attractive, creative environment in which music can happen spontaneously as well as to develop scheduled projects to involve students individually or in groups.

This last possibility—developing scheduled projects—should perhaps be a definitely planned strategy. There is no question but what music must be integrated with the other subjects if it is to function properly as a part of open education, but it must also be recognized that the classroom teacher is rarely qualified to integrate music successfully into the curriculum. Music is too specialized a discipline and requires the regular participation of a music specialist. Therefore, it is sug-

[21] Sister M. Tobias Hagan, "How the Teacher Functions in an Open Classroom," *Music Educators Journal*, 59:3 (November 1972), p. 44.

[22] Frances S. Redding, "Team Planning in Broward County," *Music Educators Journal*, 59:3 (November 1972), p. 28.

[23] Marvin S. Adler, "When You Climb Aboard a Bandwagon, . . ." *Music Educators Journal*, 59:3 (November 1972), p. 47.

gested that a modified open environment is more appropriate from the standpoint of the music educator. That is, the music or music-art learning center in the classroom should be supplemented by a separate music room in which scheduled activities under the supervision of the music specialist can take place. *Students should be free to go or not to go to this room as they see fit; and if they choose to go, they should be free, once there, to choose the particular type of music experience they want to become involved in from among several that are offered simultaneously.* In this way, music can still be a natural part of open education and can still be experienced under the guidance of a trained specialist.

The music teacher in an open music class, just like the general teacher in an informal classroom, is constantly evaluating on an individual basis. If he did not, he would be unable to plan for each student's needs. It does mean, of course, that nontraditional evaluative methods must be employed, that arbitrary or normative standards of achievement will furnish no guidelines for evaluation. Instead, the teacher must be guided by the idea of continuous progression, considering the student in terms of himself alone. Keeping anecdotal records on a day-to-day basis, conferring with students, and having them keep their own diaries are common devices in the British classroom that can lend themselves to evaluative procedures in the open classroom.

To make the open philosophy work in music education, it is necessary that the teacher respect each student's interests, pace, and efforts. This respect affects everything the teacher does, from selecting resource materials to facilitating learning to evaluating. As Mary Brown and Norman Precious, two English headmasters, have stated:

> It is so easy for a teacher to fall into the trap of labelling a child. "Good" is a term often used by teachers to describe the conforming child who is conscientious and well behaved (although underneath this veneer he may be excessively aggressive and disliked by the other children). This label "good" in itself is doing a disservice to the child, as so much will always be expected of him throughout his school career. If the children are valued for themselves, they will not be judged or labelled and if they are not influenced by the fear of failing they will be more eager to experiment with new things.[24]

THE NONGRADED SCHOOL

Less adventuresome and effective than open education, but more widespread because of its earlier development, is nongraded schooling. To cite its earlier development is not only to acknowledge its rapid emergence and acceptance since the late 1950s but also to recognize the fact that the earliest schools in this country were without grades and were devoted to a type of individualized instruction.

As the principle of education for all spread in the middle of the nineteenth century, grading was readily adopted as a simple, orderly way of organizing the school—of classifying swarms of enrolling children and dividing up the mass of knowledge to be taught. The idea derived from the European tradition of grouping students of the same age on the same bench. Those on the first bench, or "form" as it was called, were in the first grade; those seated on the second form were in the second grade, and so on. (The English still refer to grades as "forms.") Grades were established by John Philbrick in the twelve-room Quincy Grammar School in Boston in 1848, and within twenty-five years grading had become common practice throughout schools in the United States.

[24] Mary Brown and Norman Precious, *The Integrated Day in the Primary School* (New York: Agathon Press, Inc., 1969), p. 37.

Along with school grades came graded textbooks, which segmented subject matter according to what was deemed appropriate for children of a given age.

The realization that children do not learn in a predictable manner nor at the same rate came almost immediately on top of the broad adoption of grading. Only twenty years after the Quincy Grammar School opened, a plan was introduced in the St. Louis schools by W. T. Harris to reclassify students regularly at six-week intervals. In 1888 in Colorado, the "Pueblo Plan" was put into operation to permit students to work in a multitrack system. And by 1912, the president of San Francisco State Normal College, Frederick Burk, was writing in *Remedy for Lock-Step Schooling* that "in solid unbreakable phalanx the class is supposed to move through all the grades, keeping in locked step. This locked step is set by the 'average' pupil—an algebraic myth born of inanimate figures and an addled pedagogy."[25]

A number of plans were subsequently devised to deal with individual differences, the most promising being that of the nongraded school. A brief experiment in nongrading was tried in Bronxville, New York, in 1925; Western Spring, Illinois, introduced the concept in 1934; and Richmond, Virginia, and Athens, Georgia, have had nongraded schools in operation since 1936 and 1939 respectively. Milwaukee began a nongraded primary plan in 1942 and became the first school system to implement nongrading on a system-wide basis.

Nongrading vs. Ability Grouping

The idea behind nongrading is relatively easy to understand: Not only do children learn at different rates, but the differences among students of any selected age can be extreme. John Goodlad and Robert Anderson have pointed out that even among children in the first grade there is normally a range in mental age of up to four years, and that from the fourth grade on the span is approximately the same as the number of the grade. In other words, in grade six there may be a mental age span of six years or in grade eight a span of eight years. A tenth-grade English class, it is reported, may include students with reading levels from grade three to grade thirteen.[26] Add to this the fact that each student exhibits various levels of achievement for different subjects, and the concept of nongraded education, with each student moving ahead in each subject at his own rate, makes sense.

Nongrading is not the same, however, as ability grouping—the type of grouping that has been common even in graded schools in reading programs. Ability grouping is a form of horizontal organization that generally still adheres to grade expectations and graded texts. Nongrading, on the other hand, is a form of vertical organization, rather similar to family grouping in British primary schools, with the child making continuous progress over a period of more than one year (usually two or three years) under the guidance of *one* teacher or one team of teachers for the full span. The child in the nongraded class is often involved in multiage groups as well as individual study, rather than being among children of the same age grouped according to ability.

The major problem with nongrading is that schools and teachers have not followed through in implementing the basic principles. Some schools have removed the grade designations but have carried on with traditional

[25] Quoted in William P. McLoughlin, "Individualization of Instruction vs. Nongrading," *Phi Delta Kappan*, 53:6 (February 1972), p. 378.

[26] See John I. Goodlad and Robert H. Anderson, *The Nongraded Elementary School*, rev. ed. (New York: Harcourt Brace Jovanovich, Inc., 1963).

188

practices. Teachers have confused ability grouping with nongrading and maintained barriers to continuous progress while thinking they were indeed teaching in a nongraded system; the result of this has been normal homogeneous grouping in a self-contained class taught for one year by one teacher. In other schools, grouping has crossed class boundaries but not grade lines: Students in two or more "fifth grades," for example, have been brought together in groups divided according to achievement, but the practice has succeeded only in enlarging classes, not doing away with grades. Many other attempts have failed not only because of a misunderstanding of nongrading but also for the lack of appropriate teaching materials and staff ingenuity.

A decade after publishing the first edition of his book on the subject, Goodlad wrote in *The Schools and the Challenge of Innovation* that both teachers and administrators had picked up the label "nongraded" but were using it to describe "pitifully tired old practices."[27] By the 1970s, when William P. McLoughlin reviewed the movement, the conclusion was that ". . . virtually without exception, no substantial changes in instructional procedures accompany contemporary plans to nongrade the graded school. Reliance is placed on group instruction as the method of ministering to individual differences."[28]

Music in a Nongraded School

Whether he works in a truly nongraded school or in one that is nongraded in name only, the music teacher has a highly work-

[27] John I. Goodlad, "Thought, Invention, and Research in the Advancement of Education," in *The Schools and the Challenge of Innovation* (New York: Committee for Economic Development, 1969), p. 103.

[28] McLoughlin, *loc. cit.*

able approach at his disposal to implement nongraded music instruction—the spiral curriculum approach that we described earlier. In performance alone, it would be possible to arrange multiage, ability groupings at lower levels in the manner that has been practiced for years at the high school level (for beginning chorus, advanced chorus, madrigal singers, and so on). However, it is more practical to begin by arranging a hierarchy of perceptual experiences under several basic concepts and grouping students accordingly by their levels of perception, with frequent regrouping. For example, there might be several different groupings within which the same percepts (beat, polyrhythm, syncopation, melodic movement, sequence, dissonance, dynamics, ternary form, and others) could be examined through different levels of experience. Although students would generally be placed within a single group to experience a large number of percepts at a given level of difficulty, the teacher could reclassify certain individuals into more advanced or less advanced groups for lessons dealing with single percepts, since a student who grasps rhythmic percepts especially well may not be equally adept in dealing with harmony or form. Grouping in this way would cut across age levels.

If the teacher, working in a graded system, is able to teach lessons to, say, three grades in a middle school on a regular basis, then no more time would be required for that teacher to present three lessons at different levels in the same school to three groups that are each made up of students from perhaps all the age levels represented. Of if a teacher presented one lesson a week to four different grades in a school, he could, under a nongraded plan, also teach one basic lesson a week at four different levels to multiage groups without an increase in teaching time or class time devoted to music.

However, since nongrading is intended to

further individualized learning, and since in many instances the music teacher may not be able to spend the time necessary to present lessons on the desired number of levels, it is important that regular classroom lessons be supplemented by provisions for independent study. The types of experiences described earlier in this chapter obtainable in music labs and open classrooms are desirable as supplementary experiences in the nongraded school. Programmed tapes, single-concept cassettes, individualized learning packets, and so on all have their place in nongraded music instruction.

Discussion Questions and Projects

1. Write a brief programmed learning sequence to teach the principles of traditional chord connection (or choose your own topic). Use a branching technique.
2. What are the advantages and disadvantages of music education in a completely open classroom in a middle school? What about a modified open classroom?
3. Devise a set of unit objectives and then develop a teaching strategy to achieve these objectives in a nongraded school.
4. Explain the use of formative and summative evaluation in a music course based on the principle of mastery learning.
5. Give an explanation of the three types of programmed learning organizations and discuss when they can be used best.
6. Organize a unit of individualized instruction in Harmony II, applying the principles of mastery learning. Make the unit appropriate for the first two months of the school year.
7. Write a learning activity package dealing with meter; follow the criteria outlined in this chapter.
8. Develop an instructional management system for a unit of work in an eighth-grade general music class in which the teaching strategy is designed for individualized learning.

Selected References

BARTH, ROLAND S. *Open Education and the American School.* New York: Agathon Press, Inc., 1972.

BESSOM, MALCOLM E., ed. "Music in Open Education," special issue of *Music Educators Journal*, 60 (April 1974).

BLACKIE, JOHN. *Inside the Primary School.* New York: Schocken Books, Inc., 1971.

BLOCH, JAMES H., ed. *Schools, Society, and Mastery Learning.* New York: Holt, Rinehart and Winston, 1974.

———, and I. ANDERSON. *Mastery Learning in Classroom Instruction.* New York: Macmillan Publishing Corporation, 1975.

BLOOM, BENJAMIN. "Mastery Learning and Its Implications for Curriculum Development," in Elliot W. Eisner, ed., *Confronting Curriculum Reform.* Boston: Little, Brown and Co., Inc., 1971.

BRANDT, RONALD. "On Mastery Learning: An Interview with James H. Bloch,"*Educational Leadership*, 33:8 (May 1976), pp. 584–589.

CARLSEN, JAMES C., and DAVID BRIAN WILLIAMS. *A Computer-Annotated Bibliography: Music Research in Programed Instruction.* Reston, Virginia: Music Educators National Conference, 1978.

DAVIS, JOLL J. "Design and Implementation of an Individualized Instruction Program," *Educational Technology,* 18:7 (July 1978), pp. 36–41.

DRUMHELLER, SIDNEY J. *Handbook of Curriculum Design for Individualized Instruction—A Systems Approach.* Englewood Cliffs, New Jersey: Educational Technology Publications, 1971.

FEATHERSTONE, JOSEPH. *Schools Where Children Learn.* New York: Liveright, 1971.

FROZER, ALEXANDER. *Adventuring, Mastering, Associating.* Washington, D.C.: Association for Supervision and Curriculum Development, 1976.

GLASER, ROBERT. *The Education of Individuals.* Pittsburgh: University of Pittsburgh Press, 1966.

GOODLAD, JOHN L., and ROBERT H. ANDERSON. *The Nongraded Elementary School.* Rev. ed. New York: Harcourt Brace Jovanovich, Inc., 1963.

GROSS, RONALD, and PAUL OSTERMAN, eds. *High School.* New York: Simon & Schuster, Inc., 1971.

HERTZBERG, ALVIN, and EDWARD F. STONE. *Schools Are for Children: An American Approach to the Open Classroom.* New York: Schocken Books, 1971.

HORTON, JOHN. *Music.* In the "Informal Schools in Britain Today" series. New York: Citation Press, 1972.

"I Is In: Individualization in Music Education," *Music Educators Journal,* 59:3 (November 1972), pp. 18–54.

KAPFER, PHILIP G., and GLEN F. OVARD. *Preparing and Using Individualized Learning Packages for Ungraded, Continuous Progress Education.* Englewood Cliffs, New Jersey: Educational Technology Publications, 1978.

LANDON, JOSEPH W. *How to Write Learning Activity Packages for Music Education.* Costa Mesa, California: Educational Media Press, 1973.

MAGDISON, ERROL M. "Issue Overview: Trends in Computer-Assisted Instruction," *Educational Technology,* 18:4 (April 1978), pp. 5–8.

MESKE, EUNICE BOARDMAN, and CARROLL RINEHART. *Individualized Instruction in Music.* Vienna, Virginia: Music Educators National Conference, 1975.

NYQUIST, EWALD B., and GENE R. HAWES, eds. *Open Education: A Sourcebook for Parents and Teachers.* New York: Bantam Books, 1972.

The Open Classroom: Informal Education in America. Dayton, Ohio: Institute for Development of Educational Activities, Inc., 1972.

PEOTTER, JEAN. "Contracts," *Music Educators Journal,* 61:6 (February 1975), p. 46.

PARSONS, LESLIE BUSCH. "A Systematic Approach to Mastery Group Instruction," *Educational Technology,* 18:7 (July 1978), pp. 23–27.

PLOWDEN, LADY BRIDGET, et al. *Children and Their Primary Schools: A Report of the Central Advisory Council for Education.* 2 vols. London: Her Majesty's Stationery Office, 1967.

RATHBONE, CHARLES H., ed. *Open Education: The Informal Classroom.* New York: Citation Press, 1971.

RIDGWAY, LORNA, and IRENE LAWTON. *Family Grouping in the Primary School.* New York: Agathon Press, Inc., 1969; Ballantine Books, 1973.

ROGERS, VINCENT, ed. *Teaching in the British Primary School.* New York: The Macmillan Company, 1970.

SILBERMAN, CHARLES E. *Crisis in the Classroom: The Remaking of American Education.* New York: Random House, Inc., 1970; Vintage Books, 1971.

Vermont Design for Education. Montpelier: State of Vermont, Department of Education, 1968.

WEBER, LILLIAN. *The English Infant School and Informal Education.* Englewood Cliffs, New Jersey: Prentice-Hall, Inc., 1971.

Music
and the Student
with Special Needs

9

The music educator's role with the handicapped, then, should not be essentially different from his or her role with "normal" children. . . . Handicapped persons certainly have just as much right to learn aesthetic responsiveness as anyone else.

JERE L. FORSYTHE and JUDITH A. JELLISON[1]

THE NEED for individualized instruction is perhaps most apparent in working with exceptional children. An exceptional child is one who "deviates from the average or normal child in mental, physical, or social characteristics to such an extent that he requires a modification of school practices, or special educational services, in order to develop to his maximum capacities."[2] Thus, the term "exceptional" applies to those who are speech impaired, emotionally disturbed, mentally retarded, learning disabled, deaf or hard of hearing, blind or visually handicapped, physically handicapped, multihandicapped, or gifted.

HANDICAPPED CHILDREN

Many teachers believe that an understanding of special-education needs and practices should not concern them—that they teach only classes of "normal" students. The fact is that the majority of exceptional children are in *regular classrooms*. A 1970 report of the U.S. Office of Education indicated that fewer than 50 percent of the handicapped children in the United States were receiving the educational services needed, and the situation has hardly improved since then. Estimates vary, but

[1] Jere L. Forsythe and Judith A. Jellison, "It's the Law," *Music Educators Journal,* 64:3 (November 1977), p. 33.

[2] Samuel L. Kirk, *Educating Exceptional Children* (Boston: Houghton Mifflin Company, 1962), p. 4.

today there are close to four million handi-capped children in public schools. That is 7 percent of the total school enrollment.

It is true that the music teacher is not likely to encounter a totally deaf or totally blind child in his classes. But he will find some who are hard of hearing or who have partially impaired vision. He will have to work with students who are emotionally dis-turbed and with the one out of twenty who has a learning disability. Many exceptional students look and generally behave like or-dinary students; it is when we become in-volved in programs of instruction that we immediately sense their inability to grasp in-formation or, as in the case of the gifted stu-dent, that the materials are too elementary and inappropriate. To some extent, then, *every* music classroom must become a spe-cial-education classroom.

For many of these children, music can be a tremendously important factor in their de-velopment. Juliette Alvin, a British music therapist, has written:

> . . . physical, intellectual, emotional, and social developments are so closely interwoven that a handicap affecting only a specific area of the child's development is bound to hamper his harmonious growth. It is thought that the most valuable means of maturation are those which can integrate the different parts of the child's development and appeal to his whole being. This applies particularly well to music, since it can offer the handicapped child a vast number of sensory, emotional, intellectual, and social experiences, some of which he may not be able to get by any other means. Moreover, it is flexible enough to be adapted not only to the specific disability of the child but also to each of the stages of his maturation.[3]

It is important to distinguish between music in special education and music therapy.

The former is a definite concern of music teachers because the goal is to educate the child in music, using special understandings and techniques to break through the barrier of his handicap. The latter—music therapy—is aimed at teaching nonmusical behaviors and requires specific understandings on the part of the therapist in psychology and behavioral sciences. With some individuals, educative goals in music can be achieved; with others music experiences are primarily therapeutic—a means of advancing physical, emotional, in-tellectual, or social behaviors. Because of this, a growing body of specially trained music therapists has developed. Obviously, the aver-age music educator does not have the neces-sary training to function appropriately and effectively as a music therapist, but he should obtain at least a minimum understanding of the handicaps and needs of exceptional chil-dren in order to function effectively in the area of special education.

In the past, it was the practice to send as many handicapped children as possible to in-stitutions for special training, detaching them from the mainstream of normal living. How-ever, with the passage of the Education for All Handicapped Children Act of 1975 (P.L. 94-142) and the civil rights guarantees of Section 504 of the Rehabilitation Act of 1973, a more humane approach now is being fol-lowed. Although P.L. 94-142 has no provision for "mainstreaming" handicapped learners, it does recommend "that handicapped children should be educated with children who are not handicapped unless the nature of the severity of the handicap is such that education in the regular classroom with the use of supple-mentary aids and services cannot be achieved satisfactorily."[4] (The term "mainstreaming" means moving handicapped children out of the segregated, special education classes and

[3] Juliette Alvin, *Music for the Handicapped Child*, 2d ed. (London: Oxford University Press, 1976), p. 25.

[4] "Mainstreaming," *Today's Education*, 65:2 (March/April 1976), pp. 64–68.

integrating them with students in the regular classrooms.)

Supporting the basic concept of mainstreaming and P.L. 94-142, the National Education Association passed a resolution in 1977 stating that the following areas must be considered if P.L. 94-142 is to be effectively implemented:

a. A favorable learning experience must be created both for handicapped and non-handicapped students.

b. Regular and special education teachers and administrators must share equally in planning and implementation for the disabled.

c. All staff should be adequately prepared for their roles through in-service training and retraining.

d. All students should be adequately prepared for the program.

e. The appropriateness of educational methods, materials, and supportive services must be determined in cooperation with classroom teachers.

f. The classroom teacher(s) should have an appeal procedure regarding the implementation of the program, especially in terms of student placement.

g. Modifications should be made in class size, using a weighted formula, scheduling, and curriculum design to accommodate the demands of the program.

h. There must be a systematic evaluation and reporting of program developments using a plan which recognizes individual differences.

i. Adequate funding must be provided and then used exclusively for this program.

j. The classroom teacher(s) must have a major role in determining individual educational programs and should become members of school assessment teams.

k. Adequate released time must be made available for teachers so that they can carry out the increased demands upon them.

l. Staff reduction will not result from implementation of the program.

m. Additional benefits negotiated for handicapped students through local collective bargaining agreements must be honored.

n. Communication among all involved parties is essential to the success of the program.[5]

Educational psychologists tell us that exceptional students should be treated, for the most part, as normal students are treated. They should be considered regular members of the school community, and—in terms of interpersonal relationships between teachers and students or with other students—they should interact as they would in any type of normal situation. As far as music is concerned, there are more similarities in the curriculum than there are differences. The fostering of aesthetic sensitivity through an understanding of basic concepts of music is still the foundation of the program (except in those cases where the children are involved in a program of music therapy). The differences lie in the selection of materials to be used, the mode of presentation of these materials, and—of considerable importance—the expectations that can be realized.

The Speech Impaired

Over two million children suffer from speech impairment, with more than half of these revealing defects in articulation. Both lisping and lallation are commonly found, and in most instances where articulation is a problem the lower jaw is used improperly. Music educators who customarily teach a relaxation of the jaw in singing can offer valuable help to such students while promoting music-education goals. In addition, music specialists, in teaching regular music classes and in working with classroom teachers, can devise singing games and exercises that will serve both music

---

[5] "NEA Resolution 77-33: Education for All Handicapped Children," *Today's Education*, 66:3 (September/October 1977), p. 25.

and speech ends. For example, Richard M. Graham has suggested:

> The child having difficulties with the "p" sound can be helped with thin paper cut into the shapes of quarter notes and suspended from low (left) to high (right). The notes can be made to flutter if the child steps before each of them in order and sings the pitches of the diatonic scale using the syllable "puh." The child can move to the next note in the scale if the paper is made to flutter as a result of singing the syllable on the proper pitch.[6]

This exercise is typical of many that can be used.

Stuttering is another speech problem that can be aided by music experiences. For some reason that is not completely understood, stutterers often find that their problem is temporarily alleviated during singing. That is, stutterers will usually sing without any noticeable speech defect, but will resume stuttering when they start speaking again. The well-known country-western singer Mel Tillis is an excellent example of what a stutterer can accomplish with music. It is possible that realizing they can eliminate stuttering in certain instances may aid the students in coping with this defect in normal speech situations.

In dealing with these and other defects, such as delayed speech or cleft-palate speech, the music teacher should obtain the advice of a speech therapist. Many procedures that a therapist uses can be transferred to a music context to aid the student in the music classroom.

The Emotionally Disturbed

The emotionally disturbed child (approximately 2 percent of the school-age popula-

tion) may exhibit any of a wide range of behavioral characteristics. He may be the student whom the teacher identifies as a chronic misbehaver—one prone to constant disruptive action and even physical aggression. On the other hand, he may be an extremely withdrawn child who seems to make no effort to participate in class activities.

Although such students exhibit asocial behavior, it is not uncommon for them to be above average in mental age. Sometimes there is a tendency for a teacher to relate emotional disturbance to below-average intelligence. There is no justification for this except in certain individually diagnosed cases. The music teacher must realize that these students are, as a whole, quite capable of understanding music concepts, and that their real problems are in communication, socialization, and, most important, in developing positive self-concepts and confidence in their abilities.

Severely disturbed children will ordinarily be found in special classes, where they receive help from therapists and teachers trained in special education. Mildly disturbed students, however, can often be found in the typical general music class. In working with them, the music teacher should provide for individualized experiences in listening to music (by use of headphones at a listening center), making music (both free exploration and guided instruction on instruments, of which percussion, keyboard, and guitar are particularly suitable; and socializing experiences through participation in small groups), and creating music (through unrestricted compositional experiences, which, like instrumental performance, can serve as a strong emotional outlet). Special attention must be given to constructing situations in which these students can build trusting relationships with the teacher and their peers, can have the opportunity to initiate activities independently, and can experience recognizable personal success.

[6] Richard M. Graham, "Seven Million Plus Need Special Attention. Who Are They?" in *Music in Special Education*, Malcolm E. Bessom, ed. (Washington, D.C.: Music Educators National Conference, 1972), p. 7.

The Mentally Retarded

Mental retardation is a neurological condition and not a disease; it is *not* the same as mental illness. The causes may be (1) organic, through a defect or abnormality in the brain or nervous system occurring before, during, or after birth; (2) genetic, through some biological abnormality that is inherited; or (3) cultural, through the effects of growing up in an environment that depresses intelligence. Retardates are classified either as trainable mentally retarded (TMR), having IQs below 50, or educable mentally retarded (EMR), having IQs in the range from 50 to 85.

TMRs are incapable of becoming involved in any type of academic program. They are placed in special classes where they learn about self-care activities and where they are taught to function in small-group situations such as the home, classroom, and neighborhood. They are also taught to become contributing members of their families and perhaps trained to work in sheltered workshops. Ordinarily, this group is institutionalized, but there are some school systems that provide special classes for them. If the music teacher is called upon to provide music experiences, he will find that his chief objective is to instill a sense of excitement and enjoyment related to music activity. TMRs have to be taught to respond to music. Their motor development is at a low level, but they can accomplish basic movements to music. They can also learn to sing very simple songs and to play simple rhythmic patterns on percussion instruments or one- or two-note melodies on melodic instruments *on cue*. Activities need to be organized for small groups of five or six children.

EMRs can acquire minimum abilities in writing, arithmetic, and reading, and can learn to operate rather independently, making satisfactory social adjustments. They can also acquire certain abilities in specialized vocations so that they can support themselves partially or totally after they have completed their prescribed school program. Although they are generally placed in special classes, many educators believe that the more advanced EMRs can benefit from participating in regular classroom activities.

In either case, the music teacher will find that music can be of significant value to the educable mentally retarded child in building his coordination, developing his concentration, and helping him to discover his abilities. The EMR can participate in performing groups, though at a lower level of achievement than the normal child. At higher levels, he can be taught almost anything that is usually included in an elementary school music curriculum. Although regular elementary-level music books can often be used with EMRs, it is important for the teacher to recognize the implications of the student's chronological age as opposed to his mental age. These two factors will determine which music materials are appropriate in terms of subject matter and the expectations of achievement resulting from certain experiences. Physiologically, these students will compare favorably with their normal peers of the same chronological age. They will be comparable in size, have the same types of feelings, and have many of the same social and physical needs, interests, and desires. Their level of understanding and capacity for learning, on the other hand, are directly related to their mental age. Thus, if an EMR is fifteen years old and has a mental age of eight, his social interests will naturally prohibit the use of much material from a typical third-grade textbook. The music teacher will need to consult with the special education teacher to determine chronological and mental ages of the students and then structure his program accordingly.

When mentally retarded children are mainstreamed into a regular class, the teacher must be aware of their learning limitations. For example, they (1) are easily distracted from their assigned learning tasks; (2) have a limited attention span; (3) are unable to comprehend abstract concepts; (4) do not always know when they have completed a task successfully; (5) have memory difficulties; (6) have difficulty transferring skills learned in one situation to a different situation; (7) have difficulty with verbal communication; (8) are confused and do not know how to react in some classroom situations; and (9) are hesitant about participating in classroom activities as a result of past failures.[7]

The Learning Disabled

In recent years, a new classification of handicapped students has emerged—those with learning disabilities. The National Advisory Committee on Handicapped Children, organized by the U.S. Department of Health, Education and Welfare, has defined a learning disability as "a disorder in one or more of the basic psychological processes involved in understanding or in using spoken or written language. These may be manifested in disorders of listening, thinking, talking, reading, writing, spelling, or arithmetic. They include conditions which have been referred to as perceptual handicaps, brain injury, minimal brain dysfunction, dyslexia, developmental aphasia, and so on. They do not include learning problems which are due primarily to visual, hearing, or motor handicaps, to mental retardation, emotional disturbance or to environment deprivation."[8] Estimates of the number of learning disabled (LD) children in

school have been as conservative as one percent of all school-age children. A more likely figure, as pointed out by Dorothy Drysdale Campbell, who has been Coordinator of the Learning Disabilities Program at the University of Georgia at Athens, is 5 percent, with another 10 percent rated as borderline cases.[9]

Quite often the LD child is either hypo- or hyperactive, and it is important not to interpret these conditions themselves as the main problems. Hypo- and hyperactivity may simply be mechanisms for the reduction of stress in children who lack communication skills. Their real problems are difficulties in information processing, abstract thinking, organizing, and conceptualizing. Such a child generally wants everything to be in order, to be predictable; changes disturb him. He may exhibit an initiatory delay in responding to a stimulus, or may find his senses overloaded by stimuli so that his nervous system is unable to integrate them to distinguish between less-important and more-important items that he sees and hears. He may not be able to relate an object to its symbol or to categorize objects in customary ways. And he may be unable to shift set, thus functioning quite successfully in one situation but not in another where the skills or activities seem similar.

Music, and especially the element of rhythm, can be a major aid to LD children. Recent studies have shown that man is much more of a rhythmic being than had formerly been thought—that rhythm is central to body processes and to the functioning of the brain.[10] The LD child, then, may respond to

[7] See Janet Perkins Gilbert, "Mainstreaming in Your Classroom: What to Expect," *Music Educators Journal*, 63:6 (February 1977), pp. 64–68.

[8] National Advisory Committee on Handicapped Children, *First Annual Report, Special Education for Handicapped Children* (Washington, D.C.: U.S. Department of Health, Education and Welfare, Office of Education, 1968).

[9] See Dorothy Drysdale Campbell, "One Out of Twenty: The LD," in *Music in Special Education, op. cit.*, p. 22.

[10] See, for example, Gay Gaer Luce, *Body Time: Physiological Rhythms and Social Stress* (New York: Pantheon Books, 1971); and R. R. Ward, *The Living Clocks* (New York: Alfred A. Knopf, Inc., 1971).

music stimuli much more readily than to other stimuli. George A. Giacobbe has reported a number of studies that indicate "music rhythm has a profound effect on brain rhythm and thus on brain function."[11] Music acts as an organizing force that may lead the student to success he might not otherwise experience. For example, an LD child who is unable to speak a particular sequence of words may very often be able to sing those words. Another who is ordinarily hyperactive may remain still for an extended period of time while listening to music.

Betty T. Welsbacher has offered an important clue to how music teachers can work with the learning disabled:

> Bruner's analysis of the process of education is as valid for the neurologically handicapped student as it is for the normal child. He, too, can perceive differences in pitch, duration, timbre, intensity, and texture, even though he may not verbalize his perceptions. In this respect, he does not differ from any child, for in the process of learning a subject, the information on which the concepts are based is received through the sensory pathways. The difference lies, not in the learning process, but in the stage of development at which the teacher finds him, in the consistency with which he forms and retains basic concepts, in the variety of responses available to him, and in the time required to develop and "possess" a concept.[12]

Although all the usual types of activities of the music class are appropriate for the LD child, teaching materials must be selected carefully. Music literature should be chosen in which a particular concept to be understood is evidenced through a particularly prominent element. For example, if some aspect of rhythm is being taught, then a composition that is melodically, harmonically, or instrumentally complex would be confusing to the student. The teacher needs to be patient in generating a response and needs to use a variety of materials to present a given concept in different settings. Because of the selection of materials and the time involved before the student may respond, it is desirable for the LD student to make use of equipment such as a listening center that will help individualize his learning program.

The Deaf and Hard of Hearing

Of approximately 350,000 students in the public schools who have hearing loss, almost one out of seven is deaf, meaning that his sense of hearing is nonfunctional; the remainder are hard of hearing, meaning that the loss is educationally significant but low enough so that speech can still be interpreted, sometimes with the help of a hearing aid. It would be natural to assume that of all the handicapped, the deaf must be cut off the most from the aural art of music. That a person with a complete loss of hearing can respond to music is practically unthinkable; but he can!

Most of us, at one time or another, have experienced the low tones of an organ by not only hearing the sounds but also feeling the sympathetic vibrations of the floor beneath our feet. In the same way, a deaf person can learn to feel sound vibrations with various parts of his body and with a great degree of sensitivity. A totally deaf youth was seen dancing frenetically to rock music; his step was rhythmically precise and inventive, and his enjoyment visually obvious. Through an interpreter who knew sign language, the youth was asked how he did it. "I don't know," he replied. "I just do it." So advanced was his response to vibrations received by the body, dancing had become second nature.

[11] See George A. Giacobbe, "Rhythm Builds Order in Brain-Damaged Children," in *Music in Special Education, op. cit.*, pp. 24–27.

[12] Betty T. Welsbacher, "More Than a Package of Bizarre Behaviors," in *Music in Special Education, op. cit.*, p. 12.

The teacher should realize that hearing losses have an immediate and profound effect upon speech and language development. But at the same time, deaf students can be aided in their communication skills by a variety of auditory, speech, lip-reading, and sign-language training programs. In addition, they are aided in their perceptive capabilities by the compensatory development of other senses. On nonverbal intelligence tests, aurally handicapped students have ranged from mentally retarded through superior, with the majority being slightly below average intelligence.

The degree of hearing loss and the success of compensatory training will determine the type of music experiences that can be offered to deaf and hard-of-hearing students. Rhythmic activities are naturally the most common. A deaf student can feel pulsation and accent by placing his hands on the piano or other instruments, and if the volume is sufficient he can feel rhythm without direct contact with the sound source. Rhythm bands can be formed, Autoharps can be played, and experiences in dance and free bodily movement can become highly pleasurable and instructive. Those with only partial hearing loss may be able to sing or to listen to music, although they will be sensitive mostly to low and middle frequencies.

In some cases, deaf students have played in school instrumental groups along with normal students. A deaf clarinetist may have some problems with intonation (which can be helped by firming up the embouchure), but he may still be able to perform adequately in the clarinet section because of his sensitivity to rhythmic pulsation and his reliance on seeing the group and conductor in action. One girl, who lost her hearing totally in an accident, learned to function superbly as a percussionist in a concert band. Visual awareness of the conductor's gestures and of other students' responses and facial expressions contributed substantially to both her competence in performance and her enjoyment. She concluded that "a person does not have to hear music in order to enjoy, appreciate, and perform it."[13]

The Visually Handicapped

Because of the special training they need, most blind students are taught in special schools. Nevertheless, there are more than 60,000 in the public schools. Strangely, the sighted person often reacts to the blind person as though he had lost other senses as well. They sometimes feel that they must communicate through a third person, which is, of course, not only unnecessary but demeaning. The first thing the teacher must understand, then, is that the blind student needs challenges, not sympathy. He must be made to feel that he is a full person with his own identity and with capabilities in many areas.

The blind student usually develops a keen sense of hearing, and can often do well in music. He can be as capable as any other student in both solo and ensemble performance. The difference is in how he learns the music. In some cases, as in participating in a chorus, the student may simply listen to his part and memorize it. In other instances, he may make use of the wide variety of music that is available in braille.

However, in order to use braille music, the student must first be proficient with literary braille, since the same symbols are used. He also needs a background in music theory because of the way in which the music is printed. Braille music symbols are arranged on a single line rather than vertically as on a staff. Each note is represented by several symbols indicating such things as the octave,

[13] Carol Epley, "In a Soundless World of Musical Enjoyment," in *Music in Special Education, op. cit.*, p. 39.

the pitch, the fingering, and the interval from the preceding note.

Numerous materials are available for the blind musician. The American Printing House for the Blind in Louisville, Kentucky, publishes music textbooks in braille and a considerable amount of music, especially for the piano. The Library of Congress, through its Division for the Blind and Physically Handicapped, makes available braille music and several music periodicals that are recorded on tape.

With the exception of watching a performance or a conductor, then, the blind student can become involved in music in just about any way that the sighted student can. He can read braille music, he can sing, he can learn to play an instrument, he can perform from a score or can improvise, he can compose, and he can listen. The music teacher can thus contribute substantially to the education of those blind students enrolled in public schools.

The Physically Handicapped

More than 300,000 students in the public schools have some form of physical impairment. Because their disabilities are often visible, there is once again the unfortunate psychological impression on observers that they are less capable than they actually are. The physically handicapped student, naturally, is able to develop his cognitive and affective responses to music—unless he has some other disability as well. In addition, his physical impairment may be minimized in performance by the careful selection of an instrument that is appropriate for him and by the use of mechanical aids to help support instruments.

Beyond this, the student may derive therapeutic benefits from music activities. His emotional and psychological needs are like those of normal students generally, although he may often have a greater need for a feeling of

social acceptance and of ego status. Successful music experiences can do much to help him integrate his outlook and focus his self-expression. In addition, body movement to music can be of benefit not only psychologically, but medically. Because of the physiological problems present, however, the music teacher should not involve the student in movement activities without the counsel and supervision of a trained physical therapist.

GIFTED AND TALENTED CHILDREN

Even gifted students are handicapped by the educational system—their needs fall outside the scope of the usual school curriculum. As Margery M. Vaughan has stated:

> Left to fend for themselves quite as much as slow learners, weighed down by unreasonable assumptions and unrealistic expectations, they customarily tend toward one of two behavior patterns—either becoming cunningly cynical players of the education game or turning their backs on a world that holds out little promise of recognizing the gifts they themselves are often only dimly aware of. For many children, being gifted is hell.[14]

In 1972 Sidney Marland, then the U.S. Commissioner of Education, reported to the Congress that programs for the talented and gifted were nonexistent. His report had enough impact to cause Congress to create the Office of Gifted and Talented that same year and to enact, in 1974, Section 404 of P.L. 93-380, amendments to the Elementary and Secondary Acts that authorized the appropriation of $2.5 million annually to assist state and local agencies to develop programs and train personnel. A survey completed in 1977 by the Council for Exceptional Children indicated that there were more than 1,350,000

[14] Margery M. Vaughan, "A Bridge to Consciousness," in *Music in Special Education, op. cit.*, p. 54.

gifted and talented children in the United States. From this survey, the Council drew the conclusions that "(a) more students are being identified and served; (b) more states have statutes and policy documents; (c) more money is being appropriated; (d) more personnel are being assigned to work in this area; and (e) more training is available."[15]

Identifying the Musically Gifted and Talented

Gifted children, as defined by Marland, include children with "demonstrated achievement and/or potential in any of the following areas: (1) general intellectual ability; (2) specific academic aptitude; (3) creative and productive thinking; (4) leadership ability; (5) [ability in the] visual and performing arts; [and] (6) psychomotor ability."[16]

In the early 1950s, educators were concerned only with those students who exhibited academic giftedness; there was little effort to identify or provide for children who were gifted in other areas, especially in music. Today, however, the definition of giftedness has been expanded, and music teachers must know how to identify the gifted and talented, how to organize programs for them, and where to get state and federal financial assistance for these programs.

Gifted students are not all gifted in the same way. Some have exceptionally high IQs, some display unusual facility with certain skills, some exhibit considerable creative ability, and some are characterized simply by extensive curiosity, self-motivation, and broad

interests. These traits are neither mutually contingent nor independent; some students reveal all these characteristics, and others reveal only one. One of the most comprehensive lists describing the characteristics of gifted and talented students was presented by Miriam Goldberg in 1975 at the Kentucky State Conference on Gifted and Talented Children and Youth. That list is:

1. They are earlier than their peers to see relationships;
2. they deal at a higher level of abstraction;
3. they remember more and retrieve from memory easier and quicker;
4. they encode and decode readily;
5. they function at higher cognitive levels (as described by Piaget) earlier than the generality;
6. they are able to free themselves from the bounds of appearances into abstract thought;
7. they are interested in basic questions— "What is the meaning of life?";
8. they want to know why they are to do certain things and are not satisfied with "It's the rule.";
9. they have a high level of moral judgment but not necessarily moral behavior;
10. they seek out challenge;
11. they develop basic learning skills earlier;
12. some are more mature, but there is less difference here when compared to the average;
13. they learn to cope, can work out ways of coping, and learn to compensate;
14. they are able to solve problems, especially in communications;
15. due to their differences, they can become anxious about their relationships with their peers and haven't lived long enough to resolve the resultant conflict;
16. frequently they are singleminded in pursuit of that which captures their interest and are sometimes difficult to redirect into other activities;
17. they seek out the company of others with similar interests;

[15] Donald K. Erickson, "Survey Highlights," *ERIC Clearinghouse on Handicapped and Gifted Children*, 2:1 (Spring 1978), p. 3.

[16] Sidney Marland, *Education of the Gifted and Talented*, Report to the Subcommittee on Education, Committee of Labor and Public Welfare, U.S. Senate, Washington, D.C., 1972, p. 10.

18. "They have a kind of *style*, an ease of performance."[17]

In recent years, a number of instruments have been used to identify gifted and talented students. One is the *Scale for Rating Behavioral Characteristics of Superior Students*, which was developed by Joseph S. Renzulli and several of his colleagues. The scale was designed to gain data from the teacher pertaining to the child's characteristics in learning, motivation, creativity, leadership, art, music, dramatics, communication, and planning; the scale pertaining to musical characteristics is shown in Table 9-1. Scoring this scale is simple: the number of "Xs" in each column is added to obtain a column total; each column total is multiplied by the "weight" for that column to obtain the "weighted column total"; and finally the sum of these totals provides the student's score.

Organizing Learning Experiences

The least complex method of providing for the needs of the musically talented is to make special provisions for them during regular music classes. In a general music class, for example, the teacher can provide LAPs and other forms of programmed material in the gifted student's area of interest. There is also the intern approach, which provides the musically gifted with learning opportunities not available in the school. In this type of program, the student is allowed to spend a full semester with a person or an organization related to the student's area of interest. The student might work with a composer, a jazz arranger, a music theatre, a recording studio, and so on. The biggest drawback of this ap-

proach is that the student would miss an entire semester of schoolwork in other subjects, and therefore it is often difficult to sell to the administration. Still, an internship could be planned for the student's summer vacation, to meet special interests and not interfere with other areas of education.

A variation on the intern approach is the mentor program, wherein a member of the music staff, of the local community, of the music profession, or of a regional college music faculty, or someone else with expertise works with the student to achieve the student's objectives. In the mentor program, there is no predetermined curriculum. Instead, the student, under the guidance of the mentor, is free to design a special personal program. The mentor, as a resource person, helps the student develop objectives, select learning materials, organize projects, and evaluate progress, along with providing encouragement. The two meet when it is mutually convenient —before, during, or after school—and the number and frequency of meetings also is mutually determined.

Accelerating the learning schedule within the framework of the regular music class also may fulfill the needs of gifted students. For example, if a harmony class is organized on a multilevel basis, as suggested in Chapter 6, the talented student may be given the opportunity to cover class material at an accelerated rate. Furthermore, the teacher who is working with most of the class on the concrete level of knowledge, comprehension, or application could provide the musically gifted learner with opportunities for cognitive experiences on the more abstract levels of analysis, synthesis, and evaluation (see Chapter 2 for a discussion of Bloom's taxonomy of the cognitive domain).

Some school systems provide for musically talented learners by developing enrichment programs that are scheduled after school, on weekends, or during the summer vacation.

[17] In Cornelia Tongue and Charmian Sterling, *Gifted and Talented: An Identification Model* (Raleigh, North Carolina: Division for Exceptional Children, State Department of Public Instruction, 1976).

Table 9-1. SCALE FOR RATING BEHAVIORAL CHARACTERISTICS OF SUPERIOR STUDENTS[18]

Name _____ Date _____

School _____ Grade _____ Age _____
                                                                      Years   Months

Teacher or person completing this form _____

How long have you known this child? _____ Months.

Part VI: Musical Characteristics	Seldom or never	Occa-sionally	Con-siderably	Almost always
1. Shows a sustained interest in music—seeks out opportunities to hear and create music.	☐	☐	☐	☐
2. Perceives fine differences in musical tone (pitch, loudness, timbre, duration).	☐	☐	☐	☐
3. Easily remembers melodies and can produce them accurately.	☐	☐	☐	☐
4. Eagerly participates in musical activities.	☐	☐	☐	☐
5. Plays a musical instrument (or indicates a strong desire to).	☐	☐	☐	☐
6. Is sensitive to the rhythm of the music; responds through body movements to changes in the tempo of the music.	☐	☐	☐	☐
7. Is aware of and can identify a variety of sounds heard at a given moment—is sensitive to "background" noises, to chords that accompany a melody, to the different sounds of singers or instrumentalists in a performance.	☐	☐	☐	☐
Add Column Total	☐	☐	☐	☐
Multiply by Weight	(1)	(2)	(3)	(4)
Add Weighted Column Totals	☐	☐	☐	☐
Total				☐

[18]Joseph S. Renzulli, Linda H. Smith, Alan J. White, Carolyn M. Callahan, and Robert K. Hartman, *Scale for Rating Behavioral Characteristics of Superior Students* (Mansfield Center, Connecticut: Creative Learning Press, Inc., 1978).

These programs are quite diverse in content and are organized to fit the needs of a particular group of learners; they vary from year to year depending on the students involved. Private study in performance, independent projects in history and analysis, and experiences in composition and arranging are all attractive to the gifted student. So, too, are opportunities to instruct other students, to organize music programs for the school and community, and to conduct or give solo performances in public.

In working with such students, an important principle is not only to build upon the strengths of each individual, but also to broaden those strengths *according to their natural inclinations* rather than to mold them according to some ill-founded educational formula, norm, or preconception of what the educated person should be.

Discussion Questions and Projects

1. If you were presenting the concept of meter to several groups of exceptional students, how would you vary your presentation to make it meaningful to (a) a blind student, (b) a deaf student, (c) a gifted student, (d) a physically handicapped student who is unable to use either arm, and (e) a learning-disabled student who has difficulty distinguishing foreground from background, important from less important?

2. Visit a school for the blind or one for the deaf, and report to the class on the type of program, the materials used, the teacher's background, and your opinion of student response to the music program.

3. Visit an institution where music is used for therapeutic purposes. Talk to the therapist and determine the objectives of the program, materials, and procedures used, the therapist's background, and the success of the program. How might what you learn from this experience improve your own teaching abilities?

4. What are some of the problems you can envision with the assignment of an emotionally disturbed child to a general music class or a performing choral group?

5. Make a survey of local communities to discover those that have programs for the musically gifted and talented. How do they identify these students, and what are the programs?

Selected References

ALVIN, JULIETTE. *Music for the Handicapped Child.* 2d ed. London: Oxford University Press, 1976.

ANDLEMAN, FREDERICK. "Mainstreaming in Massachusetts Under Law 766," *Today's Education,* 65:2 (March/April 1976), pp. 20–22.

BERRY, KEITH. *Models for Mainstreaming.* San Rafael, California: Dimensions Publishing Co., 1972.

BESSOM, MALCOLM E., ed. *Music in Special Education.* Washington, D.C.: Music Educators National Conference, 1972.

ERICKSON, MARION J. *The Mentally Retarded Child in the Classroom.* New York: The Macmillan Company, 1965.

"Fact Sheet on the Education for All Handicapped Children Act of 1975," *Today's Education*, 66:3 (September/October 1977), p. 26.

GALLAGHER, JAMES JOHN. *Teaching the Gifted Child*. Boston: Allyn & Bacon, Inc., 1975.

GASTON, E. THAYER, ed. *Music in Therapy*. New York: The Macmillan Company, 1968.

GIANGRECO, C. JOSEPH, and MARIANNA R. GIANGRECO. *Education of the Hearing Impaired*. Springfield, Illinois: Charles C. Thomas, 1970.

GINGLEND, DAVID R., and WINIFRED E. STILES. *Music Activities for Retarded Children*. Nashville: Abingdon Press, 1965.

GRAHAM, RICHARD M., ed. *Music for the Exceptional Child*. Reston, Virginia: Music Educators National Conference, 1975.

HEWETT, FRANK M. *The Emotionally Disturbed Child in the Classroom*. Boston: Allyn & Bacon, Inc., 1968.

JANKOWSKI, PAUL, and FRANCES JANKOWSKI. *Accelerated Music Programs for the Gifted*. West Nyack, New York: Parker Publishing Co., 1975.

JOHNSON, DORIS, and HELMER R. MYKLEBUST. *Learning Disabilities: Educational Principles and Practices*. New York: Grune & Stratton, 1967.

KIRK, SAMUEL A. *Educating Exceptional Children*. Boston: Houghton Mifflin Company, 1962.

LEVIN, HERBERT, and GAIL LEVIN. *Music Can Teach the Exceptional Child*. Bryn Mawr, Pennsylvania: Theodore Presser Company, 1970.

Mainstreaming the Educable Mentally Retarded. West Haven, Connecticut: National Education Association, 1976.

MARTINSON, RUTH. *The Identification of the Gifted and Talented*. Ventura, California: The Office of the Superintendent of Schools, 1974.

NORDOFF, PAUL, and CLIVE ROBBINS. *Music Therapy for Handicapped Children*. New York: Rudolf Steiner Publications, 1965.

————. *Music Therapy in Special Education*. New York: The John Day Company, Inc., 1971.

PELONE, A. J. *Helping the Visually Handicapped Child in a Regular Class*. New York: Teachers College, Columbia University, 1957.

RAYER, JOHN. "Integrating the Handicapped," *Today's Education*, 66:3 (September/October 1977), p. 25.

SIEGEL, ERNEST. *Special Education in the Regular Classroom*. New York: The John Day Company, Inc., 1969.

STUART, MELANIE, and JANET GILBERT. "Mainstreaming Needs Assessment Through a Videotape Visual Scale," *Journal of Research in Music Education*, 25:4 (Winter 1977), pp. 283–289.

"Teachers' Experiences in Massachusetts," *Today's Education*, 65:2 (March/April 1976), pp. 23–27.

TORRANCE, PAUL E. *Gifted Children in the Classroom*. New York: The Macmillan Company, 1965.

YATES, NADINE. "How MTA Helped Teachers Get Ready," *Today's Education*, 65:2 (March/April 1976), pp. 28–29.

Periodicals

G/C/T (Gifted/Creative/Talented Children). G/C/T Publishing Co., Box 66654, Mobile, Alabama 36606.

The Gifted Child Quarterly. National Association for Gifted Children, 217 Gregory Drive, Hot Springs, Arkansas 71901.

The Journal for the Education of the Gifted. Room 103, School of Education, University of Virginia, Charlottesville, Virginia 22903.

Journal of Creative Behavior. State University at Buffalo, 1300 Elwood Avenue, Buffalo, New York 14222.

Music Education Through Performance Classes

Part 3

The Vocal Music Program

There is not any musicke of instruments, whatsoever, comparable to that which is made by the voyces of men, when the voyces are good, and the same well-sorted and ordered.

WILLIAM BYRD

As EACH SCHOOL YEAR BEGINS, teachers involved in academic subject areas, industrial and practical arts, and physical education pick up their schedules, supplies, and class rosters, and they are ready to begin. There is little concern whether enough students have enrolled in a particular course; this is a matter for the guidance department, and there always seem to be more than enough students assigned to classes. In fact, if class size is reduced from the expected thirty-five to twenty-five, the reaction is usually jubilation rather than a search for the missing ten students. But such a reaction is not likely to be shared by the vocal music teacher who has planned and auditioned a mixed ensemble of thirty-five voices and then discovers that only twenty-five have been scheduled because of various conflicts, for the missing ten could be all the basses, all the tenors, or enough section leaders to render the ensemble without them nonfunctional. This is just one indication that in order to have a successful vocal program, little can be left to chance. Although the guidance department will offer some assistance, the vocal teacher must take it upon himself to organize every phase of his program—from recruitment to performance —in such a fashion that it will continuously attract students, interest them, and provide opportunities for their aesthetic growth.

ORGANIZING THE VOCAL MUSIC PROGRAM

The vocal program in the secondary school has reached a fork in the educational road. Although educators recognize the importance and educational potential of performance, many question whether the primary function of music education—the development of aesthetic sensitivity—can be achieved in the conventional performance class. It cannot be denied that some people have had peak music experiences in performance, but performance classes must be organized to ensure significantly effective experiences for all those involved. The vocal teacher has the option of continuing on the traditional road that concentrates on performance skills alone or of choosing the more challenging track that also offers students the opportunity to learn about and perceive the aesthetic components of music, which will provide the music knowledge, understanding, and skill needed to respond feelingfully to music.

Many music educators have assumed that mere participation in performance automatically increases the participant's level of aesthetic sensitivity. There is absolutely no basis for such an assumption, for most class time is spent on the development of performance skills, with scarcely any attention being given to basic music concepts and percepts. In fact, research carried out by Louis Rubin and Nicholas Erneston indicates little relationship between participation in school performance activity and later development or refinement of musical taste.[1] However, when music is performed under the direction of a teacher who can maintain a balance in promoting the achievement of choral technique (necessary for effective musical performance) and in

stimulating an understanding of the structural components of music (necessary for perception of the expressive content of the music), the performer can have a truly aesthetic experience. Moreover, when performance is a union of fine vocal technique and music understanding, the aesthetic experience that is evoked will extend beyond the composition that is performed and will become a basis for further aesthetic response. Thus, the teacher of a vocal performance class must strive to make performance educationally more valid and musically more educative.

Developing Objectives

A too common occurrence has been the laborious development and listing of objectives that are subsequently ignored. Objectives must be workable guides rather than lofty, unmanageable thoughts. They must provide direction in terms of specific immediate and long-range observable behavioral changes (to be expected of students as the result of particular learning situations) and in terms of teaching materials, modes of presentation, and methods of evaluation. The vocal music teacher, then, needs to be cognizant of the various objective levels cited on pages 32–33 in Chapter 2, forming the course and instructional objectives within this frame of reference. Table 10–1 includes some possible course objectives for the choral performance class.

The course objectives listed in Table 10–1 are by no means complete or static and can be revised to fit specific class situations more accurately. Nevertheless, the table illustrates how objectives can serve the vocal teacher as a guide for implementing a vocal program designed to develop aesthetic sensitivity—a program based on the principle that vocal technique and music understanding can and must be developed simultaneously.

---

[1] See Bennett Reimer, "New Ways for a New Age," in *Perspectives in Music Education, Source Book III*, Bonnie Kowall, ed. (Washington, D.C.: Music Educators National Conference, 1966), pp. 464–465.

Table 10-1. COURSE OBJECTIVES FOR THE CHORAL PERFORMANCE CLASS

Behavior	The musically sensitive person:
Knowledge	1. is familiar with choral music of the prebaroque, baroque, classical, romantic, modern, contemporary, contemporary popular, folk, and rock styles; 2. has a knowledge and understanding of such choral forms as the motet, madrigal, cantata, oratorio, chorale, mass, and arranged folk and popular songs; 3. has a knowledge of major choral composers of all eras and styles who have made important contributions to the development of choral literature—e.g., Palestrina, Handel, Bach, Brahms, Debussy, Thompson, Britten, and Persichetti; 4. knows that in today's society, music is a form of expression befitting many aspects of contemporary life—joy, love, sorrow, protest, worship, entertainment, and so on; 5. knows that regardless of the type of choral music performed, the basic concepts related to pitch, duration, intensity, and quality are ever present; and 6. has a knowledge of the basic principles related to fine choral technique —i.e., good posture, breath control, tonal balance, tone production, intonation, and phrasing.
Understanding	1. understands how melody, harmony, rhythm, tone color, dynamics, tempo, and good choral technique unite to produce a fine performance; 2. understands the various voice classifications with regard to range and quality; 3. understands the need for developing choral technique and how it relates to the performance of a particular composition; 4. understands the director's conducting gestures as they relate to the basic beat, dynamic and tempo changes, and so on; 5. understands that developing the ability to perceive the aesthetic components of music is an important function of the choral class; 6. recognizes the similarity of music and the arts of a particular period; 7. discriminates between good and poor performance of his own group as well as others and can verbalize why the performance was good or poor beyond the point of "I liked it" or "I didn't like it"; 8. recognizes that style and textual content influence the interpretation of each composition; and 9. understands whether he has the type of vocal ability suitable to be developed for a music career.
Skill	1. has developed some facility to interpret music notation when singing familiar and unfamiliar songs; 2. has developed the ability to recognize aurally and visually the form of a piece of music, its metric organization, its tonal organization, and so on; 3. has developed some facility with vocal technique;

The Vocal Music Program

Behavior	The musically sensitive person:
	4. follows the conductor's gestures with adequate skill; and
	5. can express his own emotions through singing.
Attitude	1. tolerates the music preferences of others;
	2. willingly participates in a discussion concerning music performed or listened to;
	3. encourages and respects the vocal abilities and expressions of others;
	4. works to increase his own vocal ability through formal and informal study;
	5. participates in school, church, and community choral activities;
	6. collects recordings of choral groups and singers;
	7. attends concerts of vocal and instrumental music;
	8. encourages friends to become members of school and community vocal groups;
	9. participates in college and community choral groups after leaving high school; and
	10. serves on committees that work toward the development of music and the other arts.
Appreciation	1. is gratified emotionally and intellectually through involvement in singing;
	2. is sensitive to the place of vocal music in American society and the need of all individuals for aesthetic reaction and expression;
	3. respects artistic vocal performance of all types of music and the skills and talents of vocal artists;
	4. enjoys his experiences with vocal music to the extent that he desires to include instrumental music as well;
	5. listens to choral music with discrimination regarding interpretation, tone quality, and so on; and
	6. is more selective in the quality of choral music he chooses to hear at concerts and on recordings.
Habits	1. attends all choir rehearsals and school concerts;
	2. takes his choir music home to practice;
	3. remembers to apply his knowledge of vocal technique to all his singing; and
	4. displays proper decorum when attending concerts.

Recruiting Students

In most secondary schools, vocal music is offered on an elective basis and the successful vocal teacher must plan his recruiting campaign along two independent lines—first, he must make students aware of what the vocal program includes, and second, he must actually contact, audition, and sign up students. In the first phase of the campaign, which is a never-ending process, the following suggestions have been successfully applied:

Communications Media

To keep the vocal music program in the minds of students and parents is an essential part of a recruitment campaign—a task that should not be restricted to in-school communications media. Local newspapers should be provided with information concerning (1) concerts, recitals, and other vocal music performances; (2) students who have been chosen for membership in district, all-state, regional, national, or other special choral organizations; (3) events such as exchange concerts, music festivals, and special individual or choir awards; (4) choral social events such as dinners, beach parties, and attendance at professional concerts; and (5) students who plan careers in music and have received scholarships or college acceptances.

The school newspaper or school magazine should also be utilized. A music reporter in charge of a column devoted partially to choral events can contribute a great deal.

Using radio and television broadcasts for appearances and public service announcements will further promote an awareness of the school's vocal program, and as with local newspapers, coverage will extend beyond the limits of the school. The use of the school intercom and closed-circuit television provides performance opportunities and direct communication with the student body. These two media can be used to campaign for additional membership, announce coming music events, and also provide the school administration with a vehicle for recognizing and complimenting the vocal groups for a job well done.

FIGURE 10-1

FIGURE 10-2

Bulletin Boards

School bulletin boards—especially in areas such as the cafeteria, the library, the student lounge, and near entrances and exits where traffic is at a maximum—can be used for posters to announce special music events and membership drives for the various choral organizations. The posters should be simple, to the point, and eye catching; they can easily be made with the cooperation of the art department, as illustrated in Figures 10-1, 10-2, and 10-3.

The bulletin board in the immediate area of the choral room should contain formal and informal pictures of the performing groups, a collection of suitable cartoons, special notices, articles and pictures from local newspapers, and most important of all, a section where the choral teacher can post comments about the progress of each group, such as those illustrated in Figure 10-4.

The vocal bulletin board must be so arranged that it will maintain interest and become a habit not only with the membership but with general students who pass by it. It should be changed often and contain information that is pertinent, interesting, and up-to-date. If the vocal teacher finds that it is impossible to maintain the bulletin board personally, then this routine should be assigned to one or two responsible students from each choral group on a rotating basis.

Assemblies

Every opportunity for performance before the student body should be taken. Whether an assembly is devoted exclusively to music or the choir is to sing just one or two selections, the impression made upon the student

FIGURE 10-3

FIGURE 10-4

body—the prospective vocal group members—can be lasting. Therefore, the director must be sure that his group looks well, sings well, and performs music that will hold the interest of the audience. A poor performance or uninteresting music not only will discourage new membership but also may bring peer ridicule upon present choir members.

In many schools, awards assemblies are presented each year to honor members of athletic organizations. It is important that any vocal music awards that are planned be presented in a similar manner so that outstanding vocal performers receive as much public recognition as is accorded members of athletic teams.

Once the student body is aware of the existence of a successful vocal program, the second phase of the recruiting process—that is, *when* to recruit and *how* to recruit—becomes easier, though not necessarily automatic. All recruiting should be done during the end of the school year so that vocal performance classes can begin in September without delay. However, it cannot be left to the last few weeks in June. Since many schools employ computer scheduling, guidance counselors and administrative staff are forced to work toward specific deadlines. The vocal teacher, then, needs to know the final date when music can be added to computer scheduling cards. When the recruiting should begin will depend upon this date and the amount of time it takes the music teacher to complete his auditions. Early recruitment also gives the vocal teacher some indication of group size and potential balance to help him in his planning. (If for some reason expected members are missing because of unforeseen schedule problems and additional recruiting must be done in September, it should be limited to four or five days; then the teacher should proceed to develop the best possible group with those students he has.)

The method of recruitment depends, to some extent, upon the vocal teacher and what works best for him in a particular situation. However, the suggestions that follow have been used successfully and can be adapted to a variety of school situations. For example, when seeking membership of elementary school youngsters for junior or middle school vocal performance groups, or of junior or middle school students for high school choral organizations, an assembly by a number of vocal groups from each respective upper level will provide prospective members with the opportunity to observe present group membership, the kinds of songs they sing, and the general reaction of the groups to the director. The assembly program also allows the teacher to explain the vocal program and outline the procedure to be followed by students who are interested in becoming members. Soon after the assembly, arrangements should be made with the administrators of the lower-level schools for auditions. On the elementary level, a visit to each classroom and a quick group audition will be suitable. In the middle or junior-high school, the high school choral director can (1) expect the vocal teacher on this level to encourage members of his performance groups to continue singing in high school, (2) seek assistance from the general music teacher and get the names of those students who are not currently enrolled in vocal performance but who show good potential, (3) contact the guidance department for the names of those students who have not elected vocal music but do have time in their schedules, and (4) put out a general call for members and then meet with interested students.

When recruiting is done from the existing student body, the vocal teacher first checks to see how many present members are returning next year and how many of these will be eligible for membership in a higher performance level group. After appraising personnel needs, the vocal teacher then announces the call for new members, using the communications media and other methods previously discussed and stating specifically when he will be available to meet with interested students.

The importance and effectiveness of the personal invitation, extended to a student to join a choral group, and of the individual interview should not be underestimated. When recruiting is left to group meetings, some students, especially the boys, may hesitate to join even though they would like to give it a try. Furthermore, the individual interview gives the student and the teacher an opportunity to appraise each other on a more personal basis. Here are some suggestions that should help to guide the successful audition-interview:

1. Tell the student where you got his name (from a friend, a guidance counselor, another teacher), and explain that the personal interview is one of the procedures used each year to enlist new members.

2. Be enthusiastic about the vocal group for which you are seeking members.

3. Show all prospective members a list of students who have signed up. Some may be friends, and this step will also assure each prospect that if he joins, he won't be alone.

4. Assure the student at the beginning of the interview that membership is *elective:* he doesn't have to join if he doesn't want to, and furthermore, if he doesn't want to join he doesn't have to give any reason why. This approach will relieve the student who doesn't want to sing from the pressure of coming up with some lame excuse for refusing.

5. Be honest in describing the purpose and activities of the various choral groups. Don't high-pressure students to join. Tell them exactly how it is, because *sincerity*, especially with high school students, is more effective than high pressure.

6. If the student wishes to join, the audition should be carried out immediately.

7. Membership for each group should be oversubscribed to counteract possible membership loss as a result of schedule conflicts.

After auditions have been completed and membership lists have been posted and sent to the guidance department for scheduling, the vocal teacher's recruitment job is usually completed. However, if he teaches in a school where there are an unusual number of conflicts, the vocal teacher should check with the principal to see when scheduling will be completed in order that he may appraise, as soon as possible, any personnel problems. If such a plan is followed, then scheduling changes can be made before the opening of school, at a time when the guidance department and the administrative staff are not inundated with opening-day problems. In one community, for example, which scheduled by computer, the vocal teacher had a highly selective ensemble of nine girls and each year the computer failed to schedule all of them. However, early in August the director would check with the principal, who would pull their cards and successfully schedule them by hand. The teacher also followed the same plan to ensure having his key singers and accompanists in other groups. While even hand scheduling failed in some instances, the percentage of successes greatly outnumbered the failures.

Auditioning Members

The effective voice audition should provide information related to the floor and ceiling of the singer's range and the basic quality of the voice, both of which are needed to determine individual part assignment and total group balance. However, the audition can extend beyond this point to determine pitch accuracy, level of sight-reading ability, tonal memory, blending potential of the voice quality, ability to sing a part independently, vocal maturity (changed, changing, or unchanged), students who have potential vocal talent, and students who are most suitable for a particular group.

The individual audition is, of course, the most accurate. However, group testing (not to exceed six singers) can serve the purpose when auditions are *not* for a highly selective group, when there is little time available for individual auditions, or when students hesitate to audition alone and can gain some degree of confidence by "trying out" with their friends. Nevertheless, during the group audition there are times when the teacher must listen individually, as in cases when it is impossible to determine to whom a problematic voice belongs or when it is necessary to determine individual tonal memory and sight-reading levels.

In the lower middle school, the ranges (approximately between B and G^2) and qualities are quite homogeneous, and part assignments are not complex. Some teachers prefer to alternate parts, giving all members the opportunity to sing both the melody and the harmony, whereas other teachers prefer permanent part assignments, stressing the advantage of having boys sing the harmony part as a preparation for the time when they will become tenors and basses. In the upper-middle school or junior-high school, classification of the adolescent voice becomes more complex, and range more than quality serves as the determining factor for part assignment. Girls' voices are still quite homogeneous in quality

at this time (thin and breathy in the seventh grade; gradually losing the breathy quality and gaining body in the eighth and ninth grades) and range extends from A to B^2. The ease with which girls sing in the upper limits of their voices will help guide the teacher in making part assignments as illustrated in Figure 10-5.

In dealing with boys, the teacher will find that the unchanged voice is far richer and more resonant than that of the girls. However, the range is primarily the same and Figure 10-5 can also be used as a guide for part designation. For initial identification of boys with changed or changing voices, the teacher can observe such physical characteristics as the enlarged larynx, the appearance of facial hair, and most obvious, the lowering of the speaking voice. The range of the boy's changing voice can be found somewhere between F and C^2. Although in many respects it does retain some of its unchanged quality in the upper register, it becomes considerably heavier as it lowers. During this period of change, the teacher must be on the alert to find singing material with suitable range, and must provide for retesting voices at regular intervals in order to ensure proper part assignments. Duncan McKenzie maintains that the "comfortable range"[2] approach is the most suitable technique for preserving the boy's voice while it is in the process of changing. As the boy's voice begins to lower he is designated as an alto-tenor and is placed in the next lowest part. When the boylike reg-

[2] Duncan McKenzie, *Training the Boy's Changing Voice* (Brunswick, New Jersey: Rutgers University Press, 1956), p. 28.

FIGURE 10-5

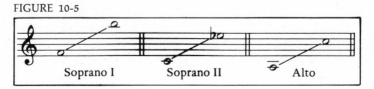

Soprano I   Soprano II   Alto

FIGURE 10-6

Bass   Tenor

FIGURE 10-7

AUDITION DATA CARD

Name _____ Grade _____
Address _____ Phone _____

_____

Do you play a musical instrument? _____
What instrument? _____
How long did you study? _____

Have you studied voice? _____ How long? _____
Teacher's name _____ Phone _____

Previous choral experience _____
_____

Part(s) sung before _____

_____
AUDITION REMARKS

Range ═══════   Part Assignment (circle)
                            S1 S2 A1 A2
                            T1 T2 B1 B2
Tone Quality _____   Group Assignment
Intonation _____   1. _____
Sight-reading _____   2. _____
Tonal Memory _____   3. _____

ister of the changing voice finally disappears and is replaced by additional tones in the lower range, the voice change is complete. If the boy is to become a bass rather than a tenor, then the change is achieved more rapidly. The delay in the final settling of the tenor voice is caused by what McKenzie calls the moving-up process, in which these boys go through still another adjustment after their voices lower. During this final adjustment, they lose some tones from the lower register and simultaneously gain some in the upper register. The range of these newly developed basses and tenors is illustrated in Figure 10-6.

At this point the reader will find it helpful to refer back to Chapter 4, pages 83 to 84, for a review of information already presented in reference to the unique character of the middle-school youngster's voice.

During the final two years of high school, most adolescent voices have reached a fairly stable level of maturity and can be satisfactorily classified according to the categories presented in Table 10-2.

The teacher who has an understanding of the ranges and qualities of voices to be auditioned must further determine what procedure, techniques, and materials are to be used, and how the data gained shall be recorded for future evaluation. While most teachers develop their own auditioning process to fit a particular situation or time limitation, the following suggestions should be helpful because of their flexibility and adaptability:

1. An audition data card should be devised to provide a maximum amount of information that can be recorded with a minimum amount of effort. An example is shown in Figure 10-7.

2. In determining range and quality, the teacher can use the vocal exercises suggested in parts (a) and (b) of Figure 10-8 to determine upper range; part (c) to discover vocal flexibility and upper range; and part (d) to locate the most comfortable lower range.

It is advisable to continue this phase of the audition by having the student sing a familiar song of his own choosing. A song performed in a medium tempo is desirable since it permits concentration on various factors related to tone quality. Both range and quality can be further defined through the song because the student must sustain vowel sounds and connect vowels and consonants in various patterns. To concentrate on range and its effect on quality, one or two phrases of the song may be selected for repeated per-

Table 10-2. HIGH SCHOOL VOICE CLASSIFICATION CHART

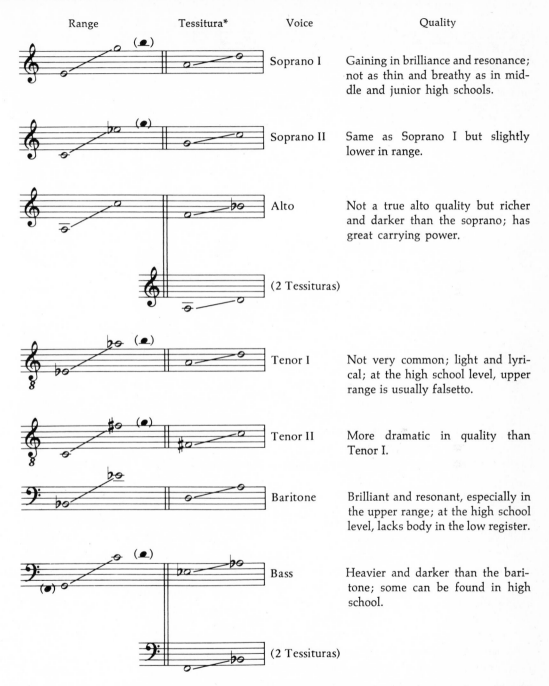

Range	Tessitura*	Voice	Quality
		Soprano I	Gaining in brilliance and resonance; not as thin and breathy as in middle and junior high schools.
		Soprano II	Same as Soprano I but slightly lower in range.
		Alto	Not a true alto quality but richer and darker than the soprano; has great carrying power.
		(2 Tessituras)	
		Tenor I	Not very common; light and lyrical; at the high school level, upper range is usually falsetto.
		Tenor II	More dramatic in quality than Tenor I.
		Baritone	Brilliant and resonant, especially in the upper range; at the high school level, lacks body in the low register.
		Bass	Heavier and darker than the baritone; some can be found in high school.
		(2 Tessituras)	

*The tessitura is that portion of the complete vocal range that is most comfortable for sustained singing; the term is also used in reference to the average position of tones in music to be sung (in contrast to the entire range of the music).

FIGURE 10-8

(a)

Ah_____   Ah_____ etc.

(b)

Ah_____   Ah_____ etc.

(c)

Ah_____   Ah_____ etc.

(d)

Ah_____   Ah_____ etc.

The teacher should feel free to use any other vowel that may be more suitable.

formance, raising and lowering the key successively by half steps.

Voices that may have questionable blending quality may also be detected at this time—for example, voices that are nasal and strident; overly breathy; forced and sharp in pitch; unfocused and unsupported, tending to be flat in pitch; and those with generally poor intonation. The young vocalist who wants to sing and falls into one of these categories can be provided with remedial attention in the general music class or a nonselective chorus.

3. A standing SATB quartet can be used to evaluate the singer's ability to carry his part independently. When this is done, the auditioning singer replaces the quartet member of his respective part. If a quartet is unavailable, the teacher may then play all of the parts on the piano excluding the one that is being sung. It is important that prior to this portion of the audition the singer have the opportunity to become familiar with the part to be sung. If the singer is required to sight-read at this time, then the level of his independence is *not* being measured. Since many students who have a low level of music reading ability are quite capable of sustaining a part independently once it has been learned, it is advisable not to couple sight-reading with this portion of the audition.

4. Singing a familiar song, as well as some ascending and descending scales and arpeggios in a comfortable range (unaccompanied), is a quick way to gain insight regarding a singer's pitch accuracy.

5. A more accurate evaluation of sight-reading ability can be attained if a number of graded pieces are used ranging from very easy to very difficult. The student should feel free to sing the melody with sol-fa syllables, numbers, a neutral syllable, or immediately with the words.

6. To evaluate how quickly and accurately

a singer can reproduce tones he hears (tonal memory), the teacher may either sing or play a series of tones on the piano or sing a short excerpt from actual choir repertoire.

7. When auditions must be given in a classroom with all the other students present, as in general music, the procedure must be so organized as not to embarrass or offend the singer. The teacher will need to assign desk work for those who are not auditioning, be in a position where class behavior is observable, and be sure that auditioning students are not facing the class.

Selecting Choral Literature

The success of many choral groups can be attributed partly to the careful selection of music literature. The search for suitable music is a difficult, time-consuming, never-ending process. The most important consideration in this search for repertoire is not to choose music without seeing it. Some music publishers and distributors have catalogs that list only composer, title, arrangement, and general level of difficulty. Such catalogs are of limited value to the busy vocal teacher since they fail to provide enough essential information to decide whether a composition meets the performance needs of a specific group. It is imperative that the teacher examine and analyze all the music being considered in terms of its specific suitability. The following questions might be raised in evaluating a choral selection:

1. Does it provide for the development of music knowledge, understanding, and skill?

2. Does it have musical worth?

3. If it is an adaptation of the original, has the adaptation retained the integrity of the composition?

4. Does it have student and audience appeal?

5. Are the ranges of all the parts suitable?

6. Are there any passages in which the tessitura lies uncomfortably high or low for an extended period of time, making the music too demanding for young voices?

7. If there are divisible parts, do they fall to weak or strong sections of the chorus? Can the group handle the additional parts?

8. Are the textual style and content suitable or are they too mature or immature?

9. Are the rhythmic, intervallic, harmonic, and interpretive difficulties within the group's capability?

10. Will student accompanists be able to play the accompaniment?

11. Does it provide variety in style, texture, harmonic content, and mood when compared with other music already chosen?

12. Does it help to balance the total selected repertoire in terms of various levels of difficulty, thus offering the group immediate success and satisfaction as well as long-range challenges?

To secure music for the purpose of analysis, the teacher will find that publishing companies, generally, will send free examination copies of most standard and new publications upon request. Notifications of such offers are sent periodically to secondary schools, and they may also be found in advertisements in professional journals. By taking advantage of these offers, the teacher can build an extensive personal reference file of choral music. Each composition can be evaluated and labeled on the cover or first page with such comments as "tenor part too high," "good for next Christmas," "unsuitable," "excellent for girls ensemble," and so on.

Other valuable sources that will help the

teacher to become familiar with suitable choral material are the following:

1. Choral workshops and clinics are sponsored by some publishing companies and by such organizations as the American Choral Directors Association.

2. Publishers exhibit at state, regional, and national music educators conventions. Free reference copies or mailing-list request forms are generally available at these exhibits.

3. Local music distributors stock music from a large number of publishers. Their stores are often staffed by knowledgeable personnel who are willing to assist teachers when they know what is needed.

4. Some publishers have made available, on a thirty-day approval basis, recordings of some of their music.

5. Music exchanges may be arranged whereby vocal teachers in neighboring communities can share music libraries.

6. Many selections can be evaluated when the teacher attends music festivals and conferences and has the opportunity to hear groups similar to his own perform.

TYPES OF VOCAL ORGANIZATIONS

There are many possible plans for organizing the vocal music curriculum in secondary schools. The program outlined in Table 10-3 is not necessarily ideal, but it offers flexibility and room for adaptation for a variety of grade-level organizations, in addition to providing for the basic assumption that *singing experiences should be available on both a nonselective and selective basis.* For example, the middle- and high-school plan of Table 10-3 is easily adaptable to the 6–3–3 plan when the fifth- and sixth-grade choirs become

part of the elementary school and when a ninth-grade girls' choir, boys' choir, and non-selective chorus are added to the seventh- and eighth-grade offerings, with the high school classes remaining basically the same. If the vocal teacher must function in a 6–2–4 grade-level grouping, the movement of the fifth- and sixth-grade choirs into the elementary program, while maintaining the rest of the plan as shown, will prove quite operational.

An open membership plan (accepting all students who wish to join without audition) should receive serious consideration when organizing nonselective groups. It provides students who would otherwise hesitate to audition with the opportunity for choral experience; it can also encourage singers who show potential to join one of the more selective groups in the future. Admittedly, with an open membership plan the teacher will have little control over group balance and the performance level will be much more limited. Therefore, it might be advantageous for the members of the nonselective mixed chorus to combine in performance with the concert choir, thus giving them the feeling that they are an integral part of a larger group made up of some of the "top singers" in the school. If the ability level of the concert choir is high, members should have little difficulty in learning the easier music of the nonselective chorus as well as their own.

The Middle School and Junior High School

Lower Middle School
The organization of choral groups in the lower middle school (grades 5 and 6), meeting once to three times a week for periods of thirty minutes, is quite valuable because it gives youngsters the opportunity to sing music and acquire understandings that are beyond the scope of the regular classroom.

Table 10-3. VOCAL MUSIC PROGRAM FOR MIDDLE AND HIGH SCHOOLS

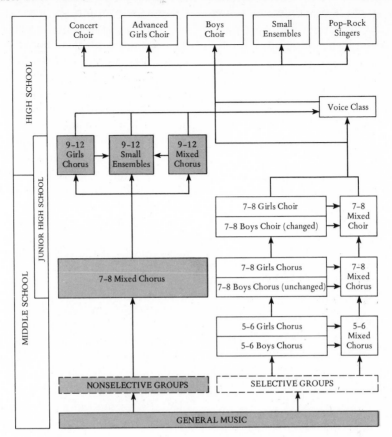

Membership at this level should not be highly selective and students should be chosen on the basis of interest rather than musical or vocal ability. Of course, in cases where several students cannot sing in tune, it is advisable that they not be chosen. These students, however, should be informed that membership is not closed and that when their singing shows improvement in the general music class they will be invited to join the choir. In situations of this kind it is very important for the teacher to follow through by (1) knowing who these students are, (2) listening to these students informally in the general music class, (3) constantly encouraging them to improve, and (4) admitting them into the choir immediately when they show suitable improvement.

Generally, at this age level girls are physically one or two years more mature than the boys and they are apt to have a more positive attitude toward singing. However, the boys are quite interested in organized group and team activity and are not averse to joining a choral group. Although most of the boys have unchanged voices, they do not like to be classified with the girls as sopranos and would much rather sing the lower part. When this is not possible, seating the boys together

225

The Vocal Music Program

reduces some of the stigma. If the schedule in a particular school is flexible enough, then it would be advisable to organize two parallel groups—one for the boys and another for the girls.

The teacher is aided in working with these groups when he is cognizant of other developmental characteristics exhibited by students in the lower middle school:

1. They have unreserved honesty. Middle-school youngsters are very free in expressing their opinions; they are either 100 percent for or against—very seldom anywhere between.

2. They need approval and receive great satisfaction when complimented by their teacher for work well done. Expressions of approval must be sincere, though, since these students are mature enough to know when they are being patronized.

3. They have a strong need for conformity. When membership in a vocal group becomes an "in" thing, recruiting members is no problem.

4. They desire to do things well. Under the direction of a capable vocal teacher who knows youngsters of this age, students can perform without difficulty to the top level of their ability.

5. They want to be liked, and in turn they want to like others.

The performance level of the lower middle-school choir can vary considerably. While some groups will be capable of performing three-part chordal and contrapuntal music with relative ease, others will be limited to unison or two-part singing. However, it must be remembered that the prime objective is not the number of parts being sung, but how artistically the chosen music is performed and what music understanding will be gained to expand the students' aesthetic sensitivity.

Authors of some of the basic book series for grades five and six have recognized the need for suitable choir music and have devoted sections of their books to such materials. However, the vocal teacher will find that he will have to turn to other sources in order to have sufficient suitable music to work with. Another source, not mentioned previously, lies in the wealth of public-domain art and folksongs that can be arranged to meet the needs of each particular group. The teacher can also create original music tailored to his chorus. If the same repertoire is used for similar groups in several middle schools throughout the system, it is possible to combine the choruses from different schools to present a mass concert at the end of the year.

Upper Middle School

At the upper middle-school level (grades 7 and 8), the organization of two nongraded boys groups can be advantageous. One would be for changed voices and the other for unchanged voices, with boys at various stages of changing placed in both groups. Using this plan, the teacher can more realistically choose suitable material, cope with the changing voice, and deal with behavioral problems. The teacher needs to be prepared for the uninhibited actions of adolescent boys at this level. Although they can be polite and cooperative, their group personality can be quite startling—especially for the beginning teacher. Their inability to sit still for extended periods of time results in such manifestations as interweaving a variety of unexpected and unusual sounds into rehearsal singing; shoving, nudging, and tripping other students; questioning the worth and value of the music being sung with such statements as "when are we going to sing some good songs?" even though they are quite satisfied with the music; wanting to quit the group because a friend has decided to leave, even though to this point they have thoroughly enjoyed singing; and, if chosen to sing a solo, constantly complaining and then enjoying every moment of the performance. Complete dictatorial regimentation might eliminate some of these problems, but it is the least satisfactory method for working with exuberant boys. Rather, the teacher needs to develop a sensitivity to their nature and know how long to work on a particular piece of music before changing pace and turning to another song or activity. He needs to recognize when a short break is required to let off a little steam. In addition, it is important that he control his temper when reprimanding a student or the whole group, and that he get to know the boys individually, treating them as adults. When working with these boys, the biggest surprise comes the evening of the concert when the teacher discovers that in spite of the many problems, the boys know all the words and music, have excellent singing positions, keep their eyes on the director, sing with great vitality, and are actually standing still.

Vocal experiences for girls at this level should also be offered on a nongraded basis. For example, after a general audition, girls showing outstanding ability can be assigned to the smaller and more highly selective girls' choir, and all other girls to the larger girls' chorus. This type of organization would help solve the teacher's dilemma of finding suitable music when there are several ability levels in one group. The music must interest and challenge all members.

The plan of having separate vocal organizations also has adaptability potential for those music educators who stress the need on this level for heterogeneous singing experiences. For example, if the girls' choir is scheduled during a given period on Monday and Wednesday and the boys' choir of unchanged voices in the same period on Tuesday and Thursday, then the two groups can be combined on Friday to perform SAB or

SATB repertoire. If the school is large enough and has two vocal teachers and two suitable rehearsal areas, both groups can be scheduled at the same time and combine whenever they so desire. Adding the boys' choir of unchanged voices to the girls' chorus is also advantageous since the fullness and resonance of the boys' voices will greatly enhance the over-all quality of the group. Scheduling can be planned similar to that of the other groups. A minimum of two class meetings a week is essential for these choruses; three meetings are desirable, while daily classes are ideal but rarely achieved.

While choral groups on all levels of the middle school can provide valuable performance and learning experiences for their members, *they should not be considered a substitute for the general music class.* Vocal performance is rather an outgrowth of the general music class, offering those students who show a special interest in singing the opportunity to broaden their experience through (1) more in-depth instruction in choral technique, which is impossible in the general music class because of the very nature of the class; (2) familiarity with vocal literature that cannot be attempted in the general music class because of limited time and class ability; and (3) public performance, which is beyond the scope and purpose of the general music class.

The High School

Ability rather than grade placement is the main criterion for membership in senior-high-school choral groups. The choral classes at this level should be offered on both a selective and nonselective basis. The open-membership plan described earlier would again be appropriate to apply in organizing the nonselective groups.

Membership in selective choruses should

be attained by audition. Here, the teacher is often faced with the decision of choosing the student with a fine voice and limited musicianship or the student with average vocal ability and a high degree of musicianship. Among choral directors there is a difference of opinion as to which choice is better. Some believe that the teacher's task is less difficult when he chooses the better musician and then proceeds to teach him vocal technique than when he tries to develop musicianship qualities (such as reading ability) with the fine singer. The logic here is that the student with limited musicianship will find the pace of a highly select group quite frustrating, as will the teacher who finds that some of his best vocalists must learn their parts by rote, thus delaying the progress and the potential of the group. Part of the rationale in this is that voices of "solo quality" are not necessary to create a good choral sound. On the other hand, some choral directors believe that as long as potential soloists are able to blend with the group, they can contribute to a better choral tone than would otherwise be possible. These same directors are often willing to devote the extra time needed in rote learning to give the top vocalists the challenge they deserve in a highly select group. Although progress may at first be slow, the end result is often as good as or better than when working with the average voices. In making this decision, much depends on how selective the teacher wants the group to be, how fast they must work, how challenging the repertoire is vocally (as opposed to the challenge of a required learning rate), and how the individual teacher best works with a group. It is possible that certain teachers may find the best solution to be a combination of both types of students—some who are outstanding singers, some who have outstanding musicianship (and, it is hoped, some who have fine voices *and* musicianship).

Mixed Chorus and Girls' Chorus

Each of these nonselective groups should meet twice weekly, and more often if the school schedule allows. It is essential that the teacher not permit the nonselective chorus to deteriorate into a community-sing period in which the main objective is to find enough easy music to keep the group singing, usually by rote. On the contrary, the purpose of the nonselective vocal group must be *educative*, and this should be stated in the course of study. In this way, the students, the administration, the guidance department, and the vocal teacher will understand that the nonselective chorus is not a place to be entertained, to escape from study halls, to pick up a few needed credits, or to gather socially, but a class in which one is expected to learn. Students should understand that in the process of preparing music for public performance they will have the opportunity to develop some knowledge, understanding, and skills related to basic vocal techniques and to concepts and percepts of the technical and formal elements of music. Organized in this manner, the nonselective chorus can provide encouragement for students who show vocal potential and also provide needed music background for those who are interested in joining one of the more selective vocal groups.

Concert Choir and Advanced Girls' Choir

The concert choir (SATB) and the advanced girls' choir (SSA or SSAA) are well-balanced, selective groups for students with high vocal potential and above-average musicianship. Membership should be limited to between thirty-five and fifty students. The determining factor regarding the actual number will depend on the availability of singers, their vocal potential, and the particular sound or balance preferred by the director in terms of the repertoire to be studied. The number of weekly meetings by each of these groups will be determined by the available time in the school schedule. However, they should rehearse at least three times a week, and a large number of high schools now offer such classes on a daily basis.

Boys' Choir

A selective all-boys group (TTB, TBB, TTBB) has the value of attracting those young men who might never consider joining a mixed group. Initially it serves to (1) show each boy that he really can sing, (2) prove that there are plenty of masculine songs through which they can attain personal satisfaction and expression, (3) demonstrate that the vocal teacher is a regular person, with a good sense of humor, who can offer the group much of value, and (4) indicate that the boys' efforts are appreciated in public performance. Once boys have had a satisfactory music experience as members of a male choir they will generally continue their membership and ask some of their friends to join. With some encouragement from the teacher, some of the boys will become interested in the challenge of a more selective group. The teacher who establishes a working rapport with boys will have little difficulty with discipline, recruitment, and their acceptance of the music. In the process of establishing rapport, the teacher should be fair, firm, and friendly in conducting the class; get to know the boys and their particular interests in and out of school; follow their suggestions in the choice of some of the repertoire; and show in class discussions that his own interests and knowledge are not limited entirely to music.

Small Ensembles

Under the direction of the vocal teacher, the most outstanding singers should have the opportunity to participate in a highly selective, small, mixed chamber ensemble of between twelve and fifteen voices. Although groups of this type have often been called "madrigal singers," their repertoire is usually expanded to include not only madrigals but other challenging choral music as well. When there is enough interest, more than one chamber group can be organized. Traditionally, small ensembles have included not only madrigal singers but also such groups as trios and quartets, double quartets of male voices, triple trios of female voices, and barbershop quartets. In recent years, folk groups and pop-rock ensembles have also been formed in the schools. (For a discussion of the organization of pop-rock singers, refer to Chapter 14.)

Although outstanding vocal ability is an important factor in choosing students for a highly select chamber ensemble, the teacher will also want to consider student interest, enthusiasm, musicianship, ability to work well with others, and the blending quality of the voice. Since the singers auditioning for such a group will have had experience with the director in one of the other vocal organizations, choosing the right combination of students should be no problem.

The small ensemble should have the opportunity to rehearse at least three times weekly. However, because of the high level of the members' musical abilities, it is not always necessary for the vocal teacher to attend each meeting. Instead, the students can work independently under their own student director. Permitting each member to have a turn as conductor of the group can contribute effectively to the students' understanding of the music, because as an individual tackles his conducting chores he becomes involved in a personal analysis of the music—of the relationship of parts, of rhythmic, melodic, and harmonic elements, of tempo, dynamics, and general stylistic interpretation, and of the blending of voices.

The highly select small ensemble offers its members the opportunity to (1) develop their musical independence (since there are fewer performers on each part), (2) further their study and analysis of structural and formal components of the compositions, (3) make their own decisions in regard to interpretation and choice of repertoire, and (4) expand their understanding of the organization of a small ensemble, which can be used in forming their own groups outside of school, both before and after graduation.

Small ensemble experiences, which, in the past, have been limited mostly to the musically and vocally talented, ought to be available to all students. Study periods and free periods can often be used to put together a number of small, student-directed ensembles, especially if the school operates on a modular schedule. However, when the members of an ensemble have a limited amount of vocal ability and musical competency, then the teacher must spend more time working with the group before the students will be able to function independently. When it is impossible to schedule small ensembles, the vocal teacher can organize his selective and nonselective groups into quartets (SATB) and trios (SSA) and use regular class time for such work. (With some groups it may be necessary, at first, to put more than one singer on each part until they have gained experience and confidence.) For example, after two or three weeks of rehearsing new literature, the music teacher can spend one or two periods on the same music with the class being divided into small groups. During these ensemble sessions the teacher can work, on a rotating basis, with each group around the piano, while the others are practicing on their own. Since there are a small number of singers in each group, enough rehearsal space can ordinarily be found without difficulty—in practice rooms, on stage or in its wings, in the corner of the auditorium, or in a uniform storage room.

The teacher who employs the small ensemble as a regular part of the larger vocal class will discover that he is in a much better position to judge the individual student's musical ability, needs, and growth than when the student is just a voice in a large group. Students will also gain from the ensemble experience because they will realize the necessity for developing musical independence and knowledge in order to have the skill to function adequately alone on a part. Finally, the larger vocal group will also benefit; as individuals grow in their ability to work independently, the performance level of the larger group will grow proportionately.

Voice Class

The voice class is offered for the benefit of a relatively small number of students who exhibit interest and have some vocal potential. The class is not designed to take the place of individualized vocal instruction because time limits the amount of attention that can be given to each student to solve individual vocal problems, and because all students do not progress at the same rate and class progress is thus restrictive. Nevertheless, the voice class can guide the beginning student toward:

1. discovering whether solo vocal performance is an experience that can be personally rewarding for him;

2. learning basic principles of vocal production, including correct breathing, resonance, placement, diction, and interpretation;

3. developing some discriminating taste regarding his own performance and that of others;

4. acquiring additional music knowledge, understanding, and skill;

5. becoming acquainted with a variety of solo literature; and

6. developing greater poise and stage deportment by singing for other class members.

If the voice class is to function satisfactorily, it needs to be scheduled for at least three meetings a week and to be limited to no more than fifteen students. Since some class time will necessarily have to be devoted to working on individual vocal problems, the small class size will ensure enough time for such instruction. It is, of course, essential that the teacher in charge of the voice class have more than just a superficial knowledge of vocal technique; otherwise, the class can become a breeding ground for questionable vocal habits, or it can deteriorate into just a singing session with little or no instruction of value.

DEVELOPING MUSIC UNDERSTANDING

As a music educator, the vocal teacher is responsible for organizing experiences and activities for learning that go beyond the development of choral technique and the acquisition of a limited performance repertoire. Experiences and activities in the choral class, as in all other phases of music education, must contribute to musical growth. This does not mean that technique must now be ignored; on the contrary, attention to breath usage, diction, development of flexibility, extension of range, and all the other aspects of singing technique are still essential since they influence the type of literature that can be used as well as the quality of the final performance. Therefore, with some preplanning on the part of the teacher, even the purpose of the vocal exercise can be expanded to develop music understanding, knowledge, and skill. Traditionally, for example, the vocal exercise in Figure 10-9 has been used to improve a singer's ability to sing sustained tones using the basic vowels a, e, i, o, and u; to sing and articulate basic vowel sounds when preceded

FIGURE 10-9

FIGURE 10-10

To be performed at a variety of dynamic levels and tempos:

by consonants without breaking the legato tone flow; to control the intake of breath as well as its expiration during singing; and to apply this technique while learning and performing music.

When the same exercise is reorganized as shown in Figure 10-10, students will still have the opportunity to develop technique. In addition, though, they will become aware of the function of the beat as it relates to note values and meter signatures; of the interval of an octave between the part sung by the girls and that of the boys; of the function of the staff and the clef signs in the designation of specific pitches; of the relationship of the conductor's beat to various meter signatures; of various dynamic markings; of the influence of tempo on the beat and the relative duration of note values; and of how these concepts are related to music being studied in class.

The greatest source for fostering musical growth and understanding is, of course, the literature being studied by the choral class. Its possibilities are unlimited. One plan that has been successful is the in-depth study of choral music of one particular stylistic period. Leroy Larson[3] has reported that after presenting a unit revolving around the music of the Renaissance to a high school choral group, a follow-up questionnaire revealed that 80 percent of the class felt that the presentation was interesting, worthwhile, and educational. There was also indication that students desired to continue performing music of the Renaissance the following year and to study other stylistic periods in the same way.

In his presentation, Larson began with a brief introduction that outlined the significant historical and music events of the period. Then, through the analysis of representative compositions, he developed an aural and visual understanding of the typical chordal and polyphonic styles with their suspensions and other nonharmonic tones. To reinforce what had been presented and analyzed in class, a periodic summary sheet containing all pertinent information was distributed to the students. This unit took the greater part of ten class meetings, but the analysis and performance of Renaissance music continued for the remainder of the year.

Another and more general approach is to analyze all compositions to be studied in the choral class and then determine how each can contribute to the musical growth of the singers. With this plan the teacher will discover that familiarity with all conceptual areas and their related percepts will be advantageous in determining immediate instructional objectives and the activities and experiences through which these objectives can be accomplished. This plan can also be reversed: the teacher can first determine what musical learning is to be pursued in the vocal class and then locate appropriate literature and devise suitable activities and experiences. The teacher who undertakes this type of class work will find that prior to the determination of desired learnings, the selection of music, and the organization of learning experiences, an analysis of all conceptual areas will provide an excellent point of departure for structuring musical growth in the choral class. For example, he might prepare an analysis of the concept of melody similar to the following:

1. *Concept:* In the broadest sense, a melody is a linear succession of rhythmically organized individual pitches perceived as a whole unit by the listener, each pitch having a specific duration in relation to the others, and each having a variable intensity depending on the interpretation of the over-all progression.

[3] See Leroy Larson, "More than Performance: It Can Be Done," *Music Educators Journal*, 55:6 (February 1969), p. 41.

2. *Percepts:*

a. *Movement*—A melody moves from one pitch to another by step or skip (upward or downward) or by remaining at the same pitch level.

b. *Tonality*—Most melodic movement is within a major or minor scale and related chromatic tones, with the over-all progression of pitches being strongly related to one central tone—the key- or home-tone of the scale. A melody of this sort is said to have a specific tonality, which is identified by the letter name of the central tone.

c. *Modality and Other Scalar Relationships*—Some melodies are based on scales other than the major or minor. Those based on modes, which are also scales of seven different tones having a particular relationship to a central tone, are known as modal melodies. Still others are based on a pentatonic scale (five tones), a chromatic scale (twelve tones), a whole-tone scale (six different tones), or some other specific sequence of pitches, including microtonal scales (with intervals smaller than half steps).

d. *Atonality*—When a melody is arranged in such a way that no tonal center is suggested, the result is referred to as atonality.

e. *Contour and Character*—Each melody has a definite shape or contour of varying interest, depending on repetition of tones; variety in tonal groups; the balance between similar and dissimilar, high and low, fast and slow, active and restful progressions of pitches; a point of climax; resolution of tension; and continuity and cohesiveness. Certain melodies display recognizable elements that give them specific character and style.

f. *Imitation*—When a group of tones in a melody is repeated exactly or in a similar form in the same or another voice, the progression is known as a melodic imitation.

g. *Sequence*—When a group of tones in a melody is repeated two or more times, each repetition beginning at a different pitch level but retaining the original pattern of steps and skips, the progression is known as a melodic sequence.

h. *Inversion*—When a group of tones in a melody is turned upside down in a subsequent phrase, with originally upward steps or skips now becoming comparable downward steps or skips, and vice versa, the newly developed group of tones is known as an inversion of the old.

i. *Counterpoint*—Two or more melodies combined simultaneously create what is known as counterpoint.

j. *Motif*—When a brief series of tones is used as a central idea to germinate an entire melody, that series is known as a melodic motif.

k. *Theme*—When a complete melody becomes the central idea in the development of a longer composition, the melody is known as a theme.

l. *Augmentation*—The presentation of melodic material in tones of longer duration than those used in its original statement is known as augmentation.

m. *Diminution*—The presentation of melodic material in tones of shorter duration than those used in its original statement is known as diminution.

n. *Serialization*—When the twelve tones of the chromatic scale are arranged successively, without repetition, in a row that serves as the basis for melodic development (through techniques of inversion, retrograde arrangement of the row, retrograde inversion, and so on), without reference to a tonal center, the melody is known as a serial, twelve-tone, or dodecaphonic melody.

o. *Melodic Notation*—The tones that make up a melody can be represented by graphic symbols (notes), which indicate the specific pitch and duration of each tone, as well as the intervals between successive tones. This

Table 10-4. MELODIC ANALYSIS CHART

In developing students' knowledge and understanding of the melodic structure of a composition, the following items should be considered as a guide to analysis.

1. *Tonal System*

    a. Determine the general type of tonal system
        –Tonality: major (Ionian), natural minor (Aeolian), harmonic minor, melodic minor
        –Modality: Dorian, Phrygian, Lydian, Mixolydian, Locrian
        –Pentatonic: first, second, third, fourth, or fifth mode
        –Whole-tone scale
        –Atonal
        –Blues scale
        –Other
    b. Determine the specific tonal center
    c. Determine whether there are multiple tonal systems
        –Modulation
        –Bitonality
        –Polytonality

2. *Movement*

    a. Determine the predominant type of movement
        –Step
        –Skip or leap
        –Repetition
        –Diatonic
        –Chromatic
    b. Determine the span
        –Range
        –Tessitura
    c. Determine the character
        –Contour
        –Phrasing
        –Tension and resolution
        –Climax
        –Unity and variety
        –Tempo and dynamics

3. *Organization*

    a. Determine the basic material
        –Motif
        –Phrase
        –Sentence
        –Theme
        –Subject

        –Countersubject
        –Row
   b. Determine the techniques of development
        –Repetition
        –Variation
        –Ornamentation
        –Imitation
        –Sequence
        –Inversion
        –Retrograde
        –Retrograde inversion
        –Augmentation
        –Diminution
        –Fragmentation
        –Pointillism
   c. Determine the context
        –Placement
        –Reinforcement
        –Monody
        –Counterpoint
        –Heterophony
        –Accompaniment

---

4. *Texture*

   a. Monophonic
   b. Homophonic
   c. Polyphonic

---

system of notation includes a staff, clefs, notes, key and meter signatures, and a variety of other symbols representing structural and interpretive factors to be observed in the performance of the melody.

Having outlined the concept of melody and its related percepts in this way, the teacher has a ready reference for his and the class' analysis of the melodic structure of compositions to be performed. He can transfer these percepts into a melodic analysis chart, such as that given in Table 10-4, for use as a checklist.

Similar charts can be developed for other conceptual areas to provide the choral teacher with a guide for thorough analysis. Using the charts for reference, he can then devote part of his class time to developing music understanding. If the teacher has a structural analysis of each composition at his fingertips, he can make use of it in introducing a new composition, to fill a natural break in rehearsal time, in relation to a problem that arises in the learning process, and in many other ways (see Chapter 12 for suggestions). Programmed tapes with annotated scores could be placed on reserve in the library to reinforce material presented in class.

Those teachers who have concentrated on the development of performance skills alone may hesitate to give up class time in order to concentrate on music understanding because they fear that the excellence of their group's performance level will be impaired. However, this fear cannot be justified on an educational basis; as Meyer Cahn wrote:

Imperfect performances will not kill music education. They may yet make the field into what it should have been long ago—an educational experience of breadth and depth provided for the growth and development of students who wish to learn how to learn about themselves through music, who wish to experience music as the people they are rather than as pawns in the creation of a perfect musical product.[4]

[4] Meyer M. Cahn, "More than Performance: Toward Human Interaction," *Music Educators Journal*, 55:6 (February 1969), p. 38.

Projects

1. Select a choral composition and then, using the course objectives in Table 10-1 as a guide, devise some immediate instructional objectives that can be realized through experiences with this composition.
2. Begin your choral reference library by consulting recent issues of *Music Educators Journal* and *The Choral Journal* and write to those publishing companies that offer free reference copies. When the music arrives, analyze it according to the points listed on pages 223–224, and make suitable notations on the cover page.
3. Using Figure 10-10 as a guide, demonstrate how other vocal exercises can be used to develop both vocal technique and music understanding.
4. Devise a detailed unit to develop music understanding for one of the groups cited in Table 10-2. Base the unit on one of the following topics: (a) madrigals, motets, and their composers; (b) oratorio choruses; (c) choruses of contemporary American composers; (d) choruses from Broadway musicals; (e) choral music of J. S. Bach; (f) melodic structure; or (g) aleatoric music for chorus.
5. Prepare an auditioning procedure for the following situations: (a) a nonselective group, first rehearsal of the year; (b) auditioning for an eighth grade mixed choir during a general music class, the members of which have previously done little singing; (c) individual auditions for high school madrigal singers; and (d) an audition during the general music class for a lower middle-school mixed chorus.
6. Compose a short choral work or arrange a song in the public domain for one of the following: (a) a nonselective mixed group with limited ability, SAB; (b) a lower middle-school choir with high performance level, SSA; (c) a high-school chamber ensemble with highly select voices, SATB; or (d) an upper middle-school boys' choir of changed voices with limited ability, TBB.
7. Develop analysis charts, similar to the one in Table 10-4, for other concept areas (rhythm, harmony, form, and so on). Using these charts, analyze a choral composition and evaluate the suitability of the analysis for use with a high-level performance group, an average performance group, and a low-level performance group.

Selected References

ANDREWS, FRANCES M. *Junior High School General Music*. Englewood Cliffs, New Jersey: Prentice-Hall, Inc., 1971. Chapter 3.

APPELMAN, D. RALPH. *The Science of Vocal Pedagogy*. Bloomington: Indiana University Press, 1967.

BOYD, JACK. *Rehearsal Guide for the Choral Conductor*. West Nyack, New York: Parker Publishing Co., Inc., 1970.

CHRISTY, VAN A. *Foundations in Singing*. 2d ed. Dubuque, Iowa: William C. Brown Company Publishers, 1970.

ERNST, KARL D., and CHARLES L. GARY, eds. *Music in General Education*. Washington, D.C.: Music Educators National Conference, 1965. Chapter 4.

GARRETSON, ROBERT L. *Conducting Choral Music*. 3d ed. Boston: Allyn & Bacon, Inc., 1970.

HOFFER, CHARLES R. *Teaching Music in the Secondary School*. Belmont, California: Wadsworth Publishing Co., 1964. Chapters 7 and 12.

HOWERTON, GEORGE. *Technique and Style in Choral Singing*. New York: Carl Fischer, Inc., 1958.

JIPSON, WAYNE R. *The High School Vocal Music Program*. West Nyack, New York: Parker Publishing Company, 1972.

MC KENZIE, DUNCAN. *Training the Boy's Changing Voice*. New Brunswick, New Jersey: Rutgers Press, 1956.

MELLALIEU, W. N. *The Boy's Changing Voice*. New York: Oxford University Press, 1957.

NEIDIG, KENNETH L., and JOHN W. JENNINGS, eds. *Choral Director's Guide*. West Nyack, New York: Parker Publishing Co., Inc., 1967.

ROBINSON, RAY, ed. *Choral Music*. New York: W. W. Norton & Company, Inc., 1978.

————, and ALLEN WINOLD. *The Choral Experience*. New York: Harper & Row, 1976.

ROE, PAUL. *Choral Music Education*. Englewood Cliffs, New Jersey: Prentice-Hall, Inc., 1970.

STANTON, ROYAL. *The Dynamic Choral Conductor*. Delaware Water Cap, Pennsylvania: Shawnee Press, Inc., 1971.

SWANSON, FREDERICK. "The Proper Care and Feeding of Changing Voices," *Music Educators Journal*, 48:2 (November-December 1961), pp. 63–66.

————. "When Voices Change," *Music Educators Journal*, 46:4 (February, 1960), p. 50.

THOMSON, WILLIAM. "The Ensemble Director and Musical Concepts," *Music Educators Journal*, 54:9 (May 1968), pp. 44–46.

TRUSLER, IVAN, and WALTER EHRET. *Functional Lessons in Singing*. Englewood Cliffs, New Jersey: Prentice-Hall, Inc., 1960.

WARREN, JOSEPH. "Vocal Growth in the Human Adolescent and the Total Growth Process," *Journal of Research in Music Education*, 16:2 (Summer 1966), pp. 35–41.

————. "Vocal Growth Measurements in Male Adolescents," *Journal of Research in Music Education*, 17:4 (Summer 1970), pp. 423–426.

The Instrumental Music Program

Sometimes a thousand twangling instruments
will hum about mine ears.

WILLIAM SHAKESPEARE
The Tempest, III, 2

Is it not strange that sheep's guts should hale souls out of men's bodies?

WILLIAM SHAKESPEARE
Much Ado About Nothing, II, 3

THE INSTRUMENTAL PROGRAM, like the vocal program, is continuously involved in stimulating the flow of new members, in developing their knowledge, understanding, and skill, and in providing for a series of elective and selective organizations that will accommodate various levels of musical competencies. The ideal instrumental program arouses pupil interest at the earliest possible age and provides lessons and group performing opportunities to meet their advancing interests and needs.

ORGANIZING THE INSTRUMENTAL MUSIC PROGRAM

The decision about whether to concentrate on performance for its sake alone or to expand performance classes to include the development of knowledge and understanding, as discussed in Chapter 10, also confronts the instrumental teacher; this decision will have a definite influence on the organization of his program. The instrumental phase of the music program does have a few advantages over the vocal since its members do develop skill in playing instruments and acquire a certain level of reading ability more readily. Because the instrumental teacher is highly aware of emerging skills, he is often moved to push toward perfecting them for concert purposes, with the result that conceptual understanding is overlooked. However, if he is to make an honest effort to realize the basic goals of music education, he must, like his counterpart in vocal music, strive to make the instrumental program educationally more valid and musically more educative.

Developing Objectives

Most administrators and school-minded citizens are pleased by the prospects of large, quality music organizations in the schools. There are many thoughtful critics, however, who question the validity of traditional instrumental music programs because few students continue to play their instruments once they have graduated from high school. Festival competitions, five rehearsals a week, and playing in concerts and at football games do not in themselves give students the meaningful experiences that will carry over into adult life. Perhaps some of these activities are fun, but they have generally contributed little to musical growth and aesthetic sensitivity—factors that determine how musically involved a student will be after graduation. Thus, the instrumental teacher must give careful consideration to formulating objectives that focus on developing both musically worthy organizations and musically sensitive individuals.

Table 10-1 in the preceding chapter presents a set of course objectives that are appropriate to a secondary school vocal-music program. These can easily be modified to fit the instrumental program. Such course objectives are in no way all-inclusive or unalterable, but they can offer guidelines for providing purpose and direction. Each school should draw up its own list of long-range objectives, compatible with the program objectives of the total music curriculum. Once prepared, they should be *used* to organize each phase of instrumental instruction. The teacher will then need to consider day-to-day, week-to-week instructional objectives (behaviorally stated) that will support the course and program objectives.

Recruiting Students

The teacher cannot sit blissfully in his office and expect beginning instrumental students to come knocking on his door; he must plan a systematic recruitment program to attract students with the potential for growth through instrumental study.

First, administrative approval must be secured at the close of school in June for time and space in which to present a recruitment demonstration at the beginning of the next school year. This long-range notice will enable the administrative staff to schedule the instrumental demonstration as one of many organizational activities that occur at a very busy time of the year.

Second, a choice must be made between the classroom or assembly type of demonstration. The availability of time, space, and demonstrating musicians are factors in this decision. Either type of demonstration can be successful if it is well organized.

Third, a decision needs to be made as to whether student or professional musicians will perform the demonstration. Some teachers prefer to use students because potential student musicians are likely to relate to their peers; others prefer professional musicians because their proficiency can best demonstrate each instrument's full range, technical facility, and adaptability to various styles (pop, rock, jazz, classical).

Fourth, students should be prepared for the demonstration. Through instruction in the general music class, most students will have had the opportunity to become familiar with

FIGURE 11-1

COME BLOW
OUR HORNS
SEE MR. DUBINSKY IN
THE MUSIC SUITE

forms, and even telephone calls. When printed matter is sent home, the teacher must keep in mind that parents are deluged with letters and forms from the school, employers, organizations, and commercial sources. Therefore, a communication should be to the point and have a humanistic touch; parents should feel that it comes from a person who is interested in their child's musical development and not from a computer. Material sent home should also show parents that the music department has a well-organized program. It is difficult to present such an image when letters contain typing errors, misspelled words, and poor grammatical construction, or cannot be read because a duplicating master suitable for 100 copies was used to run off 200 copies. Figure 11-2 shows the type of letter that has been used quite successfully to provide parents with information about the beginners program.

instruments of the band and orchestra. Prior to the demonstration, the general music teacher can provide information about the opportunities offered for instrumental instruction. In addition, eye-catching posters, such as the one in Figure 11-1, should be displayed in the music room and in other strategic places around the school.

Fifth, procedures and materials to inform parents of the opportunities in the instrumental program have to be developed. Some school systems prefer to have prospective instrumentalists undergo a series of screening tests prior to sending forms to parents, whereas others prefer to have the forms completed and returned before any type of auditioning is begun. What is important is that a procedure be established and care be taken to ensure that students and parents are fully informed about each step in the series of events from expressed interest to assignment of instrument, teacher, and lesson time. Communication needs to be set up via letters,

Screening Students

In communities where the school district provides all the instruments and instruction, the teacher may face the problem each year of having more interested beginners than available instruments. Therefore, the selection of the "right" students must be based on more than a random choice in order to maintain a low dropout rate and a continued balanced instrumentation. In those schools where instruments must be puchased or rented, the selection of students is also important. Since parents will be asked to make a financial commitment, they may want to know on what basis, other than student interest, the music department recommends that their child become involved in the instrumental program. Therefore, once the student has expressed an interest in playing, and has returned the information form that is part of the initial announcement slip sent home to parents, the teacher should first check with

nosticators of success in instrumental music has not been established."[2] Hoffer further recommends that time spent teaching preband instruments could be better utilized if it were devoted to the improvement of techniques to teach regular instruments.

A unique talent exploration program was developed by Paul Paradise for the Brookline (Massachusetts) Public Schools. The program provided fifteen half-hour violin lessons to *all* third-grade students as part of their general music experience. The violin was chosen because, unlike brasses and woodwinds, it comes in various sizes and is especially adaptable to the small child. Even though this approach was string centered, there was a noticeable increase in band membership and in the number of students studying piano and guitar as a result. Reporting on 378 third-graders, Paradise found that 20 percent maintained interest and continued to play the violin, that eighty students expressed a desire to play an instrument other than the violin, and that the dropout rate for those who continued violin study was only about 3 percent.[3]

Some music educators believe that the only way to really determine student success is to provide all who are interested with the opportunity to study the instrument of their choice. Ideally, all these instruments should be provided by the school since they are a legitimate educational expense. However, were all students permitted to participate in the program, without any screening, financing the program entirely with school funds would be prohibitive in most school systems. Thus, teachers who feel that any student should have the opportunity (which is the only justifiable position, educationally) will probably have to work with an instrument rental plan. Instruments can be rented by parents for three months at a minimal charge, and during this period students, parents, and teachers should have enough time to observe student progress and determine whether it is advisable for specific individuals to continue.

Another aspect of screening is the selection of an instrument for a student. The teacher is faced with the question of whether the student alone should decide what instrument he will learn to play. In most cases the student will approach the instrumental teacher with a specific choice rather than a general request to join the instrumental program. As a result of the demonstration, a television program, or some other experience, the student's interest will usually be aroused by a particular instrument. Very often he will choose the trombone, even though his arms are not yet long enough to play beyond the fourth position; or he will want to play some other brass instrument, even though he has protruding teeth. Under such circumstances, the teacher should respect the student's choice but point out tactfully why he might be more successful with another instrument. If, however, the student has no physical characteristic that would impair his success, then he should be allowed to study the instrument of his choice. When the director has problems of balance within certain sections of his groups, he may point this out to beginners; but if they do not wish to change on their own, pressure should not be applied. When the teacher applies pressure, it is indicative of a performance-oriented philosophy (balanced instrumentation at all cost) rather than a concern for the student's interest, musical growth, and individualism. Robert W. House has aptly described the teacher's role in this phase of the screening process:

[2] Charles R. Hoffer, *Teaching Music in the Secondary Schools* (Belmont, California: Wadsworth Publishing Company, Inc., 1964), p. 286.

[3] See Paul L. Paradise, "They All Played Strings," *Music Educators Journal*, 57:7 (March 1971), pp. 53–54.

We can only hope to consult the individual's interests, broadly interpret his physiological qualifications, and hold the door of opportunity open at all times. We must be humble in this process and admit our ignorance. When asked what one should play, it is better to suggest and advise rather than prescribe.[4]

A number of general characteristics of students should be considered by the teacher in guiding them toward the appropriate selection of an instrument:

Strings—The student needs a strong sense of pitch and rhythm, as well as good finger dexterity and coordination in order to manipulate strings with the left hand, bow with the right hand, and hold the instrument with relative ease.

Flute/piccolo—The student needs a good sense of pitch and rhythm, good coordination, fingers and hands large enough to hold and finger the keys with relative ease, and well-rounded, regular lower teeth.

Oboe/bassoon—The student needs a keen sense of pitch, a good sense of rhythm, good coordination, medium to thin lips for oboe and medium to thick lips for bassoon, hands large enough to hold the instrument with ease, and fingers long enough to reach all of the keys. Uneven teeth do not create any particular problem.

Clarinet/saxophone—The student needs a good sense of pitch and rhythm, medium or thin lips, good coordination, hands large enough to hold the instrument, and fingers long enough to manipulate all the keys. Protruding teeth should not be a problem.

Horn—The student needs an exceptionally good sense of pitch, good rhythmic feeling, regularly formed upper and lower teeth, and normal to thin lip formation.

Trumpet/cornet—The student needs a good sense of pitch and rhythm, regularly formed upper and lower teeth, and normal or thin lips.

Trombone/baritone—The student needs a good sense of pitch and rhythm, regularly formed upper and lower teeth, full lips, and arms long enough to play all positions for trombone.

Tuba—The student needs a good sense of pitch and rhythm, regular upper and lower teeth, thick lips, and physical size to be able to hold the instrument.

Percussion—The student needs a keen sense of rhythm, a good sense of pitch (for timpani), and a generally well-coordinated body.

These characteristics, though helpful as guidelines, should not be overstressed. "To place extreme emphasis upon physical characteristics," Wolfgang Kuhn has pointed out, "denies the principle of adaptation. The question is not so much one of fitting the instrument to the child as it is of letting the child adapt to the instrument. . . . It is a process which has to be taught and learned as part of learning to play."[5]

Obtaining Instruments

Most beginning instrumental programs could not function without the rental plan offered by various instrument companies or music dealers. These plans are basically the same from community to community. For example, parents obtain instruments on a rent-to-buy basis for a six- to twelve-week trial period for a minimal fee. If the teacher and the parents are satisfied with the student's progress at the end of this time, and the student has maintained his interest, arrange-

[4] Robert W. House. *Instrumental Music for Today's Schools* (Englewood Cliffs, New Jersey: Prentice-Hall, Inc., 1965), p. 67.

[5] Wolfgang E. Kuhn, *Instrumental Music: Principles and Methods of Instruction* (Boston: Allyn & Bacon, Inc., 1962), p. 14.

ments can be made for the rental fee to be applied toward the purchase of the instrument or another of comparable or better quality. In some situations the rental plan can be renegotiated for an additional six to twelve weeks if those involved are not completely satisfied with the student's progress during the first rental period. Some rental plans offer parents the option, after the first rental period, of either purchasing the instrument outright or continuing to rent on a monthly basis until the instrument has been paid for. The second option is advantageous since it does not require the parent to purchase the instrument if the student loses interest and drops out before payments are completed.

In choosing a rental firm, the teacher must be certain that the instruments to be provided are of a reputable brand name and in good playing condition; that quick repair service is available, with a replacement instrument to be provided during the period of repair; that a music stand, method book of the teacher's choice, and (if appropriate) reeds (at least during the trial period) are included as part of the rental package; that instruments will not be purchased by parents until recommended by the music teacher; and that no high-pressure tactics will be employed.

Some school districts have purchased instruments and initiated their own rental program. With an initial outlay of funds and the reinvestment of rental fees into additional purchases, it is possible to accumulate a large enough quantity of instruments to accommodate the beginners program. However, such a program actually puts the music department into the rental business with all of its related procedures of collecting fees, contacting parents who have neglected to make payments, keeping up-to-date records, arranging for instrumental repairs, and other problems. The music teacher will find it extremely time-consuming and an interference with his teaching duties, unless he is provided with some clerical help to assist him in running the rental program. Even then, it is a rather questionable operation. If the school is going to get involved in purchasing instruments, it should own them and make them available to students at no cost. (No other area of the curriculum rents or charges fees for the use of instructional materials or equipment.)

Some instrumental music teachers prefer to limit their beginners to such basic instruments as trumpets, trombones, flutes, clarinets, drums, and all of the strings. At this point in the program, there is no concern for balance in instrumentation. Group instruction is facilitated by this approach, and students are able to progress more rapidly than they would if some were studying more difficult instruments. Once students have developed the skill related to playing one instrument, then it is comparatively easy to transfer to another: excess brass players can be encouraged to change to baritone, tuba, and horn, and woodwind players to oboe, bassoon, English horn, alto clarinet, bass clarinet, and saxophone. For such a program to be successful, the school *must* provide the student with the second instrument. It would be quite unreasonable to expect parents to assume the additional financial burden of another instrument. These second instruments also fall into a more expensive category and should be considered part of standard school equipment. The school should also have on hand some of the basic instruments for those beginners who are unable to rent or purchase them.

Selecting Instructional Materials and Literature

To maintain student interest and increase musical growth, it is not enough to select simply a beginner's book. Instead, a beginner's *course* should be chosen, comprising basic instructional books, solo literature, small-ensemble selections, and music for a large group. The basic book should indicate when supplementary material is appropriate, and the supplementary music must relate to the student's development at each suggested point. Table 11-1 provides a checklist for evaluating materials.

In addition to the beginner's course, instrumental literature needs to be selected for intermediate and advanced classes and for the various performing organizations at each level. This should not be left until the time when purchase orders are due. Instead, it should be handled systematically, as an ongoing practice, by listening to music performed at conferences and public concerts, examining complimentary material sent through the mail, visiting exhibits at conventions, participating in reading clinics, and seeking a good music store with a comprehensive, regularly updated collection of scores.

As the teacher examines instrumental literature, he should raise these questions:

1. Does it provide for the development of music knowledge, understanding, and skill?

2. Is the music worth performing for its over-all artistic effect?

3. Are the technical demands within the level of capabilities of both individuals and sections?

4. Does the music challenge the technical skill and reading ability of the group?

5. Is the instrumentation suitable? Can it be played without complete instrumentation? (That is, do other instruments have important cues?)

6. If the music is an arrangement or transcription, does it retain the integrity of the original?

Table 11-1. CHECKLIST FOR EVALUATING INSTRUMENTAL INSTRUCTION MATERIAL

---

1. Does the book have:

    a. Illustrated information on assembling the instrument?
    b. Information on the care of the instrument?
    c. Clear, illustrated directions on holding the instrument, hand positions, posture, embouchure, and fingering or bowing?
    d. A discussion of the principles of tone production?
    e. Clear fingering charts?
    f. An explanation of symbols of notation and music terms?
    g. A logical, sequential plan for developing theoretic and technical knowledge, understanding, and skill?
    h. A periodic review of skills and terms?
    i. Provisions for supplementary material?
    j. A format that is functional, interesting, and attractive?

---

2. Is each type of music content good, fair, or poor?

    a. Exercises?
    b. Music composed for the course?
    c. Edited material?
    d. Solo, small ensemble, and large ensemble literature?

---

7. Does the music contribute to the balance of the selected works in terms of variety of style, varying levels of difficulty, and both immediate success and satisfaction as well as long-range challenges?

8. Does it have both student and audience appeal?

Maintaining and Repairing Instruments

A specific area of the music suite should be a well-equipped facility in which simple repair and maintenance problems can be handled. Schools can purchase a "beginner's kit" of repair tools and add other equipment as the need arises. Although the instrumental teacher's time is limited, he should be available to handle such work as replacing or adjusting pads on woodwinds, replacing rotary valve strings on horns, "thawing" frozen valves and slides on brass instruments, and adjusting soundposts on strings. He should also seek out agencies in his area that handle major repairs and become familiar with the calibre of their craftsmanship.

Periodically, each instrument should be examined by the teacher to ascertain its condition and anticipate when the instrument will need minor repairs or a complete overhaul. Instruments must be kept in top condition to ensure the best possible performance on the part of the students using them.

TYPES OF INSTRUMENTAL CLASSES

The instrumental music program tends to have more diversified offerings than the vocal program. This results from the simple fact that there is a greater variety of instruments than types of voices, thus giving rise to numerous possible combinations in small and large ensembles and necessitating a number of different classes for basic instruction in the techniques of playing different instruments. The well-organized program is one with proper articulation between middle school, junior high, and senior high school classes, so that each course is part of a larger pattern that provides for continuous growth and multiple opportunities to develop perception and skill.

The Middle School and Junior High School

At the middle-school and junior-high level, the instrumental teacher works with students at several stages—beginners, intermediate students, and advanced players. He also works with them in several types of courses, including class lessons, medium- and large-sized performance groups, and small ensembles.

The Beginners Program

In designing an effective program for beginners, the teacher will be influenced by administrative decisions regarding the amount of time allotted each week to instrumental instruction, the availability of space where such instruction can take place, when the lessons are to be scheduled (before, during, or after school), whether students will be dismissed from academic classes on a rotating basis (see Chapter 16) or only from general music classes, and the number of teachers available to implement the instrumental program. With these considerations in mind, the teacher can select the type of class grouping that best fits the circumstances:

1. *Homogeneous classes* are ideal since the same instruments are grouped together, and all students are dealing with the same problems and instructional tasks.

2. *Modified homogeneous classes* group families of instruments together. Although beginners playing instruments within a single family have to overcome similar problems,

they also face problems that are unique to specific instruments—for example, different clefs, key relationships, playing techniques, and embouchures.

3. *Heterogeneous classes* are the least desirable, and should be attempted only when there is no alternative. Since all instruments are scheduled together, the problems of technique, key relationships, embouchures, and clefs will be multiplied. However, the teacher who has a workable knowledge and understanding of all instruments, as well as good instructional materials for multiple groupings, can be successful, though progress will be slower.

Also influencing the success of the grouping is the level of student ability. The homogeneous instrumental grouping with students of similar ability is naturally the best, and it can usually be achieved in the large school. In smaller schools, this is apt to be more difficult to organize. The modified plan of grouping instruments by families, but retaining a similar level of student ability, would be the next best choice. Following this, homogeneous instrumental grouping with varying ability levels and family instrumental groupings with varying ability levels are still better than heterogeneous classes.

In using either of the homogeneous plans, it is recommended that the class lesson be supplemented by one weekly large ensemble session, separating the winds and percussion from the strings. Such an arrangement provides the beginner with the opportunity to play in his first "band" or "string orchestra," to reinforce technical and theoretic concepts learned in the class lesson, to compare his progress with other beginners, and to perform a different type of literature. The students must understand that this ensemble session is an extension of their regular lessons, and the teacher must work to make it an exciting, encouraging experience. When something is

well done, the teacher should compliment; when it is not well done, he must provide directions that lead to improvement. It is very important that the members of the ensemble respect the director's opinion, and that he respect the students and their efforts.

As the beginning student progresses, provisions should be made for solo and small ensemble experiences. Duets, trios, and quartets of various instrumental combinations ought to be available to all beginners, not only to those making above-average progress. Supplementary material for this purpose, used in conjunction with the beginner's method book, can be a strong motivating factor.

Although it would be difficult to dispute that individual instruction is the most advantageous, the cost of such instruction to a school district is equally difficult to justify. Thus, class instrumental instruction has become increasingly prevalent, and some excellent group-method materials are now available that include solo and ensemble music as well as basic instructional material. With such materials, with regular classes that meet at least two times a week, and with the beginners band and string orchestra meeting once a week during an activity period or after school, the type of program diagramed in Table 11-2 can be established. It will be noticed that demonstration concerts are built into this program; these furnish the students with the necessary incentive to work on solos and ensemble literature, and provide parents with another means of evaluating student progress.

Using course objectives similar to those in Chapter 10 for vocal classes (they need only slight modification), the teacher can develop instructional objectives that provide direction over an extended period of time as well as for day-to-day planning of class lessons. In devising instructional objectives, the teacher might consider such aspects of student behavior as keeping his instrument in working

Table 11-2. BEGINNERS INSTRUMENTAL PROGRAM IN THE LOWER
MIDDLE SCHOOL

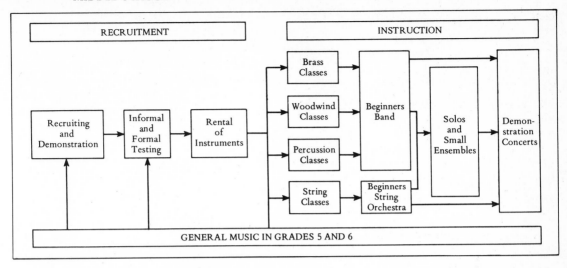

condition, being able to locate technical information in his instruction book, understanding fundamental playing techniques, understanding symbols of notation and how they relate to the actual pitches he produces on his instrument, understanding the need for good posture in performing, being able to perceive and understand basic concepts related to melody and rhythm, displaying skills related to fingering, breath control, embouchure, and hand and arm positions, exhibiting increased skills in interpreting notation, knowing when he has made a mistake in playing and being able to correct his mistake, attending all lessons with the necessary equipment and materials, practicing regularly, asking questions when concepts of theory or technique are not understood, accepting suggestions from his teacher, respecting the playing abilities of others, being willing to play his instrument for others and in general music class, and revealing an increased interest in and enjoyment of other music experiences outside of class.

In organizing a specific procedure for class instruction, much will depend on the individual teacher's background, personality, and understanding of class teaching techniques. Regardless of a teacher's individualism, however, the following are necessary factors in designing effective instruction: (1) making a careful selection of experiences and materials to bring about the desired behaviors stated in the teacher's objectives, (2) applying the principles of learning that were presented in Chapter 2, pages 29–30, (3) developing a routine that integrates solo and ensemble experiences with class instruction on a regular basis, (4) giving equal emphasis to the development of playing technique and conceptual understanding, (5) evaluating each student's progress regularly to determine areas of strength and weakness, and (6) keeping parents informed of their child's progress. A typical form to report progress to parents is shown in Figure 11-3.

In using the class approach to instruction, the teacher must remember that he is still teaching individuals, and that learning will take place at different rates. Therefore, it may be necessary at some point to supplement class lessons with private instruction to meet

FIGURE 11-3. Instrumental Progress Report

INSTRUMENTAL PROGRESS REPORT

Dear Parent:

After _____ weeks of instruction

___(student's name)_____ 's progress on

___(instrument)_____ has been

☐ outstanding.

☐ average.

☐ below average.

Recommendation:

☐ Continue without reservation

☐ Continue with the following suggestions:

  ☐ More practice

  ☐ Better attendance at lessons

  ☐ Purchase of a better instrument

  ☐ Repair of instrument

☐ Discontinue

If there are any questions, call 475-0151.

Cordially,

___(teacher's name)_____

---

the needs of individual students. The teacher must also consider the effect of his own absence on individuals rather than on the class. A scheduled lesson canceled without notification can be discouraging to a student and infuriating to parents. The student who has prepared his lesson, carried his instrument to school, and found his teacher absent may eventually look for more rewarding experiences in some other area of the school program. The teacher has the responsibility to be at every music lesson or to notify students in advance when it is necessary to cancel. Of course, equally frustrating to the teacher is the student who comes to class with such excuses as "I forgot my instrument," "I don't have a reed," or "my second valve is stuck." Many problems are alleviated when the teacher maintains a supply of extra instruction books, reeds, mouthpieces, and even instruments that can be used for a single lesson.

Innovative String Approaches

For many decades, bands and wind ensembles multiplied in number and size in the public schools, while interest in string playing declined. In recent years, however, string programs have been revitalized through the efforts of such educators as Shinichi Suzuki of Japan and George Bornoff of the United States.

The Suzuki method is a natural and logical approach in applied psychology that has implications for general learning beyond string instruction. The child learns to play the violin in the same way that he acquires facility with speech—in the natural setting of his home, by imitating his parents and other family members. He sees the violin as a natural part of family life. Learning through imitation is traditional in many of the world's cultures, including Japan where members of a family share in a child's education. In the Suzuki approach, parents—usually mothers—observe private lessons and ensemble classes, and learn to play the instrument themselves, usually beginning instruction three months prior to the child's instruction. The parents also play recordings of selected repertoire for the child and practice at home with him. Although most American students begin to learn the instrument when they are about ten years old, in Japan, Suzuki's Talent Education program starts children as early as two years of age.

In practicing and performing, the students stand, free of chairs and music stands (since all music is memorized); they walk and move rhythmically to the music. These games of mobility, along with extensive listening experiences, help them in developing an awareness of and responsiveness to tone, rhythm, and structure. Note reading is introduced as the students advance—usually after two or three years if they begin early, but sooner if they start a few years older. The more advanced students often play with the younger ones to encourage them and assist in their instruction. Under this system, students advance rapidly, and by age ten many are playing such works as the Vivaldi concerto and the Bach double concerto. Interestingly, scale studies and etudes are not introduced until a student has passed the level of Suzuki's tenth manual, with repertoire including Mozart's fourth and fifth concertos.

Thus, the key elements of Suzuki's method are that the parent functions as a teacher, the child learns by rote for an extended period of time, he accepts the violin as a natural part of family life, he learns a great deal by listening to others and to recorded literature, and he is involved physically, intellectually, and emotionally in the total learning experience. Obviously, this approach deviates from conventional violin methods in many ways. However, some of the most apparent technical differences are that the student is instructed to place his weight on his left leg rather than the right, he is allowed to place his thumb outside the frog of the bow to reduce tension in the right hand, he is permitted to use the upper part of the bow, and he is aided by markers placed on the fingerboard to ensure playing in tune.

In the method developed by George Bornoff, beginners work simultaneously from two books—one providing technique-building material and the other offering solo literature. Before the books are introduced, however, students are exposed to an extended period of rote instruction, during which they learn to play with various bowings and become familiar with the five finger patterns that are basic to the system. The five patterns place the fingers in various positions on the strings to produce different pitch sequences of whole and half steps. The basic patterns are then combined in a carefully worked-out progression of technical studies and solo music. Bornoff's materials are well organized, can be adapted to individual or class instruction, provide for the development of playing and reading skill, and offer enough flexibility so that they are adaptable to a variety of teaching situations.

Intermediate Band and Orchestra

To provide for the multiplicity of playing levels that exist in the middle and junior high school, small and large ensemble experiences need to be provided on both intermediate and advanced levels. Membership in these groups should be based on the student's ability rather than grade-level placement. The idea of playing in a band or orchestra is a great motivating factor because it represents an immediate reward for the beginning instrumentalist. Whereas the beginners band and orchestra are merely extensions of class lessons, the intermediate organizations represent the first "real" band or orchestra that the novice can join. Membership at this level should be non-selective, and almost all second-year instrumentalists should be accepted, with only those few students who would become discouraged by not keeping up with others being denied membership temporarily. Achieving a balanced instrumentation at this point is not important. What is important is maintaining student interest and developing skills and understanding. The group experience offers the student the opportunity to apply what he continues to learn in class lessons and helps to expand his knowledge of music through the performance of ensemble literature.

Advanced Band and Orchestra

An advanced band and orchestra is both possible and advisable in many middle and junior high schools. These groups are selective in both membership and instrumentation and perform music at a higher level of sophistication. Auditioning students for these groups is considerably easier than it is for similar vocal organizations because the instrumental teacher has generally worked with the students in previous ensembles or in class lessons. He can also contact the student's present teacher for information regarding ability, attitude, practice habits, and understanding. A comprehensive appraisal should still be made, however, through a formal audition. Auditions should be announced well in advance to permit the student ample time to prepare. The student should also be told what the audition will consist of, such as a prepared selection to be played with or without piano accompaniment, technical studies (scales, arpeggios), and sight-reading material of the calibre of music to be performed by the organization. A relaxed atmosphere at the audition can be created by giving the student complete attention while he is performing and by allowing him to perform the portions of the audition materials in any order he wishes. Attention to the student's comfortable playing range, blending tone quality, level of reading ability, and technical facility should provide enough data for determining assignment to an organization, assignment to a specific chair, and assignments for small ensemble experiences.

In those schools where both intermediate and advanced organizations cannot be formed and one group must serve all students regardless of ability level, the teacher will find that he is providing for the "average" and neglecting those with limited or advanced playing ability. To improve this situation, the teacher might still organize small ensemble experiences for his advanced students during the same time that the large group rehearses. Since the music of the large ensemble will be comparatively simple, advanced students can well afford to miss a number of rehearsals.

252
Music Education Through Performance Classes

Table 11-3. INSTRUMENTAL MUSIC PROGRAM IN THE MIDDLE AND
JUNIOR HIGH SCHOOL

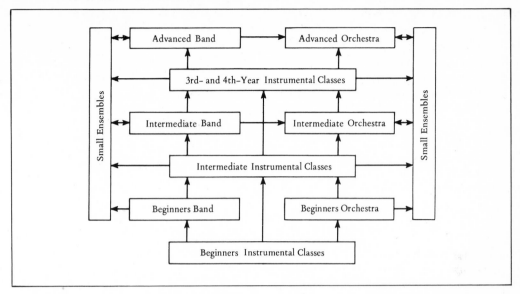

For the student with limited ability, the teacher might provide more attention through after-school sectional rehearsals or individual and small-group sessions during lunch and free periods. Table 11-3 illustrates one of the many possibilities for organizing the instrumental program at the middle or junior high school level.

The High School

The ability levels of instrumentalists are even more diverse in the high school, and the music department must provide a comprehensive program of both selective and nonselective groups. It would be inappropriate to offer instrumental instruction over a period of time and then drop the student in the senior high school because he is unable to qualify for one of the select music organizations. Yet, some instrumental teachers find themselves concentrating exclusively on selective organizations because of the demands on their time and the pressure from the school

to produce top-quality groups. As a result, difficult music, restrictive instrumentation, and extensive rehearsal time have often become the hallmarks of high school performing groups. Under such circumstances, many students are left holding their instruments with no organizations in which to participate. The high school program must enable *all* students to realize their fullest musical potentials. Table 11-4 shows one way of organizing a comprehensive program at this level.

Beginning, Intermediate, and Advanced Groups

If the teacher is truly interested in the musical development of individuals rather than of his "prize group," then beginners should be encouraged even as late as their senior year in school. Very often, however, unless the school is a large one, these students will have to rely on private instruction (which all instrumentalists should be having from their later middle-school years). Piano and guitar classes are often offered for beginners

Table 11-4. INSTRUMENTAL MUSIC PROGRAM IN THE SENIOR HIGH SCHOOL

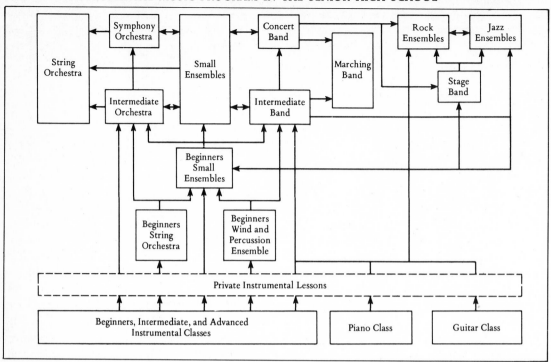

at this level, even in smaller schools, and if other classes can be accommodated in brass, woodwinds, percussion, and strings, they should be scheduled. Whenever such a program is provided, ensemble experiences should also be made available as soon as possible to reinforce the skills these beginners develop in their regular instrumental lessons. Such ensembles can be either homogeneously or heterogeneously grouped, according to the number of beginners in each instrumental family, as well as the availability of time and teaching personnel.

In many high schools intermediate instrumental groups are organized to accommodate those students who are unable to pass the auditions to become members of the concert band or symphony orchestra. While groups of this type will perform easier music, they must nevertheless maintain a high level of

expectancy within the capability of the group. The teacher must provide opportunities for public appearances so that members will feel that the intermediate group is independent and not simply a preparatory ensemble. One possibility is to establish intermediate classes of instrumental families in which students can further their individual skills, learn a second instrument if desired, and be introduced to music for woodwinds alone, brass alone, strings alone, or percussion alone. If such classes met two or three times a week, they could be joined together on remaining days to form the intermediate orchestra and wind-and-percussion ensemble. Sometimes the intermediate group will include some very capable performers who failed to gain membership in an advanced group only because of instrumentation limitations. Whenever possible, then, members of intermediate and ad-

Music Education Through Performance Classes

vanced groups should also be combined, as in forming the marching band for the football season.

Advanced instrumental groups should provide the best instrumentalists with the challenge to play fine literature and to continue their musical growth. Particularly in the concert band, the teacher needs to explore the wealth of relatively unknown concert music that has been written specifically for that medium (as opposed to arrangements and transcriptions).

The form that these groups take, on all levels, will be influenced by the particular school situation. While the program in Table 11-4 is quite inclusive and can be established in its entirety, it is also possible to make adjustments and adapt portions to fit a variety of teaching circumstances.

Marching Band

The marching band deserves special consideration here because it has been an object of controversy in recent years. Opponents have pointed out that the time spent on the marching band could be used for more musical purposes—that the literature played by the band is not challenging and that a group cannot play at its best while marching. Certainly it must be admitted that the hours spent in developing intricate maneuvers on the football field contribute little to aesthetic sensitivity. The proponents, on the other hand, contend that the marching band is an art in itself, a combination of several disciplines, and that it deserves respect for its own values. Being the music department's "most effective public relations vehicle" is generally the chief value claim. Since it is seen by more members of the community than any other music organization in the school, the marching band supposedly musters community support for the music department and its other programs. This is an entirely false concept. The marching band musters support for the marching

band. It is, by itself, a rather poor form of public relations because it presents a distorted view of the total music program, and it has seldom won community support for anything other than its own perpetuation. The group does provide good public relations for the school department, but not for music education.

There is nothing wrong with a marching band as long as it is kept in proper perspective like every other music class and performing group in the curriculum. (It would be just as unwise, for example, to build up the school's symphony orchestra as the image for music education.) The problems arise when every member of the concert band is required to be in the marching band (rather than making the marching unit an elective open to members of both intermediate and advanced ensembles), when it replaces the concert band throughout the fall season (rather than rehearsing the nonmusic aspects outside of class time and rehearsing the relatively simple music during one regular rehearsal a week; or at least establishing some other plan to maintain concert band classes), and when the music teacher is burdened with such nonmusic tasks as handling marching drills and preparing baton twirlers. It must be recognized that many communities with outstanding marching bands also have excellent concert bands; the two are not incompatible when proper perspective is maintained.

Regardless of the point of view the instrumental teacher takes toward the marching band, he must accept the fact that it is deeply entrenched in the school curriculum and work with it realistically. Each September the band director is faced with the need to prepare pregame and half-time shows, and in some school districts the first football game is scheduled ten days after the opening of school. In order to field the marching band, he will need to have adequate rehearsal time, adequate rehearsal facilities, sufficient assistance, and good incentives for the students. Those school districts with outstanding marching bands have demanded considerable time commitments of their students. In many cases, rehearsals are scheduled during the school day *and* after school, and some districts rehearse regularly during the summer months or concentrate their efforts into the two weeks prior to the opening of school by organizing "band camps." The amount of rehearsal time will be the largest determining factor in the complexity and quality of half-time shows.

Since the band director is faced with the problems of selecting music (a sufficient amount so that the same numbers are not repeated week after week); rehearsing the music; outfitting the students in uniforms; drilling them in marching routines; creating, writing, and rehearsing scripts for half-time shows; arranging for transportation and chaperones; and organizing baton squads, dancing groups, and color guards, it is necessary that he have some faculty assistance. His assistants need not be members of the music department. The most desirable assistance would be in the form of a drill master to develop the show around the music that has been chosen and a coach for the baton twirlers. A number of successful bands have now simplified the entire process by adopting a practice used for many years by drum and bugle corps, which is the development of *one* complex show that is used throughout the entire football season. It is also important that the band have the use of the football field for practice. The student must be able to develop the feel for a predetermined number of steps to each five-yard line. Working on the lined field is also essential in developing intricate routines, for the students need the lines as points of demarcation.

Since the marching band demands so much time, a student's desire to participate without coercion is important. To elicit this major commitment from students, band directors have tried a variety of incentives. For example, band camps are sometimes established in which the students have the opportunity to spend some time away from home, learn their music and routines, and have time for social and recreational activities. Participation in marching competitions is another device used to maintain interest, and very often field trips are arranged so that the band can appear in Thanksgiving or Christmas parades or in half-time shows at professional games. For these purposes, the band director will have to procure sufficient funds—and not necessarily from the school budget. Although such extrinsic (nonmusic) incentives can be quite successful, the band director must determine the extent to which they are necessary within the framework of his particular music program and community.

Half-time shows have become a staple in pop culture, and because of the exposure given to college and professional football, some high school band directors feel that they must emulate the types of shows seen on network television. Common sense, however, indicates that the typical high school stadium is not like the Rose Bowl, and many intricate maneuvers and formations will work only with the perspective gained from high-rise seating. Simpler marching patterns can be interesting if done well. Therefore, while attempting to prepare a show that has visual interest, the director still should concentrate on the quality of the musical performance. Show movements should be built around the selection of music rather than the reverse. If a certain selection is somewhat difficult or meant to be showcased, the band members should maintain a stationary position or move a bare minimum. If a selection is relatively easy, on the other hand, simple but precise marching maneuvers can produce a complementary visual effect. In either case, the director always should be aware of the direction the performers are facing and of the spread of the band across the field so that a cohesive musical sound is maintained.

Jazz and Rock Bands

Music educators are now placing greater emphasis on the need for, and values of, both jazz and rock bands in the instrumental program. County, state, regional, and national conferences include jazz band concerts on their programs, and select groups, composed of the best players within a certain jurisdiction, are organized. It is an encouraging sign of the maturity of the music-education profession to hear a student boast of having been chosen to play second trombone in the all-state jazz band.

Such bands serve to expand a student's experience by involving him in the jazz and rock idioms while devoting attention to proper technique, good tone quality, and other attributes of artistic performance. Within these groups, the student is often introduced to unusual and somewhat difficult rhythms that might not be encountered in other music he plays; he is encouraged to develop his independence because of his responsibility within a small group and the individualistic nature of this type of music, as well as to develop his sense of tonal balance in performing with the other members; and he is provided with a good format for developing his sight-reading skills.

These groups also engage students in improvisation, an aspect of creativity that is neglected in traditional instrumental ensembles. It is in the art of improvisation that the teacher can most significantly assist the student who shows an interest in jazz and rock. Such instruction must be well planned and be an integral part of each rehearsal.

Students must also have the opportunity to apply the improvisational techniques they have learned in actual concert performances. With instruction in improvisation, the student will soon realize the need to know the construction of chords and the relationship of various scales and modes to these chords as tools for improvising. (See Chapter 6, pages 143–148, for a discussion of improvisation.)

Initially, the school jazz band was used to reproduce the big band sound of the swing era. Band directors enthusiastically organized "stage" bands because they were able to identify with this music and offer their students very capable leadership. However, many have not progressed beyond this point, and they have failed to offer students the experience of playing some of the fine jazz-rock arrangements that are currently available and of creating their own arrangements of standard and original compositions.

Provisions should also be made for the rock musician in the instrumental program. It is difficult for the older music teacher who has had no experience playing in this idiom to know exactly what to do. The departure from the use of more traditional instruments to the use of amplified guitars and basses, as well as electronic equipment to enhance sound, can be frightening to the music teacher who has roots in traditional music and even to many of those who are quite comfortable with jazz. However, for some time now, universities have been graduating music teachers who are familiar with this field, and the rock combo has made a rapid development in music education. High school rock musicians spend many hours learning arrangements by ear from recordings with amazing accuracy. Such interest can be expanded to yield an understanding of music theory as it relates to the particular instrument the student plays. The ultimate goal of the teacher who works with rock musicians is to give them the knowledge, understanding, and literacy to create and play their own compositions.

Small Ensembles

Small instrumental ensembles of strings, woodwinds, brasses, percussion, or a mixed combination of families should be encouraged and provided for. These should not be limited to traditional chamber ensembles, such as string quartets and woodwind quintets. A considerable amount of interesting and challenging music is available for "odd" combinations, such as piano, percussion, trombone, and cello. Students fully enjoy the intimacy of small-group performance and the individual challenge it offers. Apart from developing performance skills, small ensembles are excellent vehicles for developing insight into the structure of music.

Since few students are involved in each ensemble, many performers are willing to rehearse before or after school if rehearsal time cannot be found during the school day. Ideally, the ensemble should develop to the point where the students carry on their own rehearsals and use the music teacher only as a consultant when they have problems. Under such circumstances, the students can rehearse wherever and whenever they wish.

The music teacher must not allow these ensembles to become forgotten segments of the instrumental program; he needs to provide them with suitable opportunities for public performance. The importance of such groups can hardly be overstressed because of their excellent potential for the carry-over of music experiences into adult life. Whereas the post-high-school musician will not attempt to organize a concert band or orchestra, it is within his means to get together with two or three other musicians in his own living room to make music.

The Guitar Class

The guitar is an excellent instrument not only for performance but for the development of music understanding. Since it is the instrument most closely associated with the youth culture, it is readily accepted at all levels of the secondary school, and it also has potential for the carry-over of performance experiences into adult life.

Some schools offer guitar instruction as a part of the general music class, but others have recognized the degree of student interest and organized regular guitar classes. In the general music class, the objective is usually of an exploratory nature—giving students the opportunity to familiarize themselves with the instrument before considering more serious study. In the guitar class, on the other hand, students learn enough about notation and playing technique to be able to carry on instruction by themselves.

In organizing the class, it is not essential for each student to have a guitar. Student progress is quite satisfactory when students work in teams of two to an instrument. (This also keeps down the initial cost.) The next step is to find a guitar method book, organized for class instruction, that familiarizes the student with the fingerboard, introduces notation through simple exercises and tunes, begins chord development with simple three-string chords (not involving wide stretches of the fingers), and has enough ensemble music that combines single-string and chord technique. The teacher must also provide students who do not have guitars at home with practice facilities, since individual progress will be related to the amount of out-of-class practice.

Student interest in the guitar can be expanded through an exposure to such artists as Julian Bream, Andres Segovia, Chet Atkins, Django Reinhardt, Charlie Christian, Barney

Kessel, Johnny Smith, Kenny Burrel, and Wes Montgomery. Recordings should be available in the library for student use.

DEVELOPING MUSIC UNDERSTANDING

In order to develop music understanding in an instrumental class, it is not necessary to change the basic character of the rehearsal. Skill in performance is still one of the prime objectives. Rather, understanding should be fostered within the regular framework of the rehearsal by augmenting the students' involvement with the repertoire.

For many years, students have assumed that in the band or orchestra one merely played music, and that it was not necessary to "learn" anything. Thus, if a teacher suddenly realizes that his principal task is teaching music understanding, and he follows through with this realization in class, his plans may not be greeted enthusiastically by his students. They are, after all, sophisticated enough to know that any departure from the playing rehearsal means additional work and responsibility for them. Thus, attention to concepts and percepts must be made interesting. The development of music learnings cannot be left to chance with an occasional fragment of information being thrown in here and there. Since every composition played contains the basic concepts of music, and related percepts, the instrumental teacher will find a continuous stream of opportunities to use his imagination in presenting pertinent information.

The five-point organizational diagram for planning conceptual development, found on page 75 of Chapter 4, is quite applicable to the instrumental class. The teacher following this scheme must define the concept and its related percepts, determine the behaviors he would like to see exhibited, select suitable experiences and literature that will effect behavioral changes, and devise a method of evaluating the degree to which behavioral change has occurred.

As another example of how concepts and percepts can be defined (see also the discussions in Chapters 4, 7, and 10 regarding rhythm, form, and melody, respectively), let us consider the organization of the concept of harmony. Once again, it should be stressed that the development of conceptual understanding will be superficial unless each area is studied in relation to other areas.

1. *Concept:* Harmony is the simultaneous occurrence of two or more tones, and in a larger sense, the relationship of such a combination to the successive sounding of other groups of simultaneous tones.

2. *Percepts:*

a. *Harmonic interval*—The "distance" (more correctly, the ratio of vibrations per second) between two tones sounded simultaneously is referred to as a harmonic interval; consequently, the two tones, as a distinct entity, are themselves identified collectively as an "interval."

b. *Chord*—Three or more tones sounded simultaneously comprise a chord. A grouping of at least four different tones is sometimes referred to as an "extended chord."

c. *Consonance*—When the tones of an in-interval or chord are in "agreement" and evoke a feeling of restfulness and repose—admittedly, a relatively subjective identification—the effect is one of consonance.

d. *Dissonance*—When the tones of an interval or chord are in "conflict" and evoke a feeling of restlessness, tension, or activity, the subjective effect is known as dissonance.

e. *Harmonic progression*—A series of chords in succession, usually involving both active and inactive chords in a pattern of tension and relaxation, is a progression.

f. *Harmonic rhythm*—Since harmonies in a progression do not necessarily change as the melody changes from tone to tone, a distinct and separate time pattern of harmonic changes occurs that is known as harmonic rhythm.

g. *Cadence*—A short harmonic progression that creates a feeling of pause—either temporary or permanent—at the end of a phrase, a larger section, or an entire work, is a cadence.

h. *Homophony*—A harmonic texture in which all the voices or parts move together in the same rhythm or substantially the same rhythm, resulting in a progression of chords, is called homophony. The term also identifies the texture of monodic music, in which a single melody is supported by a series of chords functioning primarily as accompaniment.

i. *Polyphony*—A harmonic texture in which two or more voices or parts of individual design, and sometimes of relatively equal importance, are heard simultaneously, moving independently as melody and rhythm and overlapping in articulation, but functioning collectively to create harmony, is called polyphony.

j. *Arpeggio*—If the notes of a chord are sounded individually instead of simultaneously, but closely enough together to be heard as a harmonic entity, the broken chord that results is an arpeggio.

k. *Diatonic harmony*—Chords derived solely from the tones of a diatonic scale, without the use of chromatics, constitute diatonic harmony.

l. *Chromatic harmony*—Chords that include one or more tones that are foreign to a given diatonic scale constitute chromatic harmony.

m. *Modal harmony*—Chords derived from and functioning within a modal system, rather than a system of tonality, create modal harmony.

n. *Tertian harmony*—Chords that are based predominantly on the interval of a third, whether diatonic, chromatic, or modal, constitute tertian harmony.

o. *Nontertian harmony*—More commonly called post-tertian harmony (because its development marked a new era in harmonic usage and a break from the traditional system of tertian harmony), nontertian harmony consists of chords that are *not* based on the interval of a third. This broad category of harmonic practice includes "secundal harmony" (chords based on the interval of a second), "tone clusters" (a dissonant group of tones that are close together), "quartal harmony" (chords based on the interval of a fourth), "quintal harmony" (chords based on the interval of a fifth), "polytonal harmony" (chords that derive their tones from two or more keys and suggest more than one tonality), "atonal harmony" (chords in which the tones, individually or in combination with other chords, suggest no key), and "serial harmony" (chords in which the tones are derived from a twelve-tone row).

p. *Simultaneity*—All concurrent sounds, regardless of the harmonic components, style, or usage, are sometimes referred to collectively as simultaneity. ("Simultaneity" and "harmony" are synonymous, although the former term is used predominantly for nontraditional harmonic systems and usages.)

From this type of analysis of harmonic percepts, the teacher can then select the behaviors he would like to elicit through class instruction. These might include the ability to (1) recognize homophonic and polyphonic texture; (2) aurally and visually recognize authentic, plagal, and half cadences; (3) determine whether a particular composition includes diatonic, chromatic, or modal harmonies, or a combination; (4) understand the structure of tertian harmony and recognize its use in compositions; (5) recognize the use of nontertian harmonies; (6) understand the meaning of the terms "consonance" and "dissonance" and recognize their effect in music; and (7) sense the harmonic rhythm of a composition and compare it to the melodic rhythm. Other behaviors related to harmonic perception might suggest themselves depending on the selection of literature to be studied.

Because students in an instrumental class have music-reading ability, or are in the process of acquiring it, it should be possible for the teacher to develop understanding on a more abstract level than in a vocal performance group. In the beginners band, for example, an explanation of cadence might be limited to pointing out that it produces a feeling of pause, and cadences can be located within a particular selection. In more advanced groups, however, an understanding of cadence would probably reach a more abstract level through involvement in identifying the chords, their structure, and their function, as well as the type of cadence employed.

As in the general music class, the evaluation process should determine the extent to which students have grasped certain percepts and determine the teacher's own success in organizing and presenting his lessons. Student evaluation is possible through group discussion, analysis of familiar and new repertoire, observations of individual awareness and interest both in and out of class, and written examination. In the process of self-evaluation, the teacher should consider those points discussed in Chapter 4, pages 100–101.

Discussion Questions and Projects

1. Modify the course objectives presented in Table 10-1, making them suitable for an instrumental music class, and based on these, write a set of behavioral objectives for (a) a high school percussion ensemble, (b) a lower middle-school class of beginners on the trumpet, or (c) an advanced string ensemble of junior high school students.

2. You have received administrative approval to spend $10,000 for instruments that parents are not likely to buy. The instruments are to be used in a junior high school of 1,100 students. The only instruments presently owned by the school are a bass drum, cymbals, and two timpani, which are all shared by the band and string orchestra since they rehearse at separate times. Determine what instruments should be purchased, investigate brands and prices, and decide how the money will be spent.

3. Make a study of clarinet method books and related course materials at a music store. Select the course that you would use for a beginners class and state your reasons.

4. Prepare a statement to be presented to the superintendent or board of education to convince them that the school system should underwrite a program of class violin instruction using the Suzuki method. The program would be instituted in a lower middle school of 650 students. Outline a plan for the procurement of instruments, the time required, the personnel needed, how parents are to be involved, the cost involved, and other factors that you feel are important.

5. Compile a list of compositions employing aleatoric techniques that would be suitable for a high school concert band.

6. Determine the instrumentation you would desire for (a) an advanced orchestra in a high school of 900 students, and (b) an advanced concert band in a high school of 2,700 students.

7. Your 55-member high school concert band, which rehearses three times a week, is also the school's marching band. Sixteen of the students, including all but one

percussionist, are not available after school because of part-time jobs. Before-school hours are restricted because most students arrive by school buses. What plan would you devise for rehearsing the marching band for football season, while maintaining a concert-band program?

8. Your students have petitioned the school to organize a stage band and the administration has given its approval. You have had no experience in the jazz idiom. How would you go about organizing and directing it?

Selected References

BARTLETT, HARRY R. *Guide to Teaching Percussion.* Dubuque, Iowa: William C. Brown Company, Inc., 1964.

BINION, W. T., JR. *The High School Marching Band.* West Nyack, New York: Parker Publishing Company, Inc., 1973.

BOBBITT, RICHARD. *Harmonic Technique in the Rock Idiom.* Belmont, California: Wadsworth Publishing Company, 1976.

COLWELL, RICHARD J. *Teaching Instrumental Music.* New York: Appleton-Century-Crofts, Inc., 1969.

DEVOE, ROBERT A. *Electronmusic: A Comprehensive Handbook.* Vernon, Connecticut: Electronic Music Laboratories, Inc., 1977.

DEYOUNG, DONALD. "Music Literature for Band and Wind Ensemble," *Music Educators Journal*, 64:4 (December 1977), pp. 26–29.

DUVALL, W. CLYDE. *The High School Band Director's Handbook.* Englewood Cliffs, New Jersey: Prentice-Hall, Inc., 1960.

FERGUSON, TOM, and SANDY FELDSTEIN. *The Jazz-Rock Ensemble: A Conductor's and Teacher's Guide.* Port Washington, New York: Alfred Publishing Company, 1976.

GOLDMAN, RICHARD FRANKO. *The Wind Band: Its Literature and Technique.* Boston: Allyn & Bacon, Inc., 1961.

GOODMAN, HAROLD. *Instrumental Music Guide.* Provo, Utah: Brigham Young University Press, 1977.

GOTTIKER, IRVIN. *Complete Book of Rehearsal Techniques for the High School Orchestra.* West Nyack, New York: Parker Publishing Company, Inc., 1977.

GREEN, ELIZABETH A. H. *Teaching Stringed Instruments in Classes.* Englewood Cliffs, New Jersey: Prentice-Hall, Inc., 1966.

HOLZ, EMIL A., and ROGER F. JACOBI. *Teaching Band Instruments to Beginners.* Englewood Cliffs, New Jersey: Prentice-Hall, Inc., 1966.

HOUSE, ROBERT W. *Instrumental Music for Today's Schools.* Englewood Cliffs, New Jersey: Prentice-Hall, Inc., 1965.

HUNT, NORMAN. *Guide to Teaching Brass.* Dubuque: William C. Brown Company, Inc., 1968.

INTRAVAIA, LAWRENCE J. *Building a Superior School Band Library.* West Nyack, New York: Parker Publishing Company, Inc., 1972.

KENDALL, JOHN. *The Suzuki Violin Method in American Music Education.* Washington, D.C.: Music Educators National Conference, 1973.

KOHUT, DANIEL L. *Instrumental Music Pedagogy.* Englewood Cliffs, New Jersey: Prentice-Hall, Inc., 1973.

KUHN, WOLFGANG E. *Instrumental Music: Principles and Methods of Instruction,* 2d ed. Boston: Allyn & Bacon, Inc., 1969.

————. *The Strings: Performance and Instructional Techniques.* Boston: Allyn & Bacon, Inc., 1967.

LABUTA, JOSEPH A. *Teaching Musicianship in the High School Band.* West Nyack, New York: Parker Publishing Company, Inc., 1972.

LACY, GENE M. *Organizing and Developing the High School Orchestra.* West Nyack, New York: Parker Publishing Company, Inc., 1971.

LAWRENCE, IAN. *Brass in Your School.* New York: Oxford University Press, 1975.

LEE, JACK. *Modern Marching Band Techniques.* Winona, Minnesota: Hal Leonard Music Co., 1968.

LOVE, BEATRICE. "The Guitar in the Junior High School," *Music Educators Journal,* 60:7 (March 1974), pp. 36–37.

NEIDIG, KENNETH L., ed. *The Band Director's Guide.* Englewood Cliffs, New Jersey: Prentice-Hall, Inc., 1964.

OTTO, RICHARD A. *Effective Methods for Building the High School Band.* West Nyack, New York: Parker Publishing Company, Inc., 1971.

PIZER, RUSSELL A. *Administering the Elementary Band.* West Nyack, New York: Parker Publishing Company, Inc., 1971.

RIGHTER, CHARLES B. *Teaching Instrumental Music.* New York: Carl Fischer, Inc., 1959.

ROBINSON, HELENE, and RICHARD JARVIS, eds. *Teaching Piano in Classroom and Studio.* Washington, D.C.: Music Educators National Conference, 1967.

ROTHROCK, CARSON. *Training the High School Orchestra.* West Nyack, New York: Parker Publishing Company, Inc., 1971.

SMITH, NORMAN, and ALBERT STOUTAMIRE. *Band Music Notes.* Lake Charles, Louisiana: Band Music Notes, 1977.

SPOHN, CHARLES L. *The Percussion: Performance and Instructional Techniques.* Boston: Allyn & Bacon, Inc., 1967.

————, and RICHARD W. HEINE. *The Marching Band: Comparative Techniques in Movement and Music.* Boston: Allyn & Bacon, Inc., 1969.

STARR, WILLIAM. *The Suzuki Violinist.* Knoxville, Tennessee: Kingston Ellis Press, 1976.

The String Instruction Program in Music Education. Washington, D.C.: Music Educators National Conference, 1957.

TIEDE, CLAYTON. *Practical Band Instrument Repair Manual.* Dubuque: William C. Brown Company, Inc., 1962.

TIMM, EVERETT R. *The Woodwinds: Performance and Instructional Techniques.* Boston: Allyn & Bacon, Inc., 1964.

WARWICK, JAMES. "Heads Up, Shoulders Straight, Stick and Twirl Together," *Music Educators Journal,* 64:3 (November 1977), pp. 48–51.

WEERTS, RICHARD. *Developing Individual Skills for the High School Band.* West Nyack, New York: Parker Publishing Company, Inc., 1969.

WESTPHAL, FREDERICK W. *A Guide to Teaching Woodwinds.* Dubuque: William C. Brown Company, Inc., 1962.

WINTER, JAMES H. *The Brass Instruments: Performance and Instructional Techniques.* 2d ed. Boston: Allyn & Bacon, Inc., 1969.

WISKIRCHEN, GEORGE. *Developmental Techniques for the School Dance Band Musician.* Boston: Berklee Press, 1961.

WRIGHT, AL. *Marching Band Fundamentals.* New York: Carl Fischer, Inc., 1963.

The
Effective
Rehearsal

12

In fearless youth we tempt the heights of Arts,/While from the bounded level
of our mind,/Short views we take, nor see the lengths behind. . . .

ALEXANDER POPE
The Essay on Criticism

"ART IS LONG," wrote Longfellow, "and time is fleeting." He was referring, of course, to the endurance of finished art, not its preparatory
period; but he might very well have penned the same words about rehearsals. For when the days have passed almost unnoticed, and Christmas
looms two weeks away or the spring concert is pressing fast on the calendar, we are apt to hear some common thoughts echoed in rehearsal rooms
from school to school: "Will they ever be ready in time?" "If only we
had one more week to work on the overture!"

It seems as though there is never quite enough time to complete the
job of preparing for a public concert—never enough time to finish what
we are trying to do. Undoubtedly, time is a persistent problem in conducting rehearsals, but the more important factor here is "what we are
trying to do." The process of rehearsing school performance groups is
too often confused with that of rehearsing professional organizations.
In the world of professional music, the performance is the goal toward
which all efforts are directed. In the school, on the other hand, the
rehearsal itself is the center of interest, the vehicle for learning, and the
product for evaluation, whereas the public performance is more a *résumé*
of what has been accomplished in the real activity of the rehearsal hall.
In this sense, school rehearsals are not held as a preliminary requirement

for performance; rather, the performance is a subsequent requirement of the more important process of rehearsing—an outgrowth and natural demand of achievement in the regular learning situation.

Music educators have long acknowledged the fact that school performance groups are not intended as training grounds for professional performers. Yet, while recognizing the broader educational purpose of these groups, many have pursued a course of instruction that is directed only toward the accomplishment of performance goals. Certainly, within the rehearsal situation, the music teacher should be concerned with improving performance ability: with building musicianship by developing technical skills in the areas of tone production, intonation, articulation, balance, and interpretation. But he must also, and most importantly, be concerned with the basic goal of developing musical sensitivity and understanding. This is a central goal of all activities in music education, but it is easily overlooked when the educator's mind is overshadowed by the coembodied zeal of the musician in striving for the immediate objectives of performance. It is essential to remember we are both musicians *and* educators as we stand before a class of secondary students, and that our efforts in rehearsal should be directed toward the goals of both skillful musicianship and aesthetic musicality.

MUSIC PERCEPTION AND MUSIC PERFORMANCE

Teaching music perception requires different techniques from those employed simply to obtain accuracy in performance. Over a period of time one can draw very close to notes and rhythms without being aware of how they are put together, what their over-all shape is, how one voice relates to another, how sections of a work are connected, or how the entire selection fits into the spectrum of music as a whole. It is not unusual, for example, for a student to learn his bass part perfectly, being able to recall it exactly at a much later date, and yet have little or no idea of what the melody sounds like. More specifically, we could make a safe guess that few choral selections are performed so often in our schools, year-in and year-out, as Handel's "Hallelujah Chorus." But how many of the thousands of students who sing this work yearly are aware of the change in it from polyphonic to homophonic texture and the effect it produces; are aware of the imitation between voices; know the relationship of this chorus to the rest of the oratorio; know, indeed, what an oratorio is; know that this is an example of baroque music and that certain characteristics of it are identifiable in other baroque music; or have some idea of Handel's place in music history? These are all valid topics for presentation in the effective rehearsal designed for growth in music understanding. They are not, however, automatically introduced by attention to rhythms, pitches, and tone quality alone. William Thomson has made an interesting comparison of the typical techniques employed in rehearsals with those used in the English class:

> If the English literature class were taught by similar, quaint, old strategies, the student would read novels, short stories, essays, and plays and perhaps even perform some of the plays to get a real "feel" of the drama. But the pedagogical process would go no further than the reading or performing. No mention would be made of the nature of the experience unfolded; no discussion would follow regarding the use of metaphor or simile to yield vivid images of experience; no analysis of the function of rhetoric as a communicative technique would be broached, nor would comment arise about the author's skillful use of vocabulary for creating precise meanings for the experience. Discussion of syntax and semantics would be out of place for (this teaching rationale as-

sumes) these will be *felt* rather than *known* by the careful reader.[1]

To teach those things that will increase perception—not only of the music being performed but of other works as well—reduces the amount of time devoted to actual rehearsing. This cannot be avoided if greater music understanding is to be the goal, for perception will not simply develop as a concomitant of performance. It must be taught specifically, attentively, and methodically. Taking time for such a course of action may mean fewer public performances in those schools where a large number are scheduled each year. In schools where rehearsal time is already at a premium, it might also mean that the final performance may not be quite so perfect as it otherwise could be. Nevertheless, an increasing number of educators realize this is justifiable if a priority is to be placed on the total educative function of the rehearsal. The fact that process is sometimes more important than product may not be immediately recognizable to those administrators who judge the music program only by the standard of clever parade routines, A-1 ratings, and auditorium showmanship; but excellence is achieved by more than exploitative means and rests ultimately with the individual teacher's accomplishments toward music understanding. As Meyer Cahn has pointedly stated: "It takes boldness and courage to present a less-than-perfect performance. In fact, to pay attention to human process, even at the expense of perfect performance, takes a kind of wisdom that has not yet become the norm of music education."[2]

[1] William Thomson, "The Ensemble Director and Musical Concepts," *Music Educators Journal*, 54:9 (May 1968), p. 45.

[2] Meyer Cahn, "More than Performance: Toward Human Interaction," *Music Educators Journal*, 55:6 (February 1969), p. 37.

Does this mean that the pursuit of music understanding will lower the level of performance ability? Not necessarily. The teacher must approach the rehearsal in an efficient, organized, objective manner, making the best use of time in developing performance skills, and at the same time introducing nonperformance instruction at points where relationship is natural and easily understood. This requires that he give careful thought to planning and conducting rehearsals, using techniques such as those described in the following sections of this chapter. It is important, however, to understand first the particular relationship that exists between teaching perception and teaching performance.

Educators disagree about whether the teaching of perception will lower performance quality because of the time taken from practice, or whether it will raise the quality over a period of time because of the performer's higher level of insight. Much depends not only on the way time is used but also on the type and level of the group being rehearsed. A beginning instrumental group in the middle school or junior high school will suffer much more from a decreasing amount of practice time than will a senior-high group whose members have several years of instrumental experience behind them. Similarly, an instrumental group might be expected to advance more quickly than a vocal group with an equal cut in time, because of a higher level of reading proficiency. Advanced groups might also be expected to have the advantage in the long run from the effect of increased perception on performance ability, for these groups (because of their technical level) could apply understandings much more readily.

There is also some question as to whether the performance situation can really develop music perception efficiently. The skills involved are not in themselves aesthetic; yet, without developing these skills, performance in the rehearsal room will not reach a level where aesthetic experience can rseult. Thus, a large part of the effort that goes into performance is unproductive from the standpoint of aesthetic perception. One must also consider here what Bennett Reimer has called the "ability lag."[3] That is, a student's ability in the technical skills of performance is generally exceeded by his capacity for music perception. Unless he is an artist of the highest calibre, his sensitivity will be of a much greater degree than his performance alone indicates. There is no question, therefore, that the student can develop understandings in a rehearsal, beyond his power of execution, that can contribute to this over-all musical sensitivity —and hopefully to the development of his performance ability. But these understandings may result mainly from observation and from the comments and relationships drawn by the director. Direct influence by sound—the reverse process of performance increasing perception—is less substantial, although aesthetic experience through performance may still occur for the individual student at the higher level produced by the entire organization rather than at the level of his own contribution.

Both performance and nonperformance activities, then, *can* increase perception in the rehearsal situation. The fact that they may not do so equally and the fact that perception and performance may not contribute to *each other* to an equal degree are of little importance. This is true for two reasons. First, while we would hope that increased perception would raise the student's performance ability, time out from performance should not be judged only on this basis; we must not disregard the more far-reaching application of perception in listening—the need of developing the performer as a consumer, which is a recognition of the role of performance groups

as just one means of reaching the basic goal of music understanding. Second, examining the relationship from the opposite side, many educators believe that performance is a valuable activity regardless of the extent to which it promotes aesthetic sensitivity. This view is a valid one based on the fact that the mastery of skills and materials is in itself a source of tremendous satisfaction to an individual.

What, then, should be the teacher's perspective regarding how much time and effort he shall devote to perception on the one hand and performance skills on the other? Clearly, he should not change the rehearsal into a replica of the general music class, for this would sacrifice the exceptional values inherent in an intense involvement in music performance. But at the same time, he *should* introduce nonperformance instruction in small but frequent doses during breaks and at calculated points in rehearsal where such information will be most beneficial. The desirable balance toward which the teacher ought to strive has been well stated by Reimer:

> The role of school performance groups is to provide the greatest possible degree of aesthetic sensitivity and musical mastery in the available time. The crucial point in teaching for both musical perception and musical mastery is *the dependence of one on the other.* The unique value of performance is its potential for fostering musical perception *through musical mastery.* If one concentrates on perception to the extent that skilled performance is forgotten, he loses the peculiar benefit that performance offers. On the other hand, musical mastery *must serve the cause of musical perception.* Mastery alone can be a sterile, terminal thing.[4]

PLANNING THE REHEARSAL

The teacher who is assigned to both performance groups and more formal classroom subjects, such as general music or music the-

[3] Bennett Reimer, "Performance and Aesthetic Sensitivity," *Music Educators Journal,* 54:7 (March 1968), p. 109.

[4] *Ibid.,* p. 112.

ory, will very often approach each type of class with a different concept of preparation. For a general music class he will usually make detailed plans, with a step-by-step presentation worked out, a careful analysis of materials completed, and with possible problems, substitute techniques, and motivational ideas thought through. Yet, the same teacher may walk into a rehearsal with no more preparation than to collect a batch of music under his arm and pull out a baton that hasn't become too splintered from constant tapping on a music stand. This teacher's apparent reasoning is that he is a trained musician who will be working in rehearsal with nothing more than notes that he can easily read, fingering patterns that he has learned long ago, and sounds that for the next fifty minutes require no special stylistic or harmonic analysis. He is, of course, misleading himself and misjudging the needs of his students.

To conduct an effective rehearsal, the teacher must plan his work as carefully as if he were developing a lesson plan on the fugue. He must pull the music apart, work out a musically and psychologically satisfying progression of activities, and analyze his goals and the obstacles before them—all before he meets his students.

Preparing the Music

The director who is a successful planner knows his music intimately before the first rehearsal. In preparing the music, it is necessary to analyze everything that will contribute to the ultimate sound the teacher desires from his students. On a large scale this means he must develop his own feeling for the style of the work and its interpretation; if necessary, he may have to do some research to determine the exact pronunciation of that Latin text or to determine the proper handling of tempo in a certain contemporary

work. With an over-all concept, he can then concentrate on details. Here it is helpful to mark in the conductor's score important dynamic effects, tempo changes, phrasings, and cues. Some directors like to color-code these marks so that they can see at a glance what is coming up. That is, red may be used for dynamics, blue for important entrances, and so on. Others find this type of marking confusing. It is true that one can over-mark a score to the point where so many arrows, circles, and commas appear on a page that nothing stands out any longer. A little experimentation will lead the director to the type of marking that is most effective for him.

Instrumental directors will find it helpful to write in occasional bowings and alternate fingerings at potential trouble spots. Choral directors often mark breathing points and notes that are possible pitch problems. The latter are sometimes marked with arrows pointing upward (if the pitch is apt to be sung flat) or pointing downward (if it may be sharp). Cue marks and accents are particularly effective devices for inclusion. Even rests may be circled—particularly in polyphonic music where, with some voices continuing, they may go unnoticed. Whatever marks are used, the important thing is to know the score so well that it will be used mainly for reference in rehearsal; otherwise, *eye contact with the students, which is essential, cannot be maintained.* Frequently, it is the teacher who does not maintain eye contact who is constantly complaining that his students do not watch *him* in rehearsals.

In preparing a score, it is important to check through individual parts, not just general interpretive elements that may affect whole sections at a time. It is only by checking parts individually that the director will be able to uncover potential problems—awkward intervals, difficult rhythms, problem fingerings, and so on—and determine in advance techniques for avoiding or overcoming them. This practice is also important because wrong clefs, noncanceled accidentals, missing notes, discrepancies in rehearsal numbers, and other errors in the printed score are much more common than many teachers realize.

Finally, it is valuable to practice conducting each number before rehearsals begin. Practicing the conducting of necessary tempo and meter changes, cues, abrupt breaks, free rhythms, phrase styles, and awkward patterns is time well spent, for on-the-spot improvisation in conducting can easily become habit, and may remain unclear to students.

During the time the music is being prepared, the teacher should make notes on those factors in a given work that should be brought out to increase the students' general understanding. He might, for example, list such things as the melodic sequence that occurs in the clarinet part; the melodic pattern that is repeated successively in the upper woodwinds, then the saxophones, and finally the brass; the contrast produced by the sustained line sung by the tenors and basses while the soprano and alto parts move in a quickly-flowing phrase; the counterpoint in this section and the strong chordal texture in that; or the rhythmic motif that underlies the entire composition, appearing at various times in almost every voice. He should also note significant elements of structural development and the over-all form of the work. Stylistic characteristics pertaining to the period in which the work was written, the type of work as it fits into the composer's total contributions or into music history, and the illustration of *basic concepts* in music understanding can also be noted. All these items can then be worked into rehearsals *where they relate to work on specific sections or specific problems*, and over a period of time they will serve to increase the students' music perception.

Organizing the Rehearsal

A second aspect of effective planning is working out the sequence of materials to be used in each rehearsal. It is not good to simply begin one rehearsal at the point where the music was dropped the day before, nor to rehearse selections in a random order of presentation. The first essential is a variety of types of music—not only for curriculum balance, but also for psychological stability. Rehearsing several works of the same kind in a row reduces the students' attention span. In addition to types, there needs to be, within a single rehearsal, a variety of styles, tempos, and moods. With instrumental groups there often needs to be a change in the use of personnel, for nothing is so frustrating at times as waiting for measures on end just to play an insignificant sound. Every rehearsal must be challenging for every player.

With a good selection of material chosen, the next step is to arrange the rehearsal into a psychologically favorable sequence and an educationally balanced whole. This will consist basically of a warm-up session, the inclusion of both familiar music and music to be learned, and possibly some sight-reading material. Familiar music that is well in hand is important for the end of the rehearsal so that the students will leave with a feeling of success. If there is sufficient time, a short familiar work may also be included after warming up to open the rehearsal in a good climate. Some directors like to include a few minutes of technical studies directly after the warm-up and special sight-reading material before the familiar closing selection. In the middle, of course, will be either the introduction of a new work or detailed attention to a selection that was previously begun and is still being developed. Thus, an effective rehearsal plan might look like this:

1. Warm-up
2. Brief familiar work

3. Detailed work on music in progress
   (3a. New work)
4. Music for sight-reading
5. Familiar music

Each of these areas will be discussed more specifically in the following sections covering practical rehearsal techniques.

Other Factors in Rehearsal Organization

There are various mechanical and administrative factors that also contribute to organizing a smoothly run, functional rehearsal. For example, before students arrive the teacher should see that the room is properly prepared—that the chairs are in place in a neat arrangement, that risers are where they should be and not dangerously placed, and that the room is comfortably ventilated and well lighted. Music should be in order and distributed to the stands if possible. For this purpose, the director may be assisted by a student who has a free period or study period immediately before rehearsal. This student can see that the music is either on the stands or in marked pigeon holes or on racks near the entranceway. In the case of choral groups (and on occasion with instrumental groups), the teacher may allow the students to take their music with them each day in folders; new music, however, can still be distributed to the seats prior to rehearsal.

Before the rehearsal, the teacher should also check to see that he has the full needs of organization at his conductor's stand: scores, baton, tuning devices, pencil, grade book, attendance list, and any necessary school administrative materials. It is helpful to have a student manager to take attendance (the quick way, by checking empty seats) and to handle late slips, excuses, and passes. This may be the same person who is in charge of the library. If the director prefers to check

attendance himself, this is best left until a break in the middle of the rehearsal at which time any announcements can also be made. This allows the rehearsal to start promptly and makes use of valuable time for both work and rest simultaneously.

Another important factor in efficient operation is the establishment of a few rules at the beginning of the year. Three are basic: (1) that instrument cases, clothing, and books be kept out of the rehearsal area to allow free passage and to avoid student accidents; (2) that instruments and music be put in their proper places at the end of the rehearsal for safekeeping; and (3) that when the director steps on the podium he is to be given full attention. This last rule is the only one necessary for good discipline in rehearsals. Between selections, of course, the director should step down for a moment to allow students to relax while getting out the next piece. Naturally, occasional jokes and friendly banter would not require his constant popping up and down. If the director uses no podium, a tap of the baton or a clap of his hands may serve as a signal for attention.

Relative to student management, some directors maintain a points system for awards, with so many points being earned for regular and prompt attendance, special achievements, solo performances, and so on, and with points being lost for missed rehearsals, lateness, disruptive behavior, and other offenses. This may be an effective psychological gimmick that is needed in some situations; many teachers, however, have found that this grows more and more time consuming to keep the records straight. It is hardly the best way of motivating good discipline, and the maintenance of interest is best attained through the use of good music, good pacing, and good teaching objectives and techniques.

The final ingredient of efficient organization is sufficient time. In the early grades of a middle school, approximately thirty to forty-five minutes is appropriate for a rehearsal. In the upper grades of a middle school and at the junior-high level, forty-five to fifty minutes is a good rehearsal length, while in the senior high school, fifty to sixty minutes is effective. Double-block periods of ninety minutes to an hour and forty-five minutes, a couple of times a week, are also good if there is a break in the middle, a little after the halfway point. For a more extensive guide to matters of scheduling, refer to Chapter 16.

CONDUCTING THE REHEARSAL

In the actual conducting of a rehearsal, the teacher needs to know just how much time to spend on each section and exactly what he wishes to accomplish. He might, as a general guide—but not as a timetable to be adhered to strictly—have on a paper before him the amount of time he has planned for each part of the rehearsal. This should not read simply: "Familiar work, 7 minutes; new work, 20 minutes; sight-reading, 10 minutes." Rather, it should be specific, for easy checking by the clock: "Familiar work, 11:10-11:17; new work, 11:18-11:38," and so on.

Little time should be devoted to the *warm-up session*. It is necessary, of course, since the students will be arriving from a variety of relaxing or tensing places—including, perhaps, gym class or even lunch—and they need a few moments to acclimate themselves and warm up their instruments. Much time is often wasted, however, in the use of vocalises and instrumental scale and chord patterns. It is generally much better to warm up with some simple, known *music*, such as a chorale. Adjustments in tuning can be made during and after the music, and this will permit the students to get their instruments and voices in shape without dull, drill-like material. A student conductor may be used for the tuning and warm-up session, both for the experience and to allow the teacher to circulate among the group to check tuning. (A student conductor may also assist in other ways, of course, including the direction of certain sectional rehearsals.)

Some directors insert *technical studies* immediately after the warm-up to develop mechanical skills. To be sure, the group should try material that may be at first beyond their technical ability, but straight technical studies are often boring and ineffective. Simply because a student has learned to whip off a series of arpeggios rapidly in a study does not mean he will be able to transfer this feat when he encounters a similar spot in music. It is usually better to derive technique-building material from the music at hand. The teacher can excerpt tricky passages, and insert good, related drills within the rehearsal of a particular section. Without question, some drills are good, but these should be used as required by the demands of the music being studied—not as a separate item. It will also help student technique to vary the approach to a certain passage in the score. That is, perform it not only as written, but also with changes in tempo, in volume, in rhythmic duration, and in phrasing (by grouping different notes, or by moving from legato to staccato notes).

When *familiar music* is used to begin a rehearsal, and especially in its use at the end of a rehearsal, it is best to sing or play all the way through without stopping for corrections. There are times when details should be temporarily overlooked, and the experience of full, completely worked-out patterns of sound should be the paramount objective. When this comes early in the rehearsal, time can still be taken after the complete rendition to make adjustments in the performance.

The major portion of the rehearsal will be consumed by *music to be developed*. Here, the teacher should go directly to the spots that need work. Time is wasted by starting at the beginning each time and plodding through unmusically. If the work is new, there are two approaches to getting underway. Although some directors will first isolate what they believe to be problematic portions, the better procedure is to run through the entire selection come-what-may to get a general feeling, and then to single out and rehearse items that were most obviously wrong in the original run-through. Whether it is completely new or previously introduced music, the specific techniques presented on the following pages will be most useful in this section.

Another segment of the rehearsal may be for *sight-reading* material. Although this is valuable, if precious rehearsal time cannot be devoted to this activity, sight-reading can still be improved by other means. For example, the director can explain interpretive symbols as they appear in music currently being studied so that these symbols may be recognized and interpreted independently in other compositions. He can also run through works to be studied in the near future to provide his students with advance familiarity as well as reading experience. In addition, he can point out similar rhythmic and tonal patterns appearing in different places within a work, spot melodic sequences and repetitions, and call attention to common harmonic cadences that appear and reappear in many works. Items such as these, pulled from material other than that intended purely for sight-reading, will contribute to the development of reading skills.

Specific Techniques

1. All the problems and their solutions should not be introduced at once. Instead, rehearsals need to be paced—not only each one within itself, but the over-all plan for a series of rehearsals. The most obvious and most habit-forming errors should be concen-

trated on first. Then, other problems can be worked on over a planned period of time.

2. It is not always necessary for the director to make all rehearsal decisions. Student involvement can provide such information as where rhythmic and melodic problems are, what might be done to improve interpretation, and even which of the selections being studied might combine to make the most interesting concert. Confidence in the students' musical values is important. If they prove to be disappointing at first, this will provide another necessary dimension to be considered in teaching. What may be sacrificed in musical taste initially, because of this involvement, could eventually bring about a distinct sharpening of the students' musical discrimination and also create a rehearsal atmosphere of teacher-pupil cooperation and understanding.

3. In matters of tone quality, posture, breath support, and other production factors (as well as certain interpretive factors), it helps immensely if the students know the *why* behind an instruction. Too often the intellectual element is disregarded, and students are told to do something without an understanding of the reasoning behind the request. "Sit up straight," for example, is a more effective direction if the teacher answers their silent question, "Why? We're quite comfortable as we are."

4. Interpretation should not be left untouched until all the notes are in place, for there must be feeling to the music right from the start if the rehearsal is to be an exciting experience. There are times, however, when nothing seems to fit together in a certain spot. At these places it is usually best to concentrate on rhythm first, for rhythmic accuracy often helps other elements to take shape. Then, move on to getting the pitches right, and finally turn to phrasing and interpretation.

5. Never stop a group without giving them

a specific direction for improvement. Simply saying "let's try it again" is not enough if a change is expected. The students must know what to work on, where to concentrate their attention, what to change, and *how* to change it. Talk only when necessary, however, and avoid lengthy explanations. Return immediately to the music while the mistake is still fresh in their minds. The only way the students will learn to improve their performance is by actually playing or singing the music.

6. After stopping, if it is necessary to count measures between rehearsal letters to find the right place to start, count these measures aloud *with* the students. In this way, director and students arrive at the correct measure together. Time is saved and accuracy is more assured.

7. Repetitive problems can often be avoided by calling attention to parts that are the same and parts that differ slightly, and this will speed the learning of certain sections. Also, if one rhythmic or melodic pattern occurs in various voices throughout a work, it can be pulled out for everyone to sing or play together, at various pitches if necessary. Then, when the pattern is encountered in the respective parts, it will be familiar.

8. When material is in the early working-out stage, quick directions can often be called out to avoid unnecessary stops in performance. It also helps at this point to sing important entrances with each instrument or voice. Avoid the habit of singing along too often, however, since this restricts the amount of critical listening the director can do.

9. When the work at hand requires hearing one group of instruments or voices, do not neglect the other performers. Have them follow along by humming their own parts softly or, in early rehearsals, by having them finger the instruments silently. They may also be asked to listen critically to the performing section and make suggestions or, in a chorus, to sing the other part to help out. (For example, sopranos may assist tenors, or altos may support basses.) However, do not work with individual sections for more than a moment. Sectional rehearsals in meetings for the full ensemble waste time and often create discipline problems among the waiting students. Instead, let the members of the group know the places they should work on individually, and then schedule sectional rehearsals if possible.

10. It can be useful to plan units of concentration on individual performance elements. While not neglecting any factors, devote special attention to tone for a few weeks, then to intonation for a few weeks; follow this with special attention to articulation, or rhythmic precision, or any given item. Such concentration tends to make students more aware of how they are performing, and they will gradually build up a quantity of proper techniques that will be retained rather than learned new with each composition.

11. Many problems—not only in interpretation, but in basic mechanics of performance—arise from conducting motions that are not clear. It is not necessary to be a virtuoso conductor; it is necessary to use a clear, simple, precise style. Even when this is achieved, it may be necessary at times to count and give oral directions along with the conducting patterns. Speech should be eliminated as soon as possible, though, so that the students learn to watch the director and be guided only by his conducting. It is helpful on occasion to vary the interpretation unexpectedly so that the students get used to relying on and responding to hand motions. Such experience will prove valuable later if, during the excitement of public performance, the conductor makes an unrehearsed interpretive change.

12. Records and prerecorded tapes are useful devices to give the students an impression

of how a new work to be studied sounds. Then, while rehearsing the work, playing a tape of their own performance will provide an opportunity for immediate aural perception of what the director has been demanding of them—whether or not they have yet achieved it. On other occasions, the director may wish to record his group primarily for his own personal analysis, since (as is often the case) this allows him to listen more critically than in the actual rehearsal situation.

13. With choral groups, the pianist can offer considerable assistance to the conductor by playing voice parts rather than the regular accompaniment for support while the group is learning a piece; by playing individual parts to assist sections; or by illustrating difficult intervals and tonal patterns as the singers listen. Some accompanists are able to recognize trouble spots and jump in with the appropriate aid without being directed to do so. This is the type of accompanying the teacher should work for.

14. It is extremely important to be encouraging in comments about the students' performance. When there is improvement, it is to be praised. Faults can still be worked on constructively without discouraging remarks. However, all comments should be coupled with honesty, for such statements as "Great rehearsal today," when students and director both know otherwise, make words of encouragement on other occasions meaningless.

15. After working on small details for a large portion of the rehearsal, it is important to avoid leaving the selection up in the air. These details need to be related to each other and to the whole by having the students perform the entire section or complete work. If the details have not been worked out sufficiently to be pulled together as yet, then the conductor should perform some other section of the composition that has previously been perfected. The objective should be to leave each selection with a feeling of musical accomplishment.

16. Confusion in the performance class is often created by ambiguous verbal directions. The choral director needs to be prepared to explain such statements as "Open your mouths wider," "Take a deep breath," and "Pronounce those words more distinctly." The instrumental director is cautioned to avoid using such vague instructions as "Play with a better attack," "Let's blend that tone," or "Trumpets, play in tune." While each of these directions tells the students *what* must be done to improve performance, none informs them *how* they are to accomplish what has been asked.

Seating Plans

Each director will have his own preference for the way he seats the members of his organization. This should not, of course, be a predetermined, unalterable decision, for there is no one best plan for seating any particular type of group. It depends on the singular nature of the individual organization and the peculiar acoustical properties of the rehearsal hall and auditorium being used.

The basic principle is to devise a plan that will provide balance, blend, and ensemble sense, and one that will support weaker sections and subdue overbalanced sections by the placement of each in relation to other parts. The intonation of the entire group must also be aided by the relationship of both individual and sectional positioning. The seating plans given here should serve as practical guides in experimenting to seek the best solution; but in each case the director's ear must be the final determiner of proper arrangement.

Choruses

In choral groups it is desirable to arrange students within each section so that weaker

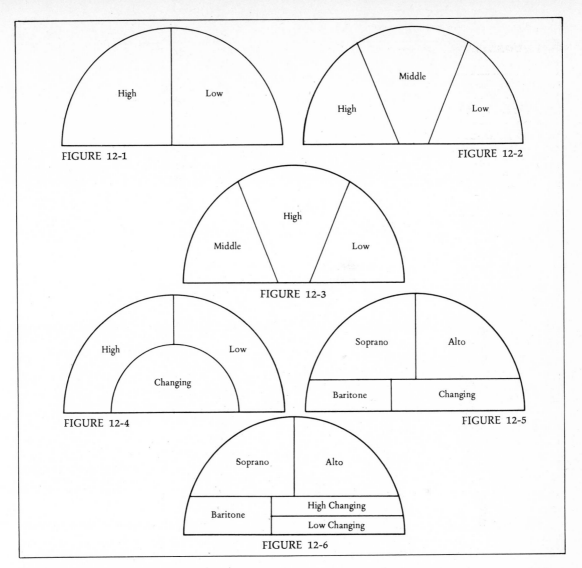

FIGURE 12-1

FIGURE 12-2

FIGURE 12-3

FIGURE 12-4

FIGURE 12-5

FIGURE 12-6

members are strategically placed next to or between those who are able to carry their parts well. Weaker sections as a whole should be brought toward the front of the group. To counter intonation problems, it may help to place the least pitch-conscious section near to the piano. More important, however, is working out a plan so that the individual sections can hear each other. Facing groups in toward the conductor at the center will help, as will the placing of outside harmonic voices next to each other (such as sopranos and basses in a mixed chorus, or first sopranos and altos in a three-part girls' chorus).

In the middle school, groups of unchanged voices are normally seated as shown in Figures 12-1, 12-2, and 12-3. In both the middle school and junior high school, groups that include a mixture of unchanged and changing voices might use the plans in Figures 12-4, 12-5, and 12-6. In each instance, the changing voices are kept toward the front of the group. Both 12-5 and 12-6 also indicate a practical placement for changed voices.

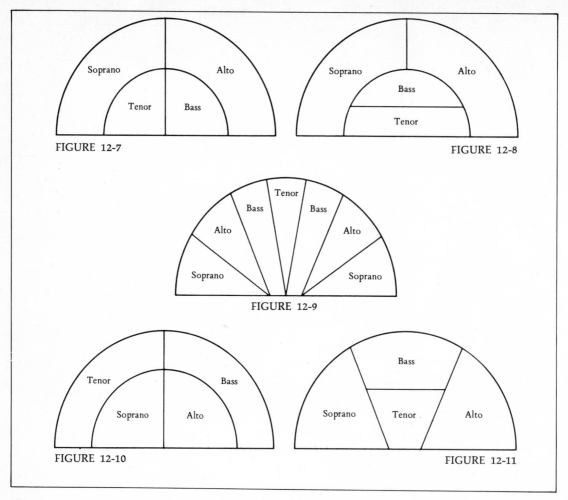

FIGURE 12-7

FIGURE 12-8

FIGURE 12-9

FIGURE 12-10

FIGURE 12-11

Mixed choruses of older students with largely changed voices can be grouped in a variety of ways, depending on individual strengths. Figures 12-7 and 12-8 show plans that aid weaker tenors and basses, and also serve to unify the soprano and alto sections. In both plans the placement of basses next to sopranos helps intonation.

The plan in Figure 12-9 can be used to strengthen the boys' sections when a divided chorus is needed.

If the bass and tenor sections are strong and the entire group is secure, Figures 12-10 and 12-11 may be used to good effect.

It is interesting to vary the seating occasionally within a given group in order to work on certain qualities. With exceptionally secure groups, for example, the members may be broken up into individual quartets, as in Figure 12-12, to work on familiar material in developing blend.

FIGURE 12-12

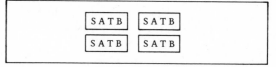

Small ensembles of mixed voices will often benefit in the same way by grouping the students in a circle around the conductor:

FIGURE 12-13

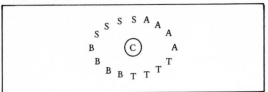

FIGURE 12-14

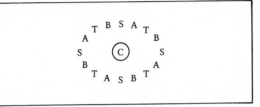

The same basic principles are applied in working out plans for all-male choruses. A boys' chorus in a middle school or in a junior high school would include a combination of unchanged and changing voices. In the junior high and in some middle schools (depending on the structure), there will also be already changed, but still-unsettled, voices. Figures 12-15 and 12-16 could then be used.

FIGURE 12-15

FIGURE 12-16

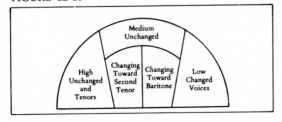

FIGURE 12-17

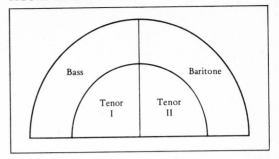

Figure 12-17 offers a good plan for the average senior high school group of largely changed voices. It strengthens the major divisions and provides harmonic support between the extreme voice parts. Still-changing voices may be seated toward the front of the second-tenor and baritone sections.

Another standardized plan at this level is given in Figure 12-18, while Figure 12-19 is an alternate that strengthens harmonic support.

FIGURE 12-18

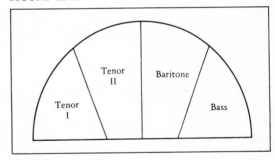

FIGURE 12-19

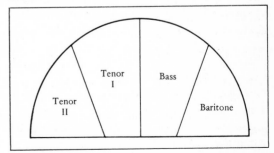

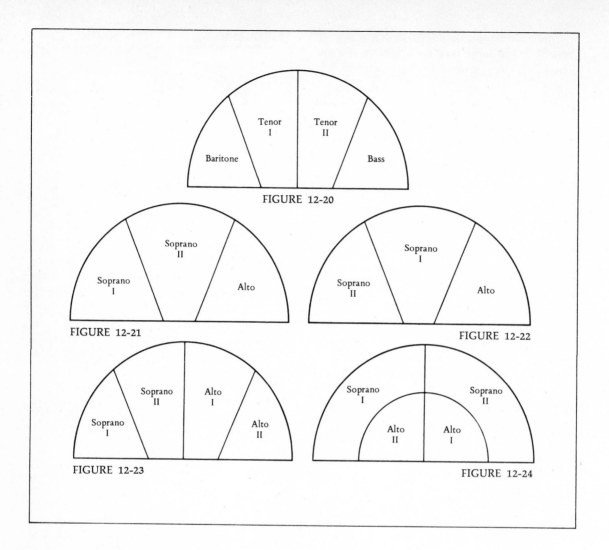

FIGURE 12-20

FIGURE 12-21

FIGURE 12-22

FIGURE 12-23

FIGURE 12-24

Smaller male ensembles consisting of secure voices might try the plan in Figure 12-20.

A standard plan for an all-female chorus is given in Figure 12-21. This plan may be used even with younger groups in which the voices have not matured into real first sopranos or altos. Less stable groups can be seated as shown in Figure 12-22.

When girls' choruses are divided into four parts, Figures 12-23 and 12-24 can be used. Figure 12-23 is standard. Figure 12-24 is good when the sopranos are especially strong.

Orchestras

With instrumental groups, seating is determined by the fundamental principles discussed generally for choruses, as well as by the size of the ensemble and the instrumentation available. A director who has no oboe or bassoon, for example, will have to make slight adjustments in some of the following plans.

Normally, violins are all placed to the conductor's left so that the f-holes of the instruments face the audience. Sometimes these are divided, with the second violins at the conductor's right; however, this requires a stronger-than-average second-violin section. Cellos are most often on the right in front; but if second violins are placed there, then cellos are moved either in back of the seconds or to the left behind the first violins, with violas filling the alternate position. In this situation, keeping the cellos on the right is preferable so that violas may have the advantage of turning toward the audience from their left-hand seats. The contrabasses should be close behind the cellos because of the frequent occurrence of octave passages.

Brass and percussion are placed at the back of the orchestra, with woodwinds forward in the center for carrying power. The horns are placed adjacent to the woodwinds for blend. Within the woodwinds, it is common to seat first-chair members of each group next to each other in a square, as shown in Figure 12-25. This plan promotes a better balance and also is practical in solo passages.

FIGURE 12-25

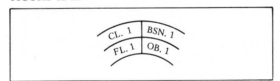

Beginning orchestras in middle and junior high schools are usually incomplete in instrumentation. There also tends to be a large number of students playing the "basic" instruments of each section, which means that the group is not proportioned in the sense of a real orchestra. Because of this, the plan in Figure 12-26 is useful. It keeps violas and cellos close to the violins for unity, and allows for the typically large number of clarinets and trumpets. Stronger beginning groups might be seated as shown in Figure 12-27.

Orchestras that approach standard instrumentation in the upper grades may be seated

FIGURE 12-26

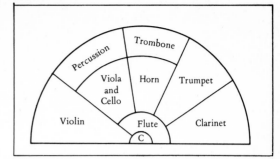

FIGURE 12-27

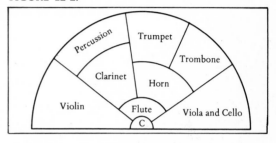

according to several other plans. Figures 12-28 and 12-29 keep all the violins on the left, the lower strings on the right. Figures

FIGURE 12-28

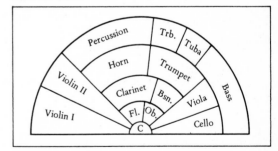

FIGURE 12-29

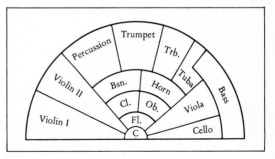

279
The Effective Rehearsal

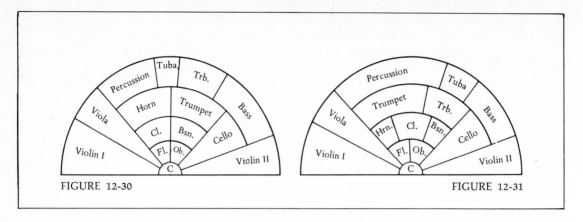

FIGURE 12-30   FIGURE 12-31

12-30 and 12-31 place the second violins on the right with the violas on the left, and show different possibilities for seating the wind sections.

Concert Bands

In the band, clarinets are seated at the conductor's left, assuming the position of the violins in the orchestra. Occasionally, when the clarinets are particularly strong and secure, they are divided left and right. Beyond the placement of this section, there is no really standardized seating plan for the concert band.

The general principle is to bring the softer instruments to the front and put the louder ones in back, arranging the inner voices to effect the best possible blend of ensemble. This depends, of course, on the number of students in each section, the completeness of instrumentation, and the strengths of students in key positions. Baritones, for example, are frequently at the back near the trombones if they are strong, but they are often brought forward as well because of solo parts. A large trumpet section may be placed not only in the back but also to the side, so that bells do not face the audience. Whatever formation is decided upon, it is a good idea not to put all the best players on the first part, but to divide them among the first chairs or stands on all

parts. This helps the weaker players and also helps the ensemble sound, since the second and third parts will have proper strength.

Ensemble sound may also be affected by the use of risers. Often, risers are used on stage for concert performance even though they may not be used in rehearsals. When this is done, the director and students will discover a distinct difference in balance, created by bringing certain instruments into prominence through their elevation. The trumpets, for example, who have played through the rest of the band from the back row, will certainly produce a more dominant sound once their position has been raised. Some band directors, however, feel that ensemble blend is better controlled by seating *all* the students on the flat stage, with balance being maintained by the shifting of sections.

A practical plan for a beginning band in a lower school is shown in Figure 12-32. This plan cuts down the volume of the cornets by having them play across the band rather than directly out toward the audience.

The cornets have a similar position in Figures 12-33 and 12-34, which also offer two possibilities for seating the inner voices. Figure 12-34, with a more complete instrumentation, is more applicable for the more experienced band.

In both Figures 12-35 and 12-36, the saxophones are brought down on the right and the cornets are moved inward toward or into the center. These plans are suitable if the saxes are relatively strong and if the ensemble of inner voices is relatively secure. The bari-

tones must also be strong since they are moved back to the outer rim of the band.

Although clarinets are not usually divided, Figure 12-37 shows how other sections may be arranged if a divided plan is desired.

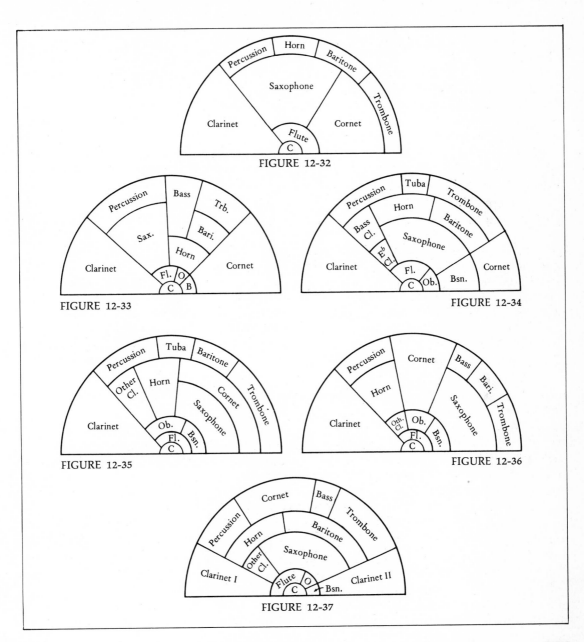

FIGURE 12-32

FIGURE 12-33

FIGURE 12-34

FIGURE 12-35

FIGURE 12-36

FIGURE 12-37

FIGURE 12-38   FIGURE 12-39

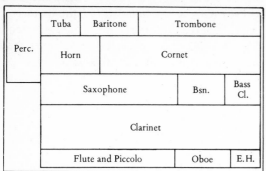

The more recent development of concert bands—known as symphonic wind ensembles—sometimes employs a straight, horizontal plan, shown in Figures 12-38 and 12-39. These groups, with smaller membership, generally spread the clarinets across the full width of the band, usually with other woodwinds in front, although the lower ones may be seated behind the clarinets near the brass section.

Discussion Questions and Projects

1. Select a composition for mixed chorus and another for concert band; compile a list of elements, techniques, and style factors in each that might be used in teaching music understanding during rehearsal.

2. Select three compositions—one each for band, orchestra, and chorus—and determine how you would mark them for effective use as conductor's scores.

3. Work out a seating plan for a senior high school chorus consisting of 35 strong sopranos, 25 altos (several of whom have consistent intonation problems), 20 basses (15 of whom are baritones, including several still-changing voices), and 12 tenors (including 2 first tenors, 5 second tenors, and 5 whose voices are still unsettled but lean toward second tenor).

4. As a first-year teacher, how would you prepare for and organize the first rehearsal with your junior high school band, high school orchestra, or high school chorus?

5. In rehearsals planned to develop music understanding, what use could you make of recordings, tapes, transparencies, and other audiovisual materials, without consuming an excessive amount of rehearsal time?

6. What arrangements could you make for involving students in the role of conductor? What might be the benefits?

7. Examine one composition for orchestra and one for chorus. Determine potential trouble spots and decide what techniques might be employed for avoiding or overcoming them. Also examine the structure of each work and the individual parts to see if there are repeated tonal and rhythmic patterns, sequences, wholly repeated sections, or somewhat similar sections; decide how these observations could be used in rehearsal to simplify the learning of the work.

Selected References

BOYD, JACK. *Rehearsal Guide for the Choral Director.* West Nyack, New York: Parker Publishing Company, Inc., 1970.

CAHN, MEYER. "More than Performance: Toward Human Interaction," *Music Educators Journal,* 55:6 (February 1969), pp. 36–39.

ERBES, ROBERT. "I Used to Direct My Rehearsals Like a Drill Sergeant: Until I Learned About Interaction Analysis," *Music Educators Journal,* 65:2 (October 1978), pp. 50–53.

GARRETSON, ROBERT L. *Conducting Choral Music.* 3d ed. Boston: Allyn & Bacon, Inc., 1970. Chapters 3 and 4.

GOTTIKER, IRVIN. *Complete Book of Rehearsal Techniques for the High School Orchestra.* West Nyack, New York: Parker Publishing Company, Inc., 1977.

GREEN, ELIZABETH A. H. *The Modern Conductor.* Englewood Cliffs, New Jersey: Prentice-Hall, Inc., 1961.

HARVEY, ARTHUR W. "A Conductor in Every Chair," *Music Educators Journal,* 58:6 (February 1972), pp. 46–47.

HOFFER, CHARLES R. *Teaching Music in the Secondary Schools.* Belmont, California: Wadsworth Publishing Company, Inc., 1964. Chapters 8 to 10.

KUHN, WOLFGANG E. *Instrumental Music: Principles and Methods of Instruction.* Boston: Allyn & Bacon, Inc., 1962. Chapter 3.

LAWSON, WARNER. "Practical Rehearsal Techniques," in *Choral Director's Guide,* Kenneth L. Neidig and John W. Jennings, eds. West Nyack, New York: Parker Publishing Company, Inc., 1967. Pp. 243–267.

MERCER, R. JACK. "Is the Curriculum the Score—or More?" *Music Educators Journal,* 58:6 (February 1972), pp. 51–53.

MOORE, RAY. "If Your Rehearsals Are Unfulfilling Experiences, Try a Choral Laboratory," *Music Educators Journal,* 59:6 (February 1973), pp. 51–52, 81–83.

REIMER, BENNETT. "Performance and Aesthetic Sensitivity," *Music Educators Journal,* 54:7 (March 1968), pp. 27–29, 107–114.

RUDOLF, MAX. *The Grammar of Conducting.* New York: G. Schirmer, Inc., 1950.

Performances

13

The value of a musical skill is most fully realized when one gives the benefit of that skill, in performance, to others.

JOSEPH A. LEEDER and WILLIAM S. HAYNIE[1]

FINDING A MEMBER of a music ensemble who does not want to share the fruits of his labors with the public is rather rare. In fact, school musicians are usually disappointed if at least a few public performances have not been scheduled on the school calendar.

Admittedly, there are times when the music teacher feels differently than his students and is envious of teachers of other subjects who do not have to cope with extra-time activities such as rehearsals, football games, concerts, festivals, and trips. But music performances are an important part of the teacher's responsibilities—a necessary adjunct of the music program that provides for educational, musical, and personal satisfaction on the part of both students and teacher. Chapter 12 explained that performances are not the goal of rehearsals, but rather a natural outgrowth and culmination of the work that goes on in performance classes. As such, they constitute a vital part of the continuum of musical growth and demand careful attention to their scheduling, programming, and realization.

[1] Joseph A. Leeder and William S. Haynie, *Music Education in the High School* (Englewood Cliffs, New Jersey: Prentice-Hall, Inc., 1958), p. 183.

Whereas professional concerts are ordinarily presented by single organizations or individuals, school music concerts generally display the achievements of several groups as they perform separately in a single program or in combined ensembles. Bringing together several groups on a program not only presents a better image of the music department to the public, but also provides for a more varied and interesting program and sometimes permits the participating students their only opportunity to enjoy the efforts of other groups in the school. It also provides the opportunity for several groups to combine forces in performing collectively. There are a number of worthwhile compositions that are suitable for a combined group effort—some that are major undertakings and would comprise the entire concert program, others that are shorter works of ten to fifteen minutes length, suitable for impressive finales.

Performances also offer opportunities for the music department to work cooperatively with other departments in the school or even with community organizations in planning programs. Although such "cooperation" is often reduced to relatively insignificant associations, with careful planning and real involvement it can add a meaningful dimension to the music department's program and strengthen the department's position in the school and the community.

As long as the public performance is recognized as an outgrowth rather than a goal of rehearsals, as long as the cost of performances is kept within reason and does not absorb a large portion of the music budget, as long as concert programs do not make excessive demands on students, and as long as they are not restricted to the "elite" among school music groups, then performances are fulfilling an appropriate and necessary function within the over-all scope of a school's music-education curriculum.

OPPORTUNITIES FOR PERFORMANCE

The opportunities for school groups to perform are bountiful—possibly too bountiful for their own good. In interviews with 222 high school band directors throughout the country, R. Jack Mercer learned that the average high school band gives performances on an average of one every two-and-a-half weeks. In high schools of over 1000 students, the average performance schedule includes 5.5 concerts, 6.6 half-time shows, and 3.3 parade appearances per year. Bands in smaller high schools of from 400 to 1000 students average 4.7 concerts, 6 half-time shows, and 3.8 parade appearances. That's 15.4 and 14.5 yearly performances, respectively, or approximately one-and-a-half performances per month during the school term.[2] Although choruses and orchestras do not have to contend with football games and parades, other demands are often made on them. These figures indicate that music teachers must weigh all the possibilities carefully, selecting only those appearances that will contribute to the educative process and perhaps those few that seem to be necessary obligations.

The evening concert is the major type of school performance, and is generally presented during the Christmas season, in late winter (the end of Feburary or early March), and in the late spring. When such concerts are scheduled, it is important that several groups participate in each in order to keep the demands on each group within reason and to spread those demands thoughout the year. If one group is required to carry the burden of a concert by itself, it may become necessary to program most, if not all, of that

[2] See R. Jack Mercer, "Is the Curriculum the Score —or More?" *Music Educators Journal*, 58:6 (February 1972), pp. 51–53.

group's repertoire to develop a presentation of adequate length. This sometimes results in an organization spending the entire fall term on seasonal music to present at the Christmas concert—a practice that is unbalanced in terms of the year's work, and one that also leaves the ensemble without any repertoire following the program. By including several groups in each program, any one group will need to prepare only a couple of selections appropriate to the seasonal event and at other times will not need to program anything but its best endeavors.

In addition to the evening concert, there are a number of other possibilities for in-school performances. These include all-music assemblies, assemblies devoted to other subjects at which an ensemble may perform one or two numbers, an annual concert of student compositions, participation in a school-sponsored music and arts festival, football games, PTA presentations, school dances (for rock and stage bands), graduation exercises, and even a series of monthly after-school recitals that may feature soloists and small groups.

Legitimate opportunities outside the school are few, but invitations are often received for parades (Thanksgiving, Christmas, New Year's Day, Easter, Memorial Day), appearances before community civic and social organizations, exchange concerts with neighboring towns, long-distance exchange concerts, educational programs for local radio and television stations, regional and state festivals and competitions, and performances at state, divisional, and national conferences.

If the music teacher were to accept all the invitations extended to his group during the course of a year, he would find that he is directing a professional performing group rather than a class for music education. In order that students not be exploited, most community invitations must be turned down. If a school policy has not already been estab-

lished, the teacher should take steps to see that one is developed. The basic principle is simply to select those opportunities that will benefit the *students* (not the inviting organization), that will not be too demanding in terms of preparation, travel, and finances, and that will not infringe on the rights of professional musicians.

A great many problems can be avoided if the music teacher and the school adhere to the Code of Ethics that has been formulated jointly by the Music Educators National Conference, the American Association of School Administrators, and the American Federation of Musicians. The Code has been in existence for many years and was revised in 1977. It recognizes and places limitations on those activities that are related to music education and those related to the field of professional music performance. The field of entertainment is the domain of the professional performer and should not be infringed upon by educational groups. Entertainment encompasses activities not organized for educational purposes (festivals, games, parades, ceremonies, and so on); functions related to private and public enterprises, chambers of commerce, and commercial groups; any occasions that are partisan or sectarian; and functions of clubs, societies, and civic and fraternal organizations. Performances that are a legitimate part of music education, on the other hand, include those for school functions; community functions organized for educational purposes; educational broadcasts for the purpose of demonstrating students' achievements or to inform the public of music education practices and events; civic occasions of such breadth that participation by school groups would not infringe upon the rights of professional musicians because the cooperation of all persons is enlisted; benefit performances in which professional musicians would also donate their services; recordings for educational purposes

Table 13-1. THE MUSIC CODE OF ETHICS: AN AGREEMENT DEFINING THE
JURISDICTIONS OF PROFESSIONAL MUSICIANS AND
STUDENT MUSICIANS[3]

Music educators and professional musicians alike are committed to the general acceptance of music as an essential factor in the social and cultural growth of our country. The music educators contribute to this end by fostering the study of music among the children, and by developing a greater interest in music.

This unanimity of purpose is further exemplified by the fact that a great many professional musicians are music educators, and a great many music educators are, or have been, actively engaged in the field of professional performance.

The members of high school instrumental groups—orchestras and bands of all types, including stage bands—look to the professional organization for example and inspiration. The standards of quality acquired during the education of these students is of great importance when they become active patrons of music in later life. Through their influence on sponsors, employers and program makers in demanding adequate musical performances, they have a beneficial effect upon the prestige and economic status of the professional musicians.

Since it is in the interest of the music educator to attract public attention to his attainments, not only for the main purpose of promoting the values of music education but also to enhance his position and subsequently his income, and since it is in the interest of the professional musician to create more opportunities for employment at increased remuneration, it is only natural that upon certain occasions some incidents might occur in which the interests of the members of one or the other group might be infringed upon, either from lack of forethought or lack of ethical standards among individuals.

In order to establish a clear understanding as to the limitations of the fields of professional music and music education in the United States, the following statement of policy, adopted by the Music Educators National Conference and the American Federation of Musicians, and approved by the American Association of School Administrators, is recommended to those serving in their respective fields:

I. MUSIC EDUCATION

The field of music education, including the teaching of music and such demonstrations of music education as do not directly conflict with the interests of the professional musician, is the province of the music educator. It is the primary purpose of all the parties signatory hereto that the professional musician shall have the fullest protection in his efforts to earn his living from the playing and rendition of music; to that end it is recognized and accepted that all music to be performed under the "Code of Ethics" herein set forth is and shall be performed in connection with non-profit, non-commercial and non-competitive enterprises. Under the heading of "Music Education" should be included the following:

1. **School Functions** initiated by the schools as a part of a school program, whether in a school building or other building.

2. **Community Functions** organized in the interest of the schools strictly for educational purposes, such as those that might be originated by the Parent-Teacher Association.

3. **School Exhibits** prepared as a part of the school district's courtesies for educational organizations or educational conventions being entertained in the district.

4. **Educational Broadcasts** which have the purpose of demonstrating or illustrating pupils' achievements in music study, or which represent the culmination of a period of study and rehearsal.

[3] Reprinted by permission of the American Federation of Musicians of the United States and Canada, AFL-CIO; the Music Educators National Conference; and the American Association of School Administrators.

Table 13-1. THE MUSIC CODE OF ETHICS (continued)

Included in this category are local, state, regional and national school music festivals and competitions held under the auspices of schools, colleges and/or educational organizations on a non-profit basis and broadcast to acquaint the public with the results of music instruction in the schools.

5. Civic Occasions of local, state or national patriotic interest, of sufficient breadth to enlist the sympathies and cooperation of all persons, such as those held by the American Legion and Veterans of Foreign Wars in connection with their Memorial Day services in the cemeteries. It is understood that affairs of this kind may be participated in only when such participation does not in the least usurp the right and privileges of local professional musicians.

6. Benefit Performances for local charities, such as the Welfare Federations, Red Cross, hospitals, etc., when and where local professional musicians would likewise donate their services.

7. Educational or Civic Services that might beforehand be mutually agreed upon by the school authorities and official representatives of the local professional musicians.

8. Student or Amateur Recordings for study purposes made in the classroom or in connection with contest, festival or conference performances by students shall be limited to exclusive use by the students and their teachers, and not offered for general sale to the public through commercial outlets. This definition pertains only to the purpose and utilization of student or amateur recordings and not to matters concerned with copyright regulations. Compliance with copyright requirements applying to recordings of compositions not in the public domain is the responsibility of the school, college or educational organization under whose auspices the recording is made.

II. ENTERTAINMENT

The field of entertainment is the province of the professional musician. Under this heading are the following:

1. Civic parades *(where professional marching bands exist), ceremonies, expositions, community concerts and community-center activities; regattas, non-scholastic contests, festivals, athletic games, activities or celebrations and the like; national, state and county fairs* (See I, Paragraphs 2 and 5 for further definition).

2. Functions for the furtherance, *directly or indirectly, of any public or private enterprise; functions by chambers of commerce, boards of trade, and commercial clubs or associations.*

3. Any occasion that is partisan *or sectarian in character or purpose.*

4. Functions of clubs, *societies, and civic or fraternal organizations.*

Statements that funds are not available for the employment of professional musicians, or that if the talents of amateur musical organizations cannot be had, other musicians cannot or will not be employed, or that the amateur musicians are to play without remuneration of any kind, are all immaterial.

This code, first entered into on September 22, 1947, is a continuing agreement which shall be reviewed regularly to make it responsive to changing conditions.

Revised, March 1977. Victor W. Fuentealba, President, American Federation of Musicians; Robert H. Klotman, President, Music Educators National Conference; Dana Whitmer, President, American Association of School Administrators.

that are limited to use by students and teachers; and any occasion upon which agreement is reached cooperatively by school authorities and representatives of the musicians' union. See Table 13-1 for the full contents of the Code of Ethics.

SCHEDULING PERFORMANCES

At the close of each school year, the teacher should plan a performance schedule for the entire year to follow. A meeting of all the secondary music teachers in the school district would be most desirable so that the timing of activities can be coordinated and any joint ventures can be considered far enough in advance. Necessary and unchangeable-time events, such as half-time shows, should be listed first. If the school is traditionally involved in any specific performances or productions, such as a spring musical show or participation in a Memorial Day ceremony, these should also be entered on the calendar immediately. When the basics have been listed, then the additional desirable performances can be sketched out in an appropriately paced sequence. The number of concerts by each ensemble will need to be considered along with the extent of involvement by each group in any one concert and the preparation time required. Time between performances should be allotted in terms of not only the preparation of program selections but also the study of music that may not be intended for public performance.

A factor that is sometimes overlooked in planning sessions is the availability of audiences. Parents, teachers, students, and the local citizenry cannot be expected to come to every concert. There are too many other activities today to attract their attention. The teacher can hardly avoid the competition of many forms of leisure-time activity, such as television, motion pictures, and professional sports events. He can, however, check the tentative schedules of known community activities, local theatre groups, and the school sports and drama departments to avoid unnecessary conflicts or the scheduling of music performances in proximity to other major activities. It pays to get the pulse of the local concert-going audience and to schedule concerts at potential peaks of school and community interest. Few things will hurt the morale of a music group more than a "poor showing" at a major performance.

When a proposed schedule has been drawn up, it must then be presented to the director of music and school principal for approval and for coordination with the activity schedules of other departments. As soon as the schedule has been accepted, arrangements should be made immediately for clearing physical facilities—scheduling rehearsal space and booking the auditorium for both the performances and one or two stage rehearsals. After the new school year has begun, the teacher should continue to keep account of newly announced community events so that conflicts can be worked out as soon as they become apparent. If changes need to be made in the schedule, they should be given prominent publicity.

PROGRAMMING

An effective concert is brought about by a good selection of literature, a good progression of elements, and a good sense of production. No organization should have to program everything that it has been studying in rehearsals, and as long as several ensembles participate this is unnecessary. The selection should be based on which compositions the group is best able to perform, tempered by which are the most artistic, which are most representative of the type of music usually studied by the group, and which make the most interesting combination.

The teachers of all the groups to appear in the program should plan the concert together so that a balance is achieved in the repertoire of not only each group by itself but all the organizations. Every program needs to have a focus, but this does not necessarily require an elaborate scheme. The focal point may be simply the variety of tonal colors produced by different vocal and instrumental ensembles, in which case this variety should be emphasized by careful attention to the sequencing of groups for distinct (and favorable) contrast. On the other hand, the focus may have to do with the literature: The music for all the groups may be selected to present a chronological sequence of music styles, or it may be all contemporary music or all American music. Another focus might be on a single major work, presented by one group or by all the ensembles as a combined unit for the finale. The major work might even be a new composition commissioned by the school from a composer in the area.

In choosing the music, thought must also be given to its progression. Even though students warm up their voices and instruments in the music room or some other area before going on stage, it must be realized that another "warming up" must usually take place in front of the audience in the sense of overcoming tension and becoming relaxed and comfortable with the audience. This is usually done through an opening number that is relatively easy for the group to execute—one that will reveal them to good advantage without excessive effort. From that point on, the sequence for each group should be arranged to contrast moods, styles, tempos, and keys, as well as to pace the group through demanding and less demanding works. A proper progression is one that benefits the students performing, interests the audience, avoids unfavorable comparisons between selections, and provides an appropriate "frame" for any soloists.

The term "showmanship" tends to have a poor connotation among some music educators, for it suggests to them a flamboyant exhibition of conducting technique by a teacher on an ego trip (sometimes accompanied by the programming of a work that is beyond the capabilities of the ensemble but looks impressive on the printed program). To be sure, the teacher should not conduct a "show" of his own, but showmanship is important in programming in the sense of having a good feel for a smoothly run, attractive, enjoyable production.

The first principle of organizing a good program from the production standpoint is to avoid an overly long concert. A concert should not run longer than one-and-one-half to one-and-three-quarters hours when several groups are involved, and considerably less when only one ensemble is being presented. Unfortunately, many teachers want to put too much on the program, feeling that the students should sing or play as many of the numbers they have rehearsed as possible; the result is a program that leaves the audience squirming for the last forty-five minutes or more. Instead, an audience should always leave wishing it could hear more, not feeling that it was subjected to an ordeal. If the concert is to run longer than an hour, it is also advisable to schedule an intermission slightly after the halfway mark. The intermission is generally five to twelve minutes long, depending on the over-all length of the program.

Second, the concert should always begin precisely at the time stated. Keeping an audience waiting is annoying, whereas beginning promptly contributes to a proper psychological set among both performers and listeners. Timing, in fact, should be worked out carefully throughout the program. With several groups performing, there generally has to be movement of risers, chairs, and music stands at some time during the evening. The logistics of moving students on and off stage and of moving equipment must be planned so that the pace of the presentation is not upset. Requiring the audience to sit for long stretches of time through such operations can ruin the effect of a production. Usually, by alternating small ensembles in front of a curtain while equipment is moved quietly behind the curtain in preparation for the next group, by making use of the orchestra pit or the steps leading to the stage, or even by using the auditorium floor for small groups, a fast-moving program can be realized.

Another aspect of good production work is briefing the performers on proper stage deportment and etiquette. Students should move onto the stage and into position with an obvious amount of organization. This might range from a precisionlike maneuver to a casual but deliberate movement toward the area of performance. Once on stage, instrumental groups ordinarily warm up briefly with sensible individual exercises, and without excessive noise; choral ensembles do not warm up on stage and should stand *comfortably* erect, ready to receive their conductor. When the group has been made ready, there should be no lull prior to the conductor's appearance. Any applause at the beginning should be acknowledged warmly, but with no more than a brief bow. If preparations have been adequately carried out, the conductor's scores will be on the stand, already opened to the first selection. After reaching the podium, the teacher immediately faces his students (and it usually helps to relax them if he also immediately smiles at them in a natural, unforced manner), and waits until the audience is quiet. Then, without looking at his score, he should begin the music in a confident manner. (It is highly desirable that no speeches by the principal, superintendent, or teacher himself intervene between the appearance of anyone on stage and the sounds of music.) Following a selection, the conductor should step down from the podium, if one is used, before acknowledging applause with a polite, brief bow. If a soloist has been featured, he should be cued to rise for recognition by the audience. Sometimes, if a single section of the ensemble has been prominent in a selection, the entire section is asked to rise for a bow. Generally, after each selection, the conductor takes a bow *on behalf of the entire ensemble*, until the end of a group of numbers, at which time he should motion to the entire group to acknowledge the audience's applause. Once in a while, during the performance of a work with several movements or other sections, the audience may begin to applaud between the movements rather than waiting until the end; when that happens, the director should remain facing his students and immediately raise his arm, as if to give a downbeat, as an indication to the audience that the music is to continue. In briefing the students on deportment, the teacher should also remind them that once on stage they should not adjust clothing and hair; that on leaving the stage, they should move quickly and quietly with the same deliberate movement used in entering; and that once off, they should remain backstage and not enter the rear of the auditorium since this often disturbs both the audience and the following groups of performers. Sometimes, students join the audience in applauding their teacher at the end of a performance and may "surprise" him with the presentation of a gift. Both practices should be discouraged on stage for they place the spotlight on the teacher rather than on the students. The teacher who displays the same type of etiquette that he requests of his students is one who directs the audience's attention to the students and away from himself.

The visual effect of a concert is also important. Part of this effect depends on how the performers are dressed. Many schools have now moved away from somber-looking robes for choruses, military-like uniforms for bands, and black skirts with white blouses for girls' ensembles. Instead, they ask the boys to wear dark jackets and ties and the girls to wear colorful, solid, pastel dresses. The result can be a less-formal climate, which is highly desirable.

The visual aspect of a concert is also affected by lighting. Many teachers merely ask for "white lights on stage" and leave it at that; although the performers will be able to read their music, such lighting may leave them looking pale and colorless. The conductor himself may be left in the dark if nothing is done to light the forestage. And sometimes, teachers go to great lengths to prepare elaborate printed programs, but then have the house lights lowered so much that the audience cannot even read the title of the next selection. The over-all effect can be enhanced considerably if taste and imagination are exercised. Sufficient lighting can be maintained in the house without making it too bright, and changing colors of blues, pinks, yellows, and so on can be achieved on stage to accompany numbers in an appropriate mood-setting manner. Occasionally, simple "scenery" in the form of mobiles or an abstract backdrop may also be employed to add interest.

A final matter of production planning is the design and content of the printed program. The cover should be simple, attractive, and appropriate to the specific type of concert; it may be straight typographical material, artistically laid out, an illustration by an art student in the school, or a preprinted cover sold by various firms with blank inner pages to be printed by the school. The program listing itself should identify at least the titles, composers and arrangers, and performing ensembles, but it may also include descriptive information about each selection. Program notes must be succinct, accurate, and nontechnical, offering information that will contribute to the listeners' understanding of the music. Often, these notes are too lengthy, filled with insignificant or irrelevant information, and awkwardly worded. When they are well prepared, they can add considerably to the enjoyment of the program and to the image of the music department. (Another technique that is sometimes used is the oral delivery of program notes in an informal manner by a student prior to each selection or group of selections.) Every effort should be made to list the names of all the participating students on the program, as well as the names of faculty and students who assisted in the production of the concert. The spelling of names should be checked and rechecked for accuracy. When space permits, it is also a good practice to use the back page or the inside cover to announce forthcoming programs and to present a paragraph about the scope of the music education program or the purpose of the music curriculum. Four samples of printed programs, illustrating both the printed format and the programming of music selections, appear in Figures 13-1, 13-2, 13-3, and 13-4.

MANAGING THE CONCERT PROGRAM

One of the secrets of performance success is the ability to organize a working team of assistants to execute managerial responsibilities with expertise and reliability. As long as excessive demands are not made on them, faculty members in other departments are often most cooperative in working with the music teacher and student committees to handle ticket sales; prepare the printed program; arrange for publicity; supervise box-office personnel, ushers, the stage crew, and other committees; arrange for custodians, police, and other personnel; assist with transportation needs; and manage other arrangements to free the music teacher for preparing his students. The music teacher, however, should make the necessary plans and decisions, inform each aide of exactly what needs to be done, and keep in touch with these people to make sure that all is progressing effectively and on schedule.

The following checklist should prove useful in seeing that everything is done in sufficient time:

End of Previous School Year
—Set tentative dates for programs.
—Book the school auditorium for both program dates and stage rehearsal dates.

PROGRAM

Overture: Fanfare And Capriccio .... Willis Schaefer
Bourne, Co. 1963
Grade 4

Polka And Fugue, From "Schwanda" .... Jaromie Weinberger
Associated Music Publishers, Inc. 1934, 1961   Arr. Glenn C. Bainum
Grade 6

Galop .... Dmitri Shostakovich
Boston Music, Co. 1971   Arr. Donald Hunsberger
Grade 5

Compendium .... Leland Forsblad
Hai Leonard Publishing, Co. 1974   Arr. Wayne Livingston
Grade 4

Where It's At .... Caesar Giovannini
Charter Publication, Inc. 1973
Grade 5

Selections From "Sweet Charity" .... Cy Coleman, Dorothy Fields
Notable Music Co., Inc. 1969   Arr. Ken Whitcomb
Grade 5

Cheerio March........................ Edwin Franko Goldman
Schirmer, Inc. 1933, 1968   Arr. Frank Erickson
Grade 4

National Band Association Grading as approached from the viewpoint
of the high school band:

Grade 1 — Training material, very easy
Grade 2 — Fairly easy, no particular technical demands
Grade 3 — Easy
Grade 4 — Of medium difficulty
Grade 5 — Difficult
Grade 6 — Very difficult

PENNSYLVANIA MUSIC EDUCATORS ASSOCIATION CONVENTION

SPRINGFIELD
Junior High School
Woodland Avenue

7th and 8th Grade

CONCERT BAND

RICHARD S. MILLER
Conductor

THE HILTON HOTEL
PITTSBURGH, PENNSYLVANIA

FRIDAY, JANUARY 10, 1975

•

12:45 P.M.

—Select the bulk of the repertoire for the following year, from which program material will later be chosen.

Three Months Before the Program
—Select the focus or the theme of the program.
—Make repertoire substitutions if necessary, based on the type of program chosen.

Two Months Before the Program
—Make a final decision on the theme.
—From those selections being studied, make a final selection of the program numbers; also select soloists as needed and any special material.
—Determine the budget for the program.

Six Weeks Before the Program
—Place the ticket order with the printer. Check the instructions to the printer for accuracy regarding date, place, time, ticket price, name of the program, name of the sponsoring organization, ticket size, weight and color of the paper stock, and delivery date.

—Have the cover design for the program prepared. Compile the list of names for the printed program and write the preliminary copy.

—Select the poster design and have the posters made.

—Line up faculty members and student assistants to help manage the production.

Five Weeks Before the Program
—Write the first publicity release, concentrating on the focus of the program, the ensembles and number of students to be featured, and the date, time, location, and availability of tickets.
—Determine the equipment, lighting, and staging needs.

Four Weeks Before the Program
—Send the first news release to the local newspapers.

—Meet with faculty and student assistants to determine progress in setting up committees and organizing work.
—Make final decisions on program selections in the event that any numbers have to be deleted.
—Compile a list of community leaders and school personnel to invite.

Three Weeks Before the Program
—Write the second publicity release, concentrating on the groups involved, the

FIGURE 13-2. Cover and Inside Page of Program of Instrumental Concert at Woodrow Wilson High School, Long Beach, California; Rolland Sandberg, Director

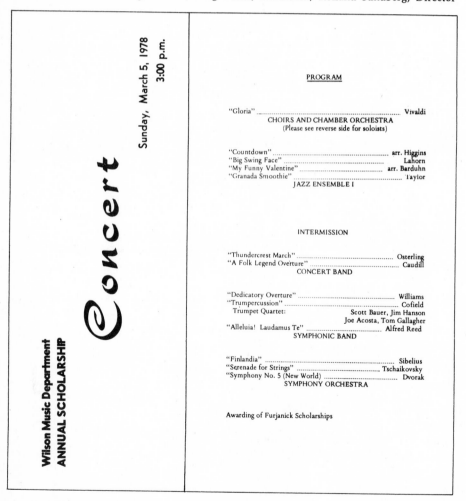

Sunday, March 5, 1978
3:00 p.m.

Concert

Wilson Music Department
ANNUAL SCHOLARSHIP

PROGRAM

"Gloria" .... Vivaldi
CHOIRS AND CHAMBER ORCHESTRA
(Please see reverse side for soloists)

"Countdown" .... arr. Higgins
"Big Swing Face" .... Lahorn
"My Funny Valentine" .... arr. Barduhn
"Granada Smoothie" .... Taylor
JAZZ ENSEMBLE I

INTERMISSION

"Thundercrest March" .... Osterling
"A Folk Legend Overture" .... Caudill
CONCERT BAND

"Dedicatory Overture" .... Williams
"Trumpercussion" .... Cofield
Trumpet Quartet: Scott Bauer, Jim Hanson
                          Joe Acosta, Tom Gallagher
"Alleluia! Laudamus Te" .... Alfred Reed
SYMPHONIC BAND

"Finlandia" .... Sibelius
"Serenade for Strings" .... Tschaikovsky
"Symphony No. 5 (New World) .... Dvorak
SYMPHONY ORCHESTRA

Awarding of Furjanick Scholarships

Music Education Through Performance Classes

FIGURE 13-3. Spring Concert Program of the Music Department of Staples High School, Westport, Connecticut

Spring Concert
April 14-15, 1978

I

SOPHOMORE BAND

Cantus Brevis. . . . . Forsblad
Fugue in G Minor . . . . J. S. Bach, arr. Moehlmann
Evergreen. . . . . Williams, Streisand, arr. Erickson
Sonata for Winds . . . . Carter

II

THE CHOIR

O, Clap Your Hands . . . . .V. Williams
        Laurel Rech, '78, Steve Rintoul, '78, Reynolds MacNary, '79: Trumpets
          Chris Guryan, '79, Bill Sielert, '78, David Rintoul, '79: Trombones
        Bill Nesbitt, '79, tuba; Russ Bassett, '78 tympani; Peter Carey, '78, cymbals

Te Deum (for the Empress Marie Therese). . . . . .Haydn
          Lynn Walkoff, '78, Robert Miller, '78   Violin I
          Emily Blau, '79, Karin Koch, '78   Violin II
          Peter Miller, '78, Laurie Woog, '78   Viola
          Sue Polk, '80, Martha Schapiro, '79   Cello
A Prayer Without Words . . . . .Rachmaninoff - edited Wilhousky
               In memory of Peter Wilhousky (1902-1978)
Teče Voda, Teče. . . . . (Waters Ripple and Flow - Czecho-Slovak Folk Song) arr. Taylor
My Bonnie Lass She Smileth . . . . German
         Gian Porro, '78   Student Conductor

Certn'y Lord! (Spiritual). . . . . arr. de Paur
        Reynolds MacNary, '79, tenor   Russell Johnson, '78, tenor
           Peter Thorsby, '78, bass

III

SYMPHONIC BAND

Amparita Roca. . . . . Spanish March - Texidor, arr. Winter
Suite, Victory at Sea. . . . . R. Rodgers - arr. Maltby
  Song of High Seas, Sunny Pacific Islands, Guadalcanal March, Beneath the Southern Cross,
    The Approaching Enemy, The Attack, Death and Debris
     Alto Saxophone Solo: Richard Steinberg, '79 - Hymn of Victory
Toccata and Fugue. . . . . Eberlin, arr. Barnes
Star Wars. . . . . Williams

INTERMISSION

IV

GIRLS GLEE CLUB

Love Learns by Laughing . . . . Morley - edited Harris
Try to Remember ("Fantasticks"). . . . . .Schmidt - Simeone
Sing to the Lord a Marvelous Song . . . . Butler

V

MALE CHORUS

Unto His Holy Name Sing Praises (Cantata No. 142) . . . . .Bach - arr. Ehret
Aura Lee. . . . . .Poulton
Li'l Liza Jane (American Folk Song) . . . . arr. Hunter - Shaw
           Chip Seadale, '78 Solo
Climbin' Up the Mountain (Spiritual). . . . . arr. Smith

VI

JAZZ ENSEMBLE

Basie Straight Ahead. . . . . .Nestico
     Linda Champagne, '79, piano   Jonathan Saxon, '79, tenor saxophone
Moonlight Serenade. . . . . .Miller - Parish
Jazz Espagnol . . . . Cobine
     Michael Wenig, '78, soprano saxophone   Russell Bassett, '78, drums
Handel with Care. . . . . .Sebesky
     Russell Bassett, '78, drums; Michael Bloom, '78, Michael Stamm, '79, trumpets
        John Dotson, '78, alto saxophone

ACKNOWLEDGMENTS

The Music Department would like to express its appreciation to The Staples Service Club: Mrs. Elly Bock, advisor; The Staples Stage and Technical Staff for Lighting: Mr. Hector Guerra, advisor; the Administration, Staff and Parents for their enthusiastic support and encouragement which makes our music program possible.

Dates to remember: Combined Concert, June 2 and 3, featuring the Staples Orchestra, the Glee Club, Male Chorus and the Sophomore Chorus. The combined choral groups and orchestra will join forces to present Peter Wilhousky's "The Battle Hymn of the Republic" in tribute to and memory of this gifted and courageous music educator who passed away this past winter.

                June 11: The Orphenians, the Chamber Orchestra and Jazz Ensemble will present their gala "Farewell Concert" before leaving for Poland July 12 at Staples High School 8:00 p. m.

The Parents Committee for the Poland trip is in the lobby to provide you the opportunity to purchase raffle tickets in support of our fund-raising efforts for Poland. Thank you for your support.

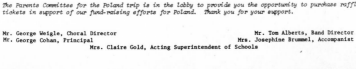

Mr. George Weigle, Choral Director   Mr. Tom Alberts, Band Director
Mr. George Cohan, Principal   Mrs. Josephine Brummel, Accompanist
               Mrs. Claire Gold, Acting Superintendent of Schools

Program

SYMPHONY NO. 2 IN D MAJOR, First Movement
.... *Joseph Haydn*

Franz Joseph Haydn (1732-1809) was one of four great composers associated with the Classical period in music and is generally credited with having established the basis of modern orchestration and the Sonata form. The Symphony No. 2 is called "The London Symphony" since it was composed during Haydn's stay in that city.

VIOLIN CONCERTO NO. 2 IN E MAJOR, First Movement
.... *J. S. Bach*

Linda Garwood, *Soloist*

The **Violin Concerto in E Major** is the second of three violin concertos written by Bach (1685-1750) for solo violin and string orchestra. The First Movement of this concerto is an excellent example of Bach's contrapuntal ingenuity and extraordinary sense of form.

Miss Garwood will attend Purdue University and will play in the university symphony orchestra.

THREE MOODS IN TWO MOVEMENTS .... *Mike Leckrone*

This rather humorous and descriptive selection was commissioned by the Wisconsin School Music Association. The two movements are subtitled I—**March For People With Uncertain Rhythm** and II—**Graduation Day.**

HUNGARIAN RHAPSODY .... *David Popper*

Lori Myers, *Violoncellist*

There are relatively few great concertos for violoncello and orchestra; however, one of the most popular and interesting violoncello solos is David Popper's **Hungarian Rhapsody** which is full of lush melody and fiery technical passages.

Miss Myers will attend college and major in music.

STAR WARS SELECTIONS .... *John Williams*

The brilliant musical score composed by John Williams for "Star Wars" is full of high adventure and soaring spirits in keeping with the character of the film itself. Arranger James H. Burden has chosen representative portions of both the main and end title themes to fashion what might be more suitably titled an overture which retains all the fire and excitement and tension and exuberance of the original score.

A FOGGY DAY .... *George Gershwin*

A new arrangement by Joe Reisman of a great popular standard written in 1937 by George and Ira Gershwin.

VIOLIN CONCERTO NO. 7 .... *Charles De Beriot*

Susan Allesee, *Soloist*

The violin concertos of Charles De Beriot are more familiar to violinists than to the general listening public. They are, however, full of lovely melody and the technical passages take full advantage of the violin's unique qualities.

Miss Allesee also is college bound and will major in music.

PRESENTATION OF AWARDS

I. Senior Keys

II. National School Orchestra Association Award

Nominees:— Susan Allesee, Linda Garwood, Lori Myers

THE KING AND I .... *Richard Rodgers*

This arrangement has been compiled and transcribed by Robert Russell Bennett who created the original Broadway Show arrangement. You will hear "**I Whistle a Happy Tune**", "**Hello Young Lovers**", "**March of the Siamese Children**", "**I Have Dreamed**", "**Getting To Know You**", "**We Kiss In A Shadow**", and "**Shall We Dance**"?

---

types of music to be heard, the titles of a few (not all) compositions that sound interesting, and the people assisting in the production.

—Confirm the program date and time with custodians and police.

—Prepare the final copy for the printed program, rechecking all the copy, including the names of students and titles of compositions.

—Determine dress for performers.

—Make final decisions on risers, equipment, lighting, logistics, and so on.

—Send complimentary tickets to community leaders and school personnel.

—Arrange for the piano to be tuned.

Two-and-a-half Weeks Before the Program
—Send the second news release to local newspapers.

—Distribute posters around the school and community.

—Have the programs printed.

—Have rehearsal photographs taken.

Two Weeks Before the Program
—Check on ticket sales.

—Check on personnel needs.

—Write the third and fourth news releases, concentrating on the students involved, program material, special features, the availability of tickets, and date, time, and location of the program.

One-and-a-half Weeks Before the Program
—Send the third news release to local newspapers, with a photograph of a few students in rehearsal.
—Send an announcement to local radio stations.
—Complete all decisions on staging and lighting.
—Arrange for a photographer at the dress rehearsal.
—Run through the entire program, in sequence, with all the ensembles.

One Week Before the Program
—Run through the staging with the stage and lighting crew.
—Check on ticket sales.
—Check the sound system, if one is to be used.

Five Days Before the Program
—Send the final news release to the local newspapers.

Four Days Before the Program
—Check all details with the performers, regarding dress, placement on program, etiquette, arrival time, and so on.
—Check all details with assistants and crews.

Two Days Before the Program
—Hold a dress rehearsal and have photographs taken.

One Day Before the Program
—Check the lighting, sound system, and other equipment.
—Give programs to ushers.
—Have the piano tuned.

Afternoon of the Program
—Check the stage to be sure it is arranged for the first ensemble.
—Be sure that the warm-up and dressing rooms are prepared.

Within One Day After the Program
—Be sure that the clean-up committee has completed its work.

Within Two Days After the Program
—Send notes of appreciation to faculty and student production assistants and to local newspapers who gave publicity.

Within Four Days After the Program
—Evaluate the performance and the production.

Within One Week After the Program
—Complete the budget report on ticket sales and make sure all bills have been received for payment.

Projects

1. Select repertoire for a concert of American music featuring a high school choir, concert band, "madrigal" ensemble, stage band, and small string orchestra.
2. Select a program for a high school orchestra, percussion ensemble, mixed chorus, and wind ensemble. Then prepare copy for a printed program featuring commentary on the selections.
3. Outline the considerations involved in bringing together junior and senior high school ensembles for a joint concert in the senior high school auditorium.
4. Compile a list of works that would be suitable for performance by (a) a high school band and chorus, and (b) a high school orchestra and chorus.

5. Make as complete a list as you can of possible performance invitations in the community that should *not* be accepted because of the MENC-AASA-AFM Code of Ethics.

Selected References

EDELSON, EDWARD. *The Secondary School Music Program from Classroom to Concert Hall.* West Nyack, New York: Parker Publishing Company, Inc., 1972. Chapters 1 and 2.

HOFFER, CHARLES. *Teaching Music in the Secondary Schools.* Belmont, California: Wadsworth Publishing Company, Inc., 1964. Chapter 11.

KUHN, WOLFGANG E. *Instrumental Music: Principles and Methods of Instruction.* Boston: Allyn & Bacon, Inc., 1962. Chapter 7.

LACY, GENE M. *Organizing and Developing the High School Orchestra.* West Nyack, New York: Parker Publishing Company, Inc., 1971. Chapter 4.

Supportive Elements in a Music Education Program

Part 4

Extraclass Activities

14

Creativity, by its very nature, refuses academic confinement.
RYLAND W. CRARY[1]

THE CONTEMPORARY CONCEPT of a curriculum is much more than a set body of subject matter or a course of study. It consists of all the experiences that the school sponsors or for which it is responsible—in or out of the regular classroom, in or out of normal school hours, and on or off the school campus. Thus, guidance services, assemblies, clubs, sports events, field trips, exchange concerts, dramatics, student government programs, and afterschool activities are all part of the curriculum. For this reason, such experiences are now often referred to as "extraclass," rather than "extracurricular" or "cocurricular," activities.

These activities can be of considerable value in providing outlets for the creative talents of students, in extending the music education program to serve more specific interests, and in involving or reaching many students who might not otherwise have contact with the music program.

INTRASCHOOL ACTIVITIES

Although many activities take the student out into the community or involve him with students from other schools, there are many oppor-

[1] Ryland W. Crary, *Humanizing the School: Curriculum Development and Theory* (New York: Alfred A. Knopf, Inc., 1969), p. 21.

tunities for worthwhile experiences within the individual school. Three of the most important are the organization of student-directed ensembles, the establishment of a music club, and the production of musical shows.

Student-Directed Ensembles

Considering the number of students who participate in formal organizations such as the school band, orchestra, or chorus, the number of small ensembles that could be put together among the same students is extensive. Because of scheduling problems and the full courses of study carried by most students, however, it is generally not possible to organize more than a few such groups to meet as formal classes. A large number could conceivably function, though, if they met before or after regular school hours, operating under the students' own direction with the music teacher serving only in an advisory capacity. Trios, quartets, quintets, and so on, of both standard and unusual instrumentation, could be formed. In schools that are unable to support a full orchestra, this can be one way of providing for the few string players who are available. Such ensembles can also draw in students who may not be active in regular school music groups.

Among the possibilities in this area, the organization of pop-rock vocal and instrumental ensembles is especially appealing to students, and there is much the teacher can do to help such groups get started. First, the teacher can facilitate the bringing together of instrumentalists. In a vocal group, these musicians must be creative enough to provide accompaniments of various styles. Finding capable rock musicians in the high school is ordinarily not difficult, but quite often, the students themselves are not aware of the number of their peers who are capable of contributing effectively to such a group.

Through the use of bulletins, the school newspaper, and personal contacts, the teacher can draw these students together and assist them in grouping themselves according to comparable abilities. Vocalists chosen for pop-rock ensembles should have above-average musicianship and tonal memory and have the ability to adapt to the stylized physical movements that are so typical of many rock singing groups. The teacher who is reluctant to get involved with choreographing movement will find that some members of the group will be quite capable (often more so than the teacher) of assuming this responsibility.

Within the group, the teacher should organize a repertoire committee that will be on a constant lookout for suitable music. Initially, the teacher may have to assume much of the arranging responsibility, but as the ensemble begins to take shape, students, with some encouragement, will be eager to help. A very successful technique for voicing is to write three parts (SSA) and have the boys sing the same parts an octave lower. This kind of voicing acts to reinforce each part, which is especially helpful when a group does a great deal of moving about or is not situated according to parts. Several books are now on the market that both the teacher and students will find helpful in creating rock-styled arrangements. After a few selections have been prepared, the members of the ensemble should be encouraged to build their repertoire by creating their own original songs in this idiom.

While the music is being learned, time can be saved by having the instrumentalists and singers rehearse separately. The teacher should appoint the best instrumentalist as the leader, confer with him regarding the type of accompaniment needed for each selection, and then leave the group on its own to work out the introduction, background accompaniment, interludes, and so on. When the teacher feels the singers are secure in their parts, then the accompaniment can be added. Choreography should be postponed until the vocalists and instrumentalists have no difficulty performing together.

To make a visual impact upon their audience, many professional singing groups dress in a unique fashion that is as contemporary as the songs they sing. High school pop-rock performers generally feel that an identifiable attire is necessary for them, too, so early in the year a decision should be made regarding suitable dress. This will allow enough time for the girls to make their own outfits and for the boys to order shirts, pants, vests, or whatever other items may be necessary to match.

As early as possible, the pop-rock ensemble should seek opportunities to perform publicly. Such groups can be scheduled into regular school concerts, but there are also numerous opportunities at the beginning of school assemblies, in talent shows, and at school dances or other functions.

Music Clubs

Clubs are not only simple to form and relatively easy to operate, but also excellent vehicles for learning experiences in an informal atmosphere. Each club needs to have a faculty adviser, but student officers should be elected to do most of the planning and to run the activities. Various music clubs can be organized depending on the size of the school and student interest. There might, for example, be a guitar club, in which students could help each other with instruction, perform for each other, share repertoire, work on guitar ensemble music, and make field trips occasionally to hear guitar programs in the community. A listeners club could be formed to make monthly trips to hear concerts and music programs in the community or in nearby communities. Folk music, jazz, and pop-rock clubs can serve the interests of students

who want to perform, listen, or learn more about music in those idioms.

A nonspecialized music club, of course, has the advantage of enlisting a larger membership and of sponsoring events that would be of interest to the entire school and to a segment of the community. One such club was organized with substantial success in a large high school of 3000 students, and drew a membership of one out of every six students. Each of the 500 members paid fifty cents in dues for the year, which went into a scholarship fund for a senior who planned to study music in college. This particular club held monthly meetings, including one each spring devoted to a concert of student compositions; two or three during the course of the year by soloists and small ensembles formed from the membership, as well as by formal school performing groups; and several featuring prominent music personalities. Through the courtesy of the local American Federation of Musicians and the use of the AFM's Music Performance Trust Fund, which pays professional musicians for educational and charitable appearances, the club sponsored appearances by such figures as Leonard Bernstein, Lukas Foss, Richard Rodgers, and local personalities. This type of activity could just as easily be carried on in schools with smaller student bodies. Meetings of a club of this sort are generally held after school, but in the case of a particularly significant presentation, arrangements could be made with the administration to present the club's program as a school assembly for the benefit of all students.

Music Theatre Productions

There are basically four types of musical shows that are commonly produced in high schools: the musical variety or talent show, the opera, the Broadway musical, and the specially written book show. Talent shows are produced in many schools on an annual basis because they permit a large number of students to perform, make use of talents that may lie dormant through most of the year for lack of an outlet, and are relatively simple to produce. The criticisms of most talent shows are that they are deadly boring, poorly staged, lacking in focus, and overly long. The well-produced talent show generally has a theme to unify the diversity of acts and a master of ceremonies to keep the show moving and help tie elements together. One school, for example, made effective use of a simple thematic idea—a chronological presentation of different styles of music, dance, and theatrical skits. Entitled "A Century of Entertainment," the show offered a sequence of acts representing entertainment from the early years of the twentieth century to the present. Within this basic framework, any type of act could be worked in logically with a little imagination. Set design was achieved in a simple manner by the use of a large abstract painting that stretched the full width of the stage, and this served as a partial backdrop throughout the performance. In addition, triangular flats were constructed by hinging together three 4' x 8' plywood sheets. Each side of a triangle was illustrated with caricatures of well-known entertainers from a specific decade, and as the show progressed, a new side of a triangle (hence a new decade) was turned to face the audience. The cost of the production was minimal, and by enlisting the services of several faculty members to work with various acts, rehearsal and production time were also reduced. Using an approach similar to this and keeping the production down to a reasonable length can turn a potentially dull show into an interesting, lively kaleidoscope of talent.

Of the other types of productions, opera presents the greatest difficulty in terms of the selection of material because of vocal and in-strumental demands. However, such operas as Aaron Copland's *Second Hurricane* and Gian Carlo Menotti's *The Telephone* have been successfully produced by high school casts. Occasionally, one still finds a music teacher who seems to attempt a compromise between the "high art" of grand opera and what he considers the "inferiority" of Broadway by reviving a Gilbert and Sullivan comic opera for still another year. There is no denying the artistry of the Gilbert and Sullivan creations, but in today's society it takes a special type of sophistication to appreciate their works. Today's high school students are certainly sophisticated, but in a different way, and for most of them Gilbert's plots and such songs as "Buttercup" and "Tit Willow" are an embarrassment.

There are also those who feel that Broadway shows, like most operas, are too demanding for high school students, either vocally or from the standpoint of production. Some of these teachers turn to musicals that have been specifically written for high schools. Although they are simpler to produce, the musical and dramatic worth of many is highly questionable.

The musical comedies and musical plays of Broadway have both their advocates and opponents among music teachers. Certainly, there are both good and poor examples of Broadway shows, but as with any music form or style, the good examples are worthy of study. One of the common criticisms of high school musicals is that the style of music is harmful to students' voices. Absolutely no justification exists for this viewpoint. Style has nothing to do with proper techniques of vocal production. There is a correct way to sing, and that way applies whether one is singing a madrigal, a mass, an art song, a folk song, or a musical-comedy number. The fact that many popular singers and Broadway entertainers do not sing correctly has nothing to do with this underlying fact. A different *style* should definitely be employed in a musical show, but the teacher who instructs his students to sing with a different *technique* in a show than in a classically oriented chorus would appear to know little about the voice.

Another common criticism of all musical productions—from the opera to the Broadway musical—is that they involve too much production time and interfere with the regular school music program. It is true that a great deal of time is involved, but proper scheduling of rehearsals can eliminate wasted time, and there need be no interference with the regular program if the teacher is well organized and holds all rehearsals after school. Occasionally, the entire school chorus is enlisted to perform in the production; this is definitely to be avoided since it ties up valuable class time in the rehearsal of the show. If all show-related activities are held in the afternoon following regular school hours and auditions are open to the entire student body, there should be no interference. Even then, a great deal of students' time is wasted by many teachers who do not know how to organize rehearsals. Common practice is to call a rehearsal for a particular scene and to expect everyone in that scene to be present; usually, the result is that some students remain idle for most of the rehearsal until the scene progresses to the point where they appear or have lines. This can be avoided by preparing a scene analysis, as illustrated in Figure 14-1. A scene analysis is a plot of the entrances and exits of each character in each scene. From this, the teacher can schedule rehearsals of portions of a scene or portions of several scenes that each involve the same nucleus of characters. This reduces the number of rehearsals that many students have to attend, and they know that when they do rehearse they will be active most of the time.

A third criticism is that a musical production costs too much. Expenses are incurred in connection with royalties, the rental of scripts and orchestration, the construction of scenery, the making of costumes, the purchase of props and makeup, the handling of lighting needs and publicity, and other items. The three main costs are royalties, scenery, and costumes. There is no way to avoid royalties and permission fees. However, many costumes can be made inexpensively, and the careful preparation of a costume plot will reduce the number of costumes needed by recombining portions of different outfits and spacing repeated costumes through the production. Although many schools build their own sets, this can be very time consuming and costly for a musical, which often calls for a large number of scene changes. Often, scenery costs can be reduced by renting backdrops and special items such as trees. Excellent, professional-looking backdrops can be rented from scenery supply houses, usually for less money than an inferior product can be built by the school. By starting early, many special props—such as bagpipes for *Brigadoon* or even a surrey with the fringe on top for *Oklahoma!*—can often be located and obtained at no cost. Because of the special costs involved, a small admission fee to the school musical is justified; and because of the community interest that usually accompanies such productions, the financial return will almost always more than cover expenses.

Still another criticism of musical productions is the demand that is often placed on faculty members outside the music department for assistance. The well-organized music teacher does not need all the assistance that one usually encounters in school shows. Ordinarily the show is scheduled for spring production, and rehearsals begin a couple of months before. If the show is selected early in the school year, the teacher has several months to draw up plans at a casual pace and prepare for many facets of the production in a way that will preclude faculty assistance. If scenery is rented, the industrial arts depart-

FIGURE 14-1. Sample Scene Analysis from *Brigadoon*

Character	I:2																			
Tommy Albright							N	—	—	X			N	—	—	—	—	—	—	X
Fiona MacLaren		N	—	—	—	—	—	—	—	X			N	—	—	—	—	—	—	X
Jeff Douglas							N	X												
Meg Brockie	AR	—	—	—	—	—	—	X												
Charlie Dalrymple									N	—	—	—	—	—	X					
Harry Beaton	AR	—	X	N	X							N	X		N	—	—	X		
Jean MacLaren		N	—	—	—	X									N	—	X			
Archie Beaton	AR	—	—	—	—	—	—	—	—	—	—	X				N	—	—	—	—
Andrew MacLaren		N	—	—	—	X									N	—	X			
Angus MacGuffie	AR	—	—	—	—	—	—	—	—	—	—	—	X			N	—	—	—	—
Sandy Dean	AR	—	—	—	—	—	—	—	—	—	—	—	X			N	—	—	—	—
Stuart Dalrymple	AR	—	—	—	—	—	—	—	—	—	—	—	X			N	—	—	—	—
Kate	AR	—	—	—	—	—	—	—	—	—	—	X				N	—	—	—	—
Maggie Anderson	AR	—	—	—	—	—	—	—	—	—	—	—	X		N	—	—	—	X	
Mixed Chorus	AR	—	—	—	—	—	—	—	—	—	—	—	X			N	—	—	—	—

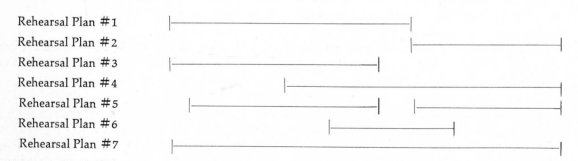

Rehearsal Plan #1

Rehearsal Plan #2

Rehearsal Plan #3

Rehearsal Plan #4

Rehearsal Plan #5

Rehearsal Plan #6

Rehearsal Plan #7

KEY: AR — Actor on stage "at rise" of curtain.
     N — Entrance
     X — Exit

Supportive Elements in a Music Education Program

Character	II:1													
Tommy Albright					N	—	—	—	X			N	—	X
Jeff Douglas					N	X								
Harry Beaton	N	—	—	X			N	X		N	X	N	—	X
Andrew MacLaren													N	X
Angus MacGuffie			N	X								N	—	X
Sandy Dean			N	X								N	—	X
Stuart Dalrymple			N	X								N	—	X
Male Chorus		N	—	X	N	—	—	—	—	X		N	—	X

Rehearsal Plan #1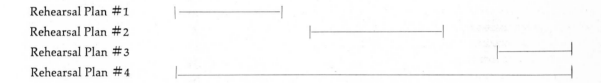
Rehearsal Plan #2
Rehearsal Plan #3
Rehearsal Plan #4

ment need not be called upon for help. If major costumes are rented, the remaining items can generally be put together by a student-directed committee without faculty assistance. In addition, the music teacher can often take the burden off the English department for dramatic direction. For some reason, there is a false assumption in most high schools that an English teacher is the best choice for the dramatic direction of a show. In some cases this is true, but in many instances, the English teacher has had no more preparation for teaching acting than the vocal music teacher has had for teaching trumpet. In schools where that is so, there is good justification for avoiding the professional approach of dividing dramatic and musical chores and for allowing the interested music teacher to handle both. Music and drama are so closely interwoven—especially in the musi-

cal play as opposed to the musical comedy—that the integration of the production is often best handled at the high school level by a single person. If the music teacher is to handle both aspects of the show, he should, of course, prepare himself by taking summer courses or workshops in theatre direction and production, or by reading books on acting, scenic design, costuming, lighting, and make-up.

In selecting the show, the teacher should seek a complementary balance between a good book and a good score. No show should be chosen simply because of its music. A show can be truly successful only if it has a good plot, good dramatic construction, and believable characters, in addition to interesting music. The selection should also be influenced by the availability of students to meet the dramatic and musical needs. Most Broadway musicals are overabundant with male parts, whereas most high schools are overabundant with females interested in auditioning. Thus, if there is a scarcity of interest or talent among boys in the school, the teacher should not decide to produce a show like *My Fair Lady*; if there is a scarcity of strong solo voices, he perhaps should not select *Oklahoma!*; if there is a scarcity of acting talent among the males, he should not consider *Camelot*; and if there is a scarcity of dancers, he should not turn to *West Side Story*. No show should be chosen that cannot be appropriately cast, dramatically and musically, for the students will derive aesthetic satisfaction from the production only to the degree that the rehearsals and performances rise. The teacher must also realize that certain shows call for good singers in the leads, whereas others call for good actors. The director who casts only in terms of musical ability in producing a show such as *Brigadoon* may realize some degree of drama in the opening scenes, but he will very likely forfeit the dramatic effect at the most crucial moment when the student sings "From This Day On" in beautiful tones rather than acting out the lyric. When the production does call for an emphasis on singing, the teacher should not be intimidated by vocal range requirements. Oddly, many teachers never think of transposition. There is no need to stop considering *Guys and Dolls*, for example, simply because the school has no tenors to handle the part of Nicely Nicely Johnson; the keys of his songs can be transposed downward. Another factor to consider in selecting a musical is the staging. Some modern schools have elaborate theatre facilities with a great deal of fly space, lighting equipment, and so on. Others can handle shows with only one or two scenes. There are ways to simplify scenic demands, but still the problem is one that may require a decision against producing a particular show.

After selecting the musical, the teacher should prepare all the details before it is time to cast and rehearse it. This involves the preparation of a production schedule, a cast analysis for distribution to interested students prior to auditions to inform them of the parts available and the requirements (see Figure 14-2), a scenery plot, a costume plot, a property list, a scene analysis (Figure 14-1), a lighting plot, a stage manager's plot, and a list of student personnel needs.

When rehearsals begin, it is usually helpful to pace them in terms of what is to be accomplished by a certain point in the production schedule. Ordinarily this procedure begins with a reading rehearsal for leads and supporting players only, for the purpose of reading through the script to gain an over-all understanding of it. At this time, it is helpful to supply the principal characters with a written character analysis so that they can see how their roles develop throughout the show. Figure 14-3 provides an example of a character analysis, drawn from the leading role of Tommy in *Brigadoon*. After the reading rehearsal, the schedule usually moves into business rehearsals (for the purpose of blocking movements on stage), characterization and line rehearsals (to concentrate on acting), pointing rehearsals (for dealing with details in acting and singing), pace rehearsals (for the purpose of tightening the show and developing a time pattern), and finally orchestra rehearsals, technical rehearsals (with stage and lighting crews), and dress rehearsals (to get used to costumes and props). An indispensable element in putting the show together is a prompt book, which should be prepared before rehearsals begin. A prompt book is rarely used today for prompting during a performance (in fact, if an actor does forget his lines on stage, it is frequently best to let him improvise until he gets back on the track rather than wait to be prompted thus creating

FIGURE 14-2. Cast Analysis from *Brigadoon*

TOMMY ALBRIGHT: A masculine figure of about thirty years—stalwart and handsome, with a thoughtful, sensitive, expressive face. He is somewhat uncertain about himself, but has a strong, determined character. Unable to conquer his doubts about love, he yields to the enchantment found in a less-than-real situation.

Speaking lines: 290   Voice: baritone
Singing lines: 103   Range: Bb_1 to $F\#^1$
Total lines: 393   Dances: none

Songs:
   "The Heather on the Hill" (with Fiona)
   "Almost Like Being in Love" (with Fiona)
   "The Chase" (with male chorus)
   "There But for You Go I" (with Fiona)
   "From This Day On" (with Fiona)
   Reprise: "From This Day On" (with Fiona)

FIONA MACLAREN: A warm and gentle young lady of twenty-two—blithe, intelligent, and to the point. She is typically Scottish in her candor and completely sincere in her personal feelings. Patient where love is concerned, she waits for a second "miracle."

Speaking lines: 152   Voice: soprano
Singing lines   107   Range: B to A^2
Total lines: 259   Dances: none

Songs:
   "Waitin' for My Dearie" (with female chorus)
   "The Heather on the Hill" (with Tommy)
   "Almost Like Being in Love" (with Tommy)
   "There But for You Go I" (with Tommy)
   "From This Day On" (with Tommy)
Reprises:
   "Come to Me"
   "Heather on the Hill"
   "From This Day On" (with Tommy)
   "MacConnachy Square" (with Charlie and the chorus)

an awkward pause). Rather, the prompt book is a looseleaf notebook containing all the information about the production. Scene and character analyses, costume and lighting plots, set designs and other materials are included. The major portion of the book, however, consists of the script, with pages of the script pasted on sheets of paper on the righthand side of the book. Each blank lefthand page is used to note all the directions pertaining to blocking, business, speech, and so on in relation to the lines that appear opposite. Circled numbers are placed beside appropriate lines in the script and keyed to the corresponding directions on the left. The lefthand pages include diagrams of the set and diagrams to show the movements and positions of actors on stage at any given time. If an over-all concept of the show is worked out by the teacher in advance and detailed in the prompt book, rehearsals will move much more smoothly and quickly right from the start. In addition, the prompt book eliminates the common problem of not remembering what direction was given to a cast member several days earlier. If a particular direction does not work out as intended, it can easily be changed and recorded in the book during rehearsals.

The production of a former Broadway musical or an opera is indeed a major undertaking, but it can be done without incurring excessive expenses, burdening faculty members, or placing extreme demands on students —if the music teacher plans the production early and is well organized. Furthermore, if it is done artistically—with the proper blend of music, drama, dance, and visual effect—it can offer the cast, and the audience, an aesthetic experience unlike any other the school provides.

FIGURE 14-3. Character Analysis from *Brigadoon*

The theme of *Brigadoon* is succinctly stated by Mr. Lundie: " 'Tis the hardest thing in the world to give everythin'; even though 'tis usually the only way to get everythin'." (II:3) And "when ye love someone deeply, anythin' is possible." (II:5) This is the frame of thought in which the conflicts of the various characters and the conflicts between characters exist. There is the conflict between the absurdity of a Brigadoon and the reality of the world we know (the setting); between the acceptance of life as it comes to you and the desire for something beyond one's existence, regardless of the consequences to others (Harry); in the reconciliation of tradition and the individual spirit (Fiona); in the uncertainty of Tommy's feelings and his sense of belonging to both the real and the unreal.

Tommy

The conflict that defines the character of Tommy is the most central to the play's theme. Throughout the drama, the entire struggle within him is one of feeling versus thought—of sensitivity versus sensibility. Not only in the words he speaks, but also in his vocal tone, facial expression, movement, actions, and mood, he must, during the course of the play, communicate a transformation from a tense, restricted containment in reason to a relaxed, fulfilled submersion in feeling.

In the opening scene we see Tommy as a sturdy, resolute, determined, yet uncertain young man—confused because he is supposedly in love but can feel nothing definite about his involvement. He is thoughtful and introspective, and the mood he must create here—one that will not be completely resolved until the end of Act II—is one in which the mind is stronger than the emotions.

In I:2 we see the first sign of the direction in which Tommy is moving. When he is alone with Fiona, his mind relaxes, and for the first time he experiences feeling rather than thought. Much of this relaxation has to come across in the song "The Heather on the Hill" in which he responds to the natural impulse of the moment. There is no thought involved here—only sensation. This

change is developed further during Tommy's absence from the stage in the third scene and is quite fully realized when he makes his next appearance in I:4. Tommy feels alive now, and his natural instinct is to ask Jeff, "Well, how do you *feel*?" Not, "what do you think?" or "what is your impression of Brigadoon?" He is not outwardly concerned with reason here—only with his immediate feelings. Yet, when he relates this feeling to his past feelings (which, toward Jane, were always more intellectual than emotional), the result is an inability to recognize love when it hits him. This is a feeling so different from what he has experienced before that he can say only that it is "*almost* like being in love." Then comes the sudden confrontation with the facts in the Bible at the end of the scene. This rips Tommy away from pure emotional response and plunges him once again into thought.

This side of the conflict continues through I:5, although he is not in the same state of thoughtfulness and introspection in which we first discovered him. Here, he is simply reasonable and reflective. This reflection is indicated by his late, quiet, and solitary entrance into the wedding scene that follows (I:6). Then, as suddenly as he was thrust backward by the Bible episode in I:4, he is thrust forward again by his stand against Harry. As the act ends, Tommy is once again more conscious of feeling than of anything else. But it is a change that must be implicit in his movements, for he says little.

Act II, Scene 1 is a continuation of his state at the end of I:6. His outlook here is stated simply in the line, "This must not end tonight." It is important that Tommy portray just the right degree of sensitivity in the beginning of the second act, for this is not the same feeling of elation that he experienced in I:4. He is still a thinking man; yet, we see more here of the sentient, tender, warm, romantic person that Tommy really is.

The real meeting of the two opposing poles within him comes in II:2 and II:3. In II:2 there is the realization finally of the true nature of the conflict within him: "I saw a man who had never known a love that was all his own." And in II:3

there is his further realization of what must be worked out. In the line "Someday if I should love, it's you I'll be dreaming of," we see that Tommy has accepted his feelings about Fiona, but still cannot accept Brigadoon.

Scene II:4 is the point of resolution—the point where he lets feeling conquer thought—and II:5 is the fulfillment of this transformation: "I found that sometimes what you believe in becomes more real to you than all the things you can explain away or understand."

To play the character of Tommy, then, the actor must be able to create an undulating mood while still moving in one direction. Words and music alone will not do this. The process will perhaps rest most of all on what can be achieved in pacing, in inflection, and in the varied intensity of the voice.

INTRACOMMUNITY AND INTERCOMMUNITY ACTIVITIES

As activities extend beyond the individual school, involving other schools or community organizations, most often those students who are active in the music department are participants (except, perhaps, for those attending concerts as members of clubs). Included among these activities are performances by selective interscholastic organizations, jamborees, exchange concerts, and arts festivals.

Selective Organizations

In large urban communities, all-city bands, orchestras, and choruses may be an integral part of the music education program. These groups are generally composed of the most outstanding musicians from each school, and membership is attained either by recommendation of the building music teacher or through competitive auditions. (Even in smaller school districts, all-city choruses and bands can be organized at the middle-school level if there are several such schools.)

Selective groups with members from a number of schools can be organized according to a variety of geographical designations. Beyond the single community, they may be representative of several neighboring communities, a county, a district of a state, a state, or a national division comprising several states. Naturally, as the area becomes larger, the

selection of students from each eligible school becomes less equitable. This is avoided sometimes in groups representing a relatively limited area by assigning a membershp quota to each school; however, this system does not produce as strong an organization as when membership is achieved by audition.

Interscholastic groups have been criticized because they sometimes involve a loss of school time and because the students in many instances bear the financial expenses. However, there is considerable value in such groups: Students are able to participate in ensembles having more balanced instrumentation or voices than is generally possible in the individual school. They may also have the opportunity to perform a better quality of literature and more difficult works, as well as give more concentrated attention to instrumental and vocal techniques and interpretive problems. Particularly at the state and national division levels—in groups organized by MENC and its affiliated state teachers associations—there is also the opportunity to work with nationally recognized conductors and music educators.

District, state, and national groups are now well established. However, the possibilities on a more local level should not be overlooked. Some music teachers have established such programs for students from four or five neighboring communities. The location of the final concert is worked out on a rotating basis, moving from community to community year by year. This plan provides for greater participation by each school, makes it possible for parents and friends to attend the concerts conveniently, and involves the teachers as active participants if the conducting chores are shared. Students also find this activity beneficial from a social standpoint: new friends are close by and visits can be arranged easily.

Planning an intercommunity program is not complex if the participating teachers schedule a meeting to make decisions on the following: (1) Where and when will the concert and rehearsals be held? This should be cleared with the administration in each school district and determined as soon as possible. (2) How will the students be chosen for membership? (3) What music will be performed and who will conduct? In the case of choral groups, accompanist duties must also be determined. (4) Will admission be charged to pay for the music, printed programs, custodians, and other personnel, or will each community share the expense? (5) Will it be necessary to make arrangements to feed the group? If so, will a school cafeteria or private homes be used? (6) What will the concert dress be? (7) What plans should be made for a student social hour after the concert? (8) What provisions must be made for transportation, chaperones, and a nurse in attendance? (9) Is a code of conduct and safety precautions available for distribution to the students? (10) Who will coordinate all the details?

Jamborees and Festivals

The jamboree is a program that brings together complete ensembles from several communities rather than selected members of each ensemble. A band jamboree, for example, might present four or five bands in a concert in a gymnasium. Although a gymnasium is not the most desirable concert hall, it does have an advantage in this case in that all the groups can be set up at once. Each band thus has the opportunity to hear the others, and after separate performances they can be joined for a finale of marches. (One caution here is that only one percussion section should be used in the combined numbers, for the echo effect can be disastrous.) Combined finales are not as advisable in jamborees of orchestras or stage bands. The planning procedure suggested in the previous section can be used as a guide in organizing a jamboree. A typical program for such an event is shown in Figure 14-4.

The regional festival, like the jamboree, involves participation by complete ensembles from each school. However, it is organized usually for the purpose of evaluating each group. Ordinarily, an ensemble performs for about fifteen minutes before two guest adjudicators, who prepare a written evaluation for the teacher and sometimes, if time permits, discuss the performance with the students involved. Quite often these evaluations are meaningless. It is common for groups to arrive with enough missing students to make the sound unbalanced. In addition, an ensemble may barely be getting warmed up and relaxed when the fifteen-minute performance is over. The time limit also rushes the adjudicators, who must complete their evaluation as the next group files on stage, and who have really not heard enough of any one group to form valid conclusions. Fortunately, most festivals have now departed from the practice of placing groups in competition with each other. Instead, top ratings can be shared by several groups. On the other hand, provisions are not always made for a group to hear other ensembles perform, which would be the one major advantage of participating in such festivals.

FIGURE 14-4. Program from the Eighth Annual North Shore Bandarama

PROGRAM

I

Beverly High School Concert Band
Lawrence P. Drouin, Conductor

Hermitage	Clifton Williams
Selections From Jonathan Livingston Seagull	Diamond - O'Reilly
Symphonic Dance No. 3	Clifton Williams

II

Danvers High School Concert Band
David Dubinski, Conductor

Selections From the Whiz	Arr. Lowden
Danzon	Arr. Krance
Rhapsody for Concert Band and Jazz Ensemble	Arr. Nestico

III

Peabody High School Concert Band
John H. Evans, Conductor

Cheerio	Goldman

Conducted by James Weaver, Salem High School '73
Berklee College of Music '77'

A Classical Overture	Grundman
Stargazing	Erb
Night Flight to Madrid	Leslie

IV

Salem High School Concert Band
Richard E. Boisvert, Robson W. Shelly, Associate Conductors

Fortinbras March	Dimitri Shostakovich
Ritual For Band	Donald O. Johnston
Godspell Medley	Schwartz - Bullock
Beguine for Band	Glenn Osser

V

McDonald's North Shore All Star Band
Paul LaValle, Conductor

"National Emblem March"	E.E. Bagley
"Overture in B Flat"	Caesar Giovannini
"Fandango"	Perkins-Werle
"Stars and Stripes Forever"	John Phillip Sousa

Paul Lavalle, now in his tenth year as head of the McDonald's All - American High School Band, is an internationally renowned music director who has also distinguished himself as a composer, arranger, and instrumentalist.

Lavalle created a number of radio programs for NBC including well - remembered 'Chamber Music Society of Lower Basin Street,' through which he introduced Dinah Shore, Lena Horne, Victor Broge, and Zero Mostel to coast to coast radio audiences.

In 1948, Paul Lavalle launched "The Band of America" which, in 1964 was appointed the official band of the New York World's Fair for two years. 1968, Lavalle became Director of Music and principle conductor of the Radio City Music Hall Symphony Orchestra.

In addition to his busy schedule of composing, arranging, and conducting, a major part of Lavalle's time is spent encouraging young musicians around the country. Throughout the year he attends as many *regional music festivals and clinics as his schedule will permit.* His appearance tonight was made possible by McDonald's of Salem, Beverly, Danvers, and Peabody.

Acknowledgements

School Administrations and City and Town Officials of the four communities for their support. The Salem Public Schools for host responsibilities Carole Cohen, Northshore Public Relations, McDonald's Corp. Ann Linblat, Arnold Advertising Agency; Alphonse Tatarunis, Director of Music, Danvers Public Schools; Dominic Mondi and students of the C.H. Patten Vocational High School- Ticket and Program printing All who participated or contributed their efforts to the success of the program.

Exchange Concerts

The exchange concert is partly a musical experience, permitting students to work with and listen to another band, chorus, or orchestra of comparable merit, and partly a social experience, often involving extensive travel and the experience of living with a family in the host community.

In planning an exchange concert, the teacher should consider the following: (1) Be sure that the music standards of the two schools are compatible. (2) Be sure that both parents and school administrators approve of the exchange, and be sure that the responsibilities involved are clearly recognized. (3) Make certain that other school activities do not conflict with the proposed dates of the exchange and that *all* members of the ensemble will be able to participate.

In planning the trip to the cooperating community, the teacher should: (1) Inform parents well in advance of the trip. (2) Secure permission slips from the parents of all participating students, realizing that such slips do not release either the school or the teacher from any legal responsibilities for the safety and welfare of students. (3) Make arrangements for transportation and secure enough chaperones (for trips of more than one day, a joint committee of MENC and the National Safety Council has recommended one adult for every ten students). (4) Be sure that parents know where the teacher will be staying (including the telephone number) in case there is an emergency, and be sure that home telephone numbers of all students are available in the event of an emergency involving a student. (5) Inform parents that if there should be a behavioral problem, the student will be sent home by public transportation at the parents' expense. (6) Be sure that each student has a schedule of all meeting times and places and has been informed of safety and conduct guidelines. (7) Meet all deadlines established by the host school.

In hosting the exchange organization in his own community, the teacher must consider the following: (1) Provide the visiting music director with a deadline for sending the names, grades, and ages of all students to be housed. (2) Organize a parents' committee to arrange housing for visiting students. (3) Secure suitable housing for the visiting music director and chaperones. (4) Inform all parents and others who are housing and boarding students of the complete schedule of events so that they will be available when needed. (5) Work out a plan for arrival-and-pickup procedures so that all concerned will be present at the right time and confusion will be avoided. (6) Be sure that all necessary school facilities and custodial services have been arranged for. (7) Provide the visiting music director with a deadline for submitting program material. (8) Inform parents, home students, and visiting students of the behavior code to be followed during the exchange. (9) Establish a curfew time for students. (10) Make seating arrangements for the home and visiting groups to have the opportunity to hear each other perform. (11) Plan for both organized social activities and free time along with rehearsal and concert activities.

Art Festivals

With the increased interest in the related arts and humanities, some schools have planned interdisciplinary festivals featuring music, drama, paintings, sculpture, graphic arts, crafts, dance, films, and so on. Such festivals are scheduled for one to three days, depending on school-community interest and the availability of sufficient school, community, and professional resources to develop an interesting and educative format. It is perhaps best to limit initial involvement in an arts festival to a one-day affair, expanding on it if it is successful, has good attendance, and thus becomes an annual event.

There are many possibilities for exhibits, concerts, and dramatic presentations at which attendants will be spectators. In addition, though, workshops and clinics can be organized to involve students and members of the community as active participants.

Planning an event of this sort requires a responsible chairman to seek out resources in the school, community, institutions of higher education, and the regional professional arts world; to put together a balanced program of activities; to coordinate times, places, materials, people, and finances; and to supervise a strong public relations program to make the festival successful. It would be desirable to have co-chairmen to coordinate details within each of the main areas of the arts.

This type of event can not only enrich the school curriculum and be educative for the community, but also enhance school–community relationships.

Projects

1. Prepare a list of organizations in your community that might lend support in organizing a school arts festival. Investigate nonorganizational resources that might be drawn on in designing such an event. For example, who are the local writers, poets, dancers, painters, actors? What are some sources of major films? What types of workshops could be organized for both students and adult members of the community?
2. Compile a set of concert locations in the local and surrounding area that are potential sites of field trips by members of a music club.
3. Visit a music store and investigate materials that would be useful to students in organizing and writing for pop-rock ensembles.
4. Make a study of operas that are suitable for production in the high school.
5. Write to licensing agencies that handle the performance rights for musical shows and request a catalog of their offerings. Then select a show and prepare a budget for its production.
6. Obtain the script to a Broadway musical, select one scene, and prepare a prompt book for that scene, detailing the set arrangement, blocking, interpretation, props needed, and so on.

Selected References

BALK, H. WESLEY. *Singing-Actor: Training for Musical Theatre*. Minneapolis: University of Minnesota Press, 1977.

CARTER, CONRAD, A. J. BRADBURY, and W. R. B. HOWARD. *Production and Staging of Plays*. New York: Arc Books, Inc., 1963.

DIETRICH, JOHN E. *Play Director*. Englewood Cliffs, New Jersey: Prentice-Hall, Inc., 1953.

NELMS, HENNING. *Play Production*. New York: Barnes & Noble, Inc., 1958.

PLUMMER, GAIL. *The Business of Show Business*. New York: Harper & Row, Publishers, Inc., 1961.

Safety for School Music Trips. Washington, D.C.: Music Educators National Conference.

WHITE, EDWIN, and MARGUERITE BATTYE. *Acting and Stage Movement*. New York: Arc Books, Inc., 1963.

WHITE, ROBERT C. "The High School Musical—Accentuate the Musical and Eliminate the Voice Abuse," *Music Educators Journal*, 64:9 (May 1978), pp. 27–33.

Measurement and Evaluation

15

Whatever exists exists in some amount and can be measured.
EDWARD L. THORNDIKE[1]

THE TERMS "measurement" and "evaluation" are often used interchange-
ably in discussing music achievement, aptitude, and performance. However, even though they are interrelated, "measurement" has a more objective connotation and generally refers to the use of some testing device to
gather quantitative data. When a junior high school student is administered a true-false test on music form and he scores "89," that student's
knowledge and understanding of form have been measured and a statistical piece of information has been obtained. "Evaluation" is a process that
follows, drawing upon measurement and other techniques in order to
appraise the student's musical growth. The score of "89," for example,
might be used along with an observation of his response to structural
elements while listening and his use of form in composing to provide
evidence for evaluating his progress toward achieving a particular objective. The information obtained from a test can provide the teacher with
some means of analyzing strong and weak areas of group and individual
achievement, of planning remedial work for students, and of evaluating
his methods of instruction and the effectiveness of teaching materials.

However, measurement devices are not limited to those that produce
only quantitative data. For example, the teacher who gives a voice test
to determine the student's assignment to a particular choral group is also

---

[1] Edward L. Thorndike, *Seventeenth Yearbook of the National Society for the
Study of Education*, Part 2 (1918); quoted in Charles Leonhard and Robert W. House,
Foundations and Principles of Music Education, 2d ed. (New York: McGraw-Hill
Book Company, Inc., 1972), p. 390.

measuring. Such a test will provide information about range, tessitura, voice quality, the ability to read, and tonal memory, instead of quantitative data; it is a measurement that provides the teacher with information used to evaluate the student's potential for membership in a given group.

In choosing and developing measuring devices to evaluate musical growth, a teacher must determine what aspect of music learning is to be measured, how it can best be measured, how to grade the results of the measurement, and how to evaluate the grade. Some areas of the music program, such as classes in theory, literature, or general music, suggest the use of tests in which the student's response involves verbal language and music symbols. In other areas, such as those involving performance, measuring techniques of the observation variety might be more suitable. The type of measurement used is sometimes reflected in the type of evaluative report that follows. Figure 15-1, for example, is a progress report based on an observation rather than a written test.

CHARACTERISTICS OF A GOOD TEST

Any test, whether it is standardized or teacher-made, should have the following interdependent attributes: (1) *validity*—the extent to which a particular test measures what it is supposed to measure; (2) *reliability*—the accuracy and consistency of a particular measuring procedure; and (3) *practicality*—such aspects of testing as ease of administration, scoring, interpretation of final results, and taking the test.

Validity

It is important to understand that validity refers to test results, not to the testing device itself. An instrumental teacher, for example,

might wish to measure the ability of a beginning student to sight-read music containing certain note values. He decides to use a test made up of a series of short excerpts taken from the beginner's method book—all of which the student has played several times before. The test results in this instance would have to be judged invalid according to the stated purpose of the test. Validity is not an "all-or-nothing" concept, however; it is generally considered in terms of various degrees—high, moderate, or low validity.

There are four types of validity commonly related to tests—content, predictive, concurrent, and construct. *Content validity* refers to how well the test measures both the content of the subject matter and the behaviors being dealt with. It is determined by simply comparing the material in the test to the items to be measured. *Predictive validity* refers to the extent that test results will predict performance at a later time. Naturally, to determine this, it is necessary to wait, measure the later performance, and then make a comparison of the test scores. *Concurrent validity* is concerned with how well test performance compares with another performance at approximately the same time. In this case, another form of measurement must be employed for the second performance, and its results are compared with the test scores. *Construct validity* concerns the extent to which test performance lends itself to psychological description, and requires experimentation to find out what influences test scores.

Reliability

Like validity, reliability refers to the *results* obtained with a measuring instrument and not to the instrument itself. There are several ways to determine a test's reliability, including the test-retest method, equivalent forms, the split-half method, and the *Kuder-Richardson Formula$_{21}$*.

FIGURE 15-1. Masconomet Regional School Music Department Instrumental Instruction Progress Report

---

This report is intended to give both parent and child a better understanding of his/her progress. If you have any questions, please feel free either to contact your child's private instructor or call me at school (telephone 887-2326).

Wayne L. Killian, Chairman
Music Department

NAME_____ Grade_____Date_____Instrument_____

Solo and Ensemble Compositions, Etudes, and Studies

a. Studying (title) _____Grade_____

b. Studying (title)_____Grade_____

c. Prepared (title)_____Grade_____

Tone Quality (actual musical sound)_____*Rhythm* (accuracy of note values)_____

Technique (technical skill): bowing_____fingering_____sticking_____range_____

sight-reading_____other_____

Articulation (use of the): tongue_____breath_____bow_____

Intonation (playing in tune)_____ *Dynamics* (controlled playing, loud, soft, and so on)_____

Interpretation: a. Phrasing (musical punctuation)_____

b. Style (legato, marcato, staccato, and so on)_____

Physical Appearance: a. Posture while playing_____

b. Embouchure (mouth muscles)_____

c. Hand and arm position_____

*Care of Equipment*_____

*Industry*_____ *Attitude*_____ *Attendance:* Lessons missed_____

Suggestions for Improvement:

Instructor's Signature_____

Key to Ratings

1. Excellent   2. Generally satisfactory   3. Poor, improvement needed   4. Generally unsatisfactory

---

318

Supportive Elements in a Music Education Program

The *test-retest method* involves the administration of the test to the same students twice within a short period of time. If there is a great variation in grades, then the reliability of the measuring instrument should be questioned. The major drawback of this method is the influence of memory and additional learning upon the results of the retest.

Equivalent forms involves the administration of two different but parallel versions of the same test to the same group. If the results of the two are quite similar, then the testing device can be considered reliable. The biggest problem in the use of equivalent forms is developing a suitable parallel exam.

The *split-half method* is the most practical means of determining reliability because the test need be administered only once. A comparison (correlation) is made between the scores of the odd-numbered items and the even-numbered items. Although this is a simpler procedure, it does tend to produce a lower estimate of reliability because the length of the test is reduced by half.

In using the *Kuder-Richardson Formula$_{21}$*, the results are less accurate. However, it does have the advantage of being relatively simple to compute as educational statistics go, and it involves the scores from only a single testing. A version of the formula is as follows:

$$KR_{21} = \frac{n}{n-1} \left[1 - \frac{M_t \left(1 - \frac{M_t}{n}\right)}{S_t^2} \right]$$

In this formula, KR_{21} is the estimated reliability; n is the number of test items; M_t is the mean (arithmetic average) of the test scores; and S_t is the standard deviation of the test scores.

A separate formula is used to compute the standard deviation:

$$\sigma = \sqrt{\frac{\Sigma x^2}{N}}$$

In this formula, the lowercase sigma represents the standard deviation; N now becomes the number of test cases (students taking the test); x is the difference between an individual's score and the group mean score; and the uppercase sigma means "the sum of." Thus, in using this formula, the teacher would follow these steps: (1) find the group mean score by dividing the sum of all the scores by the number of students; (2) compute the difference between the mean score and each individual score (x); (3) find the square of each of these differences; (4) figure the sum of the squares of the differences (Σ); (5) divide the sum arrived at in step 4 by the number of test cases (N); and (6) compute the square root of the figure arrived at in step 5. This last figure is the standard deviation, which can be used in the *Kuder-Richardson Fomula$_{21}$* to determine reliability.

Practicality

The third characteristic of a good test is the ease with which it can be used by both teacher and students. For example, the teacher who plans to give an essay-type test to two hundred general music students may find it a practical choice from the point of view of construction and administration. But its practicality is questionable when viewed in terms of scoring, grading, and the amount of non-music information and skill needed by the student to organize and express his thoughts in writing. In this instance, the teacher would probably be more successful if he were to devise a more objective type of test.

STANDARDIZED MUSIC TESTS

The purpose of standardized music tests, also referred to as norm-referenced tests, is to rank students. The test norms are structured so that half the students score above the norm and half below. It is impossible, then, for all students to attain high scores on a standardized test. In choosing the items for such a test, the test writer makes an assumption that while the items do not cover the whole area being tested, they are nevertheless representative; consequently, the teacher can conclude that the student who does well on the test has a broader knowledge and understanding of the area than what is actually covered by the test items. It is because of this assumption that data on the reliability, validity, and other procedures involved in standardization accompany all standardized tests. Norm-referenced tests are not designed to ascertain whether the student has attained the instructional objectives of a particular course. They are based on the curriculum and objectives common to many schools throughout the country; therefore, they are most useful in comparing an entire school system with other school systems or schools in one community with each other.

The two most common types of standardized measures are the achievement test, which attempts to measure what the student has learned, and the aptitude test, which attempts to measure what the student is capable of learning. Other standardized music tests have been developed to measure instrumental performance, musical attitude and interest, music appreciation, and even music taste. A listing of standardized tests of different types appears at the end of this chapter.[2]

[2] Detailed descriptions of standardized achievement, aptitude, and promotional tests are found in Richard Colwell, *The Evaluation of Music Teaching and Learning* (Englewood Cliffs, New Jersey: Prentice-Hall, Inc., 1970); Paul R. Lehman, *Tests and Measurements in Music* (Englewood Cliffs, New Jersey: Prentice-Hall, Inc., 1968); and William Whybrew, *Measurement and Evaluation in Music* (Dubuque: William C. Brown Company, Publishers, 1962).

Achievement Tests

Only two of the standardized music achievement tests available today are suitable for use in the secondary school: the Colwell *Music Achievement Tests* (1968–1969) and the *Knuth Achievement Tests in Music* (revised, 1966).

The Colwell *Music Achievement Tests* present a diversity of norm categories, making it possible to more closely relate and interpret test results in terms of the size of the community, geographic location, and whether music instruction is the responsibility of the classroom teacher or a music specialist. The author has stressed that the battery attempts to measure auditory-visual discrimination, which is only one phase of music achievement. Test items are based on the content of recent music-book series, and the tests seem to have a considerable degree of relevance to current music-education philosophy, objectives, and practice. The battery is easy to administer and to take because all directions are given on the test recording.

The *Knuth Achievement Tests* measure the student's ability to recognize and choose the last two measures of a phrase of music from a choice of four possibilities. The phrase, which is four measures long, is played on tape while the notation for the phrase beginning and four endings is presented on a filmstrip.

Neither the Colwell nor the Knuth tests is a comprehensive measure for evaluating a student's achievement, although each may be useful within its specific area. All the other achievement tests that are available suffer from antiquity and lack of revision. For example, the *Beach Music Test*, once commended by James Mursell as probably having considerable value,[3] was last revised in 1939; its

[3] See Oscar K. Buros, ed., *The Second Mental Measurement Yearbook* (Hyland Park, New Jersey: Gryphon Press, 1941), p. 174.

content has little relevancy to music education today. The *Kwalwasser-Ruch Test of Musical Accomplishment* looks quite impressive, with a high reliabiltiy coefficient of .95 (split-half), .97 based on the Spearman Brown Formula 12, and norms of standardization based upon the scores of 5415 students in grades four through twelve chosen from cities throughout the United States. However, investigation reveals that test content is based on recommendations made in the Music Supervisors' National Conference *Bulletin No. 1*, published in 1921, and it is more in keeping with the objectives and philosophy of music education of that period.

The authors of the *Diagnostic Tests of Achievement in Music* stated that the purpose of this battery is to help the teacher "(1) to determine each pupil's level of mastery of the basic theory and skills in music and (2) to locate the nature of the weaknesses or difficulties in music fundamentals for individuals as well as classes...."[4] However, since the *Diagnostic Tests* were published in 1950 and have never been revised, and since their content is based on four basic elementary music series that are no longer in print, their current usefulness is questionable. Two other well-known achievement tests that are still available but lack recent revision are the *Kwalwasser Test of Music Information and Appreciation* (1927) and the *Jones Music Recognition Test* (1949).

Aptitude Tests

There have also been efforts to devise standardized tests in order to predict a student's aptitude for music study. Many of

[4] T. L. Torgerson and M. Lila Kotick, *Diagnostic Tests of Achievement in Music*, Test Manual (Los Angeles: California Test Bureau, 1950).

these batteries attempt to measure an individual's sensory perception as it relates to such factors as tonal memory and the ability to discriminate pitch, quality, and durational and rhythmic differences in a clinical manner with no relationship to music per se. These include such tests as *The Seashore Measures of Musical Talent* (revised in 1960), the *Kwalwasser-Dykema Music Tests* (1930), and the *Kwalwasser Music Talent Test* (1953).

Other batteries, such as the Gordon *Musical Aptitude Profile* (1965), the Gaston *Test of Musicality* (revised in 1957), and the Wing *Standardised Tests of Musical Intelligence* (revised in 1961), present test items within a musical context. The latter three and the Bentley *Measures of Musical Ability* (1966), designed especially for the elementary level, should provide the music teacher with some indication of a student's musical aptitude.

In addition, many instrument manufacturers and distributors have created their own promotional aptitude tests, which are limited to those grades in which students are apt to begin studying a musical instrument (grades four through eight). Such tests are usually available free of charge or at a nominal cost. They have no norms or data related to validity or reliability. Sometimes they provide a section for information concerning such physical characteristics as jaw formation, size of lips, and other attributes that will help in determining specific instrumental suitability. Although this type of test is easy to administer and to take and is quite short, it must be recognized as a very limited prognostic device and its results evaluated accordingly.

Because research on music aptitude is still quite limited, teachers should concentrate their efforts on devising techniques to develop fully whatever musical potential a student has, rather than being overly concerned with the attributes of music aptitude. While recognizing the need for more intensive research in this area, Edwin Gordon has recommended that

> Until we discover otherwise, let us at least be content with the understanding that musical aptitude comprises various dimensions, that it is a product of innate potential and early environmental experiences, and that every student we teach can be expected to have at least some musical aptitude that will remain relatively stable somewhere after the middle elementary grades.[5]

Other Tests

Among other types of standardized tests, the best known is the *Watkins-Farnum Performance Scale* (1962), a device to measure student progress on a band instrument. The scale was originally devised by John Watkins for trumpet in 1942 and was later adapted for other band instruments. The student is required to play various graded melodies, rated from easy to very difficult. The scale can be used to measure individual growth, to test sight-reading ability, and to audition students for seat placement in the band. A scale to measure string performance has also been devised by Stephen Farnum.

CRITERION-REFERENCED TESTS

Criterion-referenced tests differ from standardized tests because the student's achievement is not being measured against a standardized group norm or even against the achievement of other students in the class. The criterion test is concerned with the individual's attainment of the instructional objectives of a particular course, unit, or lesson.

[5] Edwin Gordon, "The Source of Musical Aptitude," *Music Educators Journal*, 57:8 (April 1971), pp. 36–37.

The items used in such a test are directly related to these instructional objectives, and each item attempts to measure only what has been stated in a certain objective, nothing more. The student either answers the item 100 percent correctly or answers it wrong; the learner completely achieves the objective or does not. Evaluating the results of a criterion-referenced test, the teacher will know not only what the student has learned, but also what steps must be taken for remedial work, if necessary, and what steps must be taken to organize instruction so that the student can continue learning.

Developing good test items begins with writing instructional objectives that state precisely what behaviors are expected of the learner as a result of a segment of instruction. Then the teacher must be certain that the item asks the student to accomplish a task exactly as stated in the objective and that the task is performed under the condition specified in the objective. Moreover, the teacher must try to make each item interesting, use vocabulary that is commensurate with the student's reading ability, and test *only* what has been stated in the objectives. An application of these organizing principles is demonstrated in Figure 15-2.

CONSTRUCTING TESTS

Most teachers devise tests to measure cognitive learning, which is the least difficult to describe in behavioral terms and the least difficult to teach and evaluate. However, instruments can and should be prepared to measure psychomotor and affective course objectives as well. Although the three areas of learning tend to overlap in the teaching process, there are times when they must be separated for evaluative purposes.

FIGURE 15-2. Developing a Criterion-Referenced Test Item from an
Instructional Objective

Instructional Objective: Given a list of five contemporary composers' names and a list of seven contemporary compositions, the student will match the number preceding each composer's name with the title of that composer's composition. All five names must be matched properly with titles for the student's answer to be considered correct.
Test Item: Place the number preceding each composer's name in Column A next to the title of that composer's composition in Column B.

Column A—Composers
1. Bartók
2. Stravinsky
3. Ravel
4. Busoni
5. Křenek

Column B—Compositions
_____ *Daphnis et Chloé*
_____ *Fantasia Contrappuntistica*
_____ *Wozzeck*
_____ *Mathis der Maler*
_____ *Der Schatzgräbe*
_____ *Le Sacre du Printemps*
_____ *Mikrokosmos*

Cognitive Learning

Both subjective and objective teacher-made tests are used in measuring and evaluating cognitive learning. Subjective tests permit the student some latitude in answering questions; they consist of either written essays or oral recitation. Objective tests, which allow students no latitude because answers are limited to specific responses that are deemed right, include matching, true-and-false, multiple-choice, and completion tests.

Essay tests are generally recommended when classes are small in number, when there is considerably more time to correct the exam than to prepare it, when organizational skill and writing ability are valued but weighed only in terms of accuracy of music description, when the test is not to be used again, and when the teacher has the ability to evaluate written work objectively. Objective tests are used most successfully when groups are large, the test is prepared for reuse, test results must be reported quickly, a large amount of factual learning is to be measured, and impartiality in evaluation is desired.

In constructing either a subjective or objective test, the teacher can follow a series of steps used by professional test-makers:

1. Outline the music learnings to be measured by a particular test. These will be identified from the knowledge, understanding, and skills specified in the objectives for the class.
2. Define the test and unit objectives in terms of specific *observable* and *measurable* behaviors, the type of test to be used to demonstrate the desired behaviors, and the criteria to be used to identify acceptable performance.
3. Prepare a "table of specifications" of desired learning outcomes in terms of their relative weight and importance.

An example of the application of these steps is given in Table 15-1.

In the following pages, the various types of subjective and objective tests are related to

Table 15-1. EXAMPLE OF PROCEDURE FOR DESIGNING A TEST

1. *Desired learning outcomes related to a unit on nonharmonic tones.*

a. The student understands that nonharmonic tones are those that are not found in the basic chord but are sounded simultaneously with the chord to form a dissonance. Nonharmonic tones contribute to melodic flow, enrich music texture, and can create harmonic tension.

b. The student understands that nonharmonic tones are of two types:

–those that are decorative in nature and occur on weak beats or weak parts of beats (passing tones, auxiliary tones, anticipations, escape tones).
–those that create harmonic tension by displacing chord tones (appoggiaturas, suspensions, accented passing or auxiliary tones, and pedalpoints).

c. The student understands that passing tones are used in stepwise motion between one chord tone and the next above or below; has the ability to identify passing tones in music analysis; and has the skill to use them in his own compositions.
(and so on)

2. *Behaviors to be measured—type of testing device—criteria for acceptable performance.*

a. Behaviors

–The student will identify through music analysis all the nonharmonic tones studied in this unit.
–The student will use, with skill and understanding, all the nonharmonic tones studied in this unit in his own compositions.

b. Type of Test

–Part I: Matching music examples containing various nonharmonic tones with the following list: accented passing tone, unaccented passing tone, accented auxiliary tone, unaccented auxiliary tone, double unaccented passing tone, suspension, appoggiatura, anticipation, escape tone, pedalpoint, cambiata, échapée. Ten music examples will be matched to twelve possible choices.

–Part II: An original eight-measure composition using at least eight of the nonharmonic tones listed in Part I.

c. Criteria for Passing Test

–Minimum standard: six correct responses in each part.

3. *Table of specifications.*

a. Part I: Understanding of and ability to identify appoggiatura, accented passing tone, escape tone, suspension, anticipation, cambiata, unaccented auxiliary tone, échapée, pedalpoint, and accented auxiliary tone. Each correct answer receives two points for a total of 20.

b. Part II: Skill in using at least eight of the twelve listed nonharmonic tones in a composition. Four points for each correct use; one point deducted for each instance of awkward voice leading, incorrect doubling, and so on. Total possible score for Part II—48 points.

324

Supportive Elements in a Music Education Program

Table 15-2. BLOOM'S TAXONOMY OF COGNITIVE OBJECTIVES[6]

SIMPLE   1.00 Knowledge
                      1.10 Knowledge of Specifics
                            1.11 Knowledge of Terminology
                            1.12 Knowledge of Specific Facts
                      1.20 Knowledge of Ways and Means of Dealing with Specifics
                            1.21 Knowledge of Conventions
                            1.22 Knowledge of Trends and Sequences
                            1.23 Knowledge of Classifications and Categories
                            1.24 Knowledge of Criteria
                            1.25 Knowledge of Methodology
                      1.30 Knowledge of the Universals and Abstractions in a Field
                            1.31 Knowledge of Principles and Generalizations
                            1.32 Knowledge of Theories and Structures
       2.00 Comprehension
                      2.10 Translation
                      2.20 Interpretation
                      2.30 Extrapolation
       3.00 Application
       4.00 Analysis
                      4.10 Analysis of Elements
                      4.20 Analysis of Relationships
                      4.30 Analysis of Organizational Principles
       5.00 Synthesis
                      5.10 Production of a Unique Communication
                      5.20 Production of a Plan, or Proposed Set of Operations
                      5.30 Derivation of a Set of Abstract Relations
       6.00 Evaluation
                      6.10 Judgments in Terms of Internal Evidence
COMPLEX   6.20 Judgments in Terms of External Criteria

Bloom's taxonomy of cognitive objectives, as presented in Table 15-2.

Constructing Subjective Tests

The most commonly used subjective testing device is the essay exam. Quite often, teachers believe that this type of test must be composed of just one, two, or perhaps three questions of a broad nature that require students to write at length. It is possible, however, to construct the test with short-answer questions, thus increasing the number of items that can be included and giving students the advantage of writing briefer, more pointed answers. Table 15-3 illustrates a number of types of essay questions, based on the categorization of W. S. Monroe and R. E. Carter[7] and related to Bloom's cognitive taxonomy.

[6] From Benjamin S. Bloom et al., eds., *Taxonomy of Educational Objectives: The Classification of Educational Goals. Handbook I: Cognitive Domain* (New York: Longman Inc., 1956). Copyright © 1956 by Longman Inc. Reprinted by permission of Longman.

[7] See W. S. Monroe and R. E. Carter, "The Use of Different Types of Thought Questions in Secondary Schools and Their Relative Difficulty for Students," *University of Illinois Bulletin*, vol. 20, no. 34, *Bureau of Educational Research Bulletin No. 14* (Urbana: The University of Illinois, 1923).

Table 15-3. TYPES OF ESSAY QUESTIONS

1. *Selective recall:*
   What was the musical relationship between Mozart and Haydn? (1.12 Knowledge of Specific Facts)

2. *Evaluative recall:*
   In what way did the music of the Beatles influence the development of popular music? (1.22 Knowledge of Trends and Sequences)

3. *Comparison of two things on a designated basis:*
   Compare the two folksongs "Down in the Valley" and "Sourwood Mountain" in terms of rhythmic, melodic, and harmonic structure. (4.10 Analysis of Elements)

4. *Comparison of two things on a general basis:*
   Compare simple ternary form and compound ternary form. (1.21 Knowledge of Conventions and 2.10 Translation)

5. *Decision for or against:*
   Which of the following voicings is best for string orchestra? Why? (1.21 Knowledge of Conventions)

6. *Causes or effects:*
   Give three reasons why it is worthwhile to study music of the past. (1.24 Knowledge of Criteria)

7. *Explanation of the use or exact meaning of some phrase or passage:*
   Explain what is meant by the term "aleatoric music." (1.22 Knowledge of Trends and Sequences)

8. *Summarization:*
   Summarize in not more than one page what you have learned about the guitar. (1.12 Knowledge of Specific Facts)

9. *Analysis:*
   Select three currently popular records and define the characteristics that you believe have made them popular. (4.10 Analysis of Elements)

10. *Statement of relationships:*
    How does contrary motion in the IV-V progression avoid one of the cardinal sins of traditional harmony? Explain and illustrate with a music example. (1.21 Knowledge of Conventions)

11. *Illustration by example of principles, procedures, and so on:*
    Write an original sixteen-measure melody that shows the development of a three-tone motivic cell. Explain the techniques used to achieve variety. (3.00 Application)

12. *Classification:*
    The koto, shamisen, and biwa are instruments indigenous to what country? (1.23 Knowledge of Classifications and Categories)

13. *Application of rules or principles to new situations:*
    Write a melodic line to the following given bass line. Be sure to follow established rules for chord connection. Explain these rules. (1.21 Knowledge of Conventions and 3:00 Application)

14. *Discussion:*
    Why is breath control such an important factor in learning to sing or to play a wind instrument? (1.31 Knowledge of Principles and Generalizations)

326

15. *Statement of aims of author (composer) in selecting and organizing material:*
Why does your music-history book include so much information pertaining to political and social conditions? (1.30 Knowledge of the Universals and Abstractions in a Field)

16. *Criticism:*
Criticize, favorably or unfavorably, the aleatoric music heard in class. (6.10 Judgments in Terms of Internal Evidence)

17. *Outline:*
Outline, with examples, the techniques used in serial music. Use no more than two pages. (1.25 Knowledge of Methodology and 1.31 Knowledge of Principles and Generalizations)

18. *Reorganization of facts:*
Trace the general changes in popular music during the past twenty years. (1.22 Knowledge of Trends and Sequences)

19. *Formulation of new questions and problems:*
What obstacles prevent the immediate acceptance of experimental contemporary music? (1.31 Knowledge of Principles and Generalizations and 2.30 Extrapolation)

20. *Suggestion of new methods of procedure:*
How would you rewrite the following eight-measure SATB arrangement in a pianistic style? Explain and illustrate with a music example. (1.25 Knowledge of Methodology and 3.00 Application)

The reliability of the measurement and evaluation obtained from an essay test is heavily dependent on the teacher's skill in grading. A number of scientific studies have shown that even under the most ideal grading situations, an exam corrected by the same examiner on two separate occasions is likely to result in divergent grades, as will the same exam corrected by two experts. However, the teacher can take the following precautions in grading an essay test to achieve greater reliability.

1. Before correcting the test, prepare an ideal answer and scoring-key chart, as shown in the following example:

Question: How is sound produced on the various instruments of the woodwind family? (Total value: 9 points)
Answers should include:

    (a) The clarinets by a single reed (1 point).
    (b) The saxophones by a single reed (1 point).
    (c) The bassoon, oboe, and English horn by double reeds (3 points).
    (d) The flute and piccolo do not have a reed, and sound is produced by blowing a stream of air across the mouth-hole or embouchure (2 points).
    (e) Student's ability for creative organization in answering the question (2 points).

2. In the actual scoring, grade the same question on *all* papers at the same time. In this way comparisons can be made, and when there is any doubt the answer and scoring key can be checked.

3. Whenever possible, the names of the students should be concealed during the grading. This practice avoids what is called the "halo bias," where the teacher is influenced by his opinion of the person whose paper is being rated rather than by the answer given. This is most apt to happen when the papers of the best students in the class are corrected first.

On occasion the teacher must grade an essay test that is not of the question–answer variety. A term report is an example. Assigning grades to such papers is difficult, but the teacher can increase his objectivity by adopting a rank-rating system. First, he reads each paper and rates it as excellent, good, or fair, or by any other type of categorization. Next, he re-reads all the excellent papers and places them in rank order from the strongest to the weakest; the same procedure is followed in the other categories as well. When all papers have been ranked, each is numbered—"1" for the best, and so on. Then the teacher decides what rank numbers are to receive a specific numerical or letter grade. A natural objection to this approach is, of course, that all the papers are being judged on the same basis. This can be a problem if the topics of the reports differ. It is even more of a problem, and a critical one, if the teacher wants to consider each report in terms of individual student potential and resourcefulness. Thus, objectivity in grading is not necessary ideal.

It must be remembered that in attempting to be objective, the teacher must often build in some degree of subjective response. This is especially true when the exam asks the student to express his own ideas or interpretations of factual data rather than to cite facts alone. In this case the student's answer must be weighed in terms of his own abilities and potential rather than in terms of factual knowledge alone.

Constructing Objective Tests

Although designing an objective test is more time consuming, the objective test has two definite advantages. First, a minimum amount of writing is required of the student since his answer generally consists of a word, letter, number, or some type of symbol. Second, the time needed for correcting and grading is greatly reduced because there is only one correct answer for each question.

One form of objective test is the *matching test*, which consists of two lists of words, phrases, or music fragments that must be paired. An example is given in Figure 15-3. The matching test is not advisable when the teacher wants to measure and evaluate a student's ability to understand specific concepts or draw conclusions from a given set of ideas. It is best used to test skill and ability to recognize, identify, and classify facts, terms, and music techniques. As with all objective measuring devices, this type of test provides the student with an opportunity for guessing. However, it is a valid device and should be used when it can do the particular job required.

The *completion test* is a type that requires the student to recall and supply a missing word, date, or phrase in order to complete a statement. Figure 15-4 shows a segment of such a test. In constructing a completion test, certain practices should be avoided:

1. The initial statement should not give any hint of the correct answer. (For example: "Papageno is a character in Mozart's opera *The Magic* ———.")
2. The answer should not be suggested by a specific number (or length) of lines in the answer blank. (For example: "Marguerite and Mephistopheles are characters in the opera The Damnation of Faust.")
3. The statement should not be constructed so that more than one correct answer is possible. (For example: "The character Faust appears in an opera written by ———.")
4. The correct answer for one item should not be provided by including it as part of another item. (For example: "The opera *Carmen* was composed by ———." And later: "Georges Bizet, the composer of *Carmen,* was born in ———.")

FIGURE 15-3. Matching Test

Name_____ Date_____Test Grade_____

Test Directions: Match the instruments in Column A with the types of music listed in Column B. Write your answers on the blank lines to the right of Column B. For example, look at the first item in Column A and then find the type of music in Column B that relates *most closely* to that instrument. Write number "1" next to the answer you choose. Follow the same procedure for the other items. Do not relate any one instrument to more than one type of music; it is important to select the answer that corresponds *most closely*. If you have any questions, ask the teacher.

Column A—Instruments	*Column B—Types of Music*	
1. piano	Indian music	_____
2. koto	Australian aboriginal music	_____
3. bagpipes	Appalachian folk music	_____
4. electric guitar	ragtime	_____
5. mbira	Hungarian folk music	_____
6. tabla	jazz	_____
7. synthesizer	Russian folk music	_____
8. saxophone	rock music	_____
9. didjeridu	Spanish folk music	_____
10. balalaika	Japanese music	_____
	African music	_____
	electronic music	_____

(Note: Following Bloom's taxonomy of cognitive objectives, this test is concerned with measuring 1.10 Knowledge of Specifics—that is, the recall of terminology and specific facts.)

FIGURE 15-4. Completion Test

Test Directions: Complete the following statements by filling in a word or words on each blank at the right of the page.

1. At the beginning of the carol "Joy to the World," the melody descends by _____

2. At the beginning of the symphony* we heard in class, Mozart wrote three tones in a pattern that he used again and again to develop his music further. These notes are referred to as _____

3. The melody of "Tonal Experiment No. 1" does not relate to any key center. This melody is _____

4. At the beginning of "The Star-Spangled Banner," the melody moves by _____

5. The first two phrases of Bach's *Two-Part Invention No. 5,** which we heard in class, are closely related. This is called _____

(and so on)

* During the test, the teacher might play these opening passages again for aural identification of the answers.

(Note: Following Bloom's taxonomy of cognitive objectives, these items are concerned with measuring 2.00 Comprehension, and specifically 2.10 Translation.)

Perhaps the most widely used type of objective test is the *true–false test*. In this type, complete statements are given, and each item is either entirely true or entirely false. The student indicates his answer by marking T or a plus sign (+) beside items he believes are true, and F or a minus sign (−) beside those he considers false. Some authorities recommend that the true–false exam have at least seventy-five or eighty test items in order to have a reasonable degree of validity and reliability. The shortcoming of this kind of test is that it allows the student to guess. However, there is a formula that is often used to correct for guessing and to obtain a more accurate measure:

$$R \text{ (number right)} - W \text{ (number wrong)} = CS \text{ (corrected score)}$$

If, for example, a student takes a 100-item test, and answers 85 correctly and 10 incorrectly, his corrected score would be 75; unanswered items are not included in determining the corrected score. When this formula is used, it must be made clear to the students at the outset that they should answer a question *only* if they are sure of the answer. In that case, the student who answered 85 items correctly because he knew them, without guessing, and did not attempt any others would actually score 85. The guesser, on the other hand, who answered 85 items correctly, some by chance, and missed another 10 by guessing, would score a final 75. If this is not understood by the students when they begin the test, some students will be penalized when they should not be.

In constructing a true–false test, the teacher should consider the following points:

1. Statements should not be taken verbatim from the textbook. Rather, concepts should be presented in a new setting.
2. Statements should be short and clear, and each should deal with only one concept.

3. Words such as "sometimes" or "usually" should be avoided. Students often recognize the use of qualifying words as indicators of false statements.
4. Test items should be constructed so that they do not provide answers to other items in the same test.
5. False test items should be written to appear probable through the use of familiar terminology.

There are several variations on the true–false type of test. For example, students may be given the choice of three possible answers —true (+), false (−), and partly true (0). Other variations include underlining the part of the statement that is false, and rewriting false statements to make them true. Although these variations do not change the basic nature of the test, they do add to the complexity of answering, correcting, and grading.

In a *multiple-choice test*, items are constructed with two parts—an introduction and a conclusion, as shown in Figure 15-5. A good multiple-choice item usually includes five optional responses. Thus, the student has one chance in five of guessing the correct answer. When it is impossible to find five choices for an item, it is better to use only four than to add one that is easily classified as incorrect. Naturally, as the number of choices is reduced, the chance for the student to guess the right answer is increased. However, an increase in the number of choices beyond five, according to scientific data, does not increase the validity and reliability to any significant degree.

One of the considerations in scoring this kind of an exam is how guessing is going to be treated. A score consisting of the number of right answers might be satisfactory if the student has enough time to answer all the items; in such instances, the teacher may even encourage the students to guess if they are not sure of certain answers. However, such a procedure has been criticized as pedagog-

FIGURE 15-5. Multiple-Choice Test

Test Directions: On the line to the right of each statement, mark the letter of the answer that *best* completes the statement.

1. The *Rite of Spring* was composed by } Introduction   _____

    a. Prokofiev

    b. Stravinsky

    c. Milhaud   Conclusion

    d. Ravel

    e. Delius

2. Debussy's music was called   _____

    a. dodecaphonic

    b. neoclassical

    c. romantic

    d. impressionistic

    e. gebrauchmusik

(Note: Following Bloom's taxonomy of cognitive objectives, these test items are concerned with measuring 1.10 Knowledge of Specifics.)

---

ically unsatisfactory because it provides practice in guessing errors. When a test must be completed quickly, students will attempt only those items for which they feel reasonably sure they know the correct answers. In this case, or if the teacher wants to discourage guessing, a penalty must be assigned to incorrect answers. Therefore, the following correction formula may be used in scoring:

$$R - \frac{W}{N-1} = \text{Corrected Score}$$

The R represents the number of right responses, W the number of wrong choices, and N the total number of choices for each question. The formula is not commonly used because it is easier just to count the correct answers. In addition, it is of less value as the number of choices in the conclusion increases. When there are fewer than four choices, however, it is strongly recommended that the formula be employed.

The teacher should be mindful of several guidelines in the preparation of a multiple-choice test:

1. Each item should test relevant, important material. Avoid writing catch items that involve unimportant material or material that has received little attention in class.

2. The choices in the conclusion should be plausible and not obviously incorrect. An example of a poor test item of this sort would be: "Q—The opera *Lohengrin* was written by _____. A—(a) Richard Rodgers; (b) Burt Bacharach; (c) Richard Wagner; (d) Giuseppe Verdi; (e) Andy Williams."

3. All conclusions should be equal in length since there is a tendency on the part of students to choose responses that are either longer or shorter than the others.

4. The grammatical construction of the introduction ought not to give away the right conclusion, as it does in this exam-

ple: "Q—The composer Ralph Vaughan Williams was *an* _____. A—(a) German; (b) Canadian; (c) South African; (d) Englishman; (e) Scotsman."

5. The choices offered should all represent the same category. In the following example, the choices mix cities, countries, and continents, and more than one in this case can be considered right: "Q—Pierre Boulez is a major contemporary composer-conductor in _____. A—(a) France; (b) New York; (c) Europe; (d) the United States; (e) England."

6. Specific test directions should be included with each exam in order that students know exactly what must be done. Two examples are given in Figure 15-6.

Some tests are easier to correct than others. Regardless of the type of test involved, though, it should be corrected immediately and returned to the students for class discussion. This practice will reinforce the material that was familiar and will give the students (and the teacher) an opportunity to discuss questions they failed to answer.

Finally, in the process of determining student progress, the teacher should include some type of measure that will give the student the opportunity for self-evaluation. Much too often, the student is the last person to be considered in the evaluative process. It is important to know how the student feels about his own progress. Quite possibly, the student can help the teacher to diagnose his problems. However, this type of evaluation must go beyond the point of the teacher asking, "What's your problem?" and the student being expected to verbalize about his problem to the satisfaction of both parties. A better approach would be to prepare a checklist for a particular class or for a unit of study. The student could then use this as a guide in evaluating his own progress.

Psychomotor Learning

Although music performance does require cognitive processes, the combination of physical and mental processes involved is categorized as psychomotor learning. The results of psychomotor learning can be evaluated in terms of group or individual performance.

There are several ways of evaluating group performance skills. The group can participate in a music festival where adjudicators make a judgment according to prescribed criteria, or the teacher may ask qualified colleagues to attend a concert performance by his group and then to submit evaluations. Occasionally, an exchange concert may be arranged with a comparable group in a nearby community, permitting the students themselves to make a comparative evaluation; in such a case, a tape recording of the concert could be made for a follow-up listening session. Another means is to invite guest conductors to rehearse the group, to reinforce the teacher's evaluation or to point out problems that the teacher has missed. Small-group or sectional rehearsals may also be employed to allow the teacher to listen more critically and on a more individual basis for evaluative purposes. A periodic taping of rehearsals can also be of value, both for immediate analysis and for comparison over a period of time.

To evaluate psychomotor skills of individual students, checklists and rating scales are most useful (and they can also be used for group evaluation). For example, the Music Educators National Conference publishes adjudication forms for judging bands, orchestras, choruses, and small ensembles, including stage bands and barbershop quartets. These may be used on an individual or group basis by the teacher, an outside adjudicator, or by the students themselves. Each form includes space for comments and a numerical or letter grade in such categories as tone, intonation,

FIGURE 15-6. Test Directions

Directions: You will be shown ten slides of different music examples. The entire set of ten will be repeated twice. The specific portion of each example for consideration will appear in a box on the slide. Check the list below and put the slide number on the line next to the best answer.

_____covered octaves   _____pedaltone

_____crossed parts   _____double third
                                            (major triad)
_____suspension
                                           _____modal interchange
_____accented passing tone

_____unaccented auxiliary tone   _____appoggiatura

_____parallel fifths   _____secondary dominant

_____anticipation   _____échapée

_____half cadence   _____passing $^6_4$ chord

(Note: Following Bloom's taxonomy of cognitive objectives, this test is concerned with measuring 4.10 Analysis of Elements.)

Directions: Each of the music terms below is followed by four definitions, of which only one is entirely right. Select the best answer by writing its *letter* on the line to the left of the term.

_____   1. Enharmonic
              a. Being consonant with other tones in the chord.
              b. Pertaining to two or more notes sounded simultaneously.
              c. Having the same pitch as another note written differently.
              d. Referring to the sound of a high note on the violin.

_____   2. Dominant
              a. The fifth step of a diatonic scale.
              b. The first or primary step of a diatonic scale.
              c. The fourth step of a diatonic scale.
              d. The leading tone of a diatonic scale.

_____   3. Tritone
              a. The third step of a diatonic scale.
              b. An interval of a major ninth.
              c. A chord consisting of three tones.
              d. An interval of an augmented fourth.

(Note: Following Bloom's taxonomy of cognitive objectives, these test items are concerned with measuring 1.11 Knowledge of Terminology.)

diction, technique, balance, interpretation, and musical effect.

A teacher-made checklist can also be designed. Figure 15-7 illustrates such a form for evaluating vocal performance. Rating scales, which take somewhat longer for the teacher to develop, are intended to measure a single element of performance. For example, a rating scale to measure proficiency in instrumental sight-reading could be organized as shown in Figure 15-8.

Affective Learning

Affective learning is neither as observable nor as measurable as learning in the cognitive and psychomotor domains. Although it is possible to organize a series of lessons to develop an understanding of, say, sonata form (cognitive domain), or to prepare a series of exercises to improve a student's ability to play trumpet slurs (psychomotor domain), and then to evolve instruments for measuring what has been learned, the development of a particular affective response cannot be precisely planned and gauged. Nevertheless, the teacher needs to obtain some idea of changes in music values, attitudes, and appreciation on the part of his students.

Learning in the affective domain is influenced by the total music experience and is interrelated with learning in the other domains. Writing of this interrelationship, Rich-

FIGURE 15-7. Vocal Performance Checklist

Rating	Breath Control	Tone Quality	Intonation	Rhythmic Precision	Pronun-ciation	Enunci-ation	Phrasing	Tempo	General Interpretation
(High) 9									
8									
7									
6									
5									
4									
3									
2									
1									
(Low) 0									

FIGURE 15-8. Sight-Reading Rating Scale

Item	Scale									
Pitch Accuracy	9	8	7	6	5	4	3	2	1	0
Rhythmic Accuracy	9	8	7	6	5	4	3	2	1	0
Intonation	9	8	7	6	5	4	3	2	1	0
Steady Tempo	9	8	7	6	5	4	3	2	1	0
Articulation	9	8	7	6	5	4	3	2	1	0
Interpretation	9	8	7	6	5	4	3	2	1	0

or

Item	Excellent	Good	Fair	Poor
Pitch Accuracy				
Rhythmic Accuracy				
Intonation				
Etc.				

ard Colwell has emphasized the importance of cognitive factors in evaluating affective learning:

> In any learning situation involving musical response, an overlapping of the cognitive and the affective is necessitated by the demands of verbalization; to put into words something about music means thinking about it, using terms accurately and with understanding. . . . The fact that cognition is a legitimate part of the affective response to music helps simplify the problems of measuring affective response. Evaluation of attitudes and values, though intricate, is possible because many aspects ·can be verbalized, put into specific statements, and clearly pointed out by teacher or student.[8]

[8] Richard Colwell, *The Evaluation of Music Teaching and Learning* (Englewood Cliffs, New Jersey: Prentice-Hall, Inc., 1970), p. 129.

The use of a *self-report inventory* is one way for the teacher to determine a student's preference for a particular type of music, type of course, or certain performers, or his attitude toward classical music, membership in a choral organization, his band director's techniques, and so on. An *interest inventory* is another device used to determine student preference. The simplest form of such an inventory would be to give the students a list of compositions performed or listened to during the school year and to ask them to rank them in order of preference. This would provide the teacher with some idea of how the students feel about the music they have studied, and some generalizations might be made on this basis.

The *attitude scale* is another measuring device used in the affective domain. Figure 15-9 presents six statements from a thirty-

335
Measurement and Evaluation

FIGURE 15-9. Attitude Scale

Name _____ Date _____ Score _____

The purpose of this attitude scale is to determine how you feel about school music classes. Please make your judgments on the basis of *what these classes mean to you.* Do not worry or puzzle over each item. It is your immediate reaction and response that we want. On the other hand, do not be careless; we want your true impression. Be honest.

Directions

Read the statement and then decide whether you STRONGLY AGREE or AGREE or DISAGREE or STRONGLY DISAGREE with the statement; put an "X" in the block above your choice. For example, if you strongly agree with the following statement, your answer would go into the first block.

Statement: There is not enough music in the world.

X			
Strongly Agree	Agree	Disagree	Strongly Disagree
4	3	2	1

You are now ready to begin. Be sure to read each statement carefully.

1. I think music classes are interesting.

Strongly Agree	Agree	Disagree	Strongly Disagree
4	3	2	1

2. The material covered in the music class is a challenge to me.

Strongly Agree	Agree	Disagree	Strongly Disagree
4	3	2	1

3. Music classes are scheduled too often.

Strongly Agree	Agree	Disagree	Strongly Disagree
1	2	3	4

4. I consider myself better off for having studied music.

Strongly Agree	Agree	Disagree	Strongly Disagree
4	3	2	1

5. I always study the same thing in the music class.

Strongly Agree	Agree	Disagree	Strongly Disagree
1	2	3	4

6. Music classes deal with music I don't care about.

Strongly Agree	Agree	Disagree	Strongly Disagree
1	2	3	4

statement attitude scale used with seventh-grade general music students.[9] To establish the reliability of the scale, the test-retest method was employed with a population of ninety-three subjects. When the scores were compared using the Pearson Product Moment Correlation Formula, r was .99, indicating a high degree of reliability. The suitability of items in the scale was determined by means of a Criterion of Internal Consistency.[10] Fifty percent of the statements in the attitude scale were stated positively (statements 1, 2, and 4), and the others were stated negatively (statements 3, 5, and 6). Scoring this type of measure is simple because the individual's score is the sum of the points received for each item.

Because these rating devices are quite subjective, there is always a question of the reliability and validity of the data obtained. Even with the care taken in the development of an attitude scale, there are factors over which the teacher has no control—for example, (1) the rater's unwillingness to answer the questions honestly, (2) the rater's inability to make a valid judgment even when honestly trying, and (3) the teacher's bias in wording the statements in such a way that the outcome can be predicted before the rating is completed.

The results obtained from teacher-made measuring devices, for the affective domain, can be questionable and misleading. Therefore, the teacher must constantly scrutinize these devices and make revisions that will provide the most accurate measurement and data.

[9] Alphonse M. Tatarunis, *The Effect of Two Teaching Methods Utilizing Popular Music on the Ability of Seventh Grade Students to Perceive Aurally and Identify Musical Concepts* (unpublished doctoral dissertation, Boston University, 1975), pp. 242–243.

[10] See Tatarunis, *op. cit.*, p. 124.

GRADING PRACTICES

Determining and assigning grades is one of the most difficult, frustrating tasks that faces a music teacher. It becomes especially frustrating when the teacher realizes that no matter what system of grading is adopted, it is inadequate to truly evaluate what a student has accomplished in a music class.

A variety of grading practices are used. Some schools still adhere to the letter-grade (A, B, C, D, F) or numerical (100, 95, 75, and so on) approach that actually gives parents little information because it ranks a student on a comparative basis within an established, absolute grading scale. No reasons are given if the student is labeled a "failure"; no suggestions are offered for improvement; no indication is made of whether the student is working to capacity. A variation on this system provides parents with a little more information on the student's progress. The variation uses a combination of letters and numbers for grading. Achievement (again marked as a comparative measure) is indicated by a letter: A—excellent; B—above average; C—average; D—below average; F—failing; and I—incomplete. Conduct and effort are each indicated by a number: 1—good or excellent; 2—satisfactory; 3—improvement needed; and 4—unsatisfactory. Thus, the mark "B-2-1" would mean that a student's achievement is above average, that his conduct is satisfactory, and that his effort is excellent.

Other schools have abandoned the comparative marking system and have adopted a means of showing a student's growth according to his presumed individual potential. The so-called S-I-U system is generally used in these schools. The letter S (satisfactory) indicates that a student is progressing as well as can be expected; an I means the student is showing improvement; a U (unsatisfactory) or N (improvement needed) indicates that progress is not as great as expected. Sometimes an

O (outstanding) or H (honors) is used when a teacher wants to give special praise or recognition. A system similar to S-I-U uses numerals: 1—rapid progress; 2—satisfactory progress; 3—acceptable progress; 4—unsatisfactory or no progress. This type of marking may also be supplemented by a teacher's narrative report that provides more detailed information on the student's progress.

Another procedure that abandons the comparative marking system or any form of grading is the parent-teacher conference (which also includes students in some instances). A conference allows a detailed discussion of a student's achievement, social adjustment, and so on, and the influence of the school and home on his progress. Achievement is discussed and evaluated in terms of the student's growth since the last conference as it relates to his ability, and not in terms of an arbitrary class standard that says that a student receiving an "A" is making the best progress. The success of a parent-teacher conference depends on the teacher's skill in presenting pertinent information, creating an atmosphere conducive to open discussion, and allowing parents the opportunity to participate actively in the meeting, to question, to comment, and to evaluate along with the teacher. This type of conference is particularly worthwhile for the instrumental teacher who works with beginning students for it provides a chance to discuss the student's progress, attitude, and interest before the parents have to make a decision on purchasing an instrument.

In any of these systems of evaluating, grading, and reporting on a student's work, there is a great danger of the teacher falling into a testing trap caused by the fallacies of a marking system. It is not uncommon, for example, for teachers to give tests at regular intervals simply because the administration requires grades that fall into an established pattern. When this occurs, tests are given because tests are required, not because the tests serve some useful purpose in promoting the learning experience. Testing–grading practices can actually hinder learning if they are misused. John Holt, a prominent educator who is in favor of eliminating tests rather than improving them, has written:

> To the public—and to ourselves—we teachers say that we test children to find out what they have learned, so that we can better know how to help them to learn more. This is about 95 percent untrue. There are two main reasons that we test children: the first is to threaten them into doing what we want done, and the second is to give us a basis for handing out the rewards and penalties on which the educational system—like all coercive systems—must operate. The threat of a test makes students do their assignments; the outcome of the test enables us to reward those who seem to do it best. The economy of the school, like that of most societies, operates on greed and fear. Tests arouse the fear and satisfy the greed.[11]

Elsewhere, Holt has suggested that if one must give grades, it should be done as seldom, as privately, and as leniently as possible:

> . . . any tests that [are] not a personal matter between the learner and someone helping him learn, but [are] given instead to grade and label students for someone else's purposes (employers, colleges, evaluators of schools, administrators, anxious parents, etc.), [are] illegitimate and harmful.[12]

Unfortunately, the music teacher does not make the final decision "to mark or not to mark." This is done by the administration, and the teacher is faced with the problem of organizing his measurement-evaluation pro-

[11] John Holt, *The Underachieving School* (New York: Pitman Publishing Corporation, 1969), p. 55.

[12] From the book *What Do I Do Monday?* by John Holt. Copyright © 1970 by John Holt. Published by Elsevier-Dutton and used with their permission, p. 264.

gram to be compatible with the administrative pattern and to be as accurate and fair as possible to his students. Therefore, he should give as few tests as possible and attempt to give them in a manner that does not make a student feel that a judge and jury are waiting to hand down a verdict and determine his fate. Many students take a test with the feeling that they are their own worse witnesses—that the teacher is acting out the role of a prosecuting attorney, waiting for the slip in the defendant's testimony that will condemn him. It is difficult for the individual teacher to develop a nondefensive climate for his students because of tradition and of practices they are subjected to in other classrooms. Nevertheless, attempts can be made and *can* be successful. If, for example, the teacher employs a systems approach to instruction, it is natural to administer a pretest, prior to instruction, to determine what the students already know. Such a test should be given with the understanding that *no grades will be given*—that it is only for the teacher's use in planning instruction. Following a unit of work, when a post-test is given, it should be with the understanding that it can provide feedback information so that the teacher can determine where he has failed to clarify certain points and can take steps to recycle the individual student into the learning experience. It should be made clear that the student's mark is not based on a single test grade, but on his achievement over the period of a full marking term or year, and that whatever tests are given are for the purpose of diagnosis to help the student achieve to the maximum possible.

In addition, the teacher must establish grading criteria that indicate to both students and parents that marks are not given carelessly and inconsistently. These marks should be derived not only from test results, but also from an over-all observation of a student's work in class and from an evaluation of his achievement in terms of his individual potential. The teacher must keep clearly in mind the distinction between test measurements and final evaluation.

In some instances teachers have printed and distributed to students the evaluative criteria in order to avoid later confusion and misunderstanding. The "General Marking Standards for Nonperformance Music Classes" found in Table 15-4 should give the teacher some idea of the types of actual marking practices that are currently in use. Which of these the teacher will adopt will be determined by the particular class and teaching situation. For example, in a ninth-grade general music class, where there are many ability levels, the teacher may find a combination of student self-evaluation and student ability, as it influences achievement, a satisfactory basis for evaluation. On the other hand, in an advanced theory class, especially one for students who are planning careers in music, an arbitrary fixed standard *might* be more appropriate.

Grading in performance classes offers another set of challenges, and a variety of marking plans have been employed. The "point system," for example, gives the student various points for a wide variety of predetermined requirements, such as rehearsal attendance, playing his part without mistakes, taking private lessons, and performing solos. Although this approach has some merit, the clerical work involved can become prohibitive, especially when records must be kept for large groups. Other teachers prefer to audition students, individually or in groups, and to assign grades for tone quality, ability to carry a part, and general musicianship. These grades are then averaged with other grades the student has received for class effort, general behavior, and dependability. In those classes where the development of conceptual understanding is stressed along with performance skills, the results of a written examination

339
Measurement and Evaluation

Table 15-4. GENERAL MARKING STANDARDS FOR NONPERFORMANCE MUSIC
CLASSES

Basis for Marking	Grade Determination Procedure	Advantage	Disadvantage
Student ability	The teacher determines the final grade according to the student's achievement as it relates to his ability. (The teacher's ability to determine ability levels is often a source of parental disagreement.)	Students with limited ability do not automatically receive low grades.	The bright student and limited student both achieve on the same level; the limited student could receive an "A" and the bright student a "C."
Group standards	Individual achievement is compared with that of the group as a whole. By using the "normal curve" or some arbitrary method, a certain percentage is assigned to each grade from "A" to "F."		Students at the bottom of the scale will fail regardless of their individual effort.
Arbitrary fixed standard	Once the teacher has established the expected standard for the class, then the degree to which the standard is met determines the grade. This differs from the establishment of a group standard in that there is no predetermined percentage of grade distribution.	Students are rewarded for actual achievement.	There is an inconsistency of standards among teachers. It also discourages the limited student who makes the effort but receives the same grade as the bright student who does not work.
Self-evaluation	Students are given a printed form on which they are asked to rate their own effort and achievement.	Students learn to judge their own work.	It is of little value unless the teacher develops a valid and specific evaluation form, and unless the students are able to evaluate their work in terms of specific goals.

may also be included in the student's final average or as part of the point system.

Student achievement in music is sometimes influenced by the idea that in order to be successful one must have "musical talent." This theory states that if one does not have talent, success is impossible, and that if one does have talent, then his musical understanding, knowledge, and skill will grow with little effort on his part. The theory is, of course, foundless. The person with so-called natural musical talent as well as the average student must be made to realize that the only means to musical "success" is through concentrated effort. The effort may be easier for some than for others, but it still entails work. Throughout the entire process of measurement and evaluation, perhaps the most important

340

thought that a teacher can instill in students is that achievement in music is not limited to the gifted, but that *everyone* can increase his sensitivity to and enjoyment of music through both formal and informal performances, listening, and composition.

Projects

1. Prepare a class report on a standard music achievement and music aptitude test. Cover such factors as reliability, validity, practicality, established norms, and usefulness in terms of current music education philosophy and objectives.
2. Establish a set of behavioral objectives for one of the following units of instruction. Then, construct both a subjective and objective test to cover the same material. Discuss the suitability of each test in class.
   (a) Unit on pop music for a seventh-grade general music class with a limited ability level.
   (b) Unit on music form for a tenth- or eleventh-grade music-appreciation class that is heterogeneously grouped.
   (c) Unit on twelve-tone techniques for a senior high school class in advanced theory.
   (d) Unit on protest music for a sixth-grade general music class that is homogeneously grouped.
3. Contact four school districts to determine what systems of grading and reporting are being used. Inquire whether the grading and reporting practices are consistent on all grade levels, or in all middle schools, junior high schools, and senior high schools. If different systems are used, find out why.
4. Contact four school districts and determine whether music aptitude tests are used in the beginning instrumental programs. If they are, find out what data have been collected to indicate that their use is effective.
5. Check with music teachers who are responsible for the following classes and determine how they measure and evaluate student progress and assign grades: (a) fifth- and sixth-grade general music classes; (b) seventh- and eighth-grade general music classes; (c) beginning instrumental class; (d) a large general chorus; (e) a concert band; (f) an advanced choir; (g) a small vocal ensemble; (h) a small instrumental ensemble.
6. Write five instructional objectives for any type of music class. From these objectives develop questions to be included in a criterion-referenced test.
7. Devise a questionnaire to determine a student's attitude toward (a) a recently attended concert, (b) the selection of music played in the orchestra, and (c) the scheduling of music classes in the high school.

Selected References

BENTLEY, ARNOLD. *Musical Ability in Children and Its Measurement.* New York: October House, Inc., 1966.

BLANCHFORD, JEAN S. "A Teacher Views Criterion-Referenced Tests," *Today's Education,* 64:2 (March/April 1975), p. 36.

CHASE, CLINTON I. *Elementary Statistical Procedures.* New York: McGraw-Hill Book Company, Inc., 1967.

COLWELL, RICHARD. *The Evaluation of Music Teaching and Learning.* Englewood Cliffs, New Jersey: Prentice-Hall, Inc., 1970.

————. "Musical Achievement," *Music Educators Journal,* 57:8 (April 1971), p. 38.

DUVALL, W. CLYDE. *The High School Band Director's Handbook.* Englewood Cliffs, New Jersey: Prentice-Hall, Inc., 1960. Chapter 5.

GORDON, EDWIN. *The Psychology of Music Teaching.* Englewood Cliffs, New Jersey: Prentice-Hall, Inc., 1971.

GRONLUND, NORMAN E. *Measurement and Evaluation in Teaching.* New York: The Macmillan Company, 1966.

HAYS, WILLIAM L. *Basic Statistics.* Belmont, California: Brooks/Cole Publishing Company, 1967.

LEHMAN, PAUL R. *Tests and Measurements in Music.* Englewood Cliffs, New Jersey: Prentice-Hall, Inc., 1968.

LEONHARD, CHARLES, and ROBERT W. HOUSE. *Foundations and Principles of Music Education.* 2d ed. New York: McGraw-Hill Book Company, Inc., 1972. Chapter 11.

ODELL, C. W. *How to Improve Classroom Testing.* Dubuque, Iowa: William C. Brown Company Publishers, 1958.

SHAW, CARL N., and MARYJANE TOMCALA. "A Music Attitude Scale for Use with Upper Elementary School Children," *Journal of Research in Music Education,* 24:2 (Spring 1976), pp. 73–80.

WHYBREW, WILLIAM E. *Measurement and Evaluation in Music.* Dubuque, Iowa: William C. Brown Company Publishers, 1962.

Standardized Achievement Tests

Aliferis Music Achievement Test (James Aliferis). Minneapolis: University of Minnesota Press, 1954 revised.

Aliferis-Stecklein Music Achievement Test (James Aliferis and John E. Stecklein). Minneapolis: University of Minnesota Press, 1962 revised.

Beach Music Test (Frank A. Beach). Emporia, Kansas: Bureau of Educational Measurements, Kansas State Teachers College, 1939 revised.

Diagnostic Tests of Achievement in Music (T. L. Torgerson and M. L. Kotick). Los Angeles: California Test Bureau, 1950.

Farnum Music Notation Test (Stephen E. Farnum). New York: The Psychological Corporation, 1953.

Jones Music Recognition Test (Archie N. Jones). New York: Carl Fischer, Inc., 1949.

Knuth Achievement Tests in Music (William E. Knuth). San Francisco: Creative Arts Research Associates, 1966 revised.

Kwalwasser-Ruch Test of Musical Accomplishment (Jacob Kwalwasser and G. M. Ruch). Iowa City: Bureau of Educational Research and Service, State University of Iowa, 1927 revised.

Kwalwasser Test of Music Information and Appreciation (Jacob Kwalwasser). Iowa City: Bureau of Educational Research and Service, State University of Iowa, 1927.

Music Achievement Tests (Richard Colwell). Urbana, Illinois: MAT, 1968–1969 revised.

Snyder Knuth Music Achievement Test (Alice Snyder Knuth). San Francisco: Creative Arts Research Associates, 1965.

Strouse Music Test (Catherine E. Strouse). Emporia, Kansas: Bureau of Educational Measurements, Kansas State Teachers College, 1937.

Standardized Aptitude Tests

Conrad Instrument Talent Test (Jacques W. Conrad). New York: Mills Music, Inc., 1941.

Drake Musical Aptitude Tests (Raleigh M. Drake). Chicago: Science Research Associates, Inc., 1957 revised.

K-D Music Tests (Jacob Kwalwasser and Peter W. Dykema). New York: Carl Fischer, Inc., 1930.

Kwalwasser Music Talent Test (Jacob Kwalwasser). New York: Mills Music, Inc., 1953.

Measures of Musical Ability (Arnold Bentley). New York: October House, Inc., 1966.

Musical Aptitude Profile (Edwin Gordon). Boston: Houghton Mifflin Company, 1965.

Primary Measures of Music Audiation (Edwin Gordon). Chicago: G.I.A. Publications, Inc., 1979.

The Seashore Measures of Musical Talent (Carl Seashore, Don Lewis, and Joseph Saetveit). New York: The Psychological Corporation, 1960 revised.

Standardised Tests of Musical Intelligence (Herbert D. Wing). The Mere, Upton Park, Slough, Buckinghamshire, England: National Foundation for Educational Research, 1961 revised.

Test of Musicality (E. Thayer Gaston). Lawrence, Kansas: Odell's Instrumental Service, 1957 revised.

Promotional Aptitude Tests

Advanced Rhythm and Pitch Test (C. L. McCreery). Chicago: Lyons Band Instrument Company, Inc.

Elementary Rhythm and Pitch Test (C. L. McCreery). Chicago: Lyons Band Instrument Company, Inc.

Leblanc Music Talent Test (E. C. Moore). Kenosha, Wisconsin: G. Leblanc Corporation.

Meyers Music Aptitude Test. Detroit: Meyers Music Company.

Music Aptitude Test. Elkhart, Indiana: Conn Corporation.

Music Talent Test. Chicago: F. E. Olds and Son, Inc.

Selmer Music Guidance Survey. Elkhart, Indiana: Selmer, Inc.

Tilson-Gretsch Musical Aptitude Test (Lowell M. Tilson). Chicago: The Fred Gretsch Mfg. Company.

Administrative Factors

16

The educator's task is to maximize the occasion.

GEORGE BAINES
Headmaster, Eynsham County Primary School, Oxfordshire, England[1]

THE ADMINISTRATIVE ORGANIZATION of school districts is quite varied, and the music teacher's immediate supervisor could be the school principal, the director of music, or the music department chairman for the building in which he teaches. Regardless of the type of organization, the basic approach in dealing with the administrative staff should be one of respect and understanding for their professional responsibility as it relates to the successful operation of the total educational program and the music teacher's role within this program. Although the music teacher must be concerned from a specialist's standpoint with the operation of his classes, scheduling, curriculum organization, suitability of facilities and equipment, selection of teaching materials, and special instructional programs, he needs to remember that he must operate within the guidelines and general philosophy underlying the over-all school program. And, he must realize that in working with general administrators he will be dealing with persons who have similar concerns but who view the music curriculum as only one element among their broad responsibilities.

[1] Quoted in Charles E. Silberman, *Crisis in the Classroom: The Remaking of American Education* (New York: Vintage Books, 1970), p. 238.

WORKING WITH ADMINISTRATORS

To operate successfully within any school, the music teacher has to become familiar with his dual, interrelated responsibilities. First, he must become acquainted with the duties and procedures related to all members of the faculty and which contribute directly to the orderly function of every aspect of school life; second, he must be in command of the more specific duties and procedures related to his work as a member of the music department.

Most schools have a looseleaf teachers' handbook that provides such information as the following: (1) the general school schedule, including the number and length of periods and any changes that occur on a regular basis; (2) the floor plan of the school; (3) fire-drill regulations and procedures, which are particularly important for teachers of large performance groups; (4) the school's marking system and the procedure used for informing students and parents of impending failure; (5) the length of the school day and the reporting and dismissal time for faculty members; (6) the procedure to follow when the teacher is ill; (7) a schedule of teachers' meetings; (8) the school calendar, providing information about vacations, the end of marking periods, and the closing of school for the year; (9) the procedure for dealing with disciplinary problems; and (10) the "chain of command" that the teacher must recognize when he has a problem, wants to make curriculum changes, wants to plan a field trip, and so on. It is important for the music teacher to be familiar with the information in this guide. Busy administrators are not appreciative of queries made about school policies when the answers have already been provided by the handbook.

The administration of the music program is usually the responsibility of a director of music education. In some large school districts, however, the teacher will work more directly with a building chairman, a supervisor of vocal or instrumental music, or some other person who is in turn responsible to the director of music. The immediate music supervisor should always be available to assist the teacher when problems arise and to provide information regarding such items as (1) the existence and location of curriculum guides and resource lists; (2) the procedure to follow in making out lesson plans; (3) the availability of materials and equipment (including textbooks, music, audiovisual equipment, recordings, and transparencies); (4) the procedure involved in teacher observations and subsequent teacher-administrator conferences; and (5) the procedures for ordering new materials, making curriculum changes, changing basic textbooks, submitting budgetary requests for the following year, and making repairs to equipment.

In dealing with either the general or music administrative staff, the teacher will have little difficulty in establishing good rapport if he readily accepts and implements his responsibilities related to classroom instruction, the care of materials and equipment, and cooperation with the general faculty and other members of the music staff. The teacher should also follow general principles of human relations and be fully prepared to support and answer questions about his teaching activities. If he has any special requests or suggestions for changes and improvements, he should not present these in a fragmentary manner. Instead, each suggestion, idea, or plan should be thought through completely and his plan or project presented in as detailed a written outline as possible. When this is done, the administration has the opportunity to carefully evaluate what has been prepared and to contact the teacher for further clarification of points. The teacher will then be ready to respond to unforeseen implications, he will gain the respect of both administrators and fellow staff members, and he will avoid the embarrassment of presenting incomplete, illogical ideas.

The administrative staff is responsible for evaluating the teacher in action with his students in the classroom. Usually, the evaluative process considers the teachers' preparation, methods and skill of presentation, attitude toward and rapport with students, success in achieving the objectives set forth in the lesson plan, and overt pupil interest, which is determined by students' response and participation. Following an evaluation there is usually a conference, in which the teacher will receive commendation and encouragement for work well done as well as suggestions for techniques and materials that may make his teaching more effective. The teacher should realize that during the observation the administrator is not there to find fault or criticize. Rather, he is as eager to observe a well-planned, well-executed lesson as the teacher is to teach one. While the observation and conference are designed primarily for teacher evaluation, the astute teacher can in turn evaluate the evaluator through the level and depth of his comments and suggestions.

Finally, the teacher will find that he must coordinate his work with administrative policies in a number of ways in which he may not have any direct control over the circumstances. He must, for example, work within the general scheduling practices set forth by the administration, he must cope with credit policies that have been set forth, and he must be prepared to work within specific organizational plans for instruction.

SCHEDULING PRACTICES

Secondary school music teachers have often heard students say, "I want to take music, but I don't have time for it in my schedule." One of the main obstacles confronting stu-dents who wish to elect music but can't find the time is the lock-step plan of scheduling all "major" subjects for five meetings weekly in periods of forty-five to fifty-five minutes. Consider, for example, the high school in which band was scheduled for the first period of a six-period day. To ensure that all members of the band would be scheduled, their cards were run through the computer first. But because advanced-placement English and Biology II were also scheduled at the same time and met only once a day, and because all college-bound sophomores were required to take developmental reading, five majors, and physical education, the result was that music was out for a large number of students, and many former and prospective members could not be scheduled for band. Any attempt to move band into another period just created a new set of conflicts with other single-section courses, and in this particular school there was no reasonable solution to the sophomores' problem. The band director could meet with the unscheduled students, individually or in small groups, either after school, before school, or during study periods. This would indicate to the school principal that the teacher was making an effort to maintain his program even under such adverse conditions, and it might possibly be arranged with the principal to have these students leave their regularly scheduled classes to periodically attend one or two band rehearsals a month. Although this might help to maintain the students' interest for the year, it is hardly an ideal solution, and there is no guarantee that a better schedule would result the following year. Scheduling problems like this have been used for years by some music teachers as an excuse for inadequate performance groups; yet, other teachers, with similar problems, have managed to come up with successful programs and fine groups each year.

In a sense there is little that the music teacher can do to avoid scheduling difficulties, for the responsibility for scheduling belongs to the school principal and the administrative staff. When a basic scheduling practice has been established for the school, the music teacher must work with it and do the best he can. Nevertheless, the teacher should be cognizant of the problems and procedures involved and with the alternatives. Administrators are neither blind to nor uninterested in the problems of music scheduling and they are eager to develop a policy that is equitable to *all* areas of the curriculum. It is therefore important for music teachers to understand the different types of scheduling, know how the possibilities would affect the music pro-

gram, and be prepared to make recommendations for improvement.

Educators have recognized the need for a more flexible approach to scheduling, and their innovations have helped the performance area in many instances. For example, some schools still maintain the rigid six-period day, but major subjects are scheduled only four times a week; or a seven-period schedule is worked into a six-period day on a rotating basis by dropping one period each day (so that each class meets six times every seven days). Figures 16-1 and 16-2 illustrate this practice. Figure 16-3 offers a comparison of the first two by substituting letters for course

FIGURE 16-1. Seven-Period Schedule in a Six-Period Day

	Mon.	Tues.	Wed.	Thurs.	Fri.	Mon.	Tues.	Wed.
1	English	History	Math	Free	Science	Language	Music	English
2	History	Math	Phys. Ed.	Science	Language	Music	English	History
3	Math	Free	Science	Language	Music	English	History	Math
4	Phys. Ed.	Science	Language	Music	English	History	Math	Phys. Ed.
5	Science	Language	Music	English	History	Math	Phys. Ed.	Science
6	Language	Music	English	History	Math	Phys. Ed.	Science	Language

Schedule begins to repeat on eighth day.

FIGURE 16-2. Seven-Period Schedule in a Six-Period Day

	Mon.	Tues.	Wed.	Thurs.	Fri.	Mon.
1	English	Music	Science	Phys. Ed.	History	English
2	History	English	Language	Science	Math	History
3	Math	Free	Music	Free	Phys. Ed.	Math
4	Phys. Ed.	History	English	Language	Science	Phys. Ed.
5	Science	Math	History	Music	Language	Science
6	Language	Phys. Ed.	Math	English	Music	Language

Schedule begins to repeat on sixth day.

FIGURE 16-3. Comparison of Figures 16-1 and 16-2

Mon.	Tues.	Wed.	Thurs.	Fri.	Mon.	Tues.	Wed.
A	B	C	Free	E	F	G	A
B	C	D	E	F	G	A	B
C	Free	E	F	G	A	B	C
D	E	F	G	A	B	C	D
E	F	G	A	B	C	D	E
F	G	A	B	C	D	E	F

(From Figure 16-1)

Mon.	Tues.	Wed.	Thurs.	Fri.	Mon.
A	G	E	D	B	A
B	A	F	E	C	B
C	Free	G	Free	D	C
D	B	A	F	E	D
E	C	B	G	F	E
F	D	C	A	G	F

(From Figure 16-2)

names. It can be seen that the only real difference is that the sequence of courses is horizontal (day to day within a single time block) in Figure 16-1, whereas the sequence is vertical in Figure 16-2.

Another scheduling practice is to arrange for periods of varying lengths on different days, with an extended lunch-enrichment period that accommodates a variety of performance groups. (See Figure 16-4.) Whether the lunch-enrichment period is used in conjunction with the lock-step plan or with some innovative type of scheduling, careful planning, sufficient music personnel, and suitable rehearsal space are necessary to provide a satisfactory arrangement for the performing groups. The plan shown in Figure 16-5 is for one instrumental teacher, one vocal teacher, and two areas for rehearsal.

Scheduling instrumental beginners can be done during study periods, lunch periods, before school, or after school. Many teachers, of course, do not approve of before- or after-school scheduling, arguing that if music instruction is a legitimate part of education as a whole then it deserves to be scheduled within the school day. The reality of the situation, however, requires a different type of thinking. As new courses are continually added to an already overcrowded curriculum,

it is obvious that everything cannot be squeezed into a few morning and afternoon hours without serious conflicts. In accepting the principle of double sessions, in implementing tri-semester and quarter-semester plans, and in studying the possibilities of year-round schooling, educators have had to revise their thinking about what constitutes a school day and even what constitutes a school year. The music teacher, too, must recognize alternatives and revise his idea of what acceptable scheduling is. Why shouldn't the day be extended to earlier and later hours if it permits a more comprehensive and less conflicting curriculum?

In some instances where the general music class is scheduled two or three times a week, instrumental beginners are taken out of one of these classes; administrators readily accept this plan because it does not disrupt the academic program. This is not a desirable format since it is based on the theory that general music and performance classes are alternatives rather than complementary experiences. A more appropriate plan is to dismiss beginners from all classes (academic courses *and* music) on a rotating basis so that students will not miss the same class each week. Figure 16-6 illustrates this rotating schedule.

Another technique used to provide suffi-

FIGURE 16-4. Alternating Schedule

Time	Mon.	Tues.	Wed.	Thurs.	Fri.
8:00 9:00	English	Math	English / History	English	Math
10:00 11:00	History	Spanish	Physical Ed. / Math	History	Spanish
12:00	Lunch and Enrichment Period				
1:30 2:30	Physical Ed.	Music Theory	Spanish / Music Theory	Physical Ed.	Music Theory

FIGURE 16-5. Performance Schedule During Lunch-Enrichment Period

	Mon.	Tues.	Wed.	Thurs.	Fri.
12:00 – 12:30	Band / Advanced Mixed Choir	Orchestra / Advanced Girls Choir	Band / Advanced Mixed Choir	Orchestra / Advanced Girls Choir	Band / Nonselective Mixed Choir
1:00	String Ensemble / Small Vocal Ensemble	Brass Ensemble / Nonselective Mixed Choir	String Ensemble / Small Vocal Ensemble	Woodwind Ensemble / Nonselective Mixed Choir	String Ensemble / Advanced Mixed Choir

FIGURE 16-6. Middle School Rotating Schedule to Accommodate Beginning Instrumental Lessons

1st Monday	2nd Monday	3rd Monday
Reading	Reading	Reading
Science	Instrumental Lesson	Science
Social Studies	Social Studies	Social Studies
Phys. Ed.	Phys. Ed.	Instrumental Lesson
Instrumental Lesson	General Music	General Music
Math	Math	Math

cient time for performance groups is the extension plan, in which classes are scheduled during the first or last periods of the day and rehearsals are extended to begin thirty or forty minutes before or end thirty or forty minutes after regular school hours. The extension of the last period is particularly helpful to the band director during the football season when he is faced with the preparation of a weekly half-time show. A modification of the extension plan can be applied successfully to lunch-period rehearsals. In this case, it is possible to schedule sectional or grade-level rehearsals directly before or after lunch. Figure 16-7 shows how an extended lunch-period plan can operate at the junior high school level.

Many schools have adopted modular scheduling, which rejects the concept that all subjects require the same amount of time for study and that all major courses must meet five times a week for the same length of time. Instead, the school day is divided into modules, which may be fifteen, twenty, or twenty-five minutes long. A six-hour day that is traditionally divided into six or seven periods would therefore consist of about eighteen modules. Modules are used singly or in clusters for different classes. Major courses can meet fewer times weekly, but for three, four, or five modules at a time; or some classes can be scheduled for a different number of modules each time they meet. English or science, for example, could be scheduled once a week for five modules for large-group instruction by a team of teachers, and then meet for the rest of the week in periods of two or three modules for smaller groups under the supervision of individual teachers on the team. Similar scheduling, with modifications, can be applied to humanities or related arts courses that involve a team of teachers from several departments, or to the rehearsal of large performance groups, with segments of perhaps two modules being used for sectional rehearsals or for small-ensemble splinter groups.

The modular plan gives students the opportunity of extending their educational experience beyond four or five majors and physical education. Figure 16-8, for example, illustrates how a six-hour school day might be organized in a traditional lock-step plan, leaving the student little time for enrichment courses, and how it might be organized on the basis of twenty-minute modules, offering considerable time for elective subjects.

Although the responsibility for scheduling belongs to the administrative staff, the music teacher needs to understand the procedures and problems involved in the particular plan in operation so that he can place a check

FIGURE 16-7. Lunch-Period Extension Plan in a Junior High School

	Mon.	Tues.	Wed.	Thurs.	Fri.
Lunch		String Section		String Section	
	Lunch	Orchestra	Lunch	Orchestra	Lunch
	Band		Band		Band
		Lunch		Lunch	
	Grade 7 Band Section		Grade 8 Band Section		Grade 9 Band Section

Supportive Elements in a Music Education Program

FIGURE 16-8. Comparison of Lock-Step and Modular Scheduling

Per.	Mon.	Tues.	Wed.	Thurs.	Fri.
1	English	English	English	English	English
2	Biology	Biology	Biology	Biology	Biology
3	Phys. Ed.		Phys. Ed.		Phys. Ed.
4	French	French	French	French	French
5	Math	Math	Math	Math	Math
6	History	History	History	History	History

Mod.	Mon.	Tues.	Wed.	Thurs.	Fri.
1	English			Math	
2	English		Math	Math	Biology
3	English				
4	English	Phys. Ed.		History	
5	English				Phys. Ed.
6	French	English		English	Phys. Ed.
7	French	English	Biology	English	Phys. Ed.
8	French		Biology		
9	French		Biology		History
10	History	Biology			History
11	History	Biology	English		French
12	History	French	English		French
13	History	French	History		
14	History		History		
15					
16				French	Math
17				French	Math
18					

▨ Available Time For Enrichment

on problems as they occur and see that the music program is organized in as effective a time-plan as possible. He should be familiar with the date when students fill out their schedule cards for the following year, the deadline for making changes in schedules, the date when the first computer printout will be available for checking conflicts, the procedure to follow to remedy class conflicts, and the guidance counselors who are responsible for making out the schedules of various student groups.

CREDIT FOR MUSIC COURSES

It was not long ago that secondary music courses, particularly at the high school level, were looked upon as extracurricular when it came to granting credit. Even today, when most schools do grant credit for music study, there are some schools in which that credit is not honored toward graduation.

Credit for completion of a music course should be granted on the same basis that it is given in other subjects. This usually means that a course meeting four or five times a week, depending on the type of school schedule, is a major course and therefore receives one unit of credit. Those courses that meet two or three times a week are ordinarily given a half unit of credit. Of course, where flexible or modular scheduling is employed, a major subject might meet for only two sessions a week, but these sessions will generally be longer than traditional periods. Schools recognizing the fact that a set amount of time does not apply equally to all subjects for the completion of a given body of work must also alter the traditional guidelines by which a "major subject" is defined. Time, content, individual study requirements, objectives, and criteria for evaluation must all be considered in such cases to determine whether a particular course is a major subject or not.

When these factors indicate that the student's involvement and output are comparable to his efforts in traditionally accepted majors such as English, mathematics, history, and science, then the music course should grant the full credit of a major course. If, under these circumstances, the music course receives only half the credit, the implication is that within that school music is only half as important as other subjects. This, of course, may very well be true for certain students. However, it is also true that English is only half as important as science for some students,

351

Administrative Factors

science only half as important as industrial arts for others, and so on. Therefore, music educators should demand equal credit recognition for their courses, in whatever form it might be for that particular school.

Sometimes a school will approve a course for major credit only if it involves outside preparation on the part of the student. This is a meaningless standard since the establishment for a group of minimum time spent in homework has no relation to achievement by the individual in *any* subject. One student doing no homework may be able to achieve more than another student doing two hours of homework in that subject nightly. In those schools that insist on maintaining this requirement, it can be argued, at least in terms of performance groups, that students should qualify for full credit because of their outside practicing. (It is irrelevant that some students do not practice; some students do not do their biology homework either, but that does not negate the establishment of credit for the biology course.)

Assuming that full credit is given for courses that the music department considers major courses, music teachers must still deal with the relationship of music credit to graduation requirements. In most secondary schools, credit in music is not required for graduation. This in itself is not disturbing since a strong argument can be made for not requiring credit in most subjects. (In discussing "How We Will Raise Our Children in the Year 2000," education writer George B. Leonard even went so far as to say that "perhaps the only required courses of the future will be dance and body-energy awareness."[2]) The disturbing fact is that some schools *do not accept* music credit toward graduation. The last major survey on this problem was made in 1962 by the National Education As-

sociation; although it is out-dated and many schools have since changed their positions, the statistics from that survey indicate a situation that is still largely with us. The NEA survey revealed that a third of all secondary schools did not allow students to enroll in music courses unless they maintained a minimum grade level in required courses. (This was true of 18.4 percent of large schools—over 1000 enrollment; 44.4 percent of medium-sized schools—300 to 999 students; and 35.8 percent of small schools.) Music teachers should naturally question what right any school has to say that because a student does not achieve in certain areas he should be denied the opportunity to achieve in other areas. Some schools have offered between two and six credits toward graduation if the student is enrolled in music as a major area; 27.7 percent of the large schools and 12.5 percent of the medium-sized schools offered a kind of major in music, but some of them required that the entire three years be spent in performance groups. Most small- and medium-sized schools allowed one or two credits toward graduation for nonmajors, but a good number allowed no credit. The most favorable conditions prevailed in the large secondary schools, which usually allowed two to four credits toward graduation. Twelve percent of these schools, in fact, set no limit. However, regardless of the policy, the necessary credits required in other subjects limited the number of credits that could be acquired in music. What seems, therefore, to be a satisfactory arrangement for accepting music credits toward graduation is often negated by requiring a certain scholastic standing in other areas before music credit can be earned. Properly, a student should graduate when the school has provided all it can offer him for his particular needs and he has achieved to his best ability the objectives of these offerings—not when he has accumulated so many credits in specific courses.

[2] "How Will We Raise Our Children in the Year 2000?" *Saturday Review of Education*, 1:2 (March 1973), p. 35.

Another problem related to credit is an internal matter—that is, which students in a given music course are to be graded high enough to receive the credit allotted to that course. Whether a student receives an "A" instead of an "F," "90" instead of "60," "satisfactory" instead of "unsatisfactory," or "pass" instead of "fail" is too often an arbitrary decision based on whether the student has an outstanding voice or can play the first trumpet part rather than on whether he has learned anything or is working to capacity. Since music deals so much with the affective domain, it is impossible to say whether, how, or to what degree a student "appreciates," say, the Bach cantata that was studied in class. One can only ascertain whether a student has perceived certain structural and interpretive elements in the work—perceptions that will contribute to his own aesthetic response to the music, but cannot define that response. The student's grade, then, should be based on objective, measurable factors, not subjective factors; furthermore, the teacher must consider the student as an individual and determine how his achievement relates to his capacity to achieve, rather than to some established norm. If behavioral objectives have been written for the course, these will indicate criteria for evaluating much, but not all, of the student's work, and therefore for determining whether he is to pass or fail, and to receive credit or not. (See Chapter 2 for a discussion of behavioral objectives, as well as Chapter 15 for techniques of evaluation.)

Special factors must be considered for granting credit for private instruction in the applied music program. High school credit for private music instruction, carried on outside of the school, has been, until recently, unique in the structure of the secondary school curriculum. Regulations have to be established for the guidance of the student, the private teacher, and the school administration. An applied music program of this sort extends the walls of the school and makes available to the interested and talented student another effective learning resource in the community. It can improve the student's ability in solo performance, help him to become a more valuable member of the school's music organizations, familiarize him with more of the world's finest music for his particular instrument or voice, help to build a better foundation for the development of his special talent, and develop his desire to make use of music in filling and enjoying leisure time.

First, standards must be established to qualify private teachers for participation in the program. These standards may be set by the local school authorities upon the recommendations of the music department, and may be based on such considerations as training, degree, teaching experience, or an examination or demonstration. In some states these requirements are established by the state department of education, which may also issue permits or certification for the private teachers. Second, regulations must be established for the student's involvement in the program. One school system, for example, set forth the following guidelines:

1. Before being admitted into the applied music program, the student must have completed at least one year of successful private study in the medium in which he desires credit.

2. Application must be made on the appropriate form and returned to the music department on or before October 1.

3. Each student must take a minimum of forty lessons during the school year.

4. Each student must practice a minimum of five hours weekly, keeping a record of his practice on a music department form, which will be handed in.

5. Materials, including method books and solos, should be of appropriate difficulty and acceptable musical merit. (The music department may work out a course of study and alternatives with the private teacher.)

6. Audition-examinations will be held twice a year, in January and May. These examinations will be under the supervision of the school music staff. Examinations will be held after regular school hours, and students will be notified at least one week prior to the examination of the specific time and place.

7. Prior to the examination, the private teacher will be asked to fill out a school form that indicates the number of lessons the student has taken, the compositions studied, technique studies, scales and arpeggios studied, the teacher's general remarks, and the teacher's recommended grade for the student.

8. Each student will bring with him to the examination his personal record of practice and the private teacher's report. The examination will include the performance of two compositions (one by memory), technique studies, sight-reading, and scales and arpeggios as appropriate. Rudiments will be required for all percussion students.

9. One credit will be given to those students who complete a year's work in applied music. The student must receive a grade of "C" or better to continue this special program for the next year. Students participating in this program will ordinarily be allowed to receive only one credit per year. However, in special cases where a student is planning to enter the field of music and he is deemed capable of handling the work, he will be allowed to study more than one instrument and to receive more than one credit. In such a case, approval of the high school principal and the director of music will be necessary.

354

GUIDANCE AND CAREER EDUCATION[3]

In working with young people in the music program, the teacher will find a wide range of potentials. Some students with above-average music ability will seek information and advice from the music teacher about career possibilities, whereas others with considerable potential will reveal no interest whatsoever in a music career. The teacher should not feel obliged to sell careers in music, nor to measure success by the number of seniors each year who choose to study music at the university level. However, it is important that the teacher make available objective information on music careers for all students and give encouragement to gifted or talented students who are interested in some phase of music professionally.

Unfortunately, the careers that usually come to light through music classes are only those of the performer, composer, or teacher. Few students who otherwise might be interested in a music-related career, but are not attracted to performing, composing, or teaching, are aware of the variety of music professions and the opportunities they hold. It's possible that an individual might find a niche in music industry sales, recording studio work, acoustical design, therapy, autography, or one of many other lines of work associated with music.

Quite often, career opportunities are overlooked because they fall in the shadow of other, more prominent occupations. Think, for example, of all the people who are involved in some way with a hit recording: composer, lyricist, publisher (and the pub-

[3] Some passages in this section were written originally for *Careers and Music*, edited by Malcolm E. Bessom and John T. Aquino (Reston, Virginia: Music Educators National Conference, 1977); they are reprinted here by permission of MENC.

lisher's staff of specialists), record producer, arranger, recording artist, musicians, conductor, music contractor, recording engineer, recording technicians, pressing and packaging specialists, record company administrators, promotion specialists, lawyers, persons in performance and mechanical rights, record distributors, rack jobbers, retail salespersons, disc jockeys, record reviewers, and so on. Each has an important role to play in the "life" of that recording, but generally the only person the general public thinks of is the recording artist.

Knowing about the broad range of career possibilities is important for several reasons. First, we must face the fact that many music teachers probably should not be teaching, many performers should not be struggling with a performance career, and many persons in the music trades should not be in business. Many people who have gone into their respective fields have not been really "cut out" for their work. Such people are often unhappy in what they are doing and, consequently, do less than a good job. Perhaps they thought the work was right for them originally and then got "locked in" with no obvious way to escape. Perhaps they settled for less than they wanted because they felt inadequate for what they were really interested in. But perhaps, too, they were simply unaware of the opportunities available to them. Therefore the music student with an interest in law should know early enough that there are attorneys who specialize in music law. The student who likes manual work should know about careers in instrument crafting and instrument repair. The student with a good business sense should know about the fields of music merchandising, manufacturing, and publishing. And the student who has a flair with words should know about careers in music criticism, editing, and journalism.

Secondly, we must face the realities of the work world and the misconceptions com-monly attached to certain "public professions." A performance career, for example, can be attractive to many young people, but it also can be a great disappointment. Consider that fewer than 2 percent of the members of the American Federation of Musicians work full time in their chosen field. Not many years ago there was a strike by the AFM against the television networks—a strike that was quite noticeable to television viewers at the time; but fewer than fifty musicians were affected by it nationwide. Obviously, we should not discourage potential performers from pursuing a performance career if they wish, but we should be sure that they have the facts and know of alternatives.

In recent years, it has become commonplace for college graduates to find that the jobs they have been trained for do not exist. Today, in fact, there is an oversupply of 175,000 or more college graduates annually. High school seniors about to enter college are expressing interest in professional careers to the extent that their target professions are twice the percentage of professional jobs in our economy. These students need to be prepared psychologically for the fact that most of the jobs they want are nonexistent. They also must be prepared, both psychologically and professionally, for maneuvering on an occupational game board. The ability to adapt and the knowledge of possible moves become extremely important when you realize that the average worker in the United States not only changes jobs seven times during working life but also changes careers three times. Therefore, information on careers related to music is important to students and should be introduced into classes whenever possible.

A good way to begin career awareness is to compile a list of music-related jobs in major categories, such as performance, composition, education, recording, broadcasting, the film industry, manufacturing, merchandising, publishing, and journalism, as well as in such

355

specialized areas as law, therapy, librarianship, and community arts management. Then take stock of the professional music resources in your community. Certain professionals might be brought into the classroom as guest speakers; in other cases, field trips for either an individual student or a group might be arranged to the professional's place of business.

The general music teacher is in a good position to be first in recognizing musical talent and music-career interest and potential. Similarly, instrumental and vocal teachers at the middle- and junior-high-school levels can help in detecting, encouraging, and guiding gifted students. They should be on the watch for not only promising performers but also those who are exceptionally perceptive in aural experiences, theory, and analysis or those who are skilled in manipulating sounds in composition. Once such a student has been identified, the teacher can offer encouragement by (1) providing more challenging instructional materials; (2) extending opportunities for solo and ensemble experience; (3) making arrangements for attendance at rehearsals of high school and professional performing groups; (4) suggesting recordings for listening outside of school; (5) keeping the student informed of local concerts and community music activities; (6) showing the student that he is pleased with his progress in class; (7) informing parents of their child's music potential and progress; (8) informing the student's guidance counselor of his musical potential and interests; and (9) suggesting enrollment in special high school music courses.

At the high school level, where students are more directly faced with making vocational choices, the teacher will become more involved with guidance activities. Students expressing interest in music careers at this level generally fall into four categories:

1. *Students who express a desire to study music but seem to have little potential.* In such cases, the music teacher must explain carefully what the music requirements for college entrance are and what the student must do in preparation for entrance exams (including intensive applied study, courses in theory and literature, and the maintenance of a good academic standing). If the student then wishes to undertake the challenge of preparing for a career in music, he should have the opportunity to do so, and if the challenge proves too great it won't take long for him to discover that his interest in music should either remain avocational or be secondary to some other aspect of a profession (as in music merchandising).

2. *Students who decide late in their school careers that they want to study music, but are not adequately prepared.* In many instances, teachers feel it is too late for these students, but that is not necessarily true. For the interested, persistent student, there is almost always a way to pursue a career in music and to prove himself. For example, two students who had participated in the music program only intermittently surprised their music teacher at the end of their junior year by expressing a desire to pursue music careers after graduation. One of them played third trumpet, second chair, in the school band, and the other was an adequate "second-string" accompanist for the mixed chorus. After conferring with their teacher and guidance counselor, both students agreed to resume applied music lessons immediately, study through the summer, and enroll in the first-year theory course during their senior year. The piano student lost interest in applied study by mid-June and dropped out of the theory class by December. The trumpet player, however, as a result of his study, moved into the second chair of the first trumpet section in the band,

became first trumpet in the stage band, and had above-average success in the theory course. After two years at a community college, where he took every music course possible and played in every instrumental ensemble, he was accepted as a sophomore music major at a state university. Three years later he graduated with a degree in music.

3. *Students who have the potential but are undecided.* Early in their high school years, these students should be made aware of career opportunities and of the work related to each career. Pertinent information and evidence that the student has the potential for a successful music career should be presented to the student and his parents, but the teacher

Table 16-1. RESPONSIBILITIES OF THE TEACHER-COUNSELOR TEAM

These responsibilities are of a general nature and become more specific as they are applied to a particular student who will have his own set of problems and unique musical and academic potentials.

Music Teacher	Guidance Counselor	Together
1. Determine whether the student has the musical potential, interest, and drive needed to undertake a career in music.	1. Evaluate the student's intellectual abilities and academic achievement in relation to his probable success at the college level.	1. Help the student choose the college, university, or conservatory that best fits his particular need.
2. Guide the student in selecting music courses, applied music instruction, and performance opportunities that will contribute most effectively to his musical growth.	2. Guide the student in selecting academic courses required for college admission.	2. Keep the student and parents informed of scholarship possibilities.
3. Prepare the student for his applied entrance exam by providing opportunities to audition at solo festivals or for district and all-state groups, and to play solo recitals.	3. Arrange for the student to take the PSAT and SAT college entrance exams, as well as the advanced placement music exam.	3. Keep the student and parents informed of audition dates.
4. Help the student prepare a taped performance if that is to be used instead of an in-person audition.	4. Help the student fill out college applications on time for regular or early acceptance.	4. Evaluate the student's academic and musical growth, providing assistance as needed.
5. Keep the student, parents, and counselor informed of the student's musical growth and of any difficulties that arise.	5. Keep the student and parents informed of any academic problem that might hinder college acceptance.	
	6. Provide parents with the information and necessary forms to be completed to apply for scholarship assistance.	
	7. Keep the music teacher informed of the student's academic progress and of any impending difficulty.	

should make it clear that his judgment and advice are not infallible. Beyond this point, it is up to the student and his parents to make decisions concerning future studies, with the knowledge that the teacher and guidance counselor are available for further consultation.

4. *Students who know that they want to study music and who have the musical potential.* The teacher must help these students realize that the study of music demands extensive commitments in time and effort, help them focus their interests on specific music careers, inform them of the advantages and disadvantages of each career, and direct them toward specific areas in which they will need to develop their knowledge, understanding, and skill.

In guiding all these students, the music teacher will need to establish a working relationship with the guidance department. Both teacher and counselor must understand and respect each other's role as it relates to their mutual objective. As a member of the team, the music teacher is best prepared to evaluate musical ability and musical growth, and to suggest colleges and universities having outstanding music departments and special music majors. The counselor, on the other hand, is best prepared to gather information pertaining to the student's achievements and adjustments academically, socially, and psychologically. It will become obvious that certain functions are best accomplished by the guidance counselor alone, others by the music teacher alone, and still others by both working together (see Table 16-1).

PLANNING MUSIC ROOMS AND FACILITIES

With the exception of physical education, probably no area of the curriculum makes such specific demands as the music program

in terms of space allocations and functional facilities. Unlike educational programs in which instructors are involved exclusively in communicating information of a purely academic nature, the music program requires a physical plant that is conducive to the controlled manipulation of sounds and to accommodating large numbers of students and extensive equipment.

It is foolhardy for a music teacher or administrator to think that a comprehensive music program can be carried on effectively in an ordinary classroom. Yet, all too often, the music teacher and his students must interact in situations in which there is overcrowding, an unreasonable sharing of facilities, and near-impossible conditions for aesthetically and meaningfully experiencing music. School officials and music personnel must work cooperatively in seeking ways to improve existing conditions as well as in planning new facilities and anticipating future needs of the music program.

New facilities, especially, demand cooperative planning. First, school officials must work with the music staff in determining space, sound, and equipment needs. In turn, the architects need to work with both the administrative staff and music personnel to realize satisfactory solutions. Attention will have to be given to music classrooms, rehearsal rooms, practice rooms, a class piano room, a listening room, storage rooms, and faculty offices, as well as to shared facilities such as the auditorium, a multimedia learning center, and television and recording studios. In determining specific needs, music teachers need to consider the exact nature of the work to be done in each room; the expected enrollment of classes, including anticipated growth over at least a ten-year period; provisions for simultaneous rehearsals; the location of music rooms in relation to one another and to the rest of the school; equipment requirements; lighting needs; problems of temperature control in relation to instruments; and acoustical requirements.

Location of Facilities

Because music means "sound" instruction, music facilities are often located in some corner or end of the entire school plant. However, the fact that consideration is given to acoustical controls should obviate the supposition that the music rooms have to be away from everything. Rather, they should be located in relation to the over-all scheme in terms of student traffic patterns, accessibility, and factors related to the moving of equipment. The music suite should be apart from the main cluster of academic classrooms, but it should be within reasonable distance of the hub of student activity. Music facilities should be visible and accessible to the student body at large, serving those students who are actively involved in music and keeping music activities before the entire school public.

Rehearsal rooms need to be located in proximity to the auditorium. The movement of equipment and performers must follow an easy route, and the need of warming up a group in a rehearsal room and moving it as quickly as possible into the actual area of performance must be considered. Rehearsal rooms also need to be located on the ground floor to eliminate moving equipment up and down stairways. This would also suggest that a loading dock be accessible to the rehearsal rooms and auditorium stage. Schools with marching bands should consider access to drill and practice fields as well. Storage or equipment rooms should be located near or adjacent to rehearsal rooms; and where there are both instrumental and vocal facilities, the storage areas are best located between the rehearsal rooms for acoustical and functional reasons. Teaching studios and practice rooms are best located adjacent to the rehearsal rooms for both practical and security reasons. The cluster concept of room arrangement has considerable merit. Beyond this, each school must weigh factors that are unique to its music program.

Area and Room Requirements

Each rehearsal room should be designed with several factors in mind: the number of students to use it (possibly as many as 125 at one time), the type of activity to take place within it, the amount of stationary and portable equipment, and the acoustics.

Choral and instrumental needs differ enough so that specifications for separate rooms are desirable. For an instrumental organization, 20 to 24 square feet per student and 400 cubic feet per performer are necessary to achieve comfortable working space and proper acoustics. Ceilings should be a *minimum* of 14 feet high. If separate halls are provided for both band and orchestra, then additional consideration must be given to acoustics in order to provide less reverberation for the band than for the string group. In the choral room, 15 to 18 square feet per student is advisable; the ceiling should be higher than in a regular classroom, although it need not be as high as in the instrumental hall.

The use of risers must be decided upon early in planning, for performers on risers will create a flow of soundwaves at different heights and angles, thus affecting the acoustics of the room signficantly. In addition, if rehearsal rooms are to accommodate comprehensive learning experiences, they should be planned to include chalkboards, pianos, multipurpose chairs, tables, a stereo sound system, and storage spaces. Although rooms can be planned to cover the needs of both vocal and instrumental groups, and other music classes as well, they represent a compromise that should be avoided if at all possible.

Classrooms for general music, music literature, and music theory courses need to be larger than regular classrooms, and should include chalkboards, bulletin boards, pianos, record-tape sound sysems, and provisions for showing films, filmstrips, slides, videotapes, and transparencies. Acoustics must again be considered, although it is not such a problem here as it is in rehearsal halls.

A music-listening room, equipped with multiple turntables, tape equipment, and headphones, ought not to be considered a luxury. Recordings are to the music program what books are to the English class. Provisions should be made for the storage and dispensing of records in conjunction with this room. In some new schools where listening equipment is part of a larger multimedia learning center serving the entire school, a central control station is included in which recordings and tapes are handled exclusively by an attendant rather than by the listeners. Although a multimedia center of this type is excellent, at least a small- or medium-sized listening room should still be planned adjacent to the music classroom for use in connection with regular class lessons.

Teaching studios and practice rooms should be designed in terms of specific types of use, such as private lessons, small ensemble work, sectional rehearsals, and so on. Rooms for individual students should be 55 to 65 square feet in size, and those for small ensembles should be at least 120 square feet. Nonparallel walls are desirable to reduce reflected sound, and each room should be equipped with a piano, mirrors, tape recorder, or any other equipment that may be required for effective instruction.

A storage area for instruments should be adjacent to the rehearsal rooms, easily accessible, and planned to handle the flow of traffic as students move with their instruments before and after rehearsals or performances. The design should permit students to get their instruments at any time without disrupting instruction that is in progress. The security factor must also be considered because of the value of instruments, and equipment to maintain necessary humidity levels should be included to prevent stringed instruments from cracking. Other storage space should be provided for uniforms and robes and provision made for their protection against moths, dust, and wrinkling. This area should allow for efficient distribution and collection of apparel.

The music library does not necessarily require a separate room, although that would be desirable if the library is extensive. Music may be filed in steel cabinets or in shelving units. Sorting racks along the wall are quite useful.

Each member of the music staff should be provided with office space, including a desk, a filing cabinet, and access to a piano, tape recorder, and phonograph for use in preparing lessons.

The auditorium should be built so that performing groups sound and look their best. In many instances, an organization that sounds perfect in the rehearsal room sounds "dead" in the auditorium because of the acoustical design, the arrangement of curtains, and other factors. An auditorium, then, must be planned very carefully, with consideration being given to acoustics, seating capacity, the orchestra pit, sight-lines, stage sound shells, fly space, wings, lighting and sound equipment, dressing rooms, storage space, and facilities for handling the flow of people and equipment. It is desirable to have the grid height more than twice that of the proscenium in order that scenery can be flown completely out of sight of the audience. An audio-communications system should be provided from the area of the lighting board to both the orchestra pit and the lighting loft. The orchestra pit itself should be sunk about 5 feet into the floor, running the length of the stage and 15 feet wide, and acoustically treated to not only reduce sound but maintain balance and tone quality. A partition at the front of the pit will allow the front row of the audience to see the stage but not the orchestra. Seats in the auditorium should be raked for clear vision, with those in the front row situated so that spectators neither have to look up over the stage apron nor are able to see the stage floor clearly. Attempts to cut costs by combining auditoriums with cafeterias (cafetoriums) or gymnasiums should be avoided since they are objectionable from almost all standpoints, including those of good music facilities.

ORGANIZING THE MUSIC LIBRARY

Since a large portion of the music department's budget is spent each year on books, recordings, tapes, slides, films, filmstrips, transparencies, charts, and music for band, orchestra, and chorus, these materials must be organized and maintained so that they will not be damaged, lost, or destroyed, and so that they are readily accessible to the teaching staff and easily located within the filing system. If a system is established by which materials are safely and properly stored, thoroughly indexed, signed out when in use, and returned to place when not in use, then teachers and students are more apt to return items promptly, administrators are likely to be more willing to replace worn-out materials or purchase additions, and classroom needs will be serviced more completely and effectively.

Sometimes, teaching materials are filed in a central library that services the entire school district. This may be workable in a very small system, but the busy music teacher will make use of a wide variety of materials only if a library is maintained in the building where he works. In this case, a master inventory of all school-owned materials should be kept by the director of music, and inter-school loans of unique items should be made possible.

Within a single school, records, tapes, scores, supplementary texts, and listening rooms are occasionally located in the main school library, and responsibility for ordering, cataloging, circulation, and maintenance rests with the library staff rather than with the music department. Such a system requires each teacher to plan well ahead and is therefore not adequate for even the well-organized teacher who wishes to capitalize on unexpected opportunities in the course of teaching a lesson by switching activities or drawing upon supplementary materials. To accommodate teaching techniques of this sort, which are desirable, the music library is best located adjacent to the music and rehearsal rooms.

Music Scores

Music can be stored in several ways. Some teachers prefer to place it in expandable cardboard envelopes or in hanging folders, placed in metal filing cabinets. Cabinets are available to accommodate octavo choral music, the larger-sized instrumental scores, and the smaller-sized marching band music. A less expensive method is to store it on open shelves. The music may be placed in manila envelopes, in special storage envelopes printed on one side to record identifying information, or in filing boxes. Choral scores for large works, such as cantatas and oratorios, are generally best kept on open shelves.

There are two principal methods of arranging and cataloging scores. One is to file the music according to performance media, with subdivisions according to composer, title, or type. For example, choral music would be filed under SA, SSA, TTB, SATB, and so on, and within each main category the selections would be arranged in (1) a single intermixed group filed alphabetically by the names of composers or arrangers; (2) in a single intermixed group filed alphabetically by titles; or (3) in subdivisions such as sacred, secular, folk, and seasonal, each of which would be independently arranged alphabetically by composer or title. The same system can be used for instrumental music. In addition, a cross-index card file is maintained, with information about each selection being entered on a composer/arranger card, a title card, and a style/genre/form card, each being filed separately in its own category. The information on each card should include at least the number of copies, the arrangement, whether it is a cappella or accompanied in the case of choral works, where it is located, and preferably the name of the publisher, when it was last performed or studied, the date of acquisition, the grade of difficulty, and whether a recording of the music is available in the library. Sample filing cards are shown in Figures 16-9a and 16-9b.

The media system of organizing the library can pose a logistics problem as the library grows, for music must constantly be shifted to make room for new purchases. This problem is alleviated by the second principal method of filing: Music is numbered, and as a new selection is purchased it receives the next highest number and is placed in the last position on the shelf or in the cabinet. The same kind of card-index system is used for cataloging (see Figure 16-9c), and sometimes a single copy of each selection is pulled and filed separately in the same numerical order for easier reference. The major drawback of this system is that the teacher must rely on the card file for information. If he wants to select a folk song for SSA chorus, the cards will identify what is available, but he must then go to a number of different places to study the actual music, even in the single-copy file. The media system, on the other hand, permits him to browse through all the SSA folk songs in one place for a more convenient comparison.

Recordings

To prevent recordings from warping, they must be stored in an upright position. Special metal shelves with permanent dividers every seven or eight inches or wooden shelves with movable partitions are available for this purpose. The metal shelves are sectional and can be stacked and easily fastened into place. The initial cost of such shelving is reasonable, and as space needs increase the additional outlay is not prohibitive.

Recordings, like scores, can be filed either categorically or numerically. Categorical filing is by far the better system, for careful planning generally allows the teacher to go directly to the correct slot rather than have to consult the card index to locate a specific recording.

An effective plan is to divide the discs into several main categories: classical, jazz, ethnic-folk, pop-rock, and music theatre. In the classical and theatre sections, the recordings are arranged alphabetically by composer; jazz and pop-rock recordings are alphabetized by performers; and ethnic-folk discs are arranged alphabetically by regions or cultures (e.g., Africa, North; Australian aborigines; Brazilian Bahian cults; China; and so on). Anthologies such as *Adventures in Music* or jazz collections are placed at the beginning of the appropriate sections.

Although most recordings can be located without reference to a card file, a comprehensive card index is valuable to locate classical works on a disc that contains music by two or more composers, or specific examples of certain forms, styles, instrumental combinations, and so on. Multiple cards for a single

FIGURE 16-9

a. *Composer/arranger*
card (media system)

```
Comp./Arr._____
Title_____
Medium_____ Pub._____ No. of Copies_____
Type _____ Acquired _____

Performed/Studied      Piano acc.    ☐
_____   A cappella    ☐
                       Instrumental  ☐ _____
_____
_____   Comments _____
_____   _____
_____   _____
Recording _____   _____
```

b. *Style/genre/form*
card (media system)

```
Category_____
Title _____
Comp./Arr._____
Medium_____ Pub._____ No. of Copies_____
Acquired_____
Performed/Studied      Piano acc.    ☐
_____   A cappella    ☐
_____   Instrumental ☐ _____

_____
_____   Comments _____
_____
_____   _____
Recording _____   _____
```

c. *Media card*
(numerical system)

```
Medium _____ | No.
Title _____|
Comp./Arr._____
Type _____ Pub._____ No. of Copies _____
Acquired _____
Performed/Studied      Piano acc.    ☐
_____   A cappella    ☐
_____   Instrumental ☐ _____

_____   _____
_____   Comments _____
_____   _____
Recording_____    _____
```

FIGURE 16-10

```
Performer_____
Album Title_____
Label & No. _____    Mono □    Stereo □
Teaching Topics:            Score No. _____
_____      Filmstrip No. _____
_____      Transparency No. _____
_____
_____
_____

Condition:                  Album Location: _____
Ex. □   Gd. □   Fr. □       _____
Replace □
```

FIGURE 16-11

Programmed Tape Index Card

```
Teaching Purposes _____      Tape No.
_____
Music Exs._____      Speed _____
_____      Length _____
_____      Date made _____
_____
_____

Related Materials:
Film No. _____   Filmstrip No. _____
Transparencies _____
_____
Other _____
```

recording, then, could be filed under composer, title of composition, title of album, performer, form, period, style, and genre, depending upon the importance of each to the specific recording. Figure 16-10 shows the format of a typical card.

Reel tapes and cassettes, which should be stored in specially constructed tape cabinets, can be indexed in the same way as discs. In the case of programmed tapes, an index card should provide information about the purpose of the tape (such as illustrating a specific percept), the music examples used, tape speed, and related transparencies or filmstrips. A sample card for this purpose is shown in Figure 16-11.

Other Materials

Films, filmstrips, slides, transparencies, and videotapes are quite fragile and must be stored carefully. Filmstrips should be kept in cabinets or carrying cases designed to hold the round capsules in place. Similarly, slides should be stored in metal trays, cases, or cabinets that have numbered grooves. Films and videotapes need to be kept in metal containers, which can then be placed on open shelves or in cabinets. Transparencies can be protected by placing them in folders and filing them in metal cabinets. Professional books, supplementary texts, reference volumes, and miniature scores, if not kept in the central school library, should be located in a section of the music library that is readily accessible to students as well as members of the music staff. Shelves that are ten inches deep and thirteen inches high will accommodate most books, including oversized publications.

Films, filmstrips, and tapes lend themselves to numerical filing, with filmstrip numbers being noted on accompanying recordings as well as index cards. Cards indexing titles and subject matter should be prepared for these items. Books are generally arranged alphabetically by author within broad categories, such as reference, music history, music theory, biography, jazz, ethnomusicology, and so on. These should be cross-indexed in the card file according to author, title, and subject.

THE COPYRIGHT LAW

A teacher who discovers that a student has copied a term paper word for word from a library book, or whose own master's thesis is resubmitted in a different university under someone else's name, would immediately recognize such acts as outright plagiarism—acts that would offend any decent person. Yet many otherwise honest persons believe that as long as they give credit to the creator of a work, it is all right to make use of that work in any way they want. It definitely is *not* all right. Consider, for example, the teacher who takes students to an all-state audition with photocopies of the audition music. Or consider the teacher who has a flair for arranging and prepares a new version of a composition rather than ordering copies of

one of the half dozen arrangements in print, without requesting the publisher's permission to write the arrangement. Such teachers hardly would be willing to teach classes without being paid for their efforts. Yet they unthinkingly rob composers and publishers of their incomes—in fact, of a portion of the very revenue that makes this music available in the first place.

With the technological development of better, faster, and cheaper duplicating machines, the infringement of rights of composers, authors, and publishers has become a major problem. Coupled with the initial high costs of publishing, loss of revenue from copyright infringements has been one of the principal factors in the closure of certain publishing houses. Whether you think in terms of ethical, moral, or legal arguments, or simply consider the fact that educators and publishers need each other, it is imperative that music teachers know what can and cannot be done under Public Law 94-553 (90 Stat. 2541), the United States Copyright Act of 1976, which became fully effective on January 1, 1978.

Under the revised law, the special needs of teachers have been recognized. It is now permissible, for example, for a teacher to make *a single copy* of a chapter from a book, an article, a short story, an essay, or a poem, and from certain other copyrighted materials for that teacher's use in research, teaching, or preparation to teach a class. However, multiple copies for classroom use can be made only if the copying meets *certain tests of brevity, spontaneity, cumulative effect, and notice of copyright*. Any copying to avoid purchase, copying to create an anthology, or reproduction of consumable materials (such as workbooks and standardized tests) is strictly prohibited. Guidelines for determining permissible use of materials from books and periodicals appear in Table 16-2, taken from the House Judiciary Committee Report (H.R. Report 94-1476).

Table 16-2. GUIDELINES FOR CLASSROOM COPYING OF BOOKS AND PERIODICALS[4]

The purpose of the following guidelines is to state the minimum and not the maximum standards of educational fair use under Section 107 of H.R. 2223. The parties agree that the conditions determining the extent of permissible copying for educational purposes may change in the future; that certain types of copying permitted under these guidelines may not be permissible in the future; and conversely that in the future other types of copying not permitted under these guidelines may be permissible under revised guidelines.

Moreover, the following statement of guidelines is not intended to limit the types of copying permitted under the standards of fair use under judicial decision and which are stated in Section 107 of the Copyright Revision Bill. There may be instances in which copying which does not fall within the guidelines stated below may nonetheless be permitted under the criteria of fair use.

GUIDELINES

I. *Single copying for teachers*
A single copy may be made of any of the following by or for a teacher at his or her individual request for his or her scholarly research or use in teaching or preparation to teach a class:
  A. A chapter from a book;
  B. An article from a periodical or newspaper;
  C. A short story, short essay or short poem, whether or not from a collective work;
  D. A chart, graph, diagram, drawing, cartoon or picture from a book, periodical, or newspaper;

II. *Multiple copies for classroom use*
  Multiple copies (not to exceed in any event more than one copy per pupil in a course) may be made by or for the teacher giving the course for classroom use or discussion; *provided that:*

A. The copying meets the tests of brevity and spontaneity as defined below; *and*
B. Meets the cumulative effect test as defined below; *and*
C. Each copy indicates a notice of copyright.

Definitions
Brevity
  i. Poetry: (a) A complete poem if less than 250 words and if printed on not more than two pages or, (b) from a longer poem, an excerpt of not more than 250 words.
  ii. Prose: (a) Either a complete article, story or essay of less than 2,500 words, or (b) an excerpt from any prose work of not more than 1,000 words or 10% of the work, whichever is less, but in any event a minimum of 500 words.
  [Each of the numerical limits stated in "i" and "ii" above may be expanded to permit the completion of an unfinished line of a poem or of an unfinished prose paragraph.]
  iii. Illustration: One chart, graph, diagram, drawing, cartoon or picture per book or per periodical issue.
  iv. "Special" works: Certain works in poetry, prose or in "poetic prose" which often combine language with illustrations and which are intended sometimes for children and at other times for a more general audience fall short of 2,500 words in their entirety. Paragraph "ii" above notwithstanding such "special works" may not be reproduced in their entirety; however, an excerpt comprising not more than two of the published pages of such special work and containing not more than 10% of the words found in the text thereof, may be reproduced.

Spontaneity
  i. The copying is at the instance and inspiration of the individual teacher, and

---

[4] Developed by the Ad Hoc Committee of Educational Institutions and Organizations on Copyright Law Revision, the Authors League of America, Inc., and the Association of American Publishers, and printed in the House Judiciary Committee Report (H.R. Report 94-1476), pp. 68–70.

366

Supportive Elements in a Music Education Program

ii. The inspiration and decision to use the work and the moment of its use for maximum teaching effectiveness are so close in time that it would be unreasonable to expect a timely reply to a request for permission.

Cumulative effect

i. The copying of the material is for only one course in the school in which the copies are made.

ii. Not more than one short poem, article, story, essay or two excerpts may be copied from the same author, nor more than three from the same collective work or periodical volume during one class term.

iii. There shall not be more than nine instances of such multiple copying for one course during one class term.

(The limitations stated in "ii" and "iii" above shall not apply to current news periodicals and newspapers and current news sections of other periodicals.)

III. *Prohibitions as to I and II above*

Notwithstanding any of the above, the following shall be prohibited:

A. Copying shall not be used to create or to replace or substitute for anthologies, compilations or collective works. Such replacement or substitution may occur whether copies of various works or excerpts therefrom are accumulated or reproduced and used separately.

B. There shall be no copying of or from works intended to be "consumable" in the course of study or of teaching. These include workbooks, exercises, standardized tests and test booklets and answer sheets and like material.

C. Copying shall not:
   a. substitute for the purchase of books, publishers' reprints or periodicals;
   b. be directed by higher authority; or
   c. be repeated with respect to the same item by the same teacher from term to term.

D. No charge shall be made to the student beyond the actual cost of the photocopying.

In the case of copyrighted music, a copy of a lost part may be made in an emergency if it is subsequently replaced by a purchased part. Except in such an emergency, no copyrighted music can be reproduced for any kind of performance. For the purpose of class study, one copy per student can be made of up to 10 percent of a musical work as long as that excerpt is not a performable unit. However, *a single copy* of an entire performable unit can be made for the teacher's own use provided that it is either out of print (as confirmed by the copyright owner) or available only as part of a larger work. In addition, a single recording of a student performance for study purposes, or of aural exercises or tests made from a recording owned by the teacher or school, also can be made. In the latter instance, permissible use pertains to the copyright on the music itself and not to a separate copyright that may exist in the recording. Guidelines for the educational use of music, also from the House Report, appear in Table 16-3. One of these guidelines indicates that purchased copies may be edited or simplified if the fundamental character of the work is not changed or lyrics altered. This provision does not mean, though, that the teacher can make a new arrangement of the work; that is the exclusive right of the copyright owner (except when a recording of a previously recorded work is made, in which case the compulsory license for recording permits the making of an arrangement). The Music Educators National Conference, in cooperation with publishers and other organizations, has made available special forms to use in obtaining permission to arrange.

Table 16-3. GUIDELINES FOR EDUCATIONAL USES OF MUSIC[5]

The purpose of the following guidelines is to state the minimum and not the maximum standards of educational fair use under Section 107 of HR 2223. The parties agree that the conditions determining the extent of permissible copying for educational purposes may change in the future; that certain types of copying permitted under these guidelines may not be permissible in the future; and conversely that in the future other types of copying not permitted under these guidelines may be permissible under revised guidelines.

Moreover, the following statement of guidelines is not intended to limit the types of copying permitted under the standards of fair use under judicial decision and which are stated in Section 107 of the Copyright Revision Bill. There may be instances in which copying which does not fall within the guidelines stated below may nonetheless be permitted under the criteria of fair use.

A. PERMISSIBLE USES

1. Emergency copying to replace purchased copies which for any reason are not available for an imminent performance provided purchased replacement copies shall be substituted in due course.

2. a. For academic purposes other than performance, multiple copies of excerpts of works may be made, provided that the excerpts do not comprise a part of the whole which would constitute a performable unit such as a section, movement or aria, but in no case more than 10% of the whole work. The number of copies shall not exceed one copy per pupil.

   b. For academic purposes other than performance, a single copy of an entire performable unit (section, movement, aria, etc.) that is (1) confirmed by the copyright proprietor to be out of print or (2) unavailable except in a larger work, may be made by or for a teacher solely for the purpose of his or her scholarly research or in preparation to teach a class.

3. Printed copies which have been purchased may be edited or simplified provided that the fundamental character of the work is not distorted or the lyrics, if any, altered or lyrics added if none exist.

4. A single copy of recordings of performances by students may be made for evaluation or rehearsal purposes and may be retained by the educational institution or individual teacher.

5. A single copy of a sound recording (such as a tape, disc or cassette) of copyrighted music may be made from sound recordings owned by an educational institution or an individual teacher for the purpose of constructing aural exercises or examinations and may be retained by the educational institution or individual teacher. (This pertains only to the copyright of the music itself and not to any copyright which may exist in the sound recording.)

B. PROHIBITIONS

1. Copying to create or replace or substitute for anthologies, compilations or collective works.

2. Copying of or from works intended to be "consumable" in the course of study or of teaching such as workbooks, exercises, standardized tests and answer sheets and like material.

3. Copying for the purpose of performance, except as in A (1) above.

4. Copying for the purpose of substituting for the purchase of music, except as in A (1) and A (2) above.

5. Copying without inclusion of the copyright notice which appears on the printed copy.

---

[5] Developed by representatives of the Music Publishers' Association of the United States, the National Music Publishers' Association, Inc., the Music Teachers National Association, the Music Educators National Conference, the National Association of Schools of Music, and the Ad Hoc Committee on Copyright Law Revision, and printed in the House Judiciary Committee Report (H.R. Report 94-1476), pp. 70–71.

In recent years, many music educators have recorded student performances and distributed copies to the community. Teachers must understand that the first recording of a work can be made only with the consent of the copyright owner. Once a nondramatic musical work has been recorded and publicly distributed, however, anyone can obtain a compulsory license to record the work again. In either case, royalties must be paid to the copyright owner.

It is equally important to understand that performances of musical works are subject to the granting of permission by the copyright owners. Certain performance situations, though, are not considered infringements of the law. For example, a copyrighted work may be performed in the classroom by students or teachers in the course of face-to-face teaching activities. Similarly, nondramatic musical works can be performed at a school concert as long as there is no admission charge, performers or organizers are not compensated, and there is no commercial advantage. If there is an admission charge, the proceeds must be used for an educational or charitable purpose. Even then, the performance of a specific work is not permissible if the copyright owner objects in writing seven days prior to the scheduled performance. The performance of a dramatic musical work (such as a musical comedy or opera) is in a different class; even in the case of a performance in a nonprofit educational institution, a license to perform must be obtained from the copyright owner or agent.

Teachers should not take the copyright law lightly. In the case of an infringement, the teacher could face the payment of statutory damages between $250 and $10,000. If it is proved in court that the infringement was willful, for commercial advantage or private financial gain, the individual could be fined as much as $50,000 and imprisoned. As always, ignorance of the law is no excuse.

BUDGETS

Although the director of music is generally responsible for preparing and submitting a budget for music education throughout the school system, he relies on individual teachers in determining the financial needs of each phase of the program. There are three basic ways in which the music program is financed. One way—and the most desirable—is to include every possible expense of the system-wide music curriculum in the general school budget. A second way—which is also acceptable, though not as good—is to include music-department expenses in separate budgets prepared for each school building. The problem with this procedure is that the individual attitudes of various building principals could affect the amount budgeted in each school. The third way is to cover basic expenses (for books, teaching materials, music, equipment, and so on) in the general budget, but to maintain a separate music fund (sometimes separate band funds and vocal funds) in certain buildings for special projects, such as financing the spring musical, concerts, exchange concerts, festival fees, and field trips. In theory, the special fund is quite objectionable because it is dependent on revenue raised by the music department through ticket sales, a share in athletic receipts, and demeaning community fund-raising ventures such as car washes, bake sales, and door-to-door canvassing. Aside from the fact that this practice restricts activities unless the music department itself can raise the money, it also places the music department in the position of taxing the community twice for certain school expenses. No other school department is required to do this. Any activity sponsored by the school should be a legitimate educational activity, and as such it should be financed as a part of the school district's regular operating expenses and included in the regular school budget.

In projecting expenses, the music teacher should consider the following:

1. Instructional Supplies

a. MUSIC (for bands, orchestras, choruses, and small ensembles; for festivals and competitions; for musical shows; for any special events; and scores for theory and listening classes).

b. BOOKS(texts for general music, music history, music literature, music theory, and humanities or related arts courses; method books for voice classes and group instrumental classes; professional reference books; and supplementary reference and instructional texts).

c. RECORDING MATERIALS (discs, prerecorded tapes, blank tapes, and cassettes).

d. VISUALS (film rentals and purchases, filmstrips, transparencies, slides, videotapes, charts, photographs, and still pictures).

e. MISCELLANEOUS ITEMS (music folders, music manuscript paper, testing materials, pitchpipes, and rental of scripts and other rehearsal materials for shows).

2. Equipment

a. INSTRUMENTS (band and orchestral instruments to be purchased on a five-year plan; classroom rhythm and melody instruments; Autoharps; guitars; and pianos).

b. SOUND REPRODUCTION EQUIPMENT (portable phonographs, stereo sound systems, listening centers, portable tape recorders, tape decks, and microphones).

c. OTHER ELECTRONIC EQUIPMENT (synthesizers, tuning devices, and electronic pitch indicators for music-reading programs).

d. MISCELLANEOUS EQUIPMENT (music stands, music-stand lights, special chairs, risers, podiums, filing cabinets, storage cases and shelves, sorting racks, acoustic shells, uniforms, and robes).

e. MAINTENANCE EXPENSES (small instrumental repairs, instrument overhauling, piano tuning, instrument insurance, and uniform–robe cleaning and alterations).

3. Special projects

a. MUSICAL SHOWS (royalties, scenery, costumes, lighting, props, and special personnel).

b. TRAVEL (travel expenses to festivals, field trips, transportation costs for outside performances and exchange programs, and expenses for professional meetings and conventions).

c. FEES (royalties and commissions, clinician fees for workshops, and student fees for festivals and competitions).

d. EXPERIMENTAL TEACHING PROJECTS.

4. Office-Library Expenses

a. GENERAL SUPPLIES (letterheads, envelopes, forms, filing cards, folders, storage boxes, and staff-lined duplicator masters).

b. PRINTING EXPENSES (concert programs, bulletins, curriculum guides, and special announcements).

c. TELEPHONE.

d. EMERGENCY FUND.

If the music department receives revenues, the teacher should also pass along to the director a statement of anticipated receipts. This would include revenue from concerts, musical shows, participation in athletic events, instrument rentals, program advertising, parents' clubs, and donations by civic and social groups in the community.

In recent years, PPBS (planning, programming, budgeting systems) has emerged as an approach to budgeting. This approach, which gained recognition when Robert S. McNamara introduced it in the U.S. Defense Department, is now employed in many school districts. In addition to presenting line items in the budget, it also requires a statement of purposes, plans, and means of evaluation to determine whether each expenditure is worthwhile. In essence, PPBS is a form of educational accountability that makes possible a comparison of costs for each course or phase of the program; an analysis of costs per pupil for each subdivision of the program, course, or specific outlay for equipment and materials; and a determination of the value of objectives and outcomes. Whether a PPB system is used or not, there is no question but that the teacher must be able to support each budgetary request he makes.

PUBLIC RELATIONS

Public relations is often not acknowledged by the music teacher as being anything more than a public announcement of something that he or his students have achieved. In this sense, public relations efforts deteriorate into a form of self-initiated recognition or praise. Characteristic of this view is the teacher who remarks, "The band performed a great concert; they deserve to get their names in the paper!"

Public relations is actually much more than this. Its purpose is to (1) interpret the what, why, and how of the music program to the community; (2) foster an awareness of the place of music in general education and of aesthetic experience as an integral part of human activity; (3) obtain the public's interest in the music education program; (4) develop the community's confidence in the work being done and extend this confidence into support for continuing and improving the music program, thus promoting the concept of community partnership in the educational process; and (5) evaluate the music program

in terms of community needs. Realizing these objectives will strengthen the music curriculum and *prevent* unilateral cutbacks in the music program when the school district encounters financial problems. Thus, the public-relations effort needs to be an ongoing venture, not an occasional procedure to implement when crises occur.

Personal Contacts

Most phases of an organized public-relations program should be handled by the director of music. Nevertheless, every teacher can contribute to the effectiveness of PR work—especially in his personal contacts with students, parents, community civic and cultural leaders, and community organizations. *Good public relations begin in the classroom with good teaching.* Students who are pleased with their experiences in the classroom will transmit their feelings to parents and to other students who are not active in the school music program. Teachers should not rely only on word-of-mouth to reach parents, however. They should make an effort to talk to parents after school concerts, during "back-to-school nights," and, when the occasion warrants, by telephone (not just when there is a problem, but when there is something good to communicate about a student's work).

Other opportunities to communicate on a personal basis with both parents and non-parents exist in parent-teacher association meetings, performances before community organizations, participation in civic events, and relations with private music teachers, professional musicians, church musicians, members of the music industry, and members of arts councils, cultural organizations, and social groups. The teacher should take advantage of such opportunities to let people know about the music program—not simply to mention a forthcoming concert or how many stu-

371
Administrative Factors

dents were selected for all-state, but to explain the objectives of the music program, its scope, its importance to all students rather than just the musically talented, and the fact that the real values of a strong music-education program are transmitted in classrooms and rehearsal halls rather than in public performances.

In many communities, booster clubs or parents organizations have been organized to support music activities. It is desirable that a group of this sort not be specifically a "band parents" or "choir parents" club, but one that expresses interest in the entire music program, at least in a specific school. These groups can be of considerable assistance in conferring with the music staff about the program's needs; advising on potential trips; helping to arrange, supervise, or chaperone music activities; establishing a music awards ceremony or a music scholarship program; and influencing community awareness. It is not advisable for them to get involved in fund-raising, which unfortunately is their sole purpose in some communities. There are times (such as in planning a special trip, sponsoring a guest artist, or seeking funds for new uniforms) when the music department has no alternative but to turn to a parents' organization for assistance, but this assistance should not be through community fund-raising. Such a practice is highly questionable since all phases of education should be financed by the school. (In addition, some of the activities for which parents raise money are also questionable in terms of educational value; eliminating those activities will solve certain financial problems.) It is far better, when financial needs arise, to call on parents' clubs for support in convincing school administrators or the board of education that funds are needed and that the purpose for the funds is both legitimate and desirable.

Using the Mass Media

Some school systems have a specific procedure for sending news releases to newspapers (such as channeling releases through the principal's office for approval). Generally, releases about the music curriculum should go out of the office of the director of music, but there is no reason why individual teachers should not initiate stories.

In preparing a story, the teacher should always ask himself whether the subject will appeal to many people with varied primary interests. If the topic seems too specialized, then it is best to forget it. Stories with news interest are usually those that have a direct effect on a large number of people, describe something new or take a novel look at something old, involve conflict, relate to the future, or tell about something that is funny or of human interest.

Among the topics that may be of interest to newspaper editors (depending on the size of the community) are new school programs, new teaching techniques, unusual teaching materials, concerts, musical shows, trips, honors received at festivals or from organizations, special achievements by individual students or teachers, experimental programs, music activities that tie in with general news events, guest artists or speakers, aspects of the music program that compare favorably to recent surveys or statistical reports based on regional, statewide, or nationwide practices, the success of an alumnus in the field of music, tie-ins with state or national projects or organizations, school participation in local music events, and what students, parents, and community leaders have said in support of music education.

It is important to keep the music program visible through newspaper stories, but the music educator must be careful not to send too many releases. Selecting topics carefully, writing about them in an interesting manner, and spacing them out over a period of time will cause the local editor to look upon them more favorably.

The interesting news release is one that is brief (preferably no more than one page), gets to the point immediately, is simply worded and relatively informal in character, and is accompanied by a black and white 5″ × 7″ or 8″ × 10″ glossy photograph of something interesting. A bust shot of a staff member or a group photo of the seventy-five members of the marching band is dull to a newspaper editor. It is better to show two to five students actively involved and not looking at the camera (such as students playing guitars, painting scenery, or working at a synthesizer). The photograph should make music look enjoyable.

Radio and television should not be overlooked as means of promoting music education in the community. Both media have an obligation, under federal broadcasting regulations, to devote a certain portion of air time to public-service programming, and many program managers are eager to find new ideas in the local community to fulfill this obligation. Radio stations often carry spot announcements of special school programs, such as concerts and shows. Some might be interested in interviewing students and music personnel about current music events, trends, or issues, or in taping a concert for broadcasting. Television stations are often looking for local groups to appear in the early evening when air time is not filled by network programming. Both small ensembles and large performing groups from the school may be considered.

Whether in dealing with individuals in the community or with an invisible mass audience, the music teacher should make use of every opportunity that arises to promote the role of music in his school system. For it is only with community understanding and support that he can strengthen his current program, involve more students in the music curriculum, and realize his objectives in a far-reaching manner to promote an enlightened musical public.

Discussion Questions and Projects

1. In a high school operating on a modular schedule, with eighteen twenty-minute modules a day, what time allotments would you recommend to an administrator for (a) a concert band, (b) a percussion ensemble, (c) a theory class of twelve students, (d) a music-listening class of twenty students, and (e) a related-arts class of thirty-five students taught by a team of three teachers?

2. Given a junior high school with 750 students, a staff of two music teachers having general-vocal and general-instrumental assignments, a maximum of forty students in any instrumental ensemble and a maximum of ninety in any vocal group, what would you consider appropriate teaching facilities? Be specific and be able to justify your decisions.

3. If three students, all musically talented, expressed interest respectively in music therapy, performance, and teaching careers, what guidance would you give each one in (a) suggesting reading matter for career information, (b) describing competencies and qualifications they would need to have, (c) informing them of job opportunities and salary ranges, and (d) suggesting universities that they should consider?

4. Select a current or recent music activity or event at your college, and prepare a news release about it.

5. Plan what you would do for a thirty-minute presentation in response to a request from a junior-high-school PTA that wants to know about the school's music program.

6. You take a position as a general music teacher in a junior high school of 450 students, and learn that $1,000 has been budgeted for your classes for the year. Current resources include a set of thirty-two outdated music texts, twenty-four recordings of pretwentieth-century classical music, a piano, two pairs of bongo drums, one Autoharp, and a box of miscellaneous rhythm instruments. How would you spend the $1,000? What would you request for a budget the following year?

Selected References

BARNUM, WALTER K. "PPBS in Action," *Music Educators Journal*, 59:1 (September 1972), pp. 64–70.

BELCHEFF, KOSTE A. "Costing Out the Music Program," *Music Educators Journal*, 59:1 (September 1972), pp. 71–73.

BERANEK, LEO L. *Music, Acoustics and Architecture.* New York: John Wiley & Sons, Inc., 1962.

BESSOM, MALCOLM E. *Supervising the Successful School Music Program.* West Nyack, New York: Parker Publishing Company, 1969. Chapters 5 and 7.

————, and JOHN T. AQUINO, eds. *Careers and Music.* Reston, Virginia: Music Educators National Conference, 1977.

Careers in Music. Chicago: American Music Conference, 1976.

Careers in Music. Reston, Virginia: Music Educators National Conference, 1979.

"A Closer Look at the New Copyright Law," *Music Educators Journal*, 64:2 (October 1977), pp. 32–37.

CSIDA, JOSEPH. *The Music/Record Career Handbook.* New York: Watson-Guptill Publications, Inc., 1975.

GAINES, JOAN B. *Approaches to Public Relations for the Music Educator.* Washington, D.C.: Music Educators National Conference, 1968.

————. "Building Community Support for the Music Program," *Music Educators Journal*, 58:5 (January 1972), pp. 33–64.

GARY, CHARLES L. "What Music Educators Should Know About the New Copyright Law," *Music Educators Journal*, 63:8 (April 1977), pp. 33–38.

GEERDES, HAROLD P. *Planning and Equipping Educational Music Facilities.* Reston, Virginia: Music Educators National Conference, 1975.

HARTLEY, HARRY J. *Educational Planning-Programming-Budgeting: A Systems Approach.* Englewood Cliffs, New Jersey: Prentice-Hall, Inc., 1968.

INTRAVAIA, LAWRENCE J. *Building a Superior School Band Library.* West Nyack, New York: Parker Publishing Company, 1972.

KLOTMAN, ROBERT B., ed. *Scheduling Music Classes.* Washington, D.C.: Music Educators National Conference, 1968.

LABUTA, JOSEPH A. *Guide to Accountability in Music Education.* West Nyack, New York: Parker Publishing Company, Inc., 1974.

Music in Careers. St. Paul: Minnesota State Department of Education, Pupil Personnel Services Section Publications, 1976.

MYRICK, BARBARA. *Music Careers Chart*. Salem: Oregon Department of Education, 1976.

PETERS, MARYBETH. *General Guide to the New Copyright Act of 1976*. Washington, D.C.: Copyright Office, Library of Congress, 1978.

SMITH, RONALD O. "The McNamara Syndrome in Education," *Music Educators Journal*, 59:1 (September 1972), pp. 60–64.

TATARUNIS, ALPHONSE M., and MALCOLM E. BESSOM. "How Musical Is the Principal; How Educational the Music Teacher?" *NASSP Bulletin*, 59 (October 1975), pp. 23–30.

Index

LIBRARY
SAINT MARY'S COLLEGL
NOTRE DAME, INDIANA

DATE DUE

DEC 6 '82